Annals of Information Systems

Volume 15

For further volumes:
http://www.springer.com/series/7573

Athina A. Lazakidou
Editor

Virtual Communities, Social Networks and Collaboration

Springer

Editor
Athina A. Lazakidou
Department of Nursing
University of Peloponnese
Sparti, Greece

ISSN 1934-3221 ISSN 1934-3213 (electronic)
ISBN 978-1-4614-3633-1 ISBN 978-1-4614-3634-8 (eBook)
DOI 10.1007/978-1-4614-3634-8
Springer New York Heidelberg Dordrecht London

Library of Congress Control Number: 2012939526

Printed on acid-free paper

Springer is part of Springer Science+Business Media (www.springer.com)

Preface

Online communities are among the most obvious manifestations of social networks based on new media technology. Facilitating ad hoc communication and leveraging collective intelligence by matching similar or related users have become important success factors in almost every successful business plan.

This special issue addresses the virtual communities and collaboration among virtual participants currently proliferating across the world. Many online communities have been created to facilitate communication, enhance or express relationships, work in a common cause, seek entertainment, and network or mentor others. Others have been formed to facilitate tasks already being performed but now needing to be done virtually. Such communities and online groups span various boundaries and include networked employees, videoconferencing, gaming setups, and electronic community groups pursuing such diverse activities as friendshipping, planning, information sharing, collaborating, system developing, having fun, and advertising. Various technologies are involved, from Facebook and Twitter to teleconferencing to mobile phones and PCs.

Researchers are just beginning to understand virtual communities and collaborations. Many issues need further study, including group dynamics and outcomes, social networking implications, technical support features, group coherence and loyalty, and how organizations can better utilize the potential benefits of such communities in both internal operations and in marketing and new product development. What leads to participation and effective collaboration in these communities needs further study, as do the issues of how and why knowledge is shared among participants. Much additional research in this area is needed.

This new book presents studies from leading researchers and practitioners focusing on the current challenges, directions, trends, and opportunities associated with virtual communities and their supporting technologies.

This new book will be an excellent source of comprehensive knowledge and literature on the topic of virtual communities, social networks, and collaboration.

All of us who worked on the book hope that readers will find it useful.

Sparti, Greece — Athina A. Lazakidou

About the Editor

Athina A. Lazakidou, Ph.D., currently works at the University of Peloponnese, Department of Nursing, in Greece, as a lecturer in health informatics. She worked as a visiting lecturer at the Department of Computer Science at the University of Cyprus (2000–2002) and at the Department of Nursing at the University of Athens (2002–2007). She did her undergraduate studies at the Athens University of Economics and Business (Greece) and received her B.Sc. in Computer Science in 1996. In 2000, she received her Ph.D. in Medical Informatics from the Department of Medical Informatics, University Hospital Benjamin Franklin at the Free University of Berlin, Germany. She is also an internationally known expert in the field of computer applications in health care and biomedicine, with six books and numerous papers to her credit. Her research interests include health informatics, hospital and clinical information systems, e-learning in medicine, software engineering, graphical user interfaces, (bio)medical databases, clinical decision support systems, electronic medical record systems, telematics, and other web-based applications in health care and biomedicine.

Contents

Contributors

Penelopi Alexandrou Kingston University, London, UK

Iole Alfano University of Calabria, Cosenza, Italy

Masahiro Bessho Interfaculty Initiative in Information Studies, The University of Tokyo, Tokyo, Japan

Manuela Carini University of Calabria, Cosenza, Italy

Anargyros Chryssanthou Auditors Department, Hellenic Data Protection Authority, Ampelokipoi, Athens, Greece

Gerald Eichler Telekom Innovation Laboratories, Darmstadt, Germany

Ibrahiem M.M. El Emary Information Technology Deanship, King Abdulaziz University, Jeddah, Kingdom of Saudi Arabia

Christian Erfurth University of Applied Sciences Jena, Jena, Germany

Lorella Gabriele University of Calabria, Cosenza, Italy

S. Geronikolou Biomedical Research Foundation of Academy of Athens, Athens, Greece

Nick Glezakos Department of Nursing, Faculty of Human Movement and Quality of Life Sciences, University of Peloponnese, Sparti, Greece

Stamatia Ilioudi Department of Nursing, Faculty of Human Movement and Quality of Life Sciences, University of Peloponnese, Sparti, Greece

Kathrin Kirchner Friedrich Schiller University of Jena, Jena, Germany

Noboru Koshizuka Interfaculty Initiative in Information Studies, The University of Tokyo, Tokyo, Japan

Mary Lampri Data Processing and Automation Division, Supreme Council for Civil Personnel Selection, Athens, Greece

Charikleia Latsiou Auditors Department, Hellenic Data Protection Authority, Ampelokipoi, Athens, Greece

Athina A. Lazakidou Department of Nursing, Faculty of Human Movement and Quality of Life Sciences, University of Peloponnese, Sparti, Greece

Paul Matthews Department of Computer Science and Creative Technologies, Faculty of Environment and Technology, University of the West of England, Bristol, UK

Matthew F. Palmer Department of Comparative and International Education, Lehigh University, Bethlehem, PA, USA

Wilhelm R. Rossak Friedrich Schiller University of Jena, Jena, Germany

Ken Sakamura Interfaculty Initiative in Information Studies, The University of Tokyo, Tokyo, Japan

Volkmar Schau Friedrich Schiller University of Jena, Jena, Germany

Judith Simon Department of Philosophy, University of Vienna, Austria & Institute for Technology Assessment and Systems Analysis, Karlsruhe Institute of Technology, Germany

Christian Stolcis Navimatix GmbH, Jena, Germany

Maria Tsironi Department of Nursing, Faculty of Human Movement and Quality of Life Sciences, University of Peloponnese, Sparti, Greece

Iraklis Varlamis Department of Informatics and Telematics, Harokopio University of Athens, Athens, Greece

Lee Fueng Yap Interfaculty Initiative in Information Studies, The University of Tokyo, Tokyo, Japan

Stelios Zimeras Department of Statistics and Actuarial-Financial Mathematics, University of the Aegean, Karlovassi, Samos, Greece

Chapter 1
Health-Related Virtual Communities and Social Networking Services

Stamatia Ilioudi, Athina A. Lazakidou, Nick Glezakos, and Maria Tsironi

Department of Nursing, Faculty of Human Movement and Quality of Life Sciences, University of Peloponnese, Sparti GR-23100, Greece, mata_ilioudi@yahoo.gr; lazakid@uop.gr; nick.glezakos@gmail.com; tsironi@uop.gr

Abstract The literature indicates that a virtual community in health care as a group of people using telecommunication with the purposes of delivering health care and education, and/or providing support, covers a wide range of clinical specialties, technologies, and stakeholders. Examples include peer-to-peer networks, virtual health-care delivery, and research teams. Virtual communities (VCs) offer ubiquitous access to information and exchange possibilities for people in similar circumstances. This is especially valuable for patients with chronic/life-threatening diseases as they exhibit strong needs for information and interaction. Virtual communities and virtual relationships can improve the situation of all patients by offering them a place to establish social relationships that help them to cope with their situation. Although virtual relationships offer informational and emotional types of support, they do not seem to offer practical types of support. Therefore, virtual relationships can play an important role in complementing real-life social relationships, but they can never replace them.

Keywords Virtual communities • Social networks • Healthcare communities • Online • Electronic health records

1.1 Introduction

Virtual health-care communities aim in bringing together health-care professionals and patients in order to further improve the quality of health-care services and assist health-care professionals and researchers in their everyday activities. Patient monitoring and medical consultation – the two most popular activities inside virtual health-care communities – require members' collaboration in a secure and reliable environment.

The Internet is changing the way people access health-related information and how they search for support and interaction with peers in similar situations. There exist several ways of interaction between health-care practitioners and patients.

A.A. Lazakidou (ed.), *Virtual Communities, Social Networks and Collaboration*, Annals of Information Systems 15, DOI 10.1007/978-1-4614-3634-8_1,

In the case of a medical incident, patients receive medical treatment from doctors and nurses while at hospital and posttreatment support at home by family members and friends. In medical inquiries, patients search for information and advices on the web; their main supporters are doctors and medical institutes that provide official and valid guidance. For patients with chronicle diseases or psychological problems, the family members or professional care providers keep in contact with the patient and provide permanent support. In most cases, the health-care issue turns to be a transfer of knowledge, care, and services from health-care professionals to the patients [46].

Care providers comprise doctors and nurses, who treat and support patients as part of their work. The group is extended with researchers and scientists that produce and convey scientific knowledge. They provide guidance, medical advices, and information either in person or through the web.

Care givers comprise the friends or family of the patient who voluntarily support patients. They ask for medical advice and information regarding the problems faced by their relatives, and in several cases they are more active than the real patients.

Care consumers or "receivers" are the patients themselves. They need medical help and ask for it either directly or indirectly.

Virtual communities refer to groups of people that collaborate, discuss their issues, share experiences, consult with experts, and provide and request support by using telecommunication technologies. Virtual health-care communities employ advanced and pervasive ICT technologies in order to offer ubiquitous medical services to their members. Elder members, home care patients, or members with chronic conditions utilize different types of health-care services at different points in time, in this way bridging geographic distance and time constraints [10, 44].

Virtual health-care communities aim in bringing together health-care professionals and patients in order to further improve the quality of health-care services and assist health-care professionals and researchers in their everyday activities. Patient monitoring and medical consultation – the two most popular activities inside virtual health-care communities – require members' collaboration in a secure and reliable environment.

1.2 Online Communities and Virtual Relationships

Before looking at previous studies investigating the potential of online communities to establish social relationships there, it is important to define the two key concepts used in this research: online communities and virtual relationships. As there is no common agreement on one specific definition of online communities, for the purpose of this study they are defined using some of the key aspects that are repeatedly mentioned [12, 41]:

- Meeting and interaction of people
- Connected by a specific interest

- By means of a technical platform
- Where they have the chance to establish social relationships

Social relationships are characterized by a repeated interaction between two persons whereas the individual interaction is influenced by previous interactions as well as the expectation of future interactions [12]. To differentiate between virtual and real-world relationships, the place of the first interaction is used [39]: A virtual relationship is a relationship where the first contact took place online; a real-world relationship is a relationship where the first contact took place offline.

Especially during the early research on computer-mediated communication and web-based interaction services, numerous scholars questioned whether the characteristics of computer-mediated communication allow social relationships to be established in a virtual environment at all [38]. However, both the experience of numerous users of online interaction services and the results of several studies in this field of research document that it is possible to establish social relationships in online communities [41]. For example, Park and Floyd come to the conclusion that the emergence of social relationships through online services is common and widespread among its users. But they also discover that relationships which are initiated by virtual interaction mostly are not kept exclusively within a virtual environment but are migrated to the real world [38].

Social support plays a major role in positively influencing the well-being of patients. People join online self-help groups for the same reasons and therefore for the same problems for which people join real-world self-help groups [51]. According to Turner, the support received through online interaction services is perceived as helpful as support provided by real-world contact persons [45]. Members of online self-help groups superiorly cope with information about their disease due to the received support; furthermore, their emotional situation improves. A study conducted by Loader et al. identifies emotional as well as informational support as types of support provided by virtual relationships [30].

1.3 Patients and Virtual Health-Care Communities

Virtual communities are especially prevalent in terms of convincing communications among people who engage in similar activities. Being interested in certain activities, the concept of sharing feelings, opinions, and information is among the most distinctive characteristics of virtual communities. Present practices are shaped around the basis of establishing a web site and people becoming members of this site to share their thoughts, opinions, and experiences.

As virtual communities have started to become popular, different disciplines have started to analyze these areas in detail and obtain administrative inferences from them. One of the most important effects of the use of electronic environments in the distribution of health-care services has been the electronic prevalence of P2P (peer-to-peer) communities and virtual communities. People use health-care-related virtual

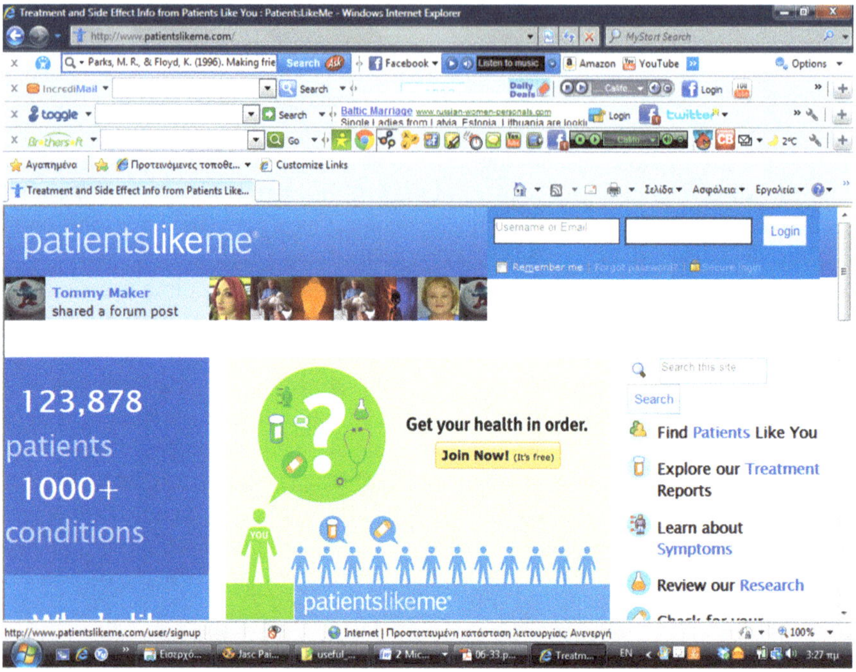

Fig. 1.1 PatientsLikeMe: http://www.patientslikeme.com

communities in accordance with their personal interests to share their experiences, to ask questions, to obtain or provide emotional support, and to obtain useful information that will help those.

As more and more people are comfortable sharing the intimate details of their lives online via blogs and social networks, the future of health-related virtual communities is looking brighter than ever – with thousands of people logging on to share side effects, treatment options, test results, and coping strategies. Data-rich virtual communities, such as PatientsLikeMe (Fig. 1.1), HealthCentral (Fig. 1.2), and CureTogether (Fig. 1.3), have been drawing a crowd in the past few years, offering a platform for patients with chronic illnesses such as fibromyalgia, depression, and multiple sclerosis to share information and connect.

PatientsLikeMe cofounders Ben and Jamie Heywood launched their site in 2008 after their brother Stephen was diagnosed with amyotrophic lateral sclerosis (ALS, also known as Lou Gehrig's disease). Earlier this year, the company tested a new design with the 100,000 members of its community and is now ready to launch the revised product to new members. CureTogether, which rates treatment options for more than 500 illnesses, boosts 26,000 members. HealthCentral, a large-scale health content site offering virtual communities, draws 17 million users to its network of health-related sites per month.

A few other virtual communities for those dealing with serious illness include Upopolis, which helps young patients, especially those in a hospital, stay wired with school friends and family in a format similar to Facebook but packed with

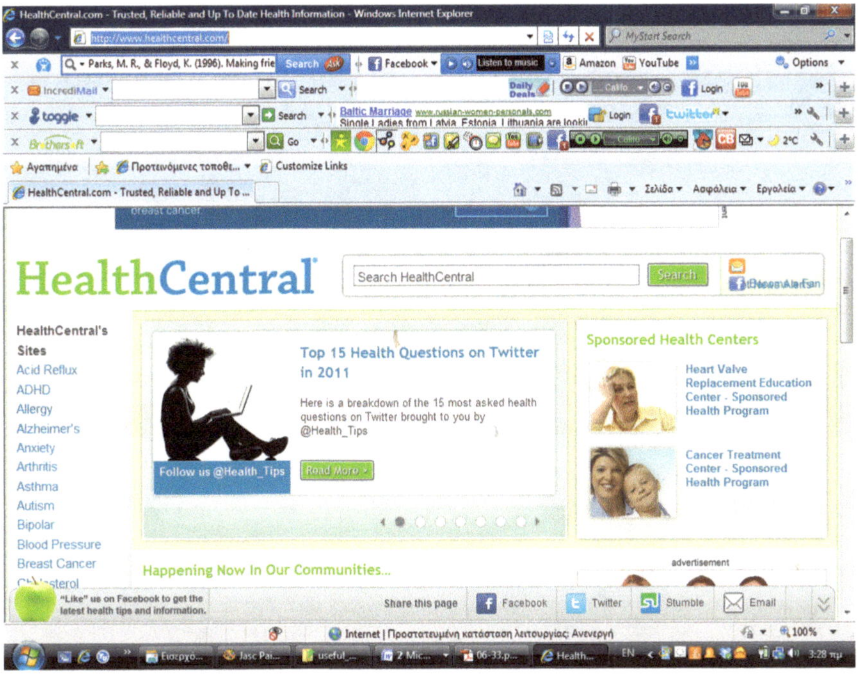

Fig. 1.2 HealthCentral: http://www.healthcentral.com

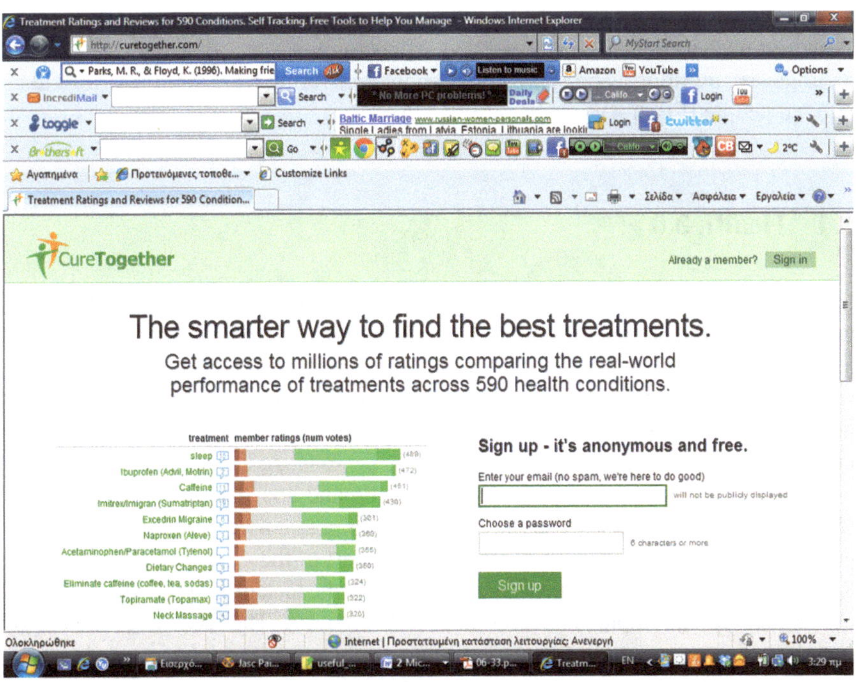

Fig. 1.3 CureTogether: http://www.curetogether.com

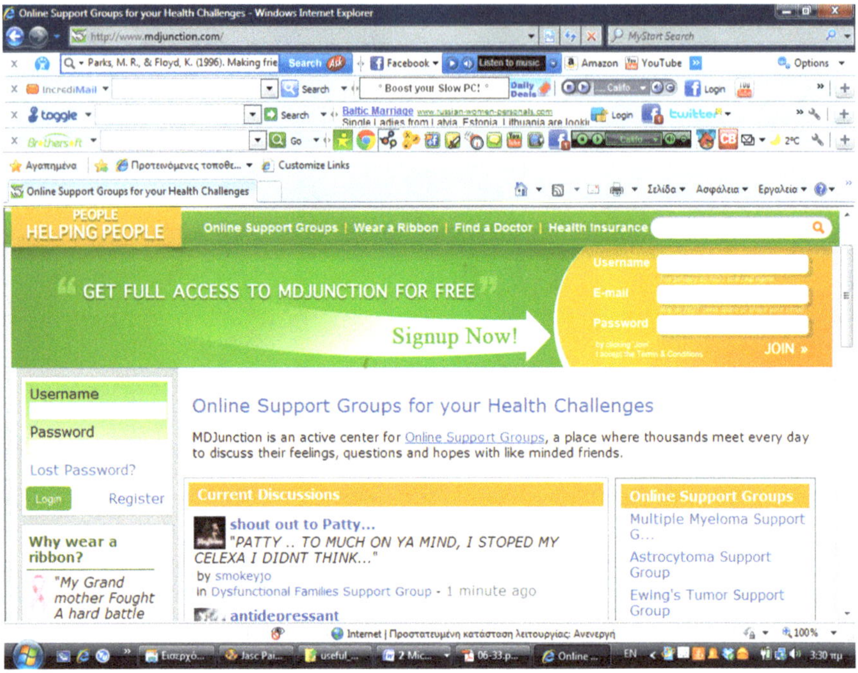

Fig. 1.4 MDJunction: http://www.mdjunction.com

"kid-friendly" tools. Also MDJunction offers online support groups to discuss feelings, ask questions, and share hopes about recovering from an illness with like-minded people (Fig. 1.4).

1.4 Health 3.0

Health 3.0 is a health-related extension of the concept of Web 2.0 whereby the users interface with the data and information available on the web is personalized to optimize their experience [2]. This is based on the concept of the Semantic Web, wherein web sites' data is accessible for sorting in order to tailor the presentation of information based on user preferences. Health 3.0 will utilize such data access to enable individuals to better retrieve and contribute to personalized health-related information within networked electronic health records and social networking resources [36, 40]. The idea was also suggested in the commentary in response to the US government's new $1.2 billion investment as a part of the American Recovery and Reinvestment Act. The commentary explains how the idea of Health 3.0 can fit in to better develop and implement electronic health records. The ideas were the use of social media and incorporation of virtual tools for enhanced interactions between health-care providers and consumers/patients [42].

Main goals of Health 3.0 are as follows:

- Improved access to health-related information on the web via semantic and networked resources will facilitate an improved understanding of health issues with the goal of increasing patient self-management, preventative care, and enhancing health professional expertise [35, 43].
- Health 3.0 will foster the creation and maintenance of supportive virtual communities within which individuals can help one another understand, cope with, and manage common health-related issues [13].
- Personalized social networking resources can also serve as a medium for health professionals to improve individuals' access to health-care expertise and to facilitate health professional-to-many-patients communication with the goal of improved acceptance, understanding, and adherence to best therapeutic options [5, 42].

1.5 A Virtual Community for Monitoring and Tele-Healthcare

Virtual communities refer to groups of people that collaborate, discuss their issues, share experiences, consult with experts, and provide and request support by using telecommunication technologies. Virtual health-care communities employ advanced and pervasive ICT technologies in order to offer ubiquitous medical services to their members. Elder members, home care patients, or members with chronic conditions utilize different types of health-care services at different points in time, in this way bridging geographic distance and time constraints [11, 47].

1.5.1 Community Members

The active members of a virtual health-care community comprise patients and doctors, as well as people with interest in the community issues, such as patients' family members, researchers, etc. Members have different roles depending on their needs and expertise: Patients and family members undertake facilitator roles, while health-care professionals become moderators for discussion and contents, facilitators and mentors for the community members. The technical administration of the community is usually performed by IT experts who must be trustful community members.

In complement to the community members, several people, in the community background, guarantee the smooth operation of the community and the uninterrupted delivery of services. The IT staff that technically supports the community, the employees of the telecommunication service provider, and the directors of the organization, company, or hospital that host the virtual community are persons that do not actually participate in the community but play a key role in its secure operation.

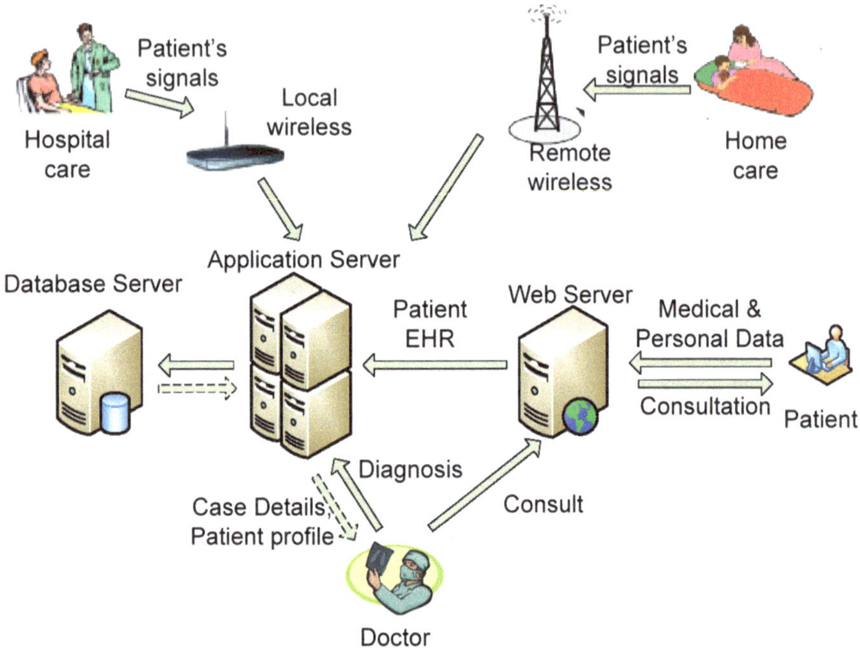

Fig. 1.5 Overview of the community interactions [8]

1.5.2 Community Activities

An overview of the interactions inside the health-care community is presented in Fig. 1.5. Health status signals are collected using wireless sensors and/or wired devices that are stored in the community servers for future reference and analysis. Patient members are also able to request for advice, diagnosis or treatment suggestion, etc., by using the community portal communication services (e-mail, forum, etc.).

The doctor from inside the hospital is able to access the patient's record (electronic health record – EHR) and make a diagnosis. The doctor replies to patients' requests but also provides consultation based on the patient's medical status signals. The hospital keeps record of patients' profiles and history, doctors' diagnoses, and of all requests and advices exchanged in the portal.

1.6 Virtual Communities for Diabetes Chronic Disease Health Care

Diabetes is classified as the world's fastest-growing chronic illness that affects millions of people. It is a very serious disease, but the bright side is that it is treatable and can be managed. Proper education in this view is necessary to achieve essential control and prevent the aggregation of this chronic sickness. In this chapter [6], the researchers describe how they have developed a health-care social network that provides methods for distance learning, opportunities for creation of virtual self-help groups where patients can get information and establish interactions among each other in order to exchange important health-care-related information, discussion forums, and patient-to-health-care specialist communication. The mission of this virtual community is to increase the independence of people with diabetes, self-management, empower them to take care of themselves, make their everyday activities easier, enrich their medical knowledge, and improve their health condition, make them more productive, and improve their communication with other patients with similar diagnoses. The ultimate goal is to enhance the quality of their life.

Virtual communities can be tools to promote health treatment strategies, to change the patient-caregiver relationship, and to reform the way health care is delivered. In fact, they already have been used to sustain healthy lifestyle changes, encourage patients' dedication in their treatment, educate, and improve the access to needed information. The proposed diabetes health-care virtual community model promotes highly effective services supported by major communication capabilities and easy information access. One of the major benefits of the health-care social network is building online social connections with peer patients, exchange experiences, share problems, and commonly search for solutions. Chat rooms, group meetings, and consultations are all virtually brought in the patient's home, anytime, anywhere. With mobile devices, the provided services are available on the go. Medical personnel are present to verify data, strengthen trust in the system, and maintain the quality of the information provided.

Virtual communities for diabetes health care play an important role in contributing to the overall effect of diabetes treatment worldwide. "A key aspect of successful chronic disease management is active partnership between consumer and provider – this is particularly important in diabetes management, where many key activities are in the hands of the patient" [48].

The benefits from the system should be attractive for both sides: health-care delivery on one hand and business perspectives so that the system can be supported on the other hand. Being a union of web application modules, mobile device applications, all based on a secure infrastructure, the proposed diabetes virtual model enables health care anywhere, at any time, and on any device.

1.7 Conclusions

The aim of this study was to examine whether online communities meet their theoretical potential to provide an environment where social relationships can be established that help patients in coping with their situation. Generally, online communities meet these potential and provide a place where patients can interact with other people, exchange information, and establish social relationships that supplement their social network.

There are several chances and challenges for virtual communities (VCs) created by new technical possibilities. Ubiquitous accesses to VCs through mobile digital devices as well as new (mobile or rather context sensitive) services for VCs are potentially very rewarding (e.g., an emergency system for cancer patients with a locating service or a mobile pill reminder). The relevance of these innovations for VCs cannot yet be assessed. The analysis of social interactions within VCs and the effects on the social network of the members have yet to be fully investigated. Research on the exact utility of health-care-oriented VCs seems to be especially promising when focusing on the measurement of the VC's influences on the perceived quality of life and the costs of treatment.

References

1. Alemi, F., Mosavel, M., Stephens, R. C., Ghadiri, A., Krishnaswamy, J., & Thakkar, H. (1996). Electronic self-help and support groups. *Medical Care, 34*, OS32–OS44.
2. Anonymous. (2009). *What is Web 3.0? Semantic Web & other Web 3.0 concepts explained in plain English*. Retrieved June 18, 2009, from http://www.labnol.org/internet/web-3-concepts-explained/8908/
3. Apostolakis, I., Chryssanthou, A., & Varlamis, I. (2009). A holistic perspective of security in health related virtual communities. In A. Lazakidou & K. Siassiakos (Eds.), *Handbook of research on distributed medical informatics and E-health* (pp. 367–381). Hershey, PA: IGI Global.
4. Bass, D. M., McClendon, M. J., Brennan, P. F., & McCarthy, C. (1998). The buffering effect of a computer support network on caregiver strain. *Journal of Aging and Health, 10*, 20–43.
5. Bellazzi, R., Montani, S., Riva, A., & Stefanelli, M. (2000). Web-based telemedicine systems for home-care: Technical issues and experiences. *Computer Methods and Programs in Biomedicine, 64*, 175–187.
6. Chorbev, I., Sotirovska, M., & Mihajlov, D. (2011). Virtual communities for diabetes chronic disease healthcare. *International Journal of Telemedicine and Applications, 2011*, 7 pages, Article ID 721654.
7. Chryssanthou, A., Latsiou, C., & Varlamis, I. (2009). Security and trust in virtual healthcare communities. In *Proceedings of the 2nd International Conference on Pervasive Technologies Related to Assistive Environments (PETRA 09), 2009 June 9–13, 2009, Corfu, Greece* (pp. 1–8). New York: ACM Press.
8. Chryssanthou, A., Varlamis, I., & Latsiou, C. (2012). A security model for virtual healthcare communities. In A. Lazakidou (Ed.), *Virtual communities, social networks and collaboration* (Annals of Information Systems Series [Special Issue]). New York: Springer.
9. Curtis, D. W., Pino, E. J., Bailey, J. M., Shih, E. I., Waterman, J., Vinterbo, S. A., et al. (2008). SMART – An integrated, wireless system for monitoring unattended patients. *Journal of the American Medical Informatics Association, 15*(1), 44–53.
10. Cyberinsecure.com. (2008). *Asprox Botnet mass attack hits governmental, healthcare, and top business websites* [2008 Jul 18, cited 2010 Jun 4]. Retrieved July 30, 2010, from http://cyberinsecure.com/asprox-botnet-mass-attack-hits-governmental-healthcare-and-top-business-websites/
11. Demiris, G., & Demiris, G. (2005). Virtual communities in health care. In B. Silverman, A. Jain, A. Ichalkaranje, & L. Jain (Eds.), *Intelligent paradigms for healthcare enterprises* (Germany-studies in fuzziness and soft computing, Vol. 184, pp. 121–137). Berlin/Heidelberg, Germany: Springer.
12. Doering, N. (2003). *Sozialpsychologie des Internet: die Bedeutung des Internet fuer Kommunikationsprozesse, Identitaeten, soziale Beziehungen und Gruppen: Internet und Psychologie* (2nd ed.). Goettingen, Germany: Hogrefe.

13. Donath, J. S. (1998). Identity and deception in the virtual community. In P. Kollock & M. Smith (Eds.), *Communities in cyberspace*. London: Routledge.
14. Dunham, P. J., Hurshman, A., Litwin, E., Gusella, J., Ellsworth, C., & Dodd, P. W. (1998). Computer-mediated social support: Single young mothers as a model system. *American Journal of Community Psychology, 26*, 281–306.
15. Eysenbach, G., Powell, J., Englesakis, M., Rizo, C., & Stern, A. (2004). Health related virtual communities and electronic support groups: Systematic review of the effects of online peer to peer interactions. *BMJ, 328*(7449), 1166.
16. Fearon, B. (2003). Enter at own risk. *Noticeboard, 11*.
17. Flatley-Brennan, P. (1998). Computer network home care demonstration: A randomized trial in persons living with AIDS. *Computers in Biology and Medicine, 28*, 489–508.
18. Frost, J. H., & Massagli, M. P. (2008). Social uses of personal health information within PatientsLikeMe, an online patient community: What can happen when patients have access to one another's data. *Journal of Medical Internet Research, 10*(3), e15.
19. Hamman, C. J. (2000). *Effect of a nurse-managed support group via an internet bulletin board on the perception of social support among adolescents with insulin-dependent diabetes mellitus*, Dissertation, Texas Tech University, Dallas, TX, pp. 1–102.
20. Houston, T. K., Cooper, L. A., & Ford, D. E. (2002). Internet support groups for depression: A 1-year prospective cohort study. *The American Journal of Psychiatry, 159*, 2062–2068.
21. Iafusco, D., Ingenito, N., & Prisco, F. (2000). The chatline as a communication and educational tool in adolescents with insulin-dependent diabetes: preliminary observations. *Diabetes Care, 23*, 1853.
22. Jones, V. M., van Halteren, A. T., Dokovski, N. T., Koprinkov, G., Peuscher, J., Bults, R., et al. (2006). Mobihealth: Mobile services for health professionals. In R. S. H. Istepanian, S. Laxminarayan, & C. S. Pattichis (Eds.), *M-health emerging mobile health systems* (pp. 237–246). New York: Springer.
23. Kaplan, D. (2009, March 2). Group unveils first-of-its-kind standard to secure patient data. *SC Magazine – NEWS*. Retrieved March 4, 2009, from http://www.scmagazineus.com/group-unveils-first-of-its-kind-standard-to-secure-patient-data/article/128168/
24. Kraut, R., Lundmark, V., Patterson, M., Kiesler, S., Mukopadhyay, T., & Scherlis, W. (1998). Internet paradox: A social technology that reduces social involvement and psychological well-being? *The American Psychologist, 53*, 1017–1031.
25. Kui, M., Yue, W., Xu, Z., Xiaochun, X., & Gengdu, Z. (2005). A trust management model for virtual communities. In *Proceedings of the 5th International Conference on Computer and Information Technology (CIT 05) 2005 Sep 21–23; Shanghai, China* (pp. 741–745). Washington, DC: IEEE.
26. Kyriacou, E., Pavlopoulos, S., Berler, A., Neophytou, M., Bourka, A., & Georgoulas, A. (2003). Multipurpose health care telemedicine systems with mobile communication link support. *Biomedical Engineering Online, 2*, 7.
27. Laleci, G. B., Dogac, A., Olduz, M., Tasyurt, I., Yuksel, M., & Okcan, A. (2008). SAPHIRE: A multi-agent system for remote healthcare monitoring through computerized clinical guidelines. In R. Annicchiarico, U. Cortés, & C. Urdiales (Eds.), *Agent technology and E-health* (Whitestein series in software agent technologies and autonomic computing, pp. 25–44). Basel, Switzerland: Birkhäuser.
28. Landro, L. (1999). Alone together. Cancer patients and survivors find treatment – and support – online: It can make all the difference. *The Oncologist, 4*, 59–63.
29. Lieberman, M. A., Golant, M., Giese-Davis, J., Winzlenberg, A., Benjamin, H., Humphreys, K., et al. (2003). Electronic support groups for breast carcinoma. *Cancer, 97*, 920–925.
30. Loader, B., Muncer, S., Burrows, R., Pleace, N., & Nettleton, S. (2002). Medicine on the line? Computer-mediated social support and advice for people with diabetes. *International Journal of Social Welfare, 11*, 53–65.
31. Lorincz, K., Malan, D. J., Fulford-Jones, T. R. F., Nawoj, A., Clavel, A., Shnayder, V., et al. (2004). Sensor networks for emergency response: Challenges and opportunities. *IEEE Pervasive Computing, 3*(4), 16–23.

32. Maji, A. K., Mukhoty, A., Majumdar, A. K., Mukhopadhyay, J., Sural, S., Paul, S., et al. (2008). Security analysis and implementation of web-based telemedicine services with a four-tier-architecture. In *Proceedings of the 2nd International Workshop on Connectivity, Mobility and Patients' Comfort (CMPC); 2008 Jan 29; Tampere, Finland* (pp 46–54). New York: ACM.
33. Mondy, J., & Torresi, M. (2008). *CIGNA creating a virtual health care community* [2008 Jul 1, cited 2010 Jun 4. Cigna website. News Releases]. Retrieved April 27, 2012, from http://newsroom.cigna.com/article_display.cfm?article_id=925
34. Mufti, M., Agouridis, D., Din, S., Mukhtar, A. (2009). Ubiquitous wireless infrastructure for elderly care. In *Proceedings of the 2nd International Conference on Pervasive Technologies Related to Assistive Environments (PETRA 09); 2009 Jun 9–13; Corfu, Greece* (pp. 1–5). New York: ACM Press.
35. Nash, D. B. (2008). Health 3.0. *P&T, 33*(2), 69–75 [PMC 2730068; PMID 19749994]. Retrieved October 3, 2011, from http://www.pubmedcentral.nih.gov/articlerender.fcgi?tool=pmcentrez&artid=2730068.
36. National Diabetes Statistics. (2011). *NIH Publication 11–3892*. Retrieved March 8, 2011, from http://diabetes.niddk.nih.gov/dm/pubs/statistics/
37. Ng, H. S., Sim, M. L., & Tan, C. M. (2006). Security issues of wireless sensor networks in healthcare applications. *BT Technology Journal, 24*(2), 138–144.
38. Parks, M. R., & Floyd, K. (1996). Making friends in cyberspace. *Journal of Communication, 46*, 80–97 [Also appearing concurrently on-line in the *Journal of Computer-Mediated Communication, 1*(4)]. Retrieved October 29, 2011, from http://jcmc.indiana.edu/vol1/issue4/parks.html
39. Parks, M. R., & Roberts, L. D. (1998). "Making MOOsic:" The development of personal relationships on-line and a comparison to their off-line counterparts. *Journal of Social and Personal Relationships, 15*, 517–538.
40. Pitsillides, A., Pitsillides, B., Samaras, G., Dikaikos, M., Christodoulou, E., Andreou, P., et al. (2004). DITIS: A collaborative virtual medical team for home healthcare of cancer patients. In R. H. Istepanian, S. Laxminarayan, & C. S. Pattichis (Eds.), *M-health: Emerging mobile healthsystems*. New York: Kluwer Academic/Plenum.
41. Rheingold, H. (2000). *The virtual community – Homesteading on the electronic frontier: Revised edition*. Cambridge, MA: MIT Press.
42. Shachak, A., & Jadad, A. R. (2010). Electronic health records in the age of social networks and global telecommunications. *Journal of the American Medical Association, 303*(5), 452–453.
43. Shaw, T. (2010). *Healthy knowledge: Semantic technology & the healthcare revolution*. Retrieved December 9, 2011, from http://www.econtentmag.com/Articles/ArticleReader.aspx?ArticleID=69404
44. Stefanov, H., Bien, Z., & Won-Chul, B. (2004). The smart house for older persons and persons with physical disabilities: Structure, technology arrangements, and perspectives. *IEEE Transactions on Neural Systems and Rehabilitation Engineering, 12*(2), 228–250.
45. Turner, J. W., Grube, J. A., & Meyers, J. (2001). Developing an optimal match within online communities: An exploration of CMC support communities and traditional support. *The Journal of Communication, 51*, 231–251.
46. Varlamis, I., & Apostolakis, I. (2006, July). *Use of virtual communities for the welfare of groups with particular needs*. 4th International Conference on Information Communication Technologies in Health, Samos, Greece.
47. Varlamis, I., & Apostolakis, I. (2010). Self-supportive virtual communities. *International Journal on Web Based Communities, 6*(1), 43–61. doi:http://dx.doi.org/10.1504/IJWBC.2010.03001
48. Warren, J., Lundstroem, M., Osborne, D., Kempster, M., Jones, S., Ma, C., et al. (2004, January). *A multi-interface, multi-profiling system for chronic disease management learning*. Proceedings of the 37th Annual Hawaii International Conference on System Sciences, Big Island, HI.
49. Wellman, B. (1997). An electronic group is virtually a social network. In S. Kiesler (Ed.), *Cultures of the internet* (pp. 170–205). Mahwah, NJ: Lawrence Erlbaum.

50. Winzelberg, A. J., Taylor, C. B., Sharpe, T., Eldredge, K. L., Dev, P., & Constantinou, P. S. (1998). Evaluation of a computer-mediated eating disorder intervention program. *The International Journal of Eating Disorders, 24*, 339–349.
51. Wright, K. (1999). Computer-mediated support groups: An examination of relationships among social support, perceived stress, and coping strategies. *Communication Quarterly, 47*(4), 402–414.

Chapter 2
Emergent Evaluation Criteria for Collaborative Learning Environment

Ibrahiem M.M. El Emary

Information Technology Deanship, King Abdulaziz University, Jeddah,
Kingdom of Saudi Arabia, omary57@hotmail.com

Abstract System and software architecture evaluation techniques have advanced significantly within last decades, but little progress has been made in the development of formalized methods and tools for distributed-collaborative architectural evaluation. Collaborative evaluation represents an effective professional development method to the degree that it sustains argumentation about the application of evidence-based design principles. The main objective of this chapter is to address an effective educational support environment and to develop meaningful collaboration learning applications. It is used for learners of educational multimedia to help them develop understanding, knowledge, and confidence and to promote the effective use of multimedia in supporting teaching and learning. This system is a framework supporting collaboration work using computers and communication vendors in a geographically distributed ubiquitous environment.

Keywords Architecture • Evaluation • Collaborative evaluation • CEVE • VE • CVE

2.1 Introduction

In the past few years and due to the evolving growth in networking and telecommunication technologies, a number of interactive virtual environments (VEs) have been developed. VEs from typical software applications can be defined as interactive, multisensory, three-dimensional, computer-synthesized environments [1]. Three-dimensional (3D) VEs come with varying features; however, typically, most provide three main components: the illusion of 3D space, avatars that serve as the visual representation of users, and an interactive chat environment for users to communicate with one another. Specific types of VEs can be distinguished based on their use or purpose. A collaborative virtual environment (CVE) is a computer-based, distributed, VE or set of places. In such places, people can meet and interact with others, with agents, or with virtual objects. CVEs are powerful and engaging

A.A. Lazakidou (ed.), *Virtual Communities, Social Networks and Collaboration*, Annals of Information Systems 15, DOI 10.1007/978-1-4614-3634-8_2,

collaborative environments for e-learning because they are capable of supporting several important learning objectives. These objectives include experiential learning, simulation-based learning, inquiry-based learning, guided exploratory learning, community-based learning, and collaborative learning (CL). It is probable that CVEs will play an important role in future education due to continuous enhancements in computer technology and the current widespread computer literacy among the public. To keep up with such expectations, e-learning systems have gone through a radical change from the initial text-based environments to more stimulating multimedia systems.

There are several reasons why producing high-quality multimedia learning resources is challenging. Many types of media, media features, and design models are available to resource developers, yet there are few standards that can guide in selecting them. Relevant research on multimedia learning has expanded, yet many developers are unaware of its full scope and value. Personnel are available who specialize in media development, instructional design, usability design, subject knowledge, and teaching, yet they are rarely coordinated so that their expertise can be effectively brought to bear. Learners usually have opinions about the resources they use, yet their opinions are rarely heard by developers. In most recent times, ubiquitous learning is characterized by providing intuitive ways for identifying right collaborators [2], right contents, and right services in the right place at the right time based on learners' surrounding context such as where and when the learners have time and space, what the learning resources and services available for the learners, and who are the learning collaborators that match the learners' needs. As a result, the effectiveness and efficiency of ubiquitous learning heavily relies on the surrounding context of learners.

Collaboration in virtual learning communities characterizes itself by heavily relying on interaction among the collaborators. The collaborators can be instructors and learners; the interaction can be resources discovery, access, and sharing, as well as group communication and discussion, or simply any collaboration which has occurred among the instructors and learners [3]. In addition, the collaboration should be enacted inside and outside of classrooms without limitation of space and time; it can be over the Internet and beyond the geographical boundary. Nevertheless, such collaboration environment is generally not supported by conventional learning environments. Typical learning services for collaboration in virtual learning communities are content, access of certain learning subjects, making studying notes and annotation on learning subjects, group discussion, brainstorming for knowledge creation, and sharing. This makes peer-to-peer network particularly suitable for implementing ubiquitous learning environments for collaborative learning.

Collaborative learning is an educational approach to teaching and learning that involves groups of students working together to solve a problem, complete a task, or create a product. Collaborative learning is based on the idea that learning is a naturally social act in which the learners talk among themselves [4]. It is through the talk that learning occurs. A set of assumptions about the learning process is described below: Learning is an active process whereby students assimilate the information and relate this new knowledge to a framework of prior knowledge. Learning requires a challenge that opens the door for the learner to actively engage his/her peers and to process and synthesize information rather than simply memorize and regurgitate it. Learners benefit when exposed to diverse viewpoints from people with varied backgrounds. Learning flourishes in a social environment where conversation between learners takes place. During this intellectual gymnastics, the learner creates a framework and meaning to the discourse [5]. In the collaborative learning environment, the learners are challenged both socially and emotionally as they listen to different perspectives, and are required to articulate and defend their ideas. In so doing, the learners begin to create their own unique conceptual frameworks and not rely solely on an expert's or a text's framework. The purpose of this collaboration is to bring interactive multimedia ubiquitous learning in real time.

As in any human computer interaction (HCI) research, educational technology designers use formative evaluation to informally understand what needs improvement in their learning environment, and guide the process of iterative design. Formative evaluation must pay attention first to usability and second to learning outcomes [6]. It is a qualitative approach, centered mostly on the operational requirements or the user requirements (learner-centered approach). Through formative evaluation, there is an assessment of the concepts and contents of the cognitive objects taught as well as of the supportive material.

According to Paramythis and Loidl-Reisinger [6], the types of formative evaluation are requirements estimation, structure definition, and development process and development fidelity. Furthermore, predictive evaluation can be part of the formative evaluation. It refers to the assessment of the quality and capabilities of the software, before its use by the target group. It is realized through means such as reports, reviews, and checklists. Expert heuristic and formative evaluations are applied in alternating cycles in the early design state of the CEVE [7]. Based on the expert's knowledge, problems concerning usability can be solved following the expert's recommendations. After these recommendations are considered in a new and better design of the CEVE, the summative evaluation is applied. The objective of the summative evaluation method is to compare different CEVEs designed with the information obtained from the User+Need Space and to determine the effectiveness of the software compared to predefined goals.

Another form of evaluation is interpretive evaluation. The main idea of this method is observation of the use of the educational software by the target group. It can be software-oriented, development-oriented, or concerning the evolving learning process through the use of the software. Bruce [7] suggested a framework constructed out of two different but complementary theoretical models: the conversational framework and the viable system model (VSM). The conversational framework is a well-known model of effective teaching practice for academic learning. The VSM is a model for the design and diagnosis of effective organizational structures drawn from management cybernetics. Bruce [7] presented a case study where place

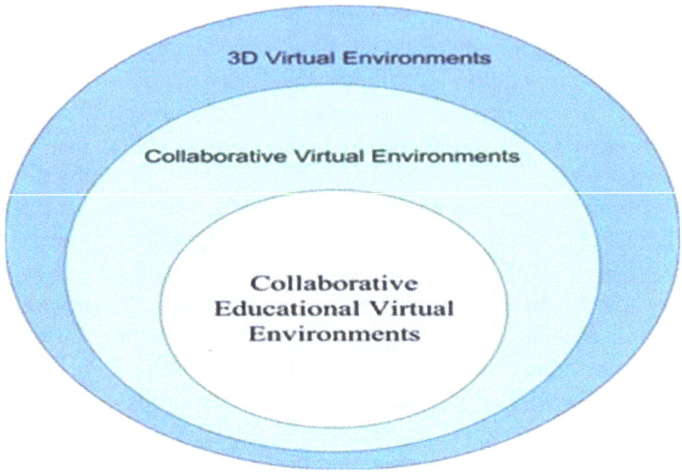

Fig. 2.1 The definition of CEVEs

metaphors in a number of 3D educational CEVEs are analyzed. The methodology followed was based on an exploratory case study and concludes that a characterization framework of 3D CEVEs could be based on the terms of learner, place, and artifact. Even though this is not an evaluation framework, we believe that it could provide guidelines toward the determination of specific metrics in an evaluation framework for CEVEs (Fig. 2.1).

Another significant work concerning the way that virtual reality aids complex conceptual learning has been presented [7]. Although this work is focused on immersive VEs, it is possible to adopt the model's main ideas for scientific investigations concerning also other types of virtual environments such as desktop-based VEs [7]. According to this model, the first step is to specify the learning concepts and which of the VEs characteristics are able to facilitate the knowledge acquisition. The next step is to gather background information on the learners.

Finally, Henda and Mohamed [8] have also observed that there is a need for a detailed theoretical framework for VR-based learning environments that could guide future development efforts. They point out that a critical step toward achieving an informed design of a VR-based learning environment is the investigation of the relationship between the relevant constructs or participant factors, the learning process, and the learning outcomes. According to the above, we can conclude that there is no focused and concrete evaluation framework for evaluating CEVEs. One the one hand, there are many techniques and evaluation frameworks for evaluating either the pedagogical or the technical nature of CSCL systems, but none of them is focused on the CEVE nature of the e-learning system. One the other hand, there are several evaluation approaches for CEVE systems. However, none of them is focused both on the pedagogical and educational nature of the e-learning system.

2.2 System Configuration

This system is a framework supporting collaboration work using computers and communication vendors in a geographically distributed ubiquitous environment, as shown in [9]. The system is structured from various layers; the layer representation of the system architecture helps one to understand the scope of each service and the relationship with other services. The system architecture can be viewed as divided in four logical parts: the infrastructure, the service functions, the advanced service functions, and the application. The system infrastructure includes operating systems and communication service module which supports data transportation among PCs in distributed collaboration environment, creates/destroys the network connections, and performs the functions controlling the QOS by detaching the network load.

Service functions include session management, floor management, concurrency management, and media management. Also, the advanced service functions include creation/deletion of shared window and creation/deletion of video window. Shared window object provides free hand line, straight line, box, and text to collaboration work learners. Application area is a collection of applications and provides a ubiquitous learning or self-learning, home education and collaboration learning, distance conference, and self-evaluation. The system provides e-learning with an intuitive shared whiteboard and application program sharing to promote group collaboration.

2.2.1 Application Human Interface

This system provided in lesson plan production, interactive lesson, and evaluation of lesson. There are four application areas that were developed [10]: self-learning or collaboration learning, self-evaluation, home study or collaboration learning, and distance conference. The floor control window controls the floor among learners, and it consists of video image window as many as the number of students who learners in the session. The video window is used for monitoring the video of a remote learner, and it displays the video image of the learner who has the floor control. The video window allows the learner to select and view the video clip. And the video window can be displayed simultaneously with a document or whiteboard information so the education can stay focused on lecture. The shared window is a window shared by all the learners, and the modification carried out by the speaker is notified to every other learners.

The local window is not shared except initial file sharing, and each learner can modify it as needed. The local window has the lecture plans which are distributed at the beginning, and enables learners to memo and browse other parts in the lesson plans, and has functions as a blackboard. The tool box provides various tools for editing contents of both the shared window and the local window. The toolbox of button is menu box for the AVI file play, Internet service, etc.. The whiteboard in top right of the screen serves as a blackboard in conventional classroom, which is an education assistant tool to write texts, draw pictures, or fill colors, and provides application program sharing with other learners and interactive education. The process for activation of collaboration learning is described below:

- The teacher prepares a lesson plan using the editor provided by the distance collaboration learning system, and the lesson plan is kept in the DB of the distance learning system.
- The teacher dispatches an invitation message of collaboration discussion to the proper students who have joined the environments.
- Each student participates in the distance collaboration learning session using his or her name.
- The teacher distributes the lesson plans to the students, and a lesson and discussion starts. After the lesson is activated, questions, answers, and discussion are done interactively in the session.

2.2.2 Advanced Service Function (Application Program Sharing)

There are two types of application program sharing. One is centralized architecture and another is replicated architecture. Since replicated architecture can only transmit management data and event data, it can reduce communication overhead. However, it has the program where the learner has to have the same application program. Software provides various execution modules through different vendors.Application program requires each student to own it. Also the problem of command serialization can be solved through invoking two applications at ones. To solve these problems, central architecture was designed and implemented [11]. The method of application-sharing program made use of windows hook function. A hook is a mechanism by which a function can intercept events (message, mouse action, key strokes) before they reach in application. Functions that received event are called event distributor and are classified according to the type of event they intercepted. Event distributor sends the event data to application program and receives processing result. The result is displayed to the own monitor and sends to remote event distributor. In case of graphic image, they are transmitted at changing of graphic image which is snatched from GDI (graphics device interface) function. GDI is communication between the application and the device driver, which performs hardware-specific functions that generate output by acting as buffer between applications and output devices. Event distributor snatches messages and sends the message to remote site for same operation.

2.2.3 Service Functions

Service functions provide the following services:

2.2.3.1 Session Management Module

Session management manages access to whole session. Session management not only restricts access, it facilities access. It can also allow learners in a session to find others and bring them into the session. Session management deals with session start/termination, join/invitation/leave, and late comers. It may also allow sub-sessions and permit to join another session. Session management has an object with various information for each session, and it also supports multi-casting with this information.

2.2.3.2 Floor Management Module

Floor management manages the learner who can talk and learner who can change the information. In this module, initially, it is set to teacher-mediated floor management, but it can be changed while in session. Mechanism of the floor management consists of brainstorming, priority, mediated, token passing, and time-out. In floor management module, it provides explicit floor management and brainstorming.

2.2.3.3 Concurrency Management Module

Concurrency management is inevitable to allow multiple learners to be in safe collaboration in distributed multimedia environment.

2.2.3.4 Window Overlays Module

This is laid by a simple sketching tool over a copied window. It provides all users with transparent background and tele-pointers. So all users can point and gesture.

2.2.3.5 Window Sharing Module

This is a combination of window copying, window overlays, floor management, and session management. All users are able to interact through application shared by them. One user is running a single user application. The other users get to see exactly what this user sees. The application can allow different users to interact with the application by selecting one of the user's keyboard and mouse as the source of input.

2.2.3.6 Media Management Module

This module manages the creation and deletion of the service object for media use and media share between remote learners. And it also limits the service by hardware constraint. Media module supports convenient module for application using the environment. Supplied module is the creation and deletion of the service object for media use. Media module limits the service by hardware constraint.

2.2.4 Communication Service Module

The communication service module is in charge of data transportation among PCs in distributed environment and used by other service modules. The communication service module creates the network connections which altogether form a collaboration work, destroy, and experiment effective system.

2.3 Evaluation Framework for CEVEs

It is important when planning an evaluation to determine which items are assessable. This is often the most complex part. This collection of items is necessary to formulate specific questionnaires and hence to find and eliminate disturbance factors from the implementation of a CEVE. The evaluation goals and the evaluation criteria are usually concurrently defined since they affect each other mutually. In our research, we discovered that criteria varied considerably between evaluations [12].

The common criteria used among the majority of researchers include effectiveness, transparency, confidence, usability, interaction, application, collaborative work, system-related criteria, and the sense of copresence. Considering all these evaluation items in one session is almost impossible since the items mentioned above evaluate too many different aspects of HCI. Also, there is no mutually accepted array of criteria or evaluation framework which is compatible with all educational software [13]. The broadness of CEVE evaluation criteria constitutes an obstruction in the evaluation process. This has been circumvented by many researchers who propose specific criteria partitioning. These partitions differ greatly in number, purpose, and scope. Some partitions simply help categorize the criteria while others constitute distinct phases or sessions of the evaluation process. Regardless of the type or model of methodology followed by the evaluator, software evaluation is comprised of certain successive phases. The adoption and utilization of CEVEs for supporting the pedagogical process requires a new type of evaluation methodology or framework. In other words, evaluation should not be limited to system and usability assessment but should also focus on the pedagogical added value of the medium, as well as the new affordances made available through its application.

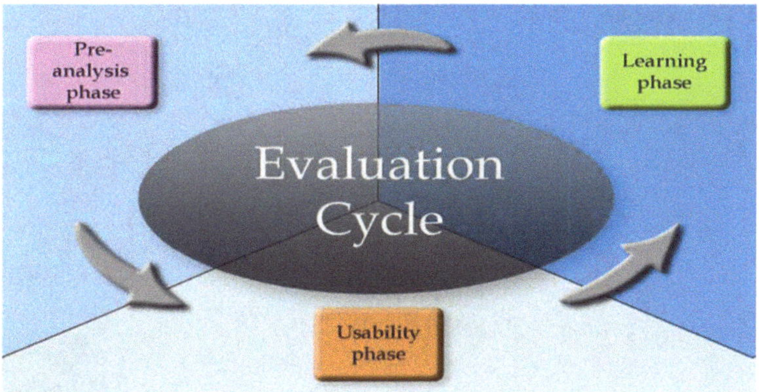

Fig. 2.2 Overview of an evaluation cycle for CEVEs

The rationale concerning the evaluation framework [14] for CEVEs is to organize the evaluation process based on the idea of iterative and incremental development process of an educational VE. An iterative and incremental development process specifies continuous iterations of design solutions together with users. According to [35], iteration includes:

(a) A proper analysis of the user requirements and the context of use
(b) A prototype design and development phase
(c) A documented evaluation of the prototype. Therefore, concerning the evaluation process, that is the main interest in this chapter, we need to conduct various evaluation cycles in order to evaluate each prototype of the system. The evaluation of each prototype system will result in suggestions for modifications in the following version of the prototype system design. In the case of a CEVE, we propose to conduct three phases in each evaluation cycle (Fig. 2.2), namely:

- Pre-analysis phase
- Usability phase
- Learning phase

A brief and general description regarding the necessity of the above phases as well as useful techniques for their successful conduct is presented in the following paragraphs.

Pre-analysis phase. Formative evaluation must pay attention first to usability and second to learning outcomes. Enhancing this idea, as shown in Fig. 2.3 [15], evaluation goals can be defined in the form of questions. Two types of questions can be formed [35]:

1. The evaluation methodology questions
2. Evaluation questions

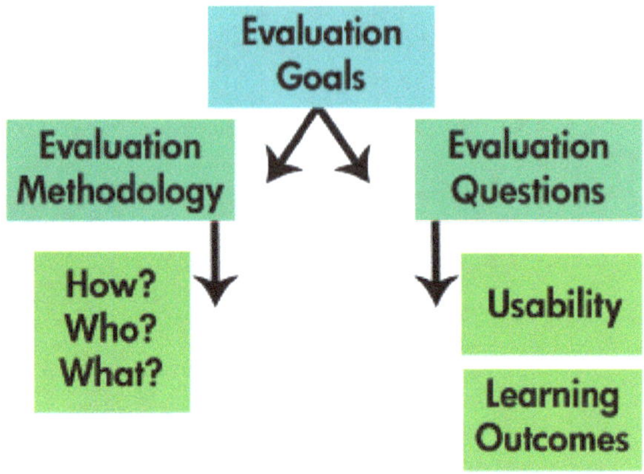

Fig. 2.3 Organizing the evaluation goals

The evaluation methodology (meta-evaluation) questions concern questions regarding the general process of evaluation [16]. Usually, the selected evaluation methodology or framework contains specific inherent goals. For example, the experimental model checks and evaluates the technical characteristics of the software, and its purpose is to reveal design issues concerning functional requirements [33]. On the other hand, the teacher-as-a-researcher model uses the teacher in order to assess the effect of the software in class and can help reveal prejudice problems, role conflicts, and student overworking.

In any case, before selecting a specific evaluation methodology, the evaluator's desired outcomes should be in consonance with the possible results of a framework [17]. A list of questions that can aid evaluators in detecting the appropriate metrics and selecting a fitting methodology was presented in [18]. The evaluation questions concern questions regarding usability and learning outcomes. Usability refers to the ability of the system to support the learning process. This covers the effectiveness, efficiency, and satisfaction with which specified users achieve specified goals in particular environments. Furthermore, in the usability questions, the characteristics of the system (e.g., avatars, nonverbal signals, and communication tools) are evaluated.

The learning outcome questions concern pedagogical research. Learning outcomes are derived from educational objectives since teaching, like research, is a purposeful activity. Learning outcomes represent the translation of aims into specific, tangible, attainable terms. For the definition of learning outcomes and objectives, [19] can be used. In order to help teachers understand and implement standard-based curriculum, Bloom's taxonomy has been revised. Classifying instructional objectives using the revised taxonomy helps to determine the levels of learning included in an instructional unit or lesson [34].

Furthermore, in this phase, the evaluator can gather information regarding the individual learning styles. This information can then be used in conjunction with questionnaire or interview results to ascertain the validity and weight of a learner's opinion recorded in the other phases. For example, during the learning phase, the tutor presents learning objects by utilizing a specific pedagogic approach. If the selected approach is not in accordance with a learner's learning style, then his or her opinion will probably bear a fair amount of subjective negativity and must therefore be judged in a lighter objective fashion. According to Edwards et al. [20], the Felder-Silverman learning style model (FSLSM) seems to be the most appropriate for use in computer-based educational systems as it describes the learning style of learners in more detail than other models. For identifying the learning styles according to FSLSM, the Index of Learning Styles, a 44-item questionnaire, can be used. Some example types of learners according to the FSLSM are [21]:

- Active learners, which learn by trying things out and working with others
- Reflective learners, which learn by thinking things through and working alone
- Visual learners, which remember best what they have seen
- Verbal learners, which get more out of words, regardless whether they are spoken or written

Usability phase. Usability inspections of the initial applications are necessary so as to uncover the main design flaws and allow a cleanup of the design, meanwhile adapting the method to 3D collaborative aspects. Usability and interaction are very much interrelated. Concerning interaction, social-arbitrary knowledge (i.e., language, values, rules, morality, and symbol systems) can only be learned in interactions with others. Several HCI rules for display design must be taken into account when implementing any e-learning system. These include consistency of data display, efficient information assimilation by the user, use of metaphors, minimal memory load on user, compatibility of data display with data entry, flexibility for user control of data display, presentation of information graphically where appropriate, standardized abbreviations, and presentation of digital values only where knowledge of numerical value is necessary and useful.

Learning phase. The main goal of the learning evaluation phase is to conduct pedagogical research. As proposed by Ogata and Yano [22], the model presented can be a useful guide in designing, developing, and evaluating a VR learning environment. Although this model is focused on immersive VEs, it could also be used in desktop CEVEs in order to address which CEVE features are appropriate, what kind of students might gain benefits through learning in CEVEs, and how CEVEs enhance learning by looking into the interaction and learning experience. Therefore, our proposed evaluation framework is based on the rationale of this model in order to test scientific hypotheses concerning learning and communicating in VEs through experimental studies.

2.4 Collaborative Argumentation in Learning Resource Evaluation and Design

There are several reasons why producing high-quality multimedia learning resources is challenging. Many types of media, media features, and design models are available to resource developers, yet there are few standards that can guide in selecting them. Relevant research on multimedia learning has expanded, yet many developers are unaware of its full scope and value. Personnel are available who specialize in media development, instructional design, usability design, subject knowledge, and teaching, yet they are rarely coordinated so that that their expertise can be effectively brought to bear. Learners usually have opinions about the resources they use, yet their opinions are rarely heard by developers.

The challenge is seen most clearly when design decisions are informed by conflicting recommendations from different specializations. Decisions about text layout are a case in point. Psychologists and educational researchers who have studied readers using computer screens to read text with a fixed number of alphabetic characters per line have observed that more characters per line (possibly up to 100) may be optimal for rapid reading, but that as few as 40 or 50 characters per line may be optimal for reading comfort and comprehension. Bhatt [23] concluded that "longer line lengths should be used when information is presented that needs to be scanned quickly and shorter line lengths should be used when text is to be read more thoroughly, rather than skimmed." Specialists familiar with this research who are designing the text components of a resource to be used for a defined learning activity might choose a fixed line length of, say, 70 characters. On the other hand, many Web developers advocate a "liquid design" for Web pages in which the number of characters per line varies according to the width of the browser window, character size, and presence of images [22]. They argue that readers can resize the browser window to the optimal width for normal reading or to a much wider width that minimizes scrolling when scanning through a large document. Because neither fixed nor liquid approaches to line length are likely to be the best choice in all design situations, an analysis of how specific circumstances play into the decision seems necessary, and that process requires knowledge of both the fixed length and flexible length strategies [24]. Finding the best design solutions and evaluating existing designs requires an exchange of specialist knowledge in relation to situated learner needs. The nature and requirements of this exchange are the concern of this chapter.

Any approach to ensuring quality in learning objects that is built around rigid standards for technologies or implementation will quickly become obsolete. Instead, what is needed is a system for evaluating learning objects that applies design principles, recognizes that the best way to operationalize these principles will change from context to context, and has a mechanism for continued interpretation and clarification of how these principles relate to specific learning objects. We maintain that continued interpretation of quality standards requires reasoned discussion or argumentation among learning object stakeholders – media developers, instructional designers, instructors, students, and so on – and that this argumentation can also serve as a form of professional development for the stakeholders. Such dialogue provides the opportunity for professionals and students to test their ideas and see the views of other stakeholders who may be approaching the same object from different professional perspectives [25].

The purpose of this chapter is to present theory and evidence that collaborative argumentation can be a powerful method for the design and evaluation of multimedia learning resources. We describe how a model of collaborative argumentation that we have developed, convergent participation, has been used to evaluate learning resources and provide professional development for learning resource designers. Before taking up this main theme, we introduce an instrument for evaluating multimedia learning resources that offers substantive guidance to collaborating reviewers.

Most learning object evaluation rubrics are designed for use by teachers and focus on content, pedagogy, and usability. For example, the evaluation rubrics used by Vicki and Jun [26] advise users to consider quality of content, potential effectiveness as a teaching tool, and ease of use. The Learning Federation (n.d.) asks users to "evaluate learning objects for educational soundness, functionality, instructional design and the overall fit to the educational purpose for which they were designed." Europe's ELEONET (n.d.), on the other hand, emphasizes a different area of quality evaluation. It evaluates technical aspects of learning objects, specifically, the metadata used to describe objects registered in a repository. LORI addresses all these areas of quality and others we believe are important. The nine LORI items broadly and concisely deal with key features of learning object quality. Because most learning object evaluators are not hired specifically to conduct reviews or formally trained in the broad range of quality issues, LORI cues reviewers to important areas of consideration. The current version of LORI has been informed by literature reviews and feedback from users in learning object quality studies and in professional development workshops for teachers and other stakeholders.

The first two items in LORI, content quality and learning goal alignment, are equally applicable to printed instructional materials and electronic resources. Content quality is usually emphasized in learning object evaluation instruments and is often given high priority by teachers. Zhang et al. [27] showed the negative impact that biases and errors in traditional textbook content can have on student understanding. In the domain of digital learning resources, where there is less regulation of content validity, reliability, and credibility, there may be even greater cause for concern about content quality. Goal alignment is a second feature that may be more neglected in multimedia resources than print textbooks. We believe that learning resource designers and evaluators should be aware of the benefits of close alignment across learning goals, learning activities, and assessments.

The next three items – feedback and adaptation, motivation, and presentation design – focus on established areas of instructional design. The feedback and adaptation item asks whether the object tailors the learning environment to the individual learner's characteristics and needs and provides feedback that is dependent on the learner's input. Feedback and adaptation has long been understood by instructional designers as an important goal for educational technology, whether manifested as simple knowledge of results on quiz items, or as adaptation of the learning environment to a sophisticated model of the learner. The motivation item [28] asks whether the object encourages learners to invest effort in working with and learning from the object. This item encourages raters to distinguish between objects that attempt to motivate by superficial complexity, such as flashing graphics, and those that engage learners existing interests and develop new ones. The presentation design item asks whether the object communicates information clearly. It draws evidence-based principles from the field of multimedia learning and established conventions for multimedia design. The presentation design item also references established stylistic conventions for clearly and concisely communicating information through graphical displays and writing.

Two items, interaction usability and accessibility, relate to learners' experience as software users. The interaction usability item assesses interface transparency, that is, how effortlessly and efficiently users can operate links, controls, and menus to navigate through the object [29]. It is important to distinguish between the challenges posed by the interface, which incur extrinsic cognitive load, and those posed by the instructional content, which may be germane to the learning goals. Any errors a student makes should be related to learning the content, not to navigational difficulties. In LORI, interaction usability is treated separately from concerns about how learners perceive and interact with the learning content. The accessibility item invites reviewers to consider the important issue of how objects can be designed to take into account differing abilities to access content. For example, Goebbels et al. [30] observed that the increasing prevalence of graphical user interfaces has produced a situation in which "blind users find the Web increasingly difficult to access, navigate, and interpret. People who are deaf and hard of hearing are served Web content that includes audio but does not contain captioning or text transcripts" (Preface: Who are you?). The Web Content Accessibility Guidelines established by the World Wide Web Consortium [31] provide useful information on how Web pages can be designed to offer consistent meaning when accessed through a range of browsers, assistive technologies, and input devices.

The final two LORI items, reusability and standards compliance, address managerial and technical matters that support the users' experience. The reusability item addresses one of the purported benefits of using learning objects: the ability for one development team to create a resource that can be reused by learners across many different courses and contexts. Finally, standards compliance addresses the need for consistent approaches to learning object metadata creation and use. Metadata (data about data) is the information that users actually search when looking for learning objects. Several organizations have been actively developing and promoting usable metadata standards. Graf and Kinshuk [32] sum up the benefits of a consistent approach to metadata creation and use: "searching becomes more specific and in-depth; managing becomes simpler and uniform; and sharing becomes more efficient and accurate."

LORI spans quality issues that are often considered the responsibility of different stakeholders, and its scope is so wide that few professionals charged with developing learning multimedia resources have detailed knowledge of all that it covers. Wherever subjective judgments of quality are applied, as they must be in using LORI, evaluations are only as good as the knowledge of the evaluators. Clearly then, the problem of advancing quality evaluation extends beyond merely translating design knowledge into evaluative criteria and overlaps significantly with problems of educating novice designers and broadening the knowledge of practicing design professionals. Next, we consider how the process of evaluation can contribute to the education of designers.

2.4.1 Evaluate to Learn

Multimedia learning resources are designed objects. As such, knowledge about how to construct them delineates a design discipline that belongs, along with engineering, computing science, architecture, among the "sciences of the artificial" described by Graf and Kinshuk [32]. With contributions from cognitive science, educational psychology, and relevant areas of educational research, a design science has emerged that advances theories, principles, and prescriptions for designing multimedia learning resources. The science informs a practice that must intentionally and reflectively bend theory to the exigencies of the situation in which the resources are used.

Educational programs for instructional designers typically present curricula in which the novice designer learns some of the theory, history, and tools of the field and is soon engaged in design projects. Of course, in the design sciences, "designing to learn" is not an innovative instructional strategy but instead a traditional and widely practiced method that is rightly regarded as a core element in design education. Designing and developing a complete learning resource can take more time than is available within a single course. As a result, students may be assigned projects that are reduced in some way; perhaps, only the design stage is completed, or only a portion of the planned content is implemented. When a student devotes much of his or her learning time to a single project, depending on the nature of that project, he or she may not have opportunity to comprehensively practice the design knowledge developed in a course. Further, design projects are often conducted individually, whether for purposes of individual evaluation, to meet unique student interests, or to allow students to design for the needs of their workplace. This can mean that students have few opportunities to discuss in detail the rationale for their design decisions.

Collaborative evaluation of learning resources can effectively complement design projects in professional development and graduate courses that teach learning resource design. The main advantage of evaluate-to-learn as an instructional strategy is that a learning object can be critiqued in less than an hour, allowing students to evaluate many cases within a single course or allowing professionals to complete evaluations within a workshop or as part of regular design work. Because real, fully developed learning resources can be evaluated, this form of case-based learning can compensate for authenticity that is lost when design projects must be scaled down to fit an academic term.

2.4.2 Collaborative Argumentation

Collaborative argumentation differs from the common understanding of argumentation as personally invested debate or persuasive rhetoric and is antithetical to the sense of argumentation as verbal conflict or quarrelling. Martens [5] claims that collaborative argumentation is the essence of discourse in science and the means by which competing theories are assessed against data and the scientific community finds agreement. Even more broadly, collaborative argumentation can be viewed as a decision-making process used in many professional fields such as medicine, engineering, and business. It is a form of productive critical thinking characterized by evaluation of claims and supporting evidence, consideration of alternatives, weighing of cost and benefits, and exploration of implications.

Researchers in the learning sciences have proposed that argumentation, particularly collaborative argumentation, can be a highly effective instructional strategy. Argumentation may help learners to understand course content, enhance their interest and motivation, and improve performance on problem solving tasks. In a study by Martens [5], students who wrote arguments about historical demographic changes in Ireland showed deeper understanding of the causes of demographic change than students who wrote summaries or explanations. Ogata and Yano [22] found that sixth grade students were more motivationally engaged in argumentative discussions of stories than in traditional recitation discussion of the stories. A review of the psychological literature on problem solving [12] concluded that people's problem solving performance is enhanced when they are instructed to generate counterarguments or alternative reasons.

Although little evidence is available about the effects of argumentation in the workplace, there is no reason to assume that its benefits for learning, motivation, and performance are restricted to formal educational settings. The collaborative argumentation process, whereby participants make their reasoning and knowledge explicit and co-elaborate their understanding of problems and situations, is likely an effective form of learning in organizations and professions. As with narrative, collaborative argumentation may be one of the activities that comprise cognitive apprenticeship.

The nature of collaborative argumentation may depend on whether the participants bring shared knowledge and fill similar roles in an organization or project or specialize in different disciplines and fill different roles. Participants from similar backgrounds often share a great deal of background knowledge that remains implicit throughout a discursive interaction. In this case, the participants are likely to develop a complex set of claims, points of evidence, and counterarguments cognate to the shared knowledge. For example, three Web developers collaborating on a learning object project may generate richly detailed arguments about image formats but have relatively little to say about learning goals. On the other hand, when the participants have differentiated expertise, the discussion may become simply an exchange of explanations rather than collaborative argumentation. For example, the subject matter expert may explain a misconception held by novices, the instructional designer may explain why a diagram might overcome the misconception, and the Web developer may explain how the diagram will be implemented. Although an explanatory discussion of this type has the needed breadth, it lacks the depth offered by collaborative argumentation in which claims are expected to be challenged and supported by evidence. For teams charged with developing learning resources, an important challenge is how to enhance the depth of analysis afforded by collaborative argumentation among team members with differentiated experience and knowledge. We believe that inviting stakeholders to commit to a set of ratings and supporting explanations in a common evaluation framework and then discuss the reasons for those ratings in a diverse team will lead to the observed benefits of collaborative argumentation. We call this process convergent participation.

2.4.3 Future Trends in Argumentation for Evaluation and Design

Until now we have investigated the use of convergent participation in graduate education and in workshops for teachers and educational technology professionals. What broader effects can be expected when the convergent participation model for collaborative evaluation is introduced into a community of learning object developers and users? First, we anticipate that participation in collaborative evaluation will facilitate adoption of quality as a communal goal. Just as there is a recognition of the need for formal approaches to ensuring quality in more traditional publishing domains, such as textbooks and journal articles, community members will become more aware of the need for quality assurance processes in learning objects and will become better informed about the detailed meanings of learning resource quality. We anticipate this will create a demand for higher quality learning resources [5].

Second, as participants become practiced in the use of evidence-based reasoning to support design decisions, they will become aware of gaps in their knowledge of relevant research evidence. Consequently, they may become more active in seeking research that bears on their design decisions. We anticipate that participants will eventually become aware of gaps or weaknesses in the available evidence, leading to an increased demand for specific research. To this point, LORI and the convergent participation model have been used only for summative evaluation. That is, resources have been assessed only after they have been completed and made available through the Internet. A natural adaptation of the model, within a community of resource developers, would be to use it formatively to support design decisions [31]. To use LORI and convergent participation for formative evaluation, one would have stakeholders collaboratively review plans and prototypes. Learning object development involves progress through phases, with only certain features developed within a phase. For example, a navigational scheme may be developed in one phase and the audiovisual content may be developed in a subsequent phase. Therefore, a formative adaptation would likely stage the assessment of the quality dimensions to parallel the development of corresponding features of the learning object.

2.5 Conclusion

Collaborative argumentation is suitable for adapting design principles because it brings to the fore the differing beliefs and knowledge of diverse stakeholders. However, without appropriate tools, protocols, and moderation, attempts at collaborative argumentation may focus on surface level explanations, without reaching the level of deep discussion. Using collaborative argumentation within a convergent participation structure may be an effective means for fostering deep, nuanced understanding of design principles because the process requires participants to explain the reasons for their decisions to apply principles in certain ways. The collaborators with certain interests and knowledge are the priority choice. We are designing our message service from a group collaboration point of view, that is, to provide message services for group collaboration, such as discussion, instant messenger, message exchange, message filtering, push message, and message synchronization within a group. In our design of group collaboration, each peer is free to initiate a special interest group and free to apply to join any special interest group initiated by other peers in the peer-to-peer network.

References

1. Graf, S., & List, B. (2005, July 5–8). *An evaluation of open source e-learning platforms stressing adaptation issues*. IEEE International Conference on Advanced Learning Technologies (ICALT 2005), Kaohsiung, Taiwan.
2. ISO. (1998). *ISO 9241–12: Ergonomic requirements for office work with visual display terminals (VDTs) – part 11: Guidance on usability*. Geneva: International Organization for Standardization.
3. Koubek, A., & Muller, K. (2002, November 16–20). *Collaborative and virtual environments for learning*. ACM SIG Proceedings, New Orleans, LA.
4. Lee, E. A. L., & Wong, K. W. (2008). A review of using virtual reality for learning, lecture notes in computer science. In Z. Pan et al. (Eds.), *Transactions on edutainment I, LNCS 5080* (pp. 231–241). Heidelberg: Springer. doi:10.1007/978-3-540-69744-2.
5. Martens, A. (2003, April). *Support cognitive processes in intelligent tutoring systems*. Proceedings of the International Conference on Cognitive Modeling, Bamberg, Germany.
6. Paramythis, A., & Loidl-Reisinger, S. (2004). Adaptive learning environments and e-learning standards. *Electronic Journal of eLearning*, *2*(1). Retrieved Jan 28, 2012, from http://www.ejel.org/volume-2/vol2-issue1/issue1-art11.htm.
7. Bruce, B. C. (2008). Ubiquitous learning. In W. Cope (Ed.), *Ubiquitous learning*. Champaign, IL: University of Illinois Press.
8. Henda, C., & Mohamed, J. (2004). PERSO: Towards an adaptive e-learning system. *International Journal of Interactive Learning Research, 15*(4), 433–447.
9. Sung, J. S. (2009). Application Protocol Design for Collaborative Learning, International Journal of u- and e- Service, Science and Technology, Vol.2, No.4. December, 2009.
10. Po-Sheng, C., Yen-Hung, K., Yueh-Ming, C., & Tzung-Shi, C. (2008, July). *A meaningful learning based U-learning evaluation model*. In 2008 Eighth IEEE International Conference on Advanced Learning Technologies, Santander, Spain.
11. Chang, C. Y., & Sheu, J. P. (2002, August 29–30). *Design and implementation of ad hoc classroom and e-schoolbag systems for ubiquitous learning*. Paper presented at the IEEE International Workshop on Wireless and Mobile Technologies in Education, Växjö, Sweden.
12. Qu, C., & Nejdi, W. "Interacting the Edutella/JXTA Peer to Peer Network with Web Services", Proceedings of the 2004 International Symposium on Applications and the Internet (SAINT'04).
13. Schilit, B., Adams, N., & Want, R, (1994, December 8–9). *Context-aware computing applications*. Paper presented at the Workshop on Mobile Computing Systems and Applications, Santa Cruz, CA.
14. Bloom, B. S. (1956). *Taxonomy of educational objectives: The classification of educational goals, Handbook 1: Cognitive domain*. New York: McKay. ISBN 978–0582280106.
15. Bruckman, A., & Bandlow, A. (2002). HCI for kids. In J. Jacko & A. Sears (Eds.), *The human-computer interaction handbook: Fundamentals, evolving technologies, and emerging applications*. Mahwah, NJ: Lawrence Erlbaum and Associates.

16. Chee, Y., & Hooi, C. (2002). C-VISions: Socialized learning through collaborative, virtual, interactive simulation. In *Proceedings of CSCL 2002: Conference on Computer Support for Collaborative Learning, Boulder, CO* (pp. 687–696). Hillsdale, NJ: Lawrence Erlbaum.
17. Churchill, E., Snowdon, D., & Munro, A. (2001). *Collaborative virtual environments: Digital places and spaces for interaction*. London: Springer. ISBN 1852332441.
18. Dickey, M. (2005). Brave new (interactive) worlds: A review of the design affordances and constraints of two 3D virtual worlds as interactive learning environments. *Interactive Learning Environments, 13*(1), 121–137.
19. Cat, K., & Peter, H. (2005). Designing agents for feedback using the documents produced in learning. *International Journal on E-Learning, 4*(1), 21–38.
20. Edwards, K., Newman, M., Sedivy, J., Smith, Y., Balfanz, D., Smetters, D. K., et al. (2002, November 16–20). *Using speakeasy for ad hoc peer-to-peer collaboration*. Paper presented at ACM 2002 Conference on Computer Supported Cooperative Work (CSCW 2002), New Orleans, LA.
21. Haruo, N., Kiyoharu, P. H., Yasufumi, K., & Shiho, M. (2003, August 13–15). *Designing ubiquitous and universal learning situations: integrating textbooks and mobile devices*. Paper presented at the 19th Annual conference on Distance Teaching and Learning, 2003, Madison, WI.
22. Ogata, H., & Yano, Y. (2004, March 23–25). *Context-aware support for computer-supported ubiquitous learning*. Paper presented at the 2nd IEEE International Workshop on Wireless and Mobile Technologies in Education, JhongLi, Taiwan.
23. Bhatt, G. D. (2001). Knowledge management in organizations: Examining the interaction between technologies, techniques, and people. *Journal of Knowledge Management, 5*(1), 68.
24. Biström, J. (2005, April). *Peer-to-peer networks as collaborative learning environments*. Paper presented at HUT T- 110.551 Seminar on Internetworking. Retrieved October 25, 2005, from http://www.sit.fi/~johnny/collp2p.pdf
25. Sung, J. S., & Lim, D. H. (2006). Adaptive tutoring and training system based on intelligent agent. *IJMUE, 1*(3), 6–11.
26. Vicki, J., & Jun, H. J. (2004, December). *Ubiquitous learning environment: An adaptive teaching system using ubiquitous technology*. Proceedings of the 21st ASCILITE Conference, Perth, Australia.
27. Zhang, J., Jin, Q., & Lin, M. (2005, March 28–30). *A framework of social interaction support for ubiquitous learning*. Paper presented at the 19th International Conference of Advanced Information Networking and Applications, Taipei, Taiwan.
28. Felder, R. M., & Soloman, B. A. (1997). *Index of learning styles questionnaire*. Retrieved July 20, 2009, from http://www.engr.ncsu.edu/learningstyles/ilsweb.html
29. Gay, L. R., Mills, G., & Airasian, P. (2000). *Education research: Competencies for analysis and application* (6th ed.). Upper Saddle River, NJ: Merrill. ISBN 978–0131185340.
30. Goebbels, G., Lalioti, V., & Göbel, M. (2003). Design and evaluation of team work in distributed collaborative virtual environments. In *Virtual Reality Software and Technology Proceedings of the ACM Symposium on Virtual Reality Software and Technology, Osaka, Japan* (pp. 231–238). New York: ACM Press.
31. Goransson, B. (2001). *Usability design: A framework for designing usable interactive systems in practice*. IT Licentiate theses 2001–06 [ISSN 1404–3203], Department of Human Computer Interaction, Information Technology, Uppsala University, Uppsala, Sweden.
32. Graf, S., & Kinshuk, K. (2006). Considering learning styles in learning management systems: Investigating the behaviour of students in an online course. *SMAP '06, First International Workshop on Semantic Media Adaptation and Personalization, Athens, Greece*. Washington, DC: IEEE Computer Society. ISBN: 0-7695-2692-6.
33. Lawton, D. (Ed.). (1978). Curriculum evaluation: New approaches. In *Theory and practice of curriculum studies* (pp. 176–185). London/Boston: Routledge. ISBN 0710000286, 9780710000286.
34. Sung, J. S. (2009) "U-Learning Model Design Based on Ubiquitous Environment", International Journal of Advanced Science and Technology, Volume 13, December, 2009
35. Tsiatos, T., Andreas, K., & Promportsis, A. (2010). Evaluation framework for collaborative educational virtual environments. *Educational Technology & Society, 13*(2), 65–77.

Chapter 3
Evaluating and Enriching Online Knowledge Exchange: A Socio-epistemological Perspective

Paul Matthews[1] **and Judith Simon**[2]

[1] Department of Computer Science and Creative Technologies, Faculty of Environment and Technology, University of the West of England, Frenchay Campus, Bristol BS16 1QY, UK, paul2.matthews@uwe.ac.uk

[2] Department of Philosophy, University of Vienna, Austria & Institute for Technology Assessment and Systems Analysis, Karlsruhe Institute of Technology, Germany, judith.simon@univie.ac.at

Abstract We apply approaches from social epistemology and social psychology to the study of knowledge in online communities. We first provide a descriptive analysis of knowledge behaviours informed by social psychology and in particular Arie Kruglanski's lay epistemics. This is followed by normative considerations concerning epistemic, i.e. knowledge-related, practices based upon insights from the philosophical field of social epistemology. In particular, we refer to the works of Alvin Goldman, Helen Longino and Miranda Fricker. Outcomes of this dual analysis are norms and evaluation criteria as well as strategies to design online knowledge exchange through avoidance of bias, stimulation of diversity and warranted recognition of epistemic authority.

Keywords Knowledge • Social epistemology • Online communities • Diversity • Social psychology • Lay epistemics • Bias • Epistemic injustice • Values in design • Social Q&A • Knowledge exchange • QA

3.1 Introduction

The social web provides access to a wealth of minds willing and able to share knowledge, and when made available in online repositories, it forms a major source for learning amongst a wider public. Knowledge thus shared may be trivial, may contribute significantly to human welfare or may help us address the most pressing issues of our time. In all cases, we should acknowledge the new power of online community in social knowledge and seek to improve how it operates.

We believe that the rising philosophical field of social epistemology has much to offer as a foundation for the evaluation and design of online knowledge systems, providing a set of norms that may act both as evaluation criteria and design principles. Social epistemology is a branch of the philosophy of knowledge that foregrounds the

A.A. Lazakidou (ed.), *Virtual Communities, Social Networks and Collaboration*, Annals of Information Systems 15, DOI 10.1007/978-1-4614-3634-8_3,

social aspects of knowledge-related processes and often strives to demonstrate its applicability to real-world social systems. As a predominantly naturalist approach, it may find support and refinement in evidence from sociological, psychological or technology-related studies. Indeed, we argue that as it progresses from the abstract to the concrete, social epistemology needs to account for all of the situated and mediated reality of human interaction—particularly issues of trust, power and justice.

Through some well-known examples and a drawing on a range of interdisciplinary evidence, this chapter aims to understand social knowledge processes and demonstrate the value of social epistemology in guiding socio-technical design. In particular, we want to demonstrate how to fruitfully combine descriptive insights from social psychology with normative considerations from social epistemology and reflections on practical issues from the perspective of values in design (VID).

We therefore first offer some insights from social psychology concerning self-efficacy, sense of community and lay epistemics which are particularly important for knowledge sharing and acquisition. We then present the work of key thinkers in the field of social epistemology, focusing on epistemological and ethical guidelines for assessing and optimizing social knowledge practices. We then return to the specificities of knowledge in online communities and look at how these might benefit from the previous analyses. First, however, we would like to set the scene with some scoping, definitions and examples of knowledge-rich communities and how they have been shown to function.

3.2 Knowledge Online: Definitions and Examples

3.2.1 Definitions and Scope

Despite several problems and continuous discussion around the philosophical definition of knowledge as justified true belief, the broad definition nonetheless has its merits for apprehending epistemic practices in knowledge-related online communities: we desire members to acquire beliefs that are grounded in evidence, which are justified and ideally true.

In contrast to most approaches in epistemology which focus on individual knowers, social epistemology foregrounds different social aspects of knowledge creation, evaluation or sharing. Goldman [21] provides a useful taxonomy of topics in social epistemology. First, there are issues around social evidence, i.e. how individuals deal with evidence provided by other agents. Second, different issues come to the fore when we shift our focus to collective epistemic agents, such as groups or networks. Here, issues of judgement aggregation and decision-making loom large. Finally, there is the perspective of system-oriented social epistemology, where social or socio-technical systems ranging from national legal systems to specific web platforms such as Wikipedia may be assessed for their epistemological merits and limits.

We propose a socio-epistemological perspective for two reasons. First, we consider epistemology to deliver deeper insights that can enhance the understanding of the different phases of knowledge lifecycles as identified in knowledge management literature. Second, within epistemology, social epistemology appears most suited to apprehend online epistemic communities for its decided focus on different social aspects of knowledge.

Quite a number of knowledge process typologies were developed in knowledge management literature to describe phases in a (desirable) lifecycle. Several of these may be conceptually combined into the four key processes of creation, capture, transfer and utilization, with creation and exchange being key processes to assess in online community [50]. As we shall see, social epistemology and social psychology can offer insights for many of these areas, though we will largely focus on two facets of exchange: *sharing* and *acquisition*. Further qualitative typologies of knowledge are common, including the distinction between the tacit and the explicit [50]. Such distinction, however, may place too much emphasis on individuals and gives insufficient weight to where knowledge is situated in a community [57].

In terms of types of knowledge actors, we consider *lay* in addition to *expert* knowledge in our analysis, not least as the interplay between experts and novices is so central to the dynamics on online communities. Moreover, we will see that there are important similarities between lay and scientific knowledge, such that analytical considerations of the latter may be similarly applicable to the former.

We further define online communities as multi-user collectives where individuals interact (actively/ repeatedly) around a common purpose, governed by a set of implicit or explicit policies [30, 50] and take the term to encompass a range of models, ranging from closed, specialist communities to open, generalist and large-scale platforms.

While earlier conceptions of community perhaps placed more weight on long-term interaction and the development of personal relationships between community members [50], there is an increasing overlap between formal, purpose built community platforms and ad hoc interactions enabled through social networking and communication tools—in the sense that these tools may be used to delineate and structure temporary yet meaningful communities we include them in our consideration.

3.2.2 *Illustrative Examples*

To open our analysis, we will briefly introduce some better known, public web communities. We chose our examples because:

1. These sites have been quite extensively studied, and there is a foundation of evidence on how they work in practice.
2. Such larger sites have important structural similarities with many smaller, specialist or private communities, and some important aspects of the research are generalizable.

Table 3.1 Traffic summary for leading social knowledge sites

Site	Estimated daily users[a]	Global ranking[b]	Reach (% of global Internet users who visit)[b]	% Coming from search[b]
Wikipedia	25 M	7	15	50
eHow	2 M	128	1	45
Answers.com	3 M	166	0.7	47
Yahoo Answers	10 M	4 (all Yahoo)	24.8 to all Yahoo. Answers accounts for 5.6% of site traffic	–

Sources: [a]Google Trends; [b]Alexa Rankings, 25 July 2011

Table 3.1 shows visitor statistics and rankings for some of the most popular knowledge platforms on the web. What is clear from current trends is that the larger collaborative, social knowledge platforms are significant in terms of audience reach and in the number of users who reach them via web search. This is significant because these sites frequently featured in the top results returned for user queries—in other words, they serve an important epistemic (knowledge-related) function.

The way knowledge is constructed and represented in these platforms varies considerably, from the anonymously co-authored Wikipedia, through information aggregation sites (Answers.com) to collaborative question answering (Yahoo Answers). We will take Wikipedia and Yahoo Answers as examples for further exploration and draw out salient points of relevance in considering their role in knowledge exchange. Our areas of focus include scale, technical functions and features, and social characteristics of participating members.

Wikipedia currently has some 3.7 million content pages, averaging 19.39 edits per page and 142,000 active users (that part of over 15 million registered active within a 30-day period) [59]. While the wiki pages themselves represent the default public view of the content, much of the community work goes on in the "Discuss" pages, where edits are proposed and commented on—and there is some evidence that those pages with more discussions may be higher quality [43]. Over time, Wikipedia articles may arrive at a certain stability where they provide the balanced objectivity the site strives toward [58]—see also Fig. 3.1 for a visualisation of article evolution—though in contested cases, it may also be that one party wins the "edit war" [48]. In terms of quality, stable Wikipedia's articles have been blind tested to favourably compare to "traditional" encyclopaedias such as Britannica, though they perhaps contain more omissions than errors [39]. Those who point to bias in Wikipedia point to geographic bias—with more coverage of the global north—and contributor bias toward the technically literate with surplus time available to contribute [26]. Persistence of content on Wikipedia may be taken as a proxy for quality, and it has been noted that some 10% of editors contribute 86% of overall value in terms of word views [43]. Dubbing this minority of coordinating editors "cool farmers", Iba et al. show how they are responsible for most content edits and comments on the talk pages over time, though this group may be further divided into mediators and zealots—either seeking conciliation or the maintenance of a radical stance [27].

Yahoo Answers by contrast is a social question-answering site, where users may pose a question and other users contribute candidate answers. Other users may vote

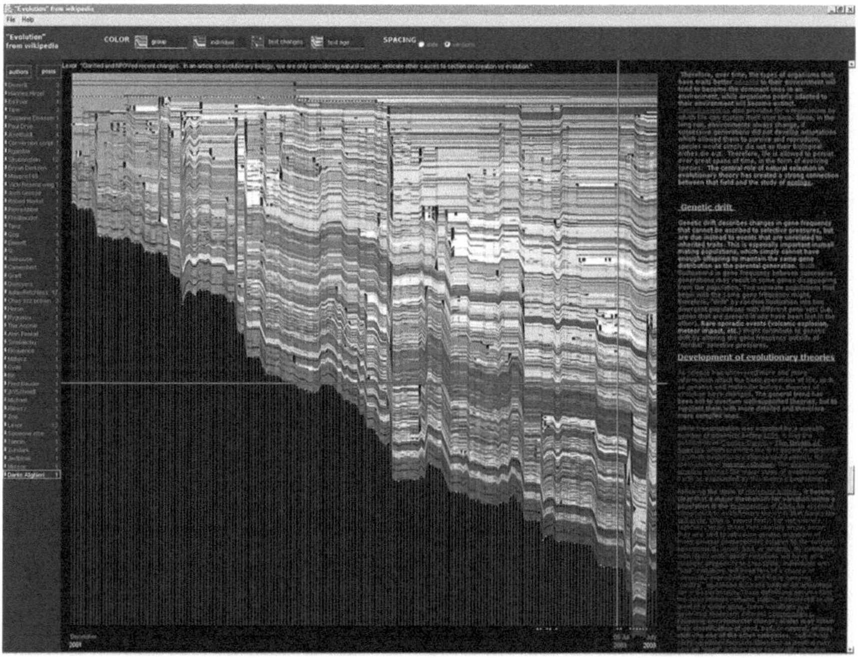

Fig. 3.1 Visualization of edits to a single Wikipedia page, showing evolution of article length (height of display) and increase in authors (each shown in a separate shade). Note persistence of contributions over time (Source: IBM History Flow Project, http://www.research.ibm.com/visual/projects/history_flow/index.htm)

the provided answers, and the original asker chooses a "best" answer amongst candidates. Content categories vary and include areas where specialized, more factual answers are common (e.g. mathematics) to broader general interest categories where answers are perhaps more a matter of opinion [1]. In exchange for supplying answers, users gain reputation points, providing several game-like interface aspects to the system. In 2009, the site was reported to have over 50 million resolved questions on its English site, with a further 5.3 million at the voting or open stage [63]. Studies of user typology on the site have revealed distinct types of answerer: those who respond from personal knowledge—"specialists"—and those who use other sources to construct answers, "synthesists". Notably, the latter tend to accumulate more reward points [16]. In terms of activity, users tend to be both contributors and consumers, and this may be taken as a sign of health of the community—as those communities with a dearth of answerers may be unsuccessful [52]. Characteristics of proffered answers may indicate likelihood of acceptance by the asker, particularly answer length and the previous number of accepted answers attributed to the user [1]. Figure 3.2 shows an example question and accepted answer pair on Yahoo Answers, with the accepted answer comment revealing the credibility cues used by the asker. In a detailed study of these acceptance criteria, Kim and Oh showed that

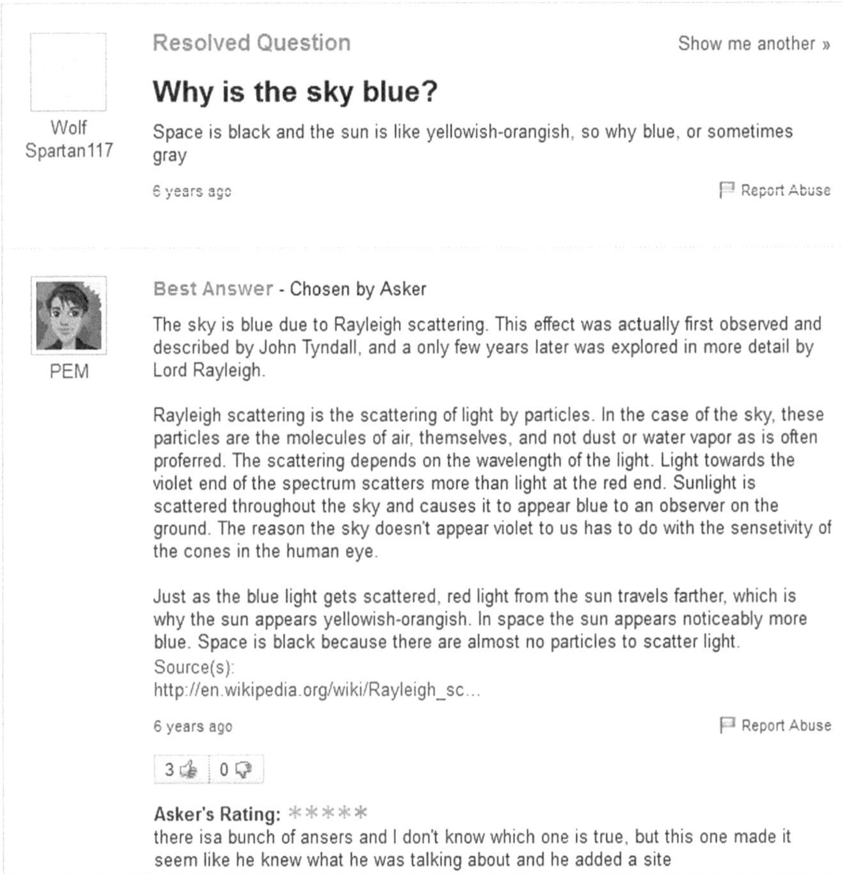
Resolved Question

Show me another »

Why is the sky blue?

Wolf Spartan117

Space is black and the sun is like yellowish-orangish, so why blue, or sometimes gray

6 years ago

Report Abuse

Best Answer - Chosen by Asker

PEM

The sky is blue due to Rayleigh scattering. This effect was actually first observed and described by John Tyndall, and a only few years later was explored in more detail by Lord Rayleigh.

Rayleigh scattering is the scattering of light by particles. In the case of the sky, these particles are the molecules of air, themselves, and not dust or water vapor as is often proferred. The scattering depends on the wavelength of the light. Light towards the violet end of the spectrum scatters more than light at the red end. Sunlight is scattered throughout the sky and causes it to appear blue to an observer on the ground. The reason the sky doesn't appear violet to us has to do with the sensetivity of the cones in the human eye.

Just as the blue light gets scattered, red light from the sun travels farther, which is why the sun appears yellowish-orangish. In space the sun appears noticeably more blue. Space is black because there are almost no particles to scatter light.

Source(s):

http://en.wikipedia.org/wiki/Rayleigh_sc...

6 years ago

Report Abuse

3 0

Asker's Rating: *****

there isa bunch of ansers and I don't know which one is true, but this one made it seem like he knew what he was talking about and he added a site

Fig. 3.2 Sample Yahoo answers question and accepted answer. Note the reasons for acceptance provided by the asker

content completeness, answer feasibility and attitude agreement/confirmation were important criteria for the asker, though emotional support, attitude and novelty of perspective or content were also significant [28].

3.3 Understanding Knowledge Exchange: Insights from Social Psychology and HCI

3.3.1 Why We Share: Motivational Aspects

A number of studies have investigated factors influencing participants' willingness to share knowledge in different types of online community. These have drawn on social psychology in addition to influential theories in sociology, communication and HCI. In her review of recent studies, Kosonen grouped facilitating factors into individual motivations, personal characteristics, technical attributes and social capital. The majority of studies in the review used questionnaires informed by "established" constructs followed by statistical modelling, while perhaps fewer have looked at participant behaviour and interaction patterns [30].

In these studies, key individual motivators include the enjoyment of helping, knowledge-sharing self-efficacy, recognition and status. Personal characteristics include comfort with online communication, sportsmanship, "hobbyist" tendencies and being a "helpful" personality. The more social influencers have been found to be interaction ties, sense of community/structural embeddedness, trust and the norm of reciprocity. Technical aspects have much in common with information systems (IS) acceptance models and have shown system quality, usability, learnability and site management to be significant [30].

Other similar studies not covered in the Kosonen review highlight sociability and usability [44] and have underlined trust (above reciprocity) and self-efficacy [9]. A key idea of Bandura's self-efficacy is that experience of mastery heightens personal efficacy, which suggests a virtuous circle associated with successful sharing, which may be reinforced with feedback and attention [62]. A form of trust termed "swift trust" may be applicable in online communities, where suspension of doubt and risk taking guides behaviour in lieu of a history of trust-building interaction [50]. Ma takes the sense of community construct further and stresses "need to belong" as an overriding factor [38]. Blanchard argues that sense of community may be elaborated to sense of virtual community (SOVC) and found positive correlation between this and trust amongst members of the website babycenter.com, a forum for new parents [7].

Aside from social aspects, Schmitz-Justin introduced a "content quality" measure and found the perception of quality in existing content to be strongly related to knowledge contribution [50]. This study also noted a relatively strong effect of professional affiliation motivation, over and above social affiliation. While this may result from the community used in the study (a higher education forum), it perhaps captures an important subjective distinction we may try to make between our social and professional personas.

3.3.2 *How We Acquire Knowledge: Insights from Lay Epistemics*

The integrative work of Arie Kruglanski in social psychology marshals a range of evidence on human belief formation under different conditions, under the banner of "lay epistemics". While not exclusive to an online setting, the work provides an empirically sound platform for understanding the dynamics of knowledge acquisition online as well as identifying frailties in the way we seek and use social evidence in knowledge processes. Kruglanski introduces the interlocking paradigms of need for cognitive closure (NFCC), the unimodel theory of social judgement and the concept of epistemic authority [32]. NFCC may be specific or non-specific—desirous of a particular epistemic outcome or not—but the results of several studies show that the higher the NFCC, the greater the tendency of human subjects to fixate on a conclusion and its associated beliefs earlier and to consult less detailed evidence in the process [31]. This may be further marked when there is increased accountability associated with the conclusion (e.g. where people are told they will have to have to justify the knowledge gained to a third party afterwards). High NFCC may be linked to more impersonal interaction styles, resistance to persuasion and intolerance of diversity [32]. NFCC also absorbs other cognitive theoretical movements such as dissonance and self-efficacy when applied to knowledge-seeking behaviour—we are motivated to seek greater predictability and avoid dissonance by confirming (or changing) our opinion, and we may only persevere in seeking when we have belief in our own effectiveness to do so [60].

The unimodel theory applies to the mechanism underlying hypothesis formation and validation. Here, Kruglanski posits an underlying syllogistic, if-then approach to the testing and assimilation of evidence, much of which comes from social sources, and it is here that an implicit hierarchy of epistemic authority applies, formed in childhood and developing in sophistication with age.

The foundational importance and interplay of the three components of lay epistemics become important in our consideration of knowledge exchange online. They reveal motivational aspects to knowledge seeking and precursors to confirmation bias and the avoidance of uncertainty, human tendencies that may be enhanced or mitigated through social and technical biases online. Notably, Kruglanski's conception of everyday belief formation is that it is fundamentally similar to the scientific method, in broad agreement with Popper—science as "common sense writ large" [32].

Studies of information-seeking behaviour tend to corroborate Kruglanski's claims, with NFCC doubtless being a key element in both formal and informal knowledge interactions. For instance, the speed, availability and convenience of online sources have been found to be important both to novice and expert seekers, to the extent of not considering options beyond those immediately available [11]. NFCC behaviours can also be linked to information satisficing, where a seeker will decide that "enough" evidence has been collected on a topic of research, in the absence of a full and rational analysis of options [46].

A note of caution is needed; however, while Kruglanski's approach provides broad brush explanations of socio-cognitive phenomena in knowledge acquisition, we should not neglect individual differences, both in experience level and cognitive style that may lead to significant differences in how individuals approach a knowledge task [12].

3.3.3 The Role of Norms: Evolution and Enaction

Community norms, overlaying and informing the development of the technical platform, provide the environment for knowledge exchange and are a crucial component to consider, as—overtly or otherwise—they represent the embodiment of the community's underlying philosophy. Norms may be captured in explicit policies, enacted in the language used and the interactions between members or applied through moderation of content. In a relatively early study of news blog communities, for instance, Lackaff illustrates how community norms may be enacted through distributed or "heterarchical" moderation schemes, where power to edit, rate and sanction contributions is devolved to community members [35]. This has been in part a response to the onerous task of maintaining "top-down" moderation and also is illustrative of the value of granting autonomy to the communities' members. In this way, community norms emerge as a combination of the rules set by the community's creators and the way these rules are enforced by users. Importantly, applying qualitative categories to posts (e.g. "useful", "informative", "funny") is necessarily subjective, but group consensus through common ground and archetyping may emerge. Lackaff shows how different communities continually adjust moderation rules and influence changes to technical features.

Other evidence shows that core community members ("Wikipedians" in the Wikipedia community) are more likely to explicitly reference community policy in justifying modification of content and therefore act as "champions" for the community's values [43].

3.4 Assessing and Improving Knowledge Exchange: Insights from Social Epistemology

Social epistemology is the philosophical discipline exploring the ways and the extent to which knowledge and epistemic practices are social. Given the goals of this chapter, it appears to be a suitable theoretical framework to apprehend knowledge practices in which multiple agents are involved.

Social epistemology as a term is mostly used to refer to a field of discourse which emerged in the 1980s in a predominantly analytic tradition, although predecessors exist within and beyond philosophy [34].

In the following, we will briefly outline several approaches within social epistemology which appear suited to shed some light on different socio-epistemic processes in online communities.

First, we present Alvin Goldman's veritistic social epistemology and argue that his approach is well suited to understand less complex testimony-related processes of knowledge exchange, whereas it appears less suited to an understanding of knowledge creation.

We then turn to Helen Longino's critical contextual empiricism, which appears better suited to apprehend communities in which new knowledge gets created. Finally, we turn Miranda Fricker's notion of epistemic injustice to emphasize a crucial problem in designing systems that serve epistemic purpose: how to avoid bias and counter epistemic injustices. Two caveats appear necessary. First of all, it is obvious that given the scope of this chapter, we can only provide a much reduced portrayal of the approaches. Second, some may consider our approach "using" different socio-epistemological approaches to shed light on difference aspects of online communities too eclectic, given that the approaches portrayed here differ profoundly in their philosophical premises. Given the scope and goals of this chapter, however, we rather wish to open up the debate and show the utility of social epistemology for online systems design and must refer to other publications for more detailed accounts of the differences between different approaches. The interested reader may confer Goldman and Whitcomb [22] for a collection of influential papers in analytical social epistemology. Overviews over the field are provided by Kusch [34] and Goldman [19]. For specific approaches within social epistemology, confer for instance Kusch [33], Longino [37] and Goldman [18].

3.4.1 Goldman's Normative Social Epistemology and Knowledge Exchange

Alvin Goldman is one of the most prominent social epistemologists, and two aspects make his work particularly relevant for this article. First of all, Goldman stressed the potential of social epistemology to provide guidance for systems design [21], and second, he explicitly addresses the role of information and communication technologies [18, 20]. However, as will also become obvious, ICT in his view are rather means of testimonial knowledge transfer conceptualized in analogy to simple sender-receiver models of information theory [53]. In the following, we will briefly outline central aspects of his veritistic social epistemology and show some of its pros and cons for systems design.

Epistemology quite generally for Goldman is "[...] a discipline that evaluates practices along truth-linked (veritistic) dimensions" and "[s]ocial epistemology evaluates specifically social practices along these dimensions" [18], and his veritistic social epistemology is specifically targeted at supporting truth and countering error and ignorance. The central concept is that of veritistic value.

Goldman argues that in everyday life as well as in science, certain value is placed on having true rather than false beliefs, and this value is what he calls veritistic value. For his assessment of epistemic social practices, it is essential that these (a) can have different veritistic outcomes, such as knowledge (positive veritistic value), error (negative veritistic value) or ignorance, and (b) that they can be evaluated according to these outcomes. Accordingly, an epistemic practice has a higher veritistic value if it yields more knowledge than another epistemic practice. While epistemic states, such as knowledge, error and ignorance, have fundamental veritistic values, epistemic practices, by contrast, have instrumental veritistic values for achieving these states [18]. Through different epistemic practices, the overall veritistic values in a society, i.e. the relationship between truth, error and ignorance, can be changed. And these changes in turn can then be used to assess the value of specific epistemic practices. Hence, the goal of epistemology in general is to evaluate practices along truth-linked dimension, and the goal of social epistemology consequently is to identify those social practices that have a comparably favourable effect on knowledge as opposed to error and ignorance.

Goldman's framework for the evaluation of social knowledge practices provides some important criteria and demonstrates his desire to progress from an egocentric to a workable social conception of knowledge. Specifically, Goldman acknowledges:

1. The core of the evaluative model, which should analyse the mechanics of the knowledge exchange practice itself: the inference practice of the "credal agent" (the believer), the speech practices of the speaker and the communication-control practice. This model is further developed in his analysis of system-oriented SE, where non-human agents may be considered part of this practice.
2. A role for personal interest as well as authority: "sensitivity to relative amounts of interest should play a modest role in assessing ... epistemic credentials" [18].
3. "Need to know": Not everybody in a community needs to know everything; instead, knowledge should be available to those who need it most.
4. Accommodation of different types of question. For questions where no agreed "true" answer exists, it might be treated in a Popperian manner—you cannot know what is true, but you can reject specific hypotheses. For this to work, however, a full range of hypotheses need to be represented. As we have seen, this is in agreement with lay epistemics, which proposes an underlying, partly subconscious, logical mechanism to reasoning and belief formation.

3.4.1.1 Testimony and ICT

Testimony in Goldman's account refers to the process of communicating knowledge from one person to another. Stating that testimony is the most elementary and universal path to knowledge, Goldman focuses on the different roles and options for action that the provider and the recipient of testimony have. He conceptualizes testimony as a four-stage process. After the initial discovery of knowledge (stage 1), someone decides to transmit a message containing this knowledge to others (stage 2). This message has then to be received (stage 3) and accepted (stage 4) by others. Only if all four stages are mastered successfully, knowledge has been transmitted from one person to another. This model strongly resembles Shannon and Weaver's mathematical theory of information [53]. And in line with such a model of testimony as signal transfer, Goldman considers testimony to be responsible solely for the spread of knowledge which has been created before. The crucial question from a veritistic point of view then is under what conditions the report of testimony will produce the largest possible change of veritistic value [18].

This veritistic perspective on knowledge transfer from one person to another also informs Goldman's analyses of ICT with respect to their potential to increase the overall veritistic value in a society or community. This can be done in two ways: either more people get to know something or something new gets known, i.e. new knowledge gets discovered.

The epistemological task for ICT usage and design then consists in finding or designing systems so that they can help in spreading knowledge fast to many people. Besides the speed and breadth of spreading knowledge, it might be of additional epistemic value that knowledge can be easily found and differentiated from non-knowledge. This aspect of quality assessment is increasingly relevant today where it is rather information overload than information scarcity which is problematic. Goldman analyses different tools, such as email, forums and the web, more generally with respect to their contribution to veritistic gain and shows how those media can either be used to raise the overall veritistic value in a society by distributing knowledge or to lower it, for example, by spreading error [18].

In a more recent paper, Goldman addresses role of blogging for democracy asking whether the web "[...] is better or worse in epistemic terms than the conventional media, in terms of public political knowledge generated by the respective communication structures" [20]. Emphasizing that conventional media often have the positive epistemic function of filtering information Goldman concludes, the veritistic impact of the blogosphere will depend on the users' motivations. Some users may use the abundance of unfiltered information to pick out only the information that corroborates their views, which are possibly biased or even utterly wrong. Others, however, might use the existing diversity to cross-check information from a variety of different sources in search for the truth in between.

Despite our general acknowledgment of Goldman's early identification of the relevance of ICT for social epistemology (and vice versa), his analyses of ICT suffer from a rather narrow perspective on ICT as being solely means of knowledge transmission. However, the web has enabled an abundance of socio-technical epistemic practices which are generative of new knowledge and not only a means of "signal transfer" under the conditions of noise. Furthermore, in neglecting issues of power, social status and trust, Goldman's social epistemology represents an "abstract social conception" [14]. There is a strong argument for philosophers to include such concerns to fully situate knowledge creation and exchange. To account for those practices, a more comprehensive and broader understanding of the socio-epistemic functions of ICT is needed, and Helen Longino's approach may be especially suited to provide guidance for the design of systems which enable knowledge creation.

3.4.2 Longino and Knowledge Creation in Communities

Helen Longino's Critical Contextual Empiricism as portrayed in her book *The fate of knowledge* also develops a social account of knowledge processes, which specifically aims at dissolving a dichotomous understanding of the social and the rational. While Longino does not explicitly address the epistemic functions of information and communication technologies, we nonetheless consider her approach particularly useful for the analysis and the design of ICT, especially for those tools that aim at knowledge creation rather than transfer of existing knowledge.

Longino acknowledges that the social dimensions of knowledge practices allow for biases and distortions in science and scientific knowledge [37]. However, sociality is not only a biasing factor—it can also deliver the means to counter such biases. The role of a social epistemologist therefore is to show "[...] how the social dimensions of cognition have resources for the correction of those epistemically undermining possibilities" [37]. And these resources for correction lie within a combination of epistemic diversity with shared standards of evaluation.

To make sure that "[t]he social is not a corrupting but a validating element in knowledge" [36], Longino proposes four social norms for social knowledge:

1. *Venues*. There must be publicly recognized forums for the criticism of evidence, of methods, and of assumptions and reasoning. [...]
2. *Uptake*. There must be uptake of criticism. The community must not merely tolerate dissent, but its beliefs and theories must change over time in response to the critical discourse taking place within it. [...] Uptake is what makes criticism part of a constructive and justificatory practice. [...]
3. *Public standards*. [...] Participants in a dialogue must share some referring terms, some principles of inference, and some values or aims to be served by the shared activity of discursive interaction. [...] A community's standards are themselves subordinated to its overall cognitive aims [...] Finally, standards are not a static set but may themselves be criticized and transformed [...] There is no particular act of adopting or establishing standards. [...]
4. *Tempered equality*. Finally, communities must be characterized by equality of intellectual authority. [36]

These four norms are more than just ethical or political nice-to-have's. If knowledge involves justification and if knowledge as an epistemological status has to be attributed to a claim by a group of people, then knowledge fundamentally rests on communities and the social mechanisms and procedures they employ. As Longino states, "[w]hile intersubjective interaction is a necessary feature of scientific cognition, not just any form of interaction will do" [37]. Rather, interaction has to be effective to yield knowledge. And the four norms exemplify those criteria that have to be met for effective criticism, for checks and balances to take place. It is only through such effective criticism that the subjective can be transformed into the objective, "[...] not by canonizing one subjectivity over others, but by assuring that what is ratified as knowledge has survived criticism from multiple points of view" [37]. Thus, effective criticism is a prerequisite of knowledge and not just an addendum.

Longino considers her four norms as recommendations for the design and constitution of scientific communities. An ideal scientific community would fulfil all these four standards to a maximum. In such a community, all hypotheses and theories would be subject to the broadest range of valid criticism by fostering epistemic diversity, by encouraging dissenting voices instead of silencing them, and by listening and responding to criticism in ways that will further increase knowledge. The effect of such transformative criticism will be that the "[...] theories and hypotheses accepted in the community will not incorporate the idiosyncratic biases (heuristic or social) of an individual or subgroup" [37]. Given that these norms represent an ideal epistemic community, real epistemic communities will hardly ever fulfil all those norms completely; the quality of epistemic communities rather comes in degrees [37].

However, the fact that ideals might never be attained does not diminish their value as goals to strive for. After all, the possibility that ultimate truth may not be attained has never hindered people to strive for it.

The utility of Longino's norms for the design of online communities should be evident. If those norms can guide and amend *scientific* knowledge creation by giving concrete recommendations of how to design interaction in scientific communities, then the same norms may well be used to design and implement other socio-technical systems that serve epistemic purposes such as online epistemic communities.

3.4.3 Fricker's Epistemic Justice and the Problem of Bias

If one acknowledges that knowledge creation is a social process, one also has to deal with the possibility of social inequalities and epistemic injustices within such processes. Therefore, a normative social epistemology has to provide guidance as to how to avoid or counter such biases. Longino's normative standards for scientific communities provide guidance in how systems can be designed to foster the positive aspects of epistemic sociality while reducing the negative side effects such as the potentiality of biases and discrimination based upon social cues.

Another philosopher who has emphasized the political nature of epistemic practices is Miranda Fricker. In her book *Epistemic Injustice*, she links epistemology to ethics in order to shed a light on issues of power and prejudice in knowing. In particular, Fricker distinguishes between testimonial and hermeneutic injustices as two instances in which someone is wronged in his or her capacity as a knower based on his or her social position. According to her, "testimonial injustice occurs when prejudice causes a hearer to give a deflated level of credibility to a speaker's word", whereas hermeneutic injustice "[...] occurs at a prior stage, when a gap in collective interpretative resources puts someone at an unfair disadvantage when it comes to making sense of their social experience" [13].

Clearly, both forms of injustice are not only taking place frequently in our offline world, but also online. Quite generally, epistemic injustice occurs when people use invalid social indicators to make judgments about the epistemic merits of someone. To avoid such epistemic injustices, reputational cues and their epistemic usage have to be critically reflected upon and be kept open for constant scrutiny and revision.

Based upon these insights, we consider the critical analysis of trust and reputation metrics and of ranking and rating mechanisms in epistemic communities to be a particularly important topic in which social epistemology and feminist social epistemology in particular has a lot to offer for community design. In short, ratings and ranking as well as more sophisticated metrics by definition create biases because they support certain agents or their content in comparison to others. However, whether or not the specific ways in which those metrics are designed is epistemically beneficial and ethically acceptable should be analysed from case to case and by taking a look into the nitty-gritty of their algorithmic foundations (cf. [55] for a socio-epistemological analysis of trust metrics).

3.5 From Theory and Evidence to Design

If we were to design systems for knowledge creation and exchange that aim at learning from social psychology and at fulfilling the normative goals of social epistemology, how should we go about it? In other words, what are the characteristics of systems that support transformative criticism and which interface features might be useful? Of course, one should not assume that one can design socio-technical systems like machines that function according to plan. According to a more performative view, socio-technical systems evolve over time and change with practice. However, by designing systems just as much as by designing technical artefacts, one sets parameters that imply certain limits and affordances that make some forms of usage more likely than others.

Despite many euphoric claims regarding the democratic nature of the web and its potential to enable everyone to contribute and participate in public discourse or in knowledge creation, the web and the design of many applications make "differences that matter" [6]. First of all, there still exists a digital divide between those possessing the resources and skills needed to participate in the web, which needs to be addressed if social inequalities on the web should be reduced.

A second risk makes this vision of the web as a neutral place where everybody has the same rights even less realistic. Many tools on the web give different weights to different agents and their contributions; they make use of ratings and rankings or of implicit forms of endorsement (downloads, page views, etc.) to generate differences between different entities. Be it Slashdot's karma model, the hierarchies introduced in Wikipedia or even the weights of links in PageRank, the vast majority of tools on the web do not treat agents (users, institutions, websites) equally. Such weighting processes indeed have their epistemic merits because they help us to navigate in a sea of information. In some communities, for instance, moderation bias to automatically hide posts that are rated down may benefit the whole community in terms of information overload and removing noise from the system [35].

However, despite such benefits, such metrics also come with different problems, especially if they lack transparency. First of all, if the underlying algorithms which decide about what is ranked up or sorted out are not accessible or understandable to users of such systems, they lack epistemic responsibility, i.e. they have to blindly trust the epistemic criteria by which the systems rank entities [41, 55]. Think of the power of Google in structuring our knowledge universe.

Moreover and here again, Google's PageRank may be instructive; the web often reproduces social inequalities and has been said to support a Matthew effect in which the rich get richer, i.e. those with many hits and links get more hits and links. Such behaviour entails epistemic as well as ethical risks, especially if the link between ascribed epistemic authority and actual epistemic authority is weak or not even assessable.

As noted before, it has been primarily feminist epistemologists who have stressed the risk of epistemic injustices and biases that can occur when invalid reputational proxies are used to assess knowledge claims without critical reflection (cf. for instance [4, 13, 49]). Feminist theoreticians have also convincingly argued that such biases and the unfair attribution of intellectual authority are not only ethical but also cognitive and epistemic failures, and have therefore requested a tempered equality of intellectual authority [37]. The crucial task in addition to raising awareness about these problems is to develop tools and strategies to counter different types of epistemic injustices. A common idea behind many feminist approaches to counter biases in socio-technical epistemic systems is to raise epistemic diversity (e.g. [4, 36, 37]). Crucially, this request for diversity is not an ethical nice-to-have, but rather an epistemic and cognitive necessity, which has not only been requested by feminist epistemologists but has also been demonstrated by computer simulations [42].

Taken together, our understanding of sharing and acquisition through the socio-epistemological lens would indicate that in design, special attention should be given to:

- Avoidance of detrimental bias, both biases crystallized in the system itself and biases inherent in the epistemic behaviour of users.
- Stimulating a diversity of members, voices and opinions, and actively recognising and incorporating dissent.
- Acknowledging authority only where warranted; criteria and mechanisms of reputation and authority attribution need to be made transparent and be bound to continuous evaluation, especially in systems where reputation attribution is automated.
- Underlining best practice along proven dimensions of usability, content quality, the empowerment of sharing and the sense of community.
- The development and support of community norms adhering to these principles.

3.5.1 Avoiding Biases and Epistemic Injustices

3.5.1.1 Pre-existent, Technical and Emergent Bias

Freedom from bias is a crucial goal for the development of any socio-technical system and much of the work in the field of science and technology studies (STS), and especially in feminist STS has focused on detecting and remedying bias in such systems. In their article on "Bias in Computer Systems", Friedman and Nissenbaum offer a taxonomy of biases that may be useful for understanding bias in online systems [15].

The two authors use bias "[...] to refer to computer systems that systematically and unfairly discriminate against certain individuals or groups of individuals in favour of others" [15]. Two notions are crucial: for bias to occur, it is not sufficient that people are treated unfairly; this treatment has to be systematic to be called bias. Moreover, the systematic distortion alone is also not considered to be bias, the distortion must also lead to unfair results. Friedman and Nissenbaum then identify three different categories of bias of relevance for computer systems, which we consider to be relevant also for our analyses: pre-existing bias, technical bias and emergent bias.

Pre-existing bias refers to "bias [which] has its roots in social institutions, practices, and attitudes" [15]. This is the type of bias that has stirred most analyses in critical science and technology studies. This form of bias is a classic example of all those societal injustices or personal prejudices that get inscribed into technology, be it intentionally or unintentionally.

Technical bias however is something different. This type of bias is not rooted in societal values, but rather arises within the process of technology design, when designers make technical decisions in certain ways and not in others, when they opt for one algorithm as opposed to another. The sources of technical bias that Friedman and Nissenbaum list are limitations of computer tools, decontextualized algorithms, methods of randomization and the biases that occur; then, human concepts have to be formalized to match the formats needed for computing.

Finally, the notion of emergent bias accounts for the fact that biases might occur later on through usage and appropriation of computer systems. Typically, such bias occurs when either the society in which the system is used changes, a process which Friedman and Nissenbaum describe as "new societal knowledge". The second reason for emergent bias has its roots in a mismatch between users and system design with respect to different expertise or values. This aspect has been empirically demonstrated by studies of Madeleine Akrich's in which technologies have been used in contexts other than the ones where they have been developed [3]. A further type of emergent bias is temporal in nature: in social question answering, for example, a delay in responding to questions may be detrimental where a ranking process is used, as rapidly provided yet relatively poor answers may rank more highly than higher quality answers provided later. This can also work at member level—long-standing community members may be conferred authority (e.g. high reputation)—though the actual quality of their contributed content does not warrant this [35].

Based on this taxonomy and the case studies they analyse, Friedman and Nissenbaum draw several conclusions concerning the necessity to avoid bias in computer systems and define tasks for designers involved in the creation of computer systems. First of all, to avoid pre-existing bias, designers have to be aware of different pre-existing biases and be sensitive to what they possibly inscribe into their systems. More precisely, they propose rapid prototyping and the inclusion of different user groups into the design process, formative evaluation and field testing as tasks that should minimize this type of bias. For technical and even more so for emergent bias, designers moreover have to envision the consequences and possible appropriations of their systems in different contexts. In order to achieve this, the authors propose the anticipation of probable contexts of usage, the articulation of constraints and the possibility to take corrective action once emergent bias becomes obvious.

3.5.1.2 Cognitive Bias

Very different types of bias are cognitive biases, such as confirmation bias and belief perseverance, which have been demonstrated in social and cognitive psychology and are central to lay epistemic theory. While some of these biases may be harder to tackle than others, a first step is to make users more aware of such human tendencies to selectively use or ignore evidence. And this is a task that can be supported in online systems.

There is some reason to believe that heightened awareness of cognitive bias (introduced through training, induction or feedback) may serve to reduce it [8]. For the belief perseverance bias—where people may cling on to a belief in the face of overwhelming contradictory evidence—a further tack where there is some supporting evidence from cognitive science is to have community members rehearse alternative explanations. In an experimental setting, subjects asked to produce counter-explanations of observed data were more likely to depart from their initial belief [5].

The risks engendered by high need for cognitive closure (Kruglanski's NFCC) could be countered by interface features that make the key arguments quickly graspable but which also make it clear when "it's complicated", that time is needed to understand the debates around a topic. Recognition of complexity is arguably itself a form of interim, nonspecific closure. Rewarding or highlighting admissions of vacillation and evidence of sophisticated personal epistemology (awareness of the nature of knowledge) may be another tack, to some extent already practiced, that may serve to make an example of unbiased knowledge-sharing behaviour.

It might be argued that the more biased belief formation processes are essentially non-epistemic, in that they are too reliant on biases such as high NFCC, desire to conform or over-credulity. They do not involve the weighing of evidence or deeper investigation into a topic. In advocating the latter as a higher value approach, we need to stress the long-term pay-offs [45]. Poulter asserts a "delayed value of truth" principle:

"The benefits of valuing truth are (usually) long-term, higher-order benefits whereas the benefits of a bias to one particular opinion are (usually) short-term, lower order benefits" [45].

Again, this principle might be enacted through induction, feedback and community norms.

3.5.2 Encouraging Diversity

3.5.2.1 Diversity of Members

A major concern with the rise of social networking has been the tendency toward homophily that similar individuals gravitate toward each other, forming a relatively cliquey subnetwork that not only shares physical attributes—age, sex and ethnicity—but also shares opinions and attitudes. Network analyses have indeed shown that this can be the case for physical attributes [56], though analyses of shared opinion have found mixed results [17], indicating that inferred shared opinion is greater than actual shared opinion between online friends. Homophily nevertheless presents a major challenge to a social epistemological ideal of diversity and may be an argument against the democratizing power of social technology [20].

The issue of homophily is tightly bound up with the design approach to identity and reputation. While taking on features from social networking tools—chiefly user profiles—may be a largely positive step in fostering an environment for knowledge sharing, it may also threaten the platform neutrality that enables dissenting voices to speak against the majority view.

A two-pronged approach of empowerment and recognition may be the key to fostering membership diversity. Examples such as Global Voices Online[1] show how contributors can be encouraged through local training initiatives, and their work may then be aggregated and amplified to become essential, widely read commentary on contemporary issues. A similar approach could work at smaller scale by targeting underrepresented groups and providing the tools and positive feedback needed to encourage sharing. Communities do have inherent scope for geographical variation that should be embraced. In specialist communities of practice, for instance, knowledge sharing is valued for enabling access to examples of practice in other locations [24].

3.5.2.2 Diversity of Views

Goldman's view on more qualitative or contested types of knowledge is that while one true answer is not achievable, we can do well by exploring and systematically ruling out possibilities [18]. The "insightful" tag in Slashdot came to serve this purpose quite well [35]. A more recent approach is shown in Opinion Space,[2] which highlights insightful comments that might be some distance from the user's own views. This needs to be weighted, however, in such a way to also indicate where consensus exists, thereby avoiding the "balance fallacy" where opposing though largely discredited views are given undue weight.

The example of Wikipedia is important in showing how the evolved idea is a balanced narrative, showing the range of opinion on both specialist and generalist topics. While this appears as a seamless whole, we have noted how the real range of views is made clear on the "discuss" pages [39]. Quora, a more recent social question-answering site,[3] combines a wiki-like topic "summary" above the individual posts and as such is perhaps more effective at making the connection between the diversity of opinion and the emergent discourse.

Where group discussion toward consensus building or decision-making is needed, genuine diversity of views militates against confirmation bias in new information seeking and assimilation [51]. In an unstructured communication environment, while

[1] http://globalvoicesonline.org/

[2] http://opinion.berkeley.edu/landing/

[3] http://www.quora.com

connections between individuals within a particular pole of a debate—homophily—may be stronger than between poles, the latter exchange can exist [64]. Importantly, metrics and increasingly network visualization can enable moderators to observe this process, forge new links between poles and recognize bridge builders in the community. Moreover, there recently has been a lot of research on diversity-based search and recommendation metrics, which also aims at providing information that not only conforms to the criteria of relevance and quality but adds the criterion of diversity of results [2, 23, 40].

3.5.3 Recognizing Authority

Online interaction provides additional barriers to epistemic authority assessment. The "calibration" of authority [29] may be more difficult as interaction may be fleeting. In the case of Wikipedia, we do not even know who has written particular passages or what their reputation is [61]. Instead, we may come to recognize the authority of a system as a whole that is "reliable enough" [54].

Authority in the online sphere is an area where different models are still being developed and tested, and as we have seen, where there may be bias and opportunities for gaming a system based on metrics which are not robust to system attacks. We can identify two possible errors in the attribution of epistemic authority:

1. Unjustly attributing authority where it is not warranted (e.g. Matthew effect), which has negative epistemic consequences
2. Unjustly denying epistemic authority, having both epistemological and ethical consequences (sensu Fricker)

We have noted how reputation metrics systems require special care since they are highly influential, often opaque, frequently bound to systematic bias and vulnerable to manipulation. While content cues alone can provide a significant amount of context regarding authority, supplementary cues may also be helpful. One innovation by the Quora question-answering platform is to allow different "topic biographies" for a single user (are they employed in the area, is it simply a hobby, etc.), thereby adding some evidence of a user's qualification to respond on a topic. When accompanied by links to other web presences, such biographies can provide a degree of verifiability (Fig. 3.3).

A specific problem occurs at the intersection of reputation and anonymity. While some users will appreciate the ability to disclose personal characteristics through their profile, anonymity (or at least minimal pseudonymity) should remain an option for others in order not to create (real or imagined) barriers to entry. Yet, irrespective of their qualities, those anonymous users may be down-ranked in systems employing reputation metrics based on the identifiability of contributors, which may be epistemically detrimental and inserts a systematic bias against anonymous users into the system.

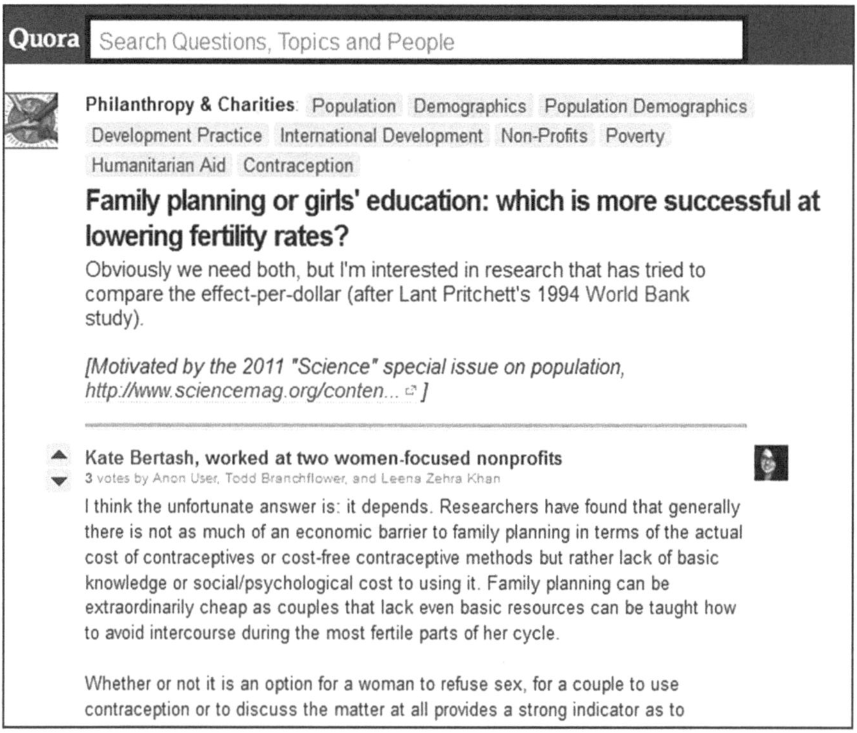

Fig. 3.3 The Quora interface showing authority cues for the highest rated answer

From a socio-epistemological perspective, several tasks for systems designers are considered crucial. First, it will be of utmost importance to design tools which not only help to assess and track authority and reputation of information sources and their providers, but which also make the criteria for authority transparent and assessable to users of varying competencies and expertise [55]. Second, the question of how to best combine traditional reputational cues (e.g. education-linked indicators) with new system-based cues (such as ratings) still needs to be fully addressed. Finally, systems need to be designed in ways to minimize the alpha and beta error of epistemic injustice: withholding epistemic authority where it would have been appropriate and attributions epistemic authority where it is not warranted.

3.5.4 Underlining Best Practice and Steering Norm Formation

Many of the principles and practices for developing a conducive environment for knowledge sharing are already well understood by community designers and managers. The motivational aspects we outline in Sect. 3.1 such as sense of community, self-efficacy and other stimuli may be encouraged through the interaction between moderators and new or experienced members. Self-efficacy, for instance, may be encouraged through welcoming new members and providing reinforcement to initial interactions with the aim of encouraging system mastery. This type of activity may be devolved with time to experienced members [47].

It is well recognized that the ideal type of community governance is a balance between top-down moderation and the fostering of bottom-up empowerment and participation in the development and enaction of community policy, leading to norms that are accepted and shared between participants. Moderators are particularly important in providing an early exemplar, "performing the public drama of the foundation myth of the community" [47]. It would therefore fall not only to systems designers, but also to moderators and founding members to embody the socio-epistemological principles we have introduced.

While there is consensus that user censorship should be light touch and that guidelines may be preferable to hard and fast rules [25], it is also recognized that for the maintenance of a fair and civil environment, a degree of policing is needed. That said, the interpretation and enforcement of guidelines and policy by community managers is often improvised and constantly reinterpreted [10].

For larger communities, content "flagging" is becoming increasingly important—users are given the ability to draw moderator's attention to content that does not conform to community policy. These data can be aggregated and provide a list of priorities for moderator attention [25]. As we see in Wikipedia, lower quality or non-compliant content thus identified may be advertised as such, providing quality cues to users. Once more, we might envisage a kind of "epistemic flagging", where topics need more input of evidence, appear biased or seem to be ignoring valid yet dissenting views.

3.6 Conclusions

This chapter has reviewed theories from social psychology and social epistemology for their contribution to a deeper understanding of knowledge practices in communities as well as for their ability to inform design practice. We have shown how both descriptive and normative insights can be brought to bear on community structure through both interface aspects and collaborative policy formation. In the process, we have highlighted a number of areas where there remains controversy and where living experiments continue to be made. We hope to have shown that, while the ideals of social epistemology may be yet to be fully realized online, a number of examples and principles exist that may be drawn on to address clear epistemic failings and promote good epistemic practice. Importantly, these go beyond what is actually encoded in social and collaborative information building to consider behaviours of knowledge providers and consumers, a holistic and, we believe, more fruitful approach.

Although much research in social epistemology focuses on scientific knowledge, the insights seem appropriate to other forms of knowledge, including the types of general knowledge exchanged on popular web platforms. It is therefore a valuable exercise to explore the work of key theorists in the field and draw lessons from them that apply as much in the diverse world of online communities as in scientific circles. Similarly, social psychology provides some quite sobering evidence of our tendencies to not behave according to good epistemic principles—even when we think we are. Our growing awareness of these biases and increased vigilance is a good first step toward their mitigation.

Acknowledgements This research was supported by the University of the West of England and the Austrian Science Fund (FWF): P 23770-G17.

References

1. Adamic, L., Zhang, J., Bakshy, E., & Ackerman, M. (2008) Knowledge sharing and Yahoo answers: Everyone knows something. In *17th international World Wide Web Conference (WWW2008), Beijing, China 2008*. New York: ACM.
2. Agrawal, R., Gollapudi, S., Halverson, A. & Leong, S. (2009). Diversifying search results. In R. E. A. Baeza-Yates (Ed.), *Proceedings of the Second ACM International Conference on Web Search and Data Mining* (pp. 5–14). New York: ACM Press.
3. Akrich, M. (1992). The de-scription of technical objects. In W. E. Bijker & J. Law (Eds.), *Shaping technology/building society: Studies in sociotechnical change*. Cambridge, MA: MIT Press.
4. Alcoff, L. M. (2001). On judging epistemic credibility: Is social identity relevant? In N. Tuana & S. Morgen (Eds.), *Engendering rationalities*. Albany, NY: SUNY Press.
5. Anderson, C. A., & Sechler, E. S. (1986). Effects of explanation and counterexplanation on the development and use of social theories. *Journal of Personality and Social Psychology, 50*, 24–34.
6. Barad, K. (2007). *Meeting the universe halfway: Quantum physics and the entanglement of matter and meaning*. Durham, NC: Duke University Press.
7. Blanchard, A. L. (2011). A model of online trust. *Information Communication Society, 14*, 76–106.
8. Burke, A. (2006). Improving prosecutorial decision making: Some lessons of cognitive science. *William & Mary Law Review, 47*, 1588–1632.
9. Chen, C., & Hung, S. (2010). To give or to receive? Factors influencing members' knowledge sharing and community promotion in professional virtual communities. *Information & Management, 47*, 226.
10. Colin, C. (2008). *Nasty as they wanna be? Policing Flickr.com – SFGate*. http://articles.sfgate.com/2008-09-29/business/17120099_1_flickr-policing-images. Accessed Sept 2011.
11. Connaway, L., Dickey, T., & Radford, M. (2011). "If it is too inconvenient, I'm not going after it": Convenience as a critical factor in information-seeking behaviors. *Library & Information Science Research, 33*, 179–190.
12. Ford, N., Wilson, T. D., Foster, A., Ellis, D., & Spink, A. (2002). Information seeking and mediated searching, Part 4: Cognitive styles in information seeking. *Journal of the American Society for Information Science and Technology, 53*, 728–735.
13. Fricker, M. (2007). *Epistemic injustice: Power and the ethics of knowing*. Oxford, England: Oxford University Press.
14. Fricker, M. (2010). Scepticism and the genealogy of knowledge: Situating epistemology in time. In A. Haddock, A. Millar, & D. Pritchard (Eds.), *Social epistemology*. Oxford, England: Oxford University Press.

15. Friedman, B., & Nissenbaum, H. (1997). Bias in computer systems. In B. Friedman (Ed.), *Human values and the design of computer technology*. Cambridge, England: Cambridge University Press.
16. Gazan, R. (2006). Specialists and synthesists in a question answering community. In Anon. (Ed.), *69th Annual Meeting of the American Society for Information Science and Technology (ASIST), Austin, US 3–8 November*. Silver Spring, MD: Richard B. Hill.
17. Goel, S., Mason, W., & Watts, D. (2010). Real and perceived attitude agreement in social networks. *Journal of Personality and Social Psychology, 99*(4), 611–621.
18. Goldman, A. I. (2003). *Knowledge in a social world*. Oxford, England: Clarendon Press.
19. Goldman, A. I. (2006). *Social epistemology*. http://plato.stanford.edu/entries/epistemology social/. Accessed Jan 2007.
20. Goldman, A. I. (2008). The social epistemology of blogging. In J. Weckert & J. V. D. Hoven (Eds.), *Information technology and moral philosophy*. New York: Cambridge University Press.
21. Goldman, A. I. (2010). Systems-oriented social epistemology. In J. Hawthorne & T. Gendler (Eds.), *Oxford studies in epistemology* (Vol. 3). Oxford, England: Oxford University Press.
22. Goldman, A. I., & Whitcomb, D. (2011). *Social epistemology: Essential readings*. New York/Oxford: Oxford University Press.
23. Hadjieleftheriou, M., & Tsotras, V. (2009). Special issue on result diversity. *Bulletin of the Technical Committee on Data Engineering, 32*, 4.
24. Hara, N., & Khe, F. H. (2007). Knowledge-sharing in an online community of health-care professionals. *Information Technology & People, 20*, 235–261.
25. Haughey, M. (2007). *Some community tips for 2007*. http://fortuito.us/2007/05/some_community_tips_for_2007. Accessed Sept 2011.
26. Holloway, T., Bozicevic, M., & Borner, K. (2007). Analyzing and visualizing the semantic coverage of Wikipedia and its authors. *Complex, 12*, 30–40.
27. Iba, T., Nemoto, K., Peters, B., & Gloor, P. A. (2010). Analyzing the creative editing behavior of Wikipedia editors: Through dynamic social network analysis. *Procedia – Social and Behavioral Sciences, 2*, 6441.
28. Kim, S., & Oh, S. (2009). Users' relevance criteria for evaluating answers in a social Q&A site. *Journal of the American Society for Information Science and Technology, 60*, 716–727.
29. Kitcher, P. (1993). *The advancement of science: Science without legend, objectivity without illusions*. New York/Oxford: Oxford University Press.
30. Kosonen, M. (2009). Knowledge sharing in virtual communities a review of the empirical research. *International Journal of Web Based Communities, 5*, 144–163.
31. Kruglanski, A. W. (1990). Lay epistemic theory in social-cognitive psychology. *Psychological Inquiry, 1*, 181–197.
32. Kruglanski, A. W., Dechesne, M., Orehek, E., & Pierro, A. (2009). Three decades of lay epistemics: The why, how and who of knowledge formation. *European Review of Social Psychology, 20*, 146–191.
33. Kusch, M. (2002). *Knowledge by agreement: The programme of communitarian epistemology*. Oxford, England: Clarendon Press.
34. Kusch, M. (2010). Social epistemology. In S. Bernecker & D. Pritchard (Eds.), *The Routledge companion to epistemology*. London: Routledge.
35. Lackaff, D. (2005). *Norm maintenance in online communities: Analysis of heterarchical moderation regimes*. MA thesis, La Trobe University, Australia.
36. Longino, H. E. (1994). The fate of knowledge in social theories of science. In F. F. Schmitt (Ed.), *Social epistemology*. Lanham, MD: Rowman & Littlefield.
37. Longino, H. E. (2002). *The fate of knowledge*. Princeton, NJ: Princeton University Press.
38. Ma, W. W. K., & Yuen, A. H. K. (2011). Understanding online knowledge sharing: An interpersonal relationship perspective. *Computers in Education, 56*, 210.
39. Magnus, P. D. (2009). On trusting WIKIPEDIA. *Epistem, 6*, 74–90.
40. Minack, E., Demartini, G., & Nejdl, W. (2009, October). *Current approaches to search result diversification*. Proceedings of the 1st International Workshop on Living Web, Washington, DC.

41. Origgi, G., & Simon, J. (2010). On the epistemic value of reputation: The place of ratings and reputational tools in knowledge organization. In C. Gnoli & F. Mazzocchi (Eds.), *Advances in Knowledge Organization, Eleventh International ISKO Conference 2010: Paradigms and conceptual systems in knowledge organization* (pp. 417–423). Würzburg, Germany: Ergon.
42. Page, S. E. (2007). *The difference: How the power of diversity creates better groups, firms, schools, and societies*. Princeton, NJ: Princeton University Press.
43. Panciera, K., Halfaker, A., & Terveen, L. (2009). Wikipedians are born, not made: A study of power editors on Wikipedia. In Anon. (Ed.), *Proceedings of the ACM 2009 International Conference on Supporting Group Work, Sanibel Island, Florida, USA* (pp. 51–60). New York: ACM.
44. Phang, C. W., Kankanhalli, A., & Sabherwal, R. (2009). Usability and sociability in online communities: A comparative study of knowledge seeking and contribution. *Journal of the Association for Information Systems, 10*, 721–747.
45. Poulter, M. (2003). *Value and belief.* Ph.D. thesis, University of Bristol, Bristol, UK.
46. Prabha, C., Lynn, S. C., Olszewski, L., & Jenkins, L. R. (2007). What is enough? Satisficing information needs. *Journal of Documentation, 63*, 74–89.
47. Rheingold, H. (1998). *The art of hosting good conversations online.* http://www.rheingold.com/texts/artonlinehost.html. Accessed Sept 2011.
48. Sanger, L. M. (2009). The fate of expertise after WIKIPEDIA. *Epistem, 6*, 52–73.
49. Scheman, N. (2001). Epistemology resuscitated: Objectivity as trustworthiness. In N. Tuana & S. Morgen (Eds.), *Engendering rationalities*. Albany, NY: SUNY Press.
50. Schmitz-Justin, F. J. (2006). *Knowledge factors: How to animate members of online communities to create knowledge-relevant content.* New York: Lang.
51. Schulz-Hardt, S., Jochims, M., & Frey, D. (2002). Productive conflict in group decision making: Genuine and contrived dissent as strategies to counteract biased information seeking. *Organizational Behavior and Human Decision Processes, 88*, 563–586.
52. Shah, C., Jung, S. O., & Oh, S. (2008). Exploring characteristics and effects of user participation in online social Q&A sites. http://firstmonday.org/htbin/cgiwrap/bin/ojs/index.php/fm/article/view/2182/2028. *First Monday, 13*(9).
53. Shannon, C. E. (1948). A mathematical theory of communication. *Bell System Technical Journal, 27*, 379–423.
54. Shirky, C. (2009). *A speculative post on the idea of algorithmic authority.* http://www.shirky.com/weblog/2009/11/a-speculative-post-on-the-idea-of-algorithmic-authority/. Accessed Sept 2011.
55. Simon, J. (2010). The entanglement of trust and knowledge on the web. *Ethics and Information Technology, 12*, 343–355.
56. Thelwall, M. (2009). Homophily in MySpace. *Journal of the American Society for Information Science and Technology, 60*, 219–231.
57. Wenger, E. (1998). *Communities of practice: Learning, meaning, and identity.* Cambridge, UK: Cambridge University Press.
58. Wikipedia. (2011a). *Wikipedia – Five pillars.* http://en.wikipedia.org/wiki/Wikipedia:Five_pillars. Accessed 27 July 2011.
59. Wikipedia. (2011b). *Wikipedia: Statistics.* http://en.wikipedia.org/wiki/Special:Statistics. Accessed July 2011.
60. Wilson, T. D. (1997). Information behaviour: An interdisciplinary perspective. *Information Processing and Management, 33*, 551.
61. Wray, K. B. (2009). The epistemic cultures of science and WIKIPEDIA: A comparison. *Epistem, 6*, 38–51.
62. Wu, F., & Wilkinson, D. H. B. (2009). *Feedback loops of attention in peer production.* Ithaca, NY: ArXiv e-prints, Cornell University Library.
63. Yahzmin (2009). *Are there statistics about "yahoo answers"?* http://answers.yahoo.com/question/index?qid=20090505082755AAW8t2U. Accessed July 2011.
64. Yardi, S., & Boyd, D. (2010). Dynamic debates: An analysis of group polarization over time on Twitter. *Bulletin of Science Technology Society, 30*, 316–327.

Chapter 4
Organizational Design of Online Communities

Nick Glezakos and Athina A. Lazakidou

Department of Nursing, Faculty of Human Movement and Quality of Life Sciences, University of Peloponnese, Orthias Artemidos & Plateon, GR-23100 Sparti, Greece, nick.glezakos@gmail.com; lazakid@uop.gr

Abstract The organizational design of online communities clearly has to embody both dimensions of what an online community stands for: an organization of a community of people (social dimension) interacting online (technology dimension). A careful balance between the two is to be realized in a social informatics service that has to be designed in order to "drive" its potential users, the community members, toward bottom-up community creation and maintenance. In order to achieve the bottom-up effect, the focus is on the design of the social informatics service. This service should entail the prerequisite characteristics that "weave" a community than to merely provide a set of rules and regulations for the service's users. It is crucial for every user to build their own environment within the online community than to be restricted by rules imported manually by other users – the technological metaphor of "bullying." Simultaneously, the characteristics of the service itself should set the boundaries of the social interaction online, thus avoiding anarchy. The chapter focuses on certain aspects of design guidelines for social informatics service designers aimed at empowering online communities with emphasis on seamless, next to "real-life" parameters and patterns. Underlining the importance of *simplicity*, *tangible value*, and *engagement*, the guidelines approach the task from two distinctive directions, the first being the governing parameters and the second being the correlating patterns.

4.1 Introduction

A social informatics online service that fosters the creation and support of an online community is a system that processes information, is based heavily on (user) feedback, and has comprehensible boundaries, and the main parameters that govern it are known to a certain extent. Frequently, it is clear that a system that aims to support such a service embodies inter-scientific knowledge combining sociological and

A.A. Lazakidou (ed.), *Virtual Communities, Social Networks and Collaboration*, Annals of Information Systems 15, DOI 10.1007/978-1-4614-3634-8_4,

technology methods and tools and, therefore, can often be quite complex. Modern approaches are usually based on complex systems that may refer to state-of-the-art technology such as enterprise systems that are addressed to large populations, user behavior forecasts, antagonistic traits such as contribution and benefits metrics, and so forth. It has become clear to designers that complexity has been established as the core characteristic of the problem base of any modern approach toward designing an online social informatics service. An efficacious way to tackle complexity is to design a service in a way that it fosters the "automatic" or "bottom-up/organic" creation of an online community. In this way, manual input (usually having to do with a set of regulations and rules and also community administration tasks) should be restrained to minimum, thus contributing in organizational and technical simplicity. Simplicity in design assures, among other benefits, smooth communication and cooperation of the actors involved. Therefore, one of the main requirements of successful designs of such systems is *simplicity*.

Another challenge of organizing a community through a social informatics service is to make each and every actor involved always aware of the *tangible value* of the interaction at hand. Users often find themselves engaging to "mechanical"-based processes in order to gain any value they anticipate from the social community. Designers should administer this problem from the initial phase of the design bringing some representation of the user's anticipated value in the center of their designs.

The final challenge (tackled by this chapter) should be the level of *engagement* of the service itself by the community. Again, bottom-up approaches give the users the opportunity to mold their online environment developing a sense of intimacy and belonging – a crucial prerequisite for community cohesion and sustainability. Thus, bottom-up approaches should first entail a sense of social intimacy in their designs, possibly as a metric, and then regulate a set of social engaging patterns to take after "real life" – the latter in order to make the whole process of socialization as seamless as possible. A clear path should be given for leadership initiatives and correlating processes for adopting them as an integral part of the service/system. Furthermore, beyond initial adoption, inceptives-based use cases and patterns should accommodate the need of sustainable socialization of an online community.

This chapter addresses the endeavor of creating meaningful and vibrant online communities in terms of *simplicity*, *tangible values*, and *engagement* focusing on two areas of the organizational design: the *governing parameters* and the correlating *engagement patterns*.

4.2 Governing Parameters

An online community bears its core parameters from the fact that it represents, in fact, an organization of people interacting online. The "organization" aspect attracts a number of people to "belong" to a general organization entity with the "online" aspect baring the traits and restrictions of online communication. Thus, an organization of people that semantically "belong" to a certain domain should indeed be characterized by a simple description of that *domain*. The definition of the domain for each case (i.e., for each separate online community) is of paramount importance [1]. In the "physical" world, this domain description would best be depicted by the community's site main message. It clearly answers the main question of the purpose of the community "who are we?" A logical extension of the question is the definition of the community's *actors*. Actors need an incentive to participate and provide fruitful contribution to the community, and this will happen when they (easily and simply) recognize *tangible value* as an immediate outcome of their interaction with the community [2].

Since there are numerous ways to tackle these definitions, the following guidelines are design propositions that try to abide to the requirement of *simplicity*, *tangible value*, and *engagement*.

4.2.1 Domain

A simple statement of the purpose of the community is impertinent to constantly remind the developers of (a) the domain area(s) the community refers to and (b) the range of the community applicability. A useful pattern for such a statement is this: "We develop a community that supports/helps/empowers <*users*> to <*do sth*>" as a verbal description of the community [3]. <*do sth*> is ideally shaped by putting a simple question to the users in a first person fashion: "what would you like to do ?" or "where would you like to be?" Often, this is quite clear and no additional effort is needed, e.g., "doctors would like to learn about the new products of a pharmaceutical company along with their uses and side effects." In this case, the community purpose statement should be: "We help doctors to learn about the new pharma products along with their uses and side effects." As trivial as this seems, it is good practice to communicate the purpose statement with everyone involved in the design and make sure that everyone has full understanding of its context. It is useful to note here, just to underline how such a simple but powerful design guideline has been neglected by social services "giants," the relevantly recent change of the home page of Twitter from the generic "follow your interests" to the more personal "Welcome to Twitter. Find out what's happening, right now, with the people and organizations you care about." Another striking example of how a simple purpose statement guides the organization of an online community (or at least guides everyone to the right direction) is the hype site of HealthTap (www.healthtap.com), an online Q&A forum that reads in the home page: "Answers from 6,000 US licensed physicians – No waiting room" (see Fig. 4.1).

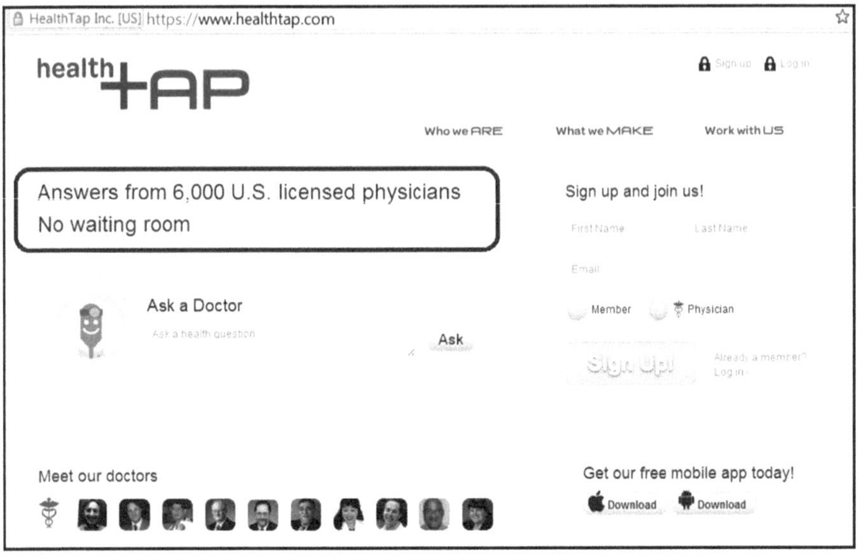

Fig. 4.1 Home page of HealthTap

4.2.2 *Actors*

Actors (or stakeholders) are the system representations of "real-life" people that handle the social informatics service and foster the online community. In order to conclude to the right definition/description of actors, the proposed guideline is to have a "bird's eye view" of the social informatics service [4]. This is plausible with a generic use case diagram shown below on Fig. 4.2 (that represents a generic social informatics service) or with just a schematic outline such as the ones showed in Fig. 4.3 (that covers an e-learning scenario) [5, 6]. The analysis of the users' interaction should just reach the depth where all actors' roles are distinct and not delve into deeper dataflow or another process-oriented analysis [7]. A good example of this "shallow" analysis is Fig. 4.3 where all additional interactions of the user/actor (apart from the obvious use case) are simply listed in comments. Following the same approach, Fig. 4.2 just outlines the main system modules (or service entities) focusing on the actors' definition.

4.2.3 *Tangible Value*

The common denominator for all actors involved in an online community and the building block of the community itself has to be *value*. The community user experience has to be crystal clear to each and every one of the actors involved regarding

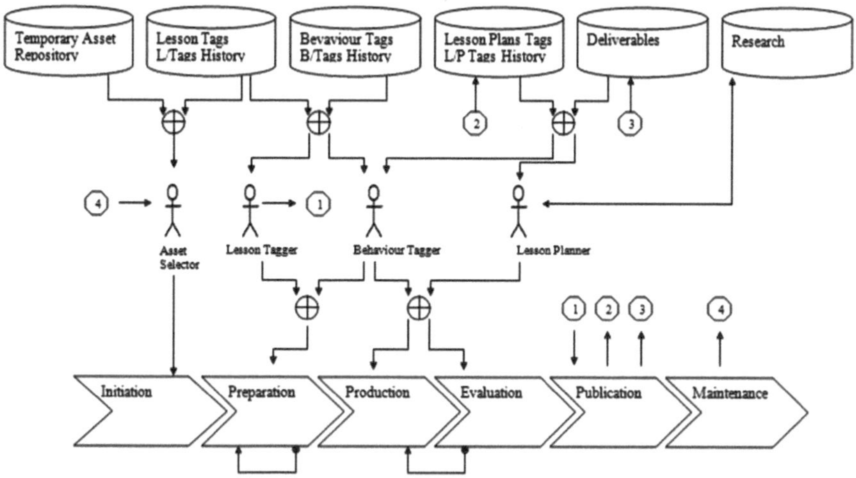

Fig. 4.2 Upper level system description of a generic social informatics service (for e-learning)

the value the online community creates and offers them. Specifically, the value has to be *tangible*; in other words, it has to be easily represented by a metric. Thus, at any given time, actors are presented with a value proposition that deals with numerical expressions of the value at hand. The latter is essential for the actors mainly due to the reason that value expressed in numbers is computable and therefore manageable, so it is fairly easy for the actor to translate the value at hand to their (personal) ecosystem specifics. Actors eventually undertake commitments (that sustain their ties with the community) based on the tangible/enumerated value that they "see" in any of the online community transactions.

The notion of the tangible value promotes a simple set of metrics on the value proposition level for each actor. A characteristic example comes from the healthcare domain, and it refers to an online community that is active in a health portal featuring a number of e-Health services (such as electronic health records (EHRs), self-management diaries, appointments, video consultations). Indicative (but not restrictive) tangible value metrics (in this case, characterizing value propositions of generic e-health applications) are the following (a more specific analysis leading to such metrics can be found in [8]):

Citizens/patients

1. Number of extra healthcare services added within a healthcare provider (hospital, medical center).
2. Financial (and other) benefits for participating in medical research by consent to personal/medical data access.
3. Financial benefits (discounts, etc.) for proven loyalty to healthcare providers (HCPs) via the EHR logs.
4. Number of personal network peers in health condition-oriented online communities.

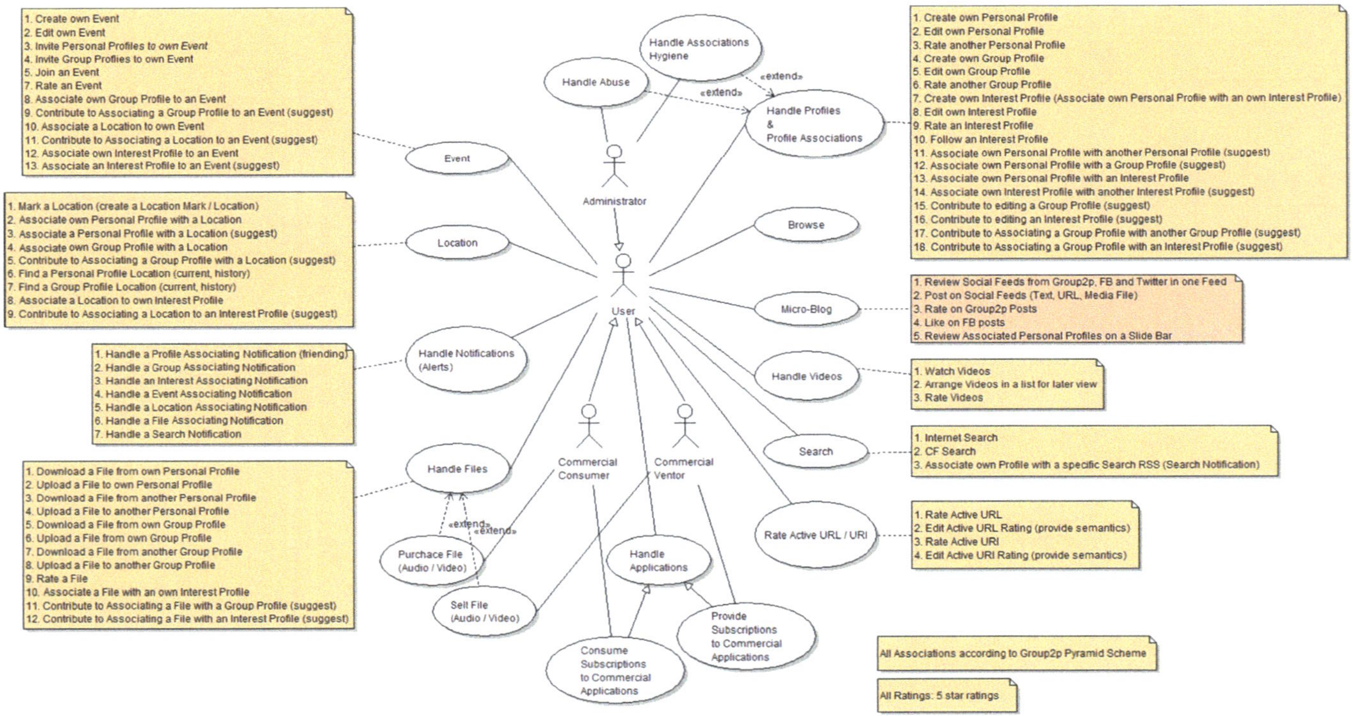

Fig. 4.3 Upper level system use case description of a generic social informatics service

5. Number of medical professionals that provide access for advice via EHR aware social media e-Health services.
6. Number of visits avoided by asynchronous communication means (paid service: less than a traditional visit).
7. Number of adverse events avoided.

Medical professionals

1. Number of extra customers added via electronic loyalty/health card schemes.
2. Volume of data access to patients' data through consent for research purposes.
3. Number of patient visits avoided by asynchronous communication means (paid service: lasts less than a traditional visit).
4. Financial benefits for providing advice in AHR aware social media under an HCP umbrella.
5. Number of feasible future customers through advice via EHR aware social media.
6. Number of extra customers from remote areas.

Payers (health insurance)

1. Number of extra customers added via electronic loyalty/health card schemes.
2. Volume of data access to patients' data through consent for statistical and cost centers monitoring purposes.
3. Costs saved by avoiding unnecessary visits.
4. Revenue from utilizing medical professionals from their networks for health advice (through portals or EHR aware social media).
5. Number of new communication/market channels analog to the number of customers on line.

Academics

1. Financial benefits for providing advice in EHR aware social media under an HCP umbrella.
2. Number of extra sources of funding for knowledge extraction and knowledge management studies (i.e., Health IT semantics).
3. Volume of data access to patients' data through consent for research purposes and number of scientific publications based on these data.

State

1. Financial benefits by saving costs on unnecessary visits to medical professionals and inpatients' time.
2. Financial benefits from public HCPs' resource management and workflow optimization.
3. Volume of data access to patients' data through consent for enriching and populating health condition-oriented national registries.
4. Volume of data access to patients' data through consent for public health statistical study purposes.

Fig. 4.4 Tangible value indices per transaction (per tweet) on Twitter

Designers should take care to "tie" each transaction with the metric/metrics associated with it by allocating a persistent block or area on the user interface clearly illustrating the "number" and "title" of the tangible value. An interesting example of applying this technique, persistent on the UI and per transaction, is the relatively new updated UI of Twitter (see Figs. 4.4 and 4.5).

4.3 Engagement Patterns

The primary object of any online community is to enhance and elevate the user experience of the average Internet user to a level that is much closer to their everyday human behavior and corresponding patterns/habits of social activity. The prime focus of the community design is to *optimally shape the use cases of the actors to take after "real-life" everyday social networking habits*. The principal strategic target is to make the users instinctively recognize familiar/everyday social activity patterns while interacting with the system. This is based on the fact that when users recognize familiar "real-life" social networking patterns, their learning curve and resistance to change toward a technology system tend to minimize. Thus, the technology control side of the user experience becomes almost completely seamless [9].

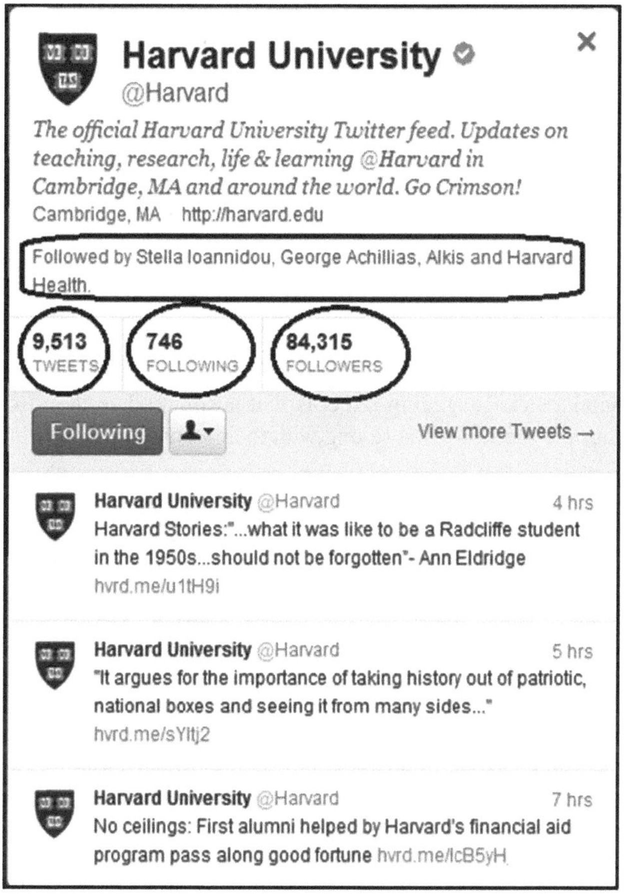

Fig. 4.5 Tangible value indices per profile on Twitter

Such design patterns that foster seamless social engagement for the social informatics service of the online community are proposed in this section. Two types are proposed: the ones applied horizontally (system/site wide) in the form of intimacy aware use cases and the ones applied vertically (in a specific section or location of the system/site) for grouping purposes.

4.3.1 Intimacy Patterns

The recurring appearance of the "horizontal" social engaging patterns and their close affiliation with "real"-life socialization ones – combined with simplicity on the UI layout and controls from the UI usability point of view – contribute to drawing the focus of the user on familiar recurring socialization processes and away from UI technology controls. In this way, the user is presented with the same set of social engaging patterns regardless the user interface active status/module. In this particular case, the use cases proposed recurrently remind the users how "close" or not they "feel" to the transaction at hand, representing a metric of intimacy [10]. A set of such "horizontal" use cases in a generic social informatics application can be applied, abiding to generic socialization patterns that bring instinctively to the user the corresponding "real-life" ones, as follows:

1. Belonging and participating.
2. Sharing experiences and opinions.
3. Defining areas/domains of social interaction.
4. Classifying and prioritizing social interaction.

The "horizontal" social engaging patterns that accommodate the aforementioned "real-life" ones are the following (along with their technological/systemic use case translations):

	Social engaging patterns	System use cases
1	Associations	Associations handling
2	Sharing	Share active URL
3	Notifications	Notifications handling
4	Rating	Rate active URL

The social engaging patterns accommodate the "real-life" socialization ones via a Likert-type scale classification scheme that represents a "social intimacy" *metric* which in turn characterizes the associations' connections among actors within the community. An illustration of such a metric in a general purpose social informatics online service is depicted in the following table:

The value of the metric (see Table 4.1) should play a significant role in the handling of the use case, thus bringing intimacy as one of the prerequisite steps to exit the use case. In this way, the users are constantly reminded, at any time, and following a similar pattern of how "close" or "distant" they "feel" doing the transaction at hand.

4.4 Grouping Patterns

Engagement in a vibrant online community is secured mainly due to patterns that govern the way users engage into groups (grouping) often expressing a tendency to follow the most active or socially exposed members (leaders) [11]. A good example of an engagement pattern that imitates "real-life" socialization grouping behavior and simultaneously fosters leadership expression is presented, introducing a notion of a separate system entity called interest profile. The interest profile is a systemic file that features a title/topic and a collection of tags. In "real life," people are made

Table 4.1 Use case intimacy metrics

	Use case	Intimacy metric (default values, changeable)	User experience	"Real-life" socialization pattern
1	Notifications handling	1. Action 2. Consideration 3. Reference 4. Neutral 5. Reject	Respond to an alert/ notification. Make priorities of my responses	Classifying and prioritizing social interaction
2	Share *[any item]*	1. Urgent 2. High importance 3. Important 4. Informative 5. Casual	Illustrate the importance and the urgency of my share	Sharing experiences and opinions
3	Rate *[any item]*	1. Most interesting 2. Fairly interesting 3. Interesting 4. Informative 5. Indifferent	Express my interest for a published item	Sharing experiences and opinions
4	Rate microblog post	1. Awesome 2. Cool 3. Like 4. Dislike 5. Oppose	Express my likeness for another person's post/opinion	Sharing experiences and opinions
5	Associations handling for user profiles	1. Me 2. Intimate 3. Friend 4. Associate 5. Acquaintance	Express how close I feel to a person	Classifying and prioritizing social interaction
6	Associations handling for group profiles	1. Me 2. Intimate 3. Friend 4. Associate 5. Acquaintance	Express how close I feel to a group	Belonging and participating
7	Associations handling for interest profiles	1. Most interesting 2. Fairly interesting 3. Interesting 4. Not interesting 5. Irrelevant	Express my affiliation to various interests	Defining areas/ Domains of social interaction

aware that they are interested in some topic by coming across a "trigger" interaction with an experience of such an interest, i.e., by reading an article, tasting a new recipe, talking to a friend about a new idea, etc., and then spend some time storing and handling information about that interest topic. A typical upgrade of the process is sharing and communicating upon this particular interest with other people (their social circles or friends) [12]. The systemic translation of the aforementioned "trigger" in a social informatics environment of an online community is a transaction that, again, may draw the user's attention at any given time while interacting with the community (or while "surfing" on the web). The service should allow the user to create an interest profile according to the following use case description:

Use case: create own interest profile

ID: 0X

Brief description: user creates an interest profile which is a web page (html file) that is characterized by an interest title and relative metadata (tags)

Primary actors: user

Secondary actors: none

Preconditions: none

Main flow:

1. User creates the html file for the new interest ("tab: create new interest")
2. A title/name is given to the interest (required)
3. Related files are associated with the interest (text, URLs, media files) (optional)
4. The user saves the interest html file in his profile account. At this stage, the interest file is accessed only by the user for further editing. It actually plays the role of a notebook
5. The user chooses to publish/associate his interest html file to personal profiles or group profiles of his choosing. At this stage, the interest can be further associated with ("followed by") the other user profiles and group profiles
6. Upon publication, the user can choose to make some of the elements of the interest file editable and let others contribute to editing them. This means that every user that has already "followed" an interest can suggest a change in any interest profile field with that comment function. The only one that can really make (finalize) the changes is the owner (or contributors that the owner has assigned) (optional)
7. Upon publication, the user can assign other users as contributors. The role of the contributors will be to edit any editable interest profile fields (optional)
8. Upon publication, the user can choose to make the interest public. This means that everyone can "follow" it (optional)

Postconditions: none

Alternative flows: none

4.5 Summary

This chapter dealt with the design guidelines that a social informatics service which empowers an online community should follow. These guidelines represent a small fraction out of a wide variety of selection abundant in literature. The main characteristic of the specific guidelines this chapter offers is that it focuses on the core aspects of meaningful online social interaction those being the ones of *simplicity*, *tangible value*, and *engagement*. The main focus is to provide straightforward and easily comprehensible guidelines to the professional designer with the use of *governing parameters* and *engagement patterns* which are set to foster bottom-up community building and avoid manual input of complex rules and regulations by site and community administrators.

References

1. Klein, D. A. (Ed.). (1998). *The strategic management of intellectual capital*. Woburn, MA: Butterworth Heinemann.
2. Chi, E. H., Munson, S., Fischer, G., Vieweg, S., & Parr, C. (2010). Advancing the design of technology-mediated social participation systems. *Computer, 43*(11), 29–35. ISSN: 0018–9162, IEEE Computer Society.
3. Denaux, R., et al. (2011). Supporting domain experts to construct conceptual ontologies: A holistic approach. *Web Semantics: Science Services and Agents on the World Wide Web, 9*(2), 113–127.
4. Monachesi, P., & Markus, T. (2010). Using social media for ontology enrichment. *The Semantic Web: Research and Applications: Lecture Notes in Computer Science, 6089*, 166–180.
5. Snae, C., & Brueckner, M. (2007). Ontology-driven e-learning system based on roles and activities for Thai learning environment. *Interdisciplinary Journal of Knowledge and Learning Objects, 3*, 1–17.
6. Anderson, T., & Elloumi, F. (2004). *Theory and practice of online learning*. Edmonton, Alberta, Canada: Athabaska University Press.
7. Rodrigues, A., Pinheiro, P. R., Rodrigues, M. M., Albuquerque, A. B., & Goncalves, F. M. (2010). Applying a multicriteria model for selection of test use cases: A use of experience. *International Journal of Social and Humanistic Computing, 1*(3), 246–260. ISSN: 1752–6124.
8. van Meijgaard, J., Fielding, J. E., & Kominski, G. F. (2009). Assessing and forecasting population health: Integrating knowledge and beliefs in a comprehensive framework. *Public Health Reports, 124*(6), 778–789.
9. Lemcke, J. (2010). Light-weight semantic integration of generic behavioral component descriptions. In G. Mentzas & A. Friesen (Eds.), *Semantic enterprise application integration for business processes: Service-oriented frameworks*. Hershey, PA: Business Science Reference. ISBN 9781605668048.
10. Andre, P., Schraefel, M. C., Dix, A., & White, R. W. (2010). Experience in social affective applications: methodologies and case study. In E. D. Mynatt & D. Schoner (Eds.), *Proceedings of the 28th of the international conference extended abstracts on human factors in computing systems*. New York: Association for Computing Machinery. ISBN 978-1-60558-930-5.
11. Bradford, S. K. (2011). Leadership, collective efficacy and team performance: A New paradigm for the next generation. *International Journal of Web-Based Learning and Teaching Technologies (IJWLTT), 6*(3), 35–45. ISSN: 1548–1093.
12. G, Pallis. (2011). Online social networks: Status and trends. In A. Vakali & L. C. Jain (Eds.), *New directions in web data management 1* (Studies in computational intelligence, Vol. 331, pp. 213–234). Berlin/Heidelberg: Springer. doi:10.1007/978-3-642-17551-0_8.

Chapter 5
A Security Model for Virtual Healthcare Communities

Anargyros Chryssanthou[1], Iraklis Varlamis[2], and Charikleia Latsiou[1]

[1]Auditors Department, Hellenic Data Protection Authority, Ampelokipoi, Athens, Greece, achrysanthou@dpa.gr; clatsiou@dpa.gr

[2]Department of Informatics and Telematics, Harokopio University of Athens, Athens, Greece, varlamis@hua.gr

Abstract Virtual healthcare communities aim in bringing together healthcare professionals and patients in order to further improve the quality of healthcare services and assist healthcare professionals and researchers in their everyday activities. Patient monitoring and medical consultation – the two most popular activities inside virtual healthcare communities – require members' collaboration in a secure and reliable environment. In this environment, patients share their medical data with doctors, expect confidentiality, and demand reliable medical consultation. Apart from a concrete policy framework, several ethical, legal, and technical issues must be considered in order to build a trustful community. This work presents the architecture of a virtual healthcare community portal, giving emphasis on the security issues that arise when attempting to manage risk inside such a community. Following a standardized risk assessment process, which identifies, estimates, and evaluates all potential security risks for the community, a security model is developed, and the community architecture is designed. Finally, a set of usage scenarios, with reference to real events, is employed in order to uncover security risks and illustrate the solutions provided by the proposed architecture.

Keywords Information security • Virtual communities • Health care • ISO 27000 family of standards • Risk assessment

5.1 Introduction

The progress in telecommunication technologies has removed several distance and time barriers and allowed virtual communities to flourish. The members of a virtual healthcare community – doctors, patients, and caregivers – collaborate in order to virtually manage the illnesses and improve the quality of patients' life. Patients submit online requests for advice and share problems and solutions with other patients; doctors cooperate with each other, supervise, and support their patients. Specialized healthcare communities, such as self-supportive patient communities

A.A. Lazakidou (ed.), *Virtual Communities, Social Networks and Collaboration*, Annals of Information Systems 15, DOI 10.1007/978-1-4614-3634-8_5,

that promote peer-to-peer patient communication and medical research communities that support the collaboration of medical professionals, can be assisted by the virtual organizational model.

The most significant issue in healthcare applications is protecting a patient's medical data from unauthorized access. In pervasive and web-based healthcare applications, medical data is transferred via wireless networks and/or across the web, so specific attention should be drawn toward building and meeting the appropriate security requirements. Therefore, it is important to protect the confidentiality of sensitive medical data, maintain its integrity, and ensure that medical data is always available to the rightful holder (patient or doctor).

Trust is another important issue in healthcare communities and requires more than a secure technological solution. Members of a virtual medical community need to trust each other and to be confident for the secure, reliable, and lawful operation of the community. Moreover, a set of trust-enabling functionalities, such as transparency, content quality control, and access rights management are desired in order to strengthen users' trust toward the community [14]. As described in [6], building of trust is a continuous process that comprises several repeating steps: achieving an appropriate security level for medical data in terms of authentication and user's certification; defining a strict user policy with roles, access rights, and limitations among community members; and providing a flexible identification mechanism, which preserves anonymity while guaranteeing identity truthfulness. Additionally, in patient monitoring cases, the community must respond quickly and reliably upon emergencies.

Continuity is the last but most important issue for any virtual community. System maintenance, based on auditing and vulnerability testing, is necessary for the stability of the community infrastructure, from a technical point of view. A reputation system may help to elicit good behavior, encourage knowledge sharing among individuals, and strengthen members' bonds to the community.

A standardized methodology for securing the community infrastructure is preferable to fragmentary solutions that answer specific parts of the problem. The ISO/IEC 27001:2005 standard defines such a methodology for planning and designing an Information Security Management System (ISMS), through a structured process which involves risk assessment, risk treatment planning, selection and implementation of security controls, etc. This structured process is complemented with ISO/IEC 27002:2005, which presents a code of practice for Information Security Management, and, in the e-health sector, with ISO/IEC 27799:2008 [23], which constitutes an ISO/IEC standard directed directly to e-health that provides guide to health information practitioners on how to protect confidentiality, integrity, and availability by implementing ISO/IEC 27002:2005. These security management methodologies combined with ISO/IEC 27005:2008, which is a specialized ISO/IEC standard belonging to the 27000 ISO family of information security standards and deals with information security risk management, are adopted in this current work in order to define a concise security model and architecture.

The contributions of this work are summarized in the following:

- A roadmap for building secure portals for virtual healthcare communities and a holistic approach in developing and maintaining a trustful and secure solution. The first step involves the description of the community structure and the design and development of the initial security model.
- A risk management model, which iteratively identifies and evaluates all the potential hazards and suggests new certification mechanisms, operational policies, and functionalities that can improve the security model, strengthen the protection of the community assets, and increase members' trust.
- A scenario-based validation process, which tests the security model against various incident scenarios that might violate the community processes and lead to loss of confidentiality, availability, or integrity in terms of a data breach on a denial of service attack.
- A study on the legal implications of security incidents involving sensitive medical data in healthcare communities and a presentation of the process followed by the Hellenic Data Protection Authority for auditing, locating, and penalizing violators.

The following section refers to related works that partially cover the need of healthcare communities for security and trust. Section 5.3 gives an overview of the community structure; illustrates the steps of the information security management life cycle, which needs to be followed when developing an Information Security Management System (ISMS); and states the need for a standardized process for developing a holistic security solution. Section 5.4 describes in detail every step of the process that was followed in order to secure the community, from recording community assets and available security controls to identifying threats and potential consequences (technical, ethical, and legal), estimating and evaluating identified risks against selected criteria, and finally forming a risk treatment plan for the community. Section 5.5 presents the community's security model and explains how the available security solutions are orchestrated. Section 5.6 analyzes the specific legal implications behind potential security incidents in a healthcare community and presents the action plan of the Hellenic Data Protection Authority. Section 5.7 presents several potential threats for the community, with reference to real cases, and focuses on the mechanisms of the community's security infrastructure that are activated to confront them. Finally, Sect. 5.8 presents conclusions from this work.

5.2 Related Work

Several projects concerning the development of virtual healthcare communities that support the pervasive participation of patients (e.g., through wireless monitoring devices) have attracted national or private funding. CIGNA [35] has launched a virtual community for nutrition and healthcare, which is situated on a Second Life island. The EU-funded project Saphire [28] has integrated wireless medical sensor data with hospital decision support systems in an attempt to provide remote monitoring of patients at their homes. Several more research works on healthcare delivery [12], patient peer support [43], virtual disease management, or medical research and collaboration through virtual medical communities have been found in the literature.

The quality of patient services is strongly related to the availability and quantity of medical information. In order to increase the quantity of medical information without burdening the patient, several sensor-based monitoring systems have been designed that allow continuous recording of patients' status, such as CodeBlue [32], Scalable Medical Alert Response Technology (SMART) [8], MobiHealth [24], etc. In such dynamic and data-rich environments, a holistic security approach ([2] and [7]) is necessary in order to guarantee confidentiality and reliability and consequently increase community trust. This approach should study the community structure, identify its assets as well as its pros (existing security controls) and cons (existing vulnerabilities), and record potential threats, in order to build a list of potential risks, which can be estimated and evaluated against selected criteria and will potentially lead to possible solutions by means of a well-formed risk treatment plan. A standardized methodology should be employed for this purpose [20–22].

The first step in building a trustful healthcare community is to provide members with a security infrastructure. Patients must be sure that their medical data remain confidential and are constantly available, and their integrity is maintained. Additionally, they must be aware of their virtual caregivers' (doctors, nurses, family or friends etc.) identity and be able to selectively provide access to their sensitive data only to the appropriate right holder. The Health Information Trust Alliance [18] released a security framework for healthcare in March 2009, which is based on well-known standards such as COBIT, NIST, and ISO/IEC 27001:2005 but only available to member organizations subsequent to paying a fee [25]. The framework supports regulations such as the Health Insurance Portability and Accountability Act (HIPAA) [47] and aims in increasing patient confidence in the security of their information. However, it is not clear whether it includes a comprehensive set of privacy principles. In the Cassandra trust management system for medical communities [5], access control is based on the member's role in the community. However, each data owner is able to define the access rights on her personal data using the prototype role-based access (RBAC) model. Access rights are validated using a Datalog extension with constraints. XML-based models have also been employed for the same task. XrML [51] allows the definition of rights and granting policies with validity restrictions. XACML [39] is another model for defining conditional access and deny policies, and policy combination rules for resolving conflicting policies (e.g., First-Applicable, Deny-Override, Permit-Override). XACML does not support delegation and is thus not well suited for decentralized authorization. Finally, the Security Policy Assertion Language

(SecPAL) [4] is another XML-based model, which builds on the notion of tunable expressiveness introduced in Cassandra.

Solving the security issues, which relate to the wireless or wired transmission of data [37], and the legal and ethical issues concerning confidentiality of patient data [45] is not always adequate for building trust in the healthcare community. According to [26], trust is subjective, bidirectional though asymmetric, non-transitive, context dependent, dynamic, and time dependent. A trust management mechanism that keeps record of the members' reputation inside the community and continuously updates it by analyzing other members' feedback can be useful in this direction. In the sections that follow, we present the structure of a healthcare community and its proposed security model and emphasize on the legal aspect of security incidents. This holistic approach and an iterative refinement of the security processes and mechanisms as explained in Sect. 5.4 will guarantee security and increase members' trust to the community.

5.3 A Virtual Community for Monitoring and Tele-Health Care

Virtual communities refer to groups of people that collaborate and discuss their issues, share experiences, consult with experts, and provide and request support by using telecommunication technologies. Virtual healthcare communities employ advanced and pervasive ICT technologies, in order to offer ubiquitous medical services to their members. Elder members, home care patients, or members with chronic conditions utilize different types of healthcare services at different points in time, in this way bridging geographic distance and time constraints [11, 49].

5.3.1 Community Members

The active members of a virtual healthcare community comprise patients and doctors, as well as people with interest in the community issues, such as patients' family members, researchers, etc. Members have different roles depending on their needs and expertise: patients and family members undertake facilitator roles, while healthcare professionals become moderators for discussion and contents, facilitators and mentors for the community members. The technical administration of the community is usually performed by IT experts who must be trustful community members.

In complement to the community members, several people, in the community background, guarantee the smooth operation of the community and the uninterrupted delivery of services. The IT staff that technically supports the community,

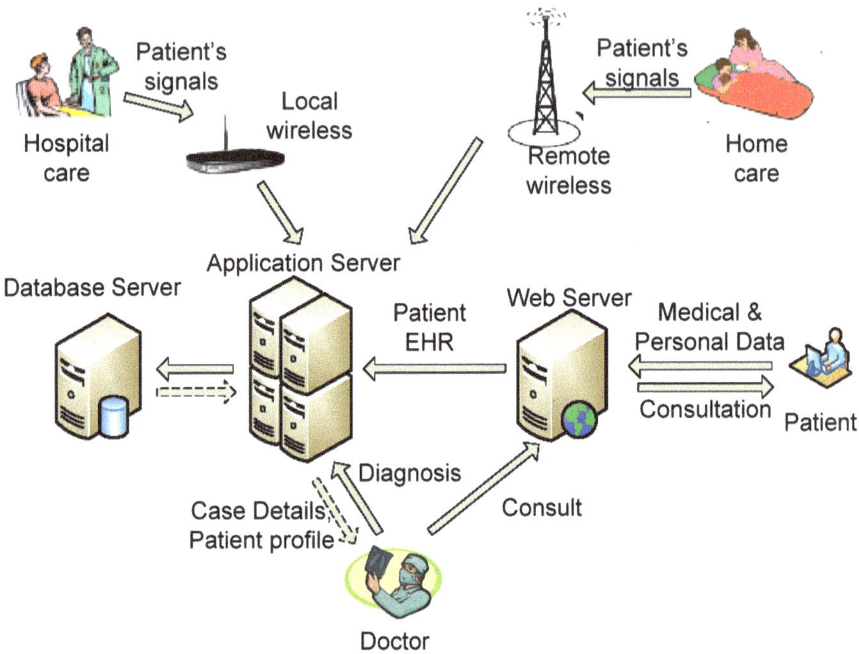

Fig. 5.1 Overview of the community interactions

the employees of the telecommunication service provider, and the directors of the organization, company, or hospital that hosts the virtual community are persons that do not actually participate in the community but play a key role in its secure operation.

5.3.2 *Community Activities*

An overview of the interactions inside the healthcare community is presented in Fig. 5.1. Health status signals are collected using wireless sensors [1, 36] and/or wired devices [46] and are stored in the community servers for future reference and analysis [27]. Patient members are also able to request for advice, diagnosis or treatment suggestion, etc., by using the community portal communication services (e-mail, forum, etc.).

The doctor from inside the hospital is able to access the patient's record (Electronic Health Record – EHR) and make a diagnosis. The doctor replies to patients' requests but also provides consultation based on the patient's medical status signals. The hospital keeps record of patients' profiles and history, doctors' diagnoses, and of all requests and advices exchanged in the portal.

5.3.3 Securing the Community

Building a security infrastructure is a bottom-up and continuous process. In order to design an effective security infrastructure for any organization, the first step the designer of the organization's Information Security Management System (ISMS) must perform is a detailed and accurate risk assessment of the organization.

A risk assessment according to ISO/IEC 27005:2008 is the overall process of risk analysis and evaluation. Risk analysis comprises of two interconnected stages, risk identification and risk estimation. Risk identification involves identifying assets to the organization, whether human, such as people, technical, such as hardware, information, such as medical data, or critical processes, such as transfers of medical signals. It includes identifying threats, existing security controls, vulnerabilities, and potential consequences. Risk estimation aims to identify a level of risk for each risk identified in the previous process. Risk evaluation comprises evaluating identified risks against selected criteria. These criteria are selected beforehand and could be legal, operational, and organizational.

In order to secure the infrastructure of the community, a specific methodology defined by ISO/IEC 27005:2008 was adopted, which supports the requirements set by ISO/IEC 27001:2005. By using this methodology, assets to the virtual community were located, while emphasis was given to patients and their sensitive medical data. Potential risks were identified by analyzing several reported incidents that relate to the exposure, damage, or loss of patient information. Lastly, these risks were assessed, and a risk treatment plan was formed which leads to selecting the security controls that are incorporated in the proposed community's security model. The community's security model effectively constitutes the community's Information Security Management System, as defined in ISO/IEC 27001:2005.

This methodology is part of a continuous cycle of procedures, which repeats itself as an organization evolves and the legal and operational environments, in which the organization operates, change. Simultaneously, the modus operandi of potential e-crime perpetrators becomes more and more sophisticated as technology evolves and newer tools are developed, which make it easier for a perpetrator to steal valuable data. This cycle consists of four stages, namely, Plan, Do, Check, and Act, as depicted in Fig. 5.2.

An Information Security Management System is a constantly evolving part of an organization, which has to be carefully designed and implemented in the Plan and Do phases. However effective the ISMS of the organization is, the implementer will have failed if he does not complete the cycle over and over again by checking the ISMS' effectiveness and correcting any identified security issues. Integral part of this cycle is the risk management methodology that is being followed by the implementer with its key product being the risk treatment plan. The latter, in the case of a medical community, produces a security model, which is the core of the community's ISMS. This security model is the key contribution of this chapter and is depicted in Sect. 5.5.

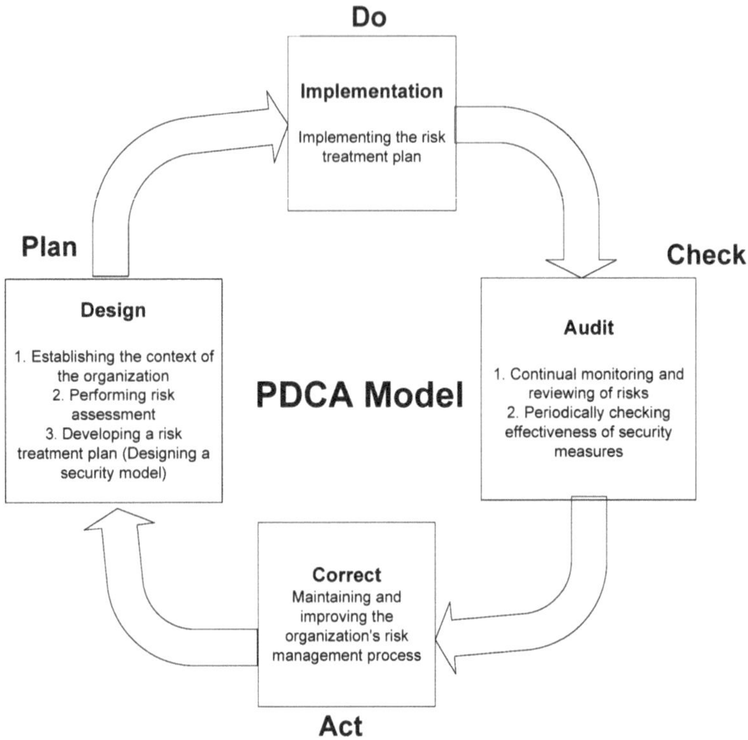

Fig. 5.2 The information security management cycle (combining ISO/IEC 27001:2005 and ISO/IEC 27005:2008)

5.4 The Risk Management Model

5.4.1 Risk Identification

The first step in the risk assessment model applied to the community, as defined by ISO/IEC 27005:2008, is risk identification which comprises the recording of (a) valuable community assets, (b) potential community threats, (c) existing security controls, (d) detected vulnerabilities, and (e) consequences of potential incident scenarios in regard to CIA (confidentiality, integrity, availability).

5.4.1.1 Community Assets

Identified assets are the active members of the community, medical data, and the internal structure of the community, which consists of information systems and physical premises. Assets need to be protected in the context of the traditional CIA model of security with CIA standing for confidentiality, integrity, and availability. Data must remain confidential, maintain their integrity, and remain constantly available. The same applies to systems. A distributed denial of service attack, for example, could render the whole community systems unavailable to patients and doctors, which could even lead to loss of human life in case of an emergency due to unavailability of a patient's electronic health record. Thus, assets need to be assessed in the context of potential threats, which are mainly technical, and consequences, which can be ethical and legal.

5.4.1.2 Threats for the Community

The threats for a virtual healthcare community are mainly technical, and their basic source is the human factor: malicious attackers, naïve users and administrators, malicious insiders, and security-unaware users. These threats have consequences that relate to potential incident scenarios which are represented in Sect. 5.4.1.5. These consequences are multifold with aspects covering technical to ethical and regulatory issues.

Technical threats target both the information repository and the operational infrastructure of the virtual medical community. A virtual medical community is susceptive to a variety of attacks. Ranging from outside malicious users gaining unauthenticated access to inside users gaining unauthorized access control to sensitive patient information, all these threats are a major issue that concerns both the CIA (confidentiality, integrity, availability) model and community trust. Identities can be stolen by phishing attacks. Denial of service attacks can render the whole community unavailable. Eavesdropping can lead to information leakage, while message disclosure can lead to breach of confidentiality. Web application attacks can damage the database or lead to major information leakage in various ways. Data breaches, security incidents that include theft, or loss of digital media, such as USB sticks containing an organization's data, constitute a phenomenon that multiplies nowadays and can have serious consequences for a virtual community.

The list of threats mentioned previously is indicative and grows as technology advances. Threats are dealt with security measures such as the ones proposed later in this chapter.

5.4.1.3 Security Controls

The identification of assets and threats is followed by a careful recording of the community shields. The security controls, which are readily available, should also be recorded. This will inform us on the state of the existing controls. The list of potential security controls contains physical, technical, and administrative solutions such as security guards, surveillance cameras and locked doors, data encryption, smart cards, network authentication, access control lists (ACLs), file integrity auditing software, security training programs, and disaster recovery plans.

In order to identify existing controls, one should read the previous information security management records, interview the people who are responsible for information security, and perform an internal on-site audit of existing security infrastructure. All the available controls will be evaluated in the following steps, depending on their cost, vulnerabilities, and application status, as well as on the criticality of the processes they guard.

5.4.1.4 Identifying Vulnerabilities

A threat can become a real danger for the community if it manages to exploit existing vulnerabilities. For this reason, the identification of vulnerabilities is an important step of the risk management procedure and should be performed in a constant basis.

The vulnerabilities may be found in the human factor (personnel), in organizational and management routines, in the technological infrastructure, and in the physical premises of the organization. The absence of an access control policy, the sharing of passwords among different users, and the lack of a secure data transmission method are some examples of vulnerabilities. Although, the existence of vulnerabilities does not necessarily mean harm, all identified weaknesses should be properly treated or else should be constantly monitored.

The answer to vulnerabilities is implementing security controls that minimize the vulnerability's effect or totally eradicate the vulnerability. For example, a patch for a vulnerability, which resides in the operating system, will fix the vulnerability and immunize the system to a potential exploit against the vulnerability in question. Additionally, one should also check whether the existing controls effectively cover the weaknesses of the system or whether they should be combined or enhanced to improve a system's defense.

5.4.1.5 Identifying Consequences

Technical threats that might breach confidentiality and corrupt integrity of medical data or cease availability of healthcare services provided by the community were analyzed in Sect. 5.4.1.3. Examining these threats, as part of our risk identification procedure, means constructing incident scenarios and identifying their consequences. These consequences will certainly include technical issues, as new security measures will have to be implemented as countermeasures to these incident scenarios; operational cost, as these security measures are not free; ethical issues depending on the nature of each incident scenario; and legal issues depending on the legal and regulatory boundaries that were taken into account when defining the ISMS policy for the virtual community (clause 4.2.1b in ISO/IEC 27001:2005). In the next two sections, mainly incident scenarios, which lead to ethical issues, will be presented (Sect. 5.4.1.5.1) as well as an overview of the regulatory framework that governs medical data and the rules that must be kept, in order for the medical virtual community to operate in compliance with data protection laws (Sect. 5.4.1.5.2).

Ethical Issues

The goal of a virtual healthcare community is mainly to provide patients with medical consultation. The community stores a whole load of medical data in its servers and grants data access to various entities based on their access role and responsibilities. For example, doctors have access to the medical profile of patients in order to provide consultations. If a particular doctor improperly uses patient information to perform genetic or biomedical experiments, or provides medications that violate accepted policies, then important ethical issues arise. The code of ethics would also be violated, in a different case scenario, by a patient who harasses other patients. Such behaviors are unethical and raise issues of trust in the community.

Legal Issues

Events that raise ethical issues usually include legal penalties. A data breach incident, including, for example, use of data for other than notified purpose, is subject to civil, administrative, and penal sanctions, which are imposed, among others, from data protection laws. Virtual healthcare communities usually cross national borders, and as such, they face several legal issues, such as licensing, accreditation, concerns of identity deception, and dependency, which are difficult to be properly addressed by legislative entities.

In the hypothetical scenario, where the administrators[1] of the virtual community illegally process medical data, they could receive administrative penalties (e.g., monetary fine) and will be obliged to modify the way they process medical data. In case of a data breach, once again, the community's administrators will be subjected to an administrative control and later, based on the control's findings, receive a monetary fine and be responsible to adjust the community's security measures, in order to avoid similar data breaches in the future.

Since the implications from a data breach incident or a denial of healthcare service may be fatal, it is important that the community's administrators are familiar with the legal consequences that might arise for them in such unfortunate incident scenarios. For this reason, the legal framework that protects members of medical and healthcare communities in respect of handling sensitive medical data and potential security violations is explained in a separate section (Sect. 5.6).

[1] The administrators of the community could be physical entities (persons) or legal entities, in terms of an authority which supervises the community. A hospital could be the authority in question.

5.4.2 Risk Estimation

Having identified threats and potential consequences, the next step consists of estimating the identified risks. Risk estimation aims to identify level of risk for each risk identified in the previous process (risk identification).

A distributed denial of service attack would be rated as severe in regard to business impact, due to loss of availability, but low in regard to likelihood of event as attackers would not normally aim to bring a medical community down. An accidental loss of community data contained in an USB stick on the other hand would be rated as severe in regard to business impact, due to loss of confidentiality, and medium to severe in regard to likelihood of event. Statistics show that data losses through lost media included 42,212,702 sensitive records with a mean of 659,573 records per incident during the last 5 years, while 3% of data loss incidents in 2008 were due to lost media. However, only 12% of these incidents concerned the medical sector [10].

5.4.3 Risk Evaluation

Risk evaluation comprises evaluating identified risks against selected criteria. These criteria are selected beforehand and could be legal, operational, and organizational. For the case of the proposed virtual community, selected criteria range from loss of human life and legal consequences to likelihood of event, with the latter one balancing the former ones.

Evaluating the above-mentioned two examples would lead to a medium level of risk for the distributed denial of service attack scenario due to low likelihood of event and a high level of risk for the data loss scenario due to the likelihood of event and the potential consequences, which can include even loss of life.

Completing the risk evaluation, existing identified risks have been successfully assessed. The next stage is forming a risk treatment plan based on the conducted risk assessment.

5.4.4 Risk Treatment Plan

Upon completion of a risk assessment, a risk treatment plan must be formed (clause 9 in ISO/IEC 27005: 2008). The plan must explain the selection of security controls in relation to identified risks.

An indicative list of security controls, which can be used to reinforce the community's security infrastructure, is listed in the following table (Table 5.1).[2]

[2] A complete list of security controls that are applicable to any kind of organization structure can be found in ISO 27001:2005 (Annex A) and in ISO 27002:2005.

Table 5.1 Selected security controls from ISO/IEC 27001:2005

Selected control	ISO/IEC 27001:2005 clause	Implemented measure
Access control	A.11	Overall access and behavior policy, all the applicable security measures in this family of controls
Audit logging	A.10.10.1	Audit logs of application and systems
Management of removable media	A.10.7.1	Endpoint security solution
Business continuity management	A.14.1	Disaster recovery plan, periodic security checks (physical and logical security, application and hardware layer)
Information security policy document	A.5.1.1 (and clause 7.2 in ISO/IEC 27799:2008)	Overall access and behavior policy
Review of the information security policy document	A.5.1.2	Policy reviewed at planned intervals of after periodic security checks
Allocation of information security responsibilities	A.6.1.3	Overall access and behavior policy, definition of community roles
Controls against malicious code	A.10.4.1	Filtering module, web application firewalls, signatures of known attacks for routers and firewalls, antivirus software (constantly updatable)
Network controls	A.10.6.1	Firewall, web application firewall, 802.1x wireless access, EAP-TLS authentication, digital certificates
Monitoring system use	A.10.10.2 (and clause 7.7.10.2 in ISO/IEC 27799:2008)	Audit logs of application and systems
Protection of log information	A.10.10.3	Encrypted log storage, two-entity access
Administrator and operator logs	A.10.10.4	Logging of administrator's access
Input data validation	A.12.2.1	Filtering module, web application firewalls
Cryptographic controls	A.12.3	Encrypted hard drives (read in the presence of hardware tokens), authentication through e-token devices
Information backup	A.10.5.1 (and clause 7.7.7.2 in ISO/IEC 27799:2008)	Periodic backup, keeping of backup tapes in separate locations
Technical vulnerabilities management	A.12.6.1	Regular updates to all devices and applications by means of a patch management suite
Data protection and privacy of personal information	A.15.1.4	Compliance to applicable data protection laws
Physical and environmental security	A.9	Supply generators, physical access only to authorized personnel (with combined use of access cards and access code)

Based on the selected controls, a security model for the community is formulated. Along with this security model, the architecture of the community's Information Security Management System is designed. This architecture is explained in the following section (Sect. 5.5).

5.5 Multitiered Security Model

5.5.1 Architecture

The process of achieving an adequate level of security in the networked environment of the virtual community is twofold. First, the *internal layer* of the community needs to be secured. This mainly comprises the database server, where the sensitive medical data reside and the *application layer* where the user requests are served. Second, it must be certified that users in the *community perimeter* (mainly patients) have an adequate level of security.

The intranet/internet model used in the past was based on the notion that a firewall is adequate to secure the inside perimeter of the system (intranet). However, the advent of pervasive and ubiquitous computing created new challenges for computer security professionals. People are connected to the internet from anywhere and make use of advanced community services without being aware of how to interact with them. Third-party applications, devices, and networks interact with the same services and access the same resources. As a consequence, an interface to these applications is necessary and a *presentation layer* for interacting with individuals is required.

The iMedik telemedicine system [33] presented a four-tier architecture comprising a web server on the demilitarized zone (DMZ), a web proxy layer in front of the firewall, and finally the application server and the database protected behind the firewall. The first level of authentication is performed on the web proxy layer. This four-tier model can solve authentication and security issues of the medical community.

In the proposed structure, the proxy layer checks the validity of a user session (whether the user is authenticated or not), the presentation layer (web server) validates the user input, and the application server checks whether user's permission on the requested data is sufficient. The user is authenticated outside the perimeter, and any invalid attempts will fail grace to the firewall (Fig. 5.3, point 3). Moreover, typical web attacks such as cross-site scripting or SQL injection, which may be performed even by a valid community member, can be detected at the presentation layer. Finally, user permissions and access rights on medical data can be verified at the application server level. This multilayer approach keeps unauthorized users outside the community's perimeter and guarantees that authorized users cannot gain invalid access to medical profiles or access the database in a disallowed mode.

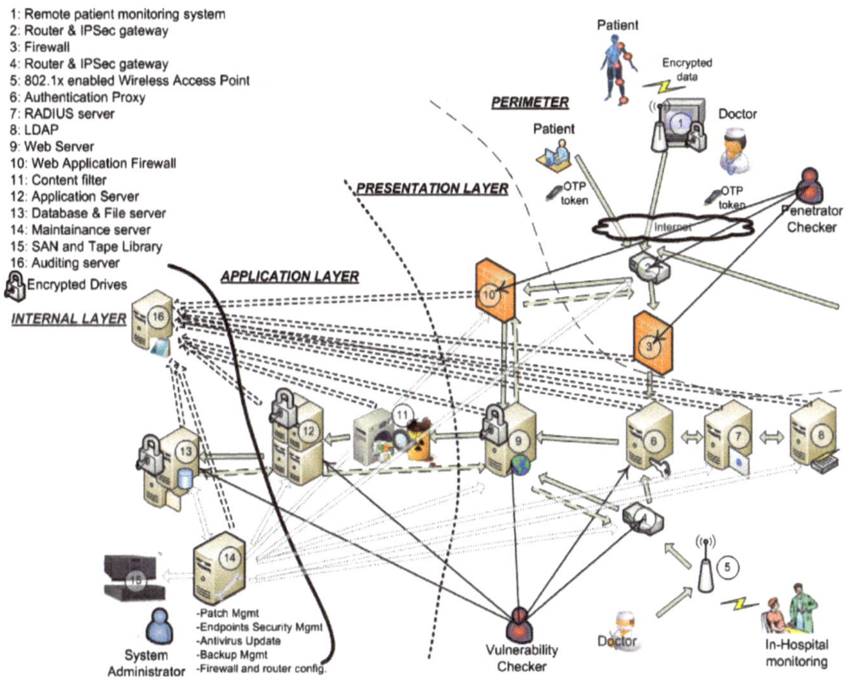

Fig. 5.3 Security-enabled architecture

Figure 5.3 presents the overview of the desired community architecture, with all the suggested servers and other security mechanisms. The subsections that follow explain the details of this architecture and the reasons behind each decision.

Doctors from inside the hospital and patients, who are treated inside the hospital, are able to enter the community through an 802.1x-enabled wireless access point (Fig. 5.3, point 5). Doctors' mobile devices and the sensors that monitor patient activity are connected to a wireless base station configured to use 802.1x protocol, and all traffic is forwarded to the authentication proxy. The proxy is configured to require 802.1x from all clients connecting through the particular wireless router and ignores any other incoming connection. The identity of the client device is forwarded to the RADIUS Server (authentication server). The authentication server sets up an EAP-TLS session with the client using digital certificates for mutual identification. If valid digital certificates are used, the client is successfully authenticated.

In the case of home-care applications, remote patient monitoring systems (Fig. 5.3, point 1), consisting of wireless sensors attached in the patient's body, need to securely communicate with the application server of the community. Off-the-shelf wireless sensor platforms with security features, such as TinyOS, can be employed given that they offer software or hardware encryption of wireless transmitted signals [52]. The encrypted signals, which are collected to the base of the remote monitoring system, can be forwarded via the secure router (Fig. 5.3, point 2) to the application server. Devices that do not support data encryption must be cable-connected to the base.

5.5.1.1 Presentation Layer

The presentation layer is the target of multiple forms of web attacks. Malicious users attack web applications using cross-site scripting, SQL injection, HTTP request smuggling, etc. In the proposed architecture, a filtering module in the application layer (Fig. 5.3, point 11) will "wash out" malicious user inputs and will block several of the aforementioned attacks. The filtering module processes user input and ensures that user requests through the web server (Fig. 5.3, point 9) do not attack the application server (Fig. 5.3, point 12). Commercial web application firewalls (Fig. 5.3, point 10) can be employed to perform input filtering, record all traffic that is directed to the database server, and distinguish between legitimate requests and potential attacks. The system administrators can configure routers and firewalls (Fig. 5.3, dotted arrows) using signatures of known attacks, provided by the firewall's manufacturer, and create additional signatures for illegitimate traffic.

5.5.1.2 Application Layer

Access to the application server is allowed only to authenticated community members, third-party applications, and devices. The primary aim of the security mechanisms in this layer is to guarantee that users are properly identified and have access only to the data they are allowed to. The role of the application server (Fig. 5.3, point 12), in terms of security and access control, is to verify that authenticated users are authorized to access the requested data.

The implementation of access policies, the definition of community roles, and the clarification of access rights and restrictions for each role are required in this layer. Concerning the access control, user roles can be distributed by the authorities of the community, and access credentials can be strengthened by asking users to log in with e-token devices and passwords. The distribution process will be performed by using appropriate registration forms, which will be processed by the community authorities, in order for the users' accounts to be opened and the corresponding credentials to be assigned. The configuration of the application server is performed in the maintenance server (Fig. 5.3, point 14) by the community administrator. Then patients can define which doctors can access their private data or which members can take part in a private held conversation using a semantic role-based policy. This access policy definition will be required by each upon registration.

All the above, can be made possible by adopting a flexible access policy model. The simplicity and extensibility of SecPAL [4] along with its PKI-based, SOAP-encoded infrastructure for exchanging policy assertions renders it ideal for access policy management in the distributed virtual community environment.

For example, when a patient needs to undergo a surgical operation, he can define an access policy that asserts full access to the entire EHR file for his doctor and only view permissions for the nurses. In the same policy model, the patient asserts that the doctor has the right to grant the full access privileges on his EHR file to the members of her medical team so that they can assist her during surgery. If the doctor decides to grant full access to an assistant or to any member of the community, all the respective asserts are activated to decide whether granting of privileges is allowed. The SecPAL model allows to define the duration of assigned roles (e.g., roles assigned to the members of the surgical team are valid only during surgery and recovery). Upon recovery of the patient, the access rights are automatically revoked. In special cases, where the normal security protocols need to be overridden due to healthcare priorities, then an access policy exception is necessary, as stated in ISO/IEC 27799:2008 (clause 7.2 in ISO/IEC 27799:2008). Such exceptions will be later incorporated in the access policy provided that they constitute a repeated scenario in everyday practice, which was not predicted during the initial design of the access policy, and not a one-time incident. The provision for such exceptions will be incorporated in the community's access policy.

An overall access and behavior policy is supplementary to the access control mechanisms mentioned earlier. The implemented access control model will be explained to the user upon registration and will be available as a written and electronic document. This written document will explain everything, from log-in procedures, password quality, and privacy rights to user roles and credentials. It will also include provisions for cases of access policy exception scenarios, which, as mentioned earlier, cause an override of the normal access control mechanisms and roles. In this way, the users have no excuse for violating other user's rights or the policy in general, and the community is protected against users' misbehavior.

Security applies to any type of data, whether sensitive or not. In the case of sensitive medical data, the required level of protection is even higher. For example, processing of sensitive data in Greece requires, apart from the users' consent, an extra permission from the Hellenic Data Protection Authority (Greek Data Protection Law 2472/1997, Article 7, par. 2 [29]). An access policy, a security plan, a Code of Deontology, and a risk analysis document are required by the Hellenic Data Protection Authority in order to grant permission for processing sensitive data.

5.5.1.3 Community Internal Network

In order to improve community trust, firstly, members' responsibilities must be defined, and consequently, it must be certified that members carry them out properly. Auditing can assist in this direction. Every single user action, either local or remote, must be logged (Fig. 5.3, dashed arrows). Logs must be securely stored, in an encrypted format, for a period of time, depending on the criticality of the application that the user uses. This criticality derives from the type of data the application processes and the type of function it performs. Access to the logs will be allowed only in presence of at least two administrative entities of the community with different roles (e.g., an IT administrator and a hospital manager), in order to avoid "accidental" or "intentional" data loss. Administrator's access must also be logged, in order to avoid abuse of administrative access. Logging of all database transactions as well as retaining the former content of data (in case of insert, update, delete actions) and the associated audit record (as mandated in clause 7.7.10.2 of ISO/IEC 27799:2008) will allow back tracing to the perpetrator in case of any improper data access and will also allow reconstructing the previous state of the patient's medical record.

All servers must run antivirus software, which is frequently updated. Community members must also have constantly updated antivirus software on their systems, in order to secure both ends of the communication. It is advisable that the server systems are equipped with encrypted hard drives, which can be read in presence of hardware tokens. Endpoint security must be in place so that no external devices (e.g., USB drives) can be connected to the sensitive modules of the system. A secure destruction policy, including provisions for secure disposal of media (used hard drives, tapes) will be in place to ensure that health information is securely destroyed when no longer required for use.

Finally, a disaster recovery plan must be designed in order to ensure that in case of a disaster, the virtual community will be operational the soonest possible.

5.5.2 Security Maintenance Processes

As a secure infrastructure is important for the operation of the virtual healthcare community, it must be ensured that the appropriate security level is attained at all times. Periodic checks are expected to detect new security vulnerabilities and confront evolving attack techniques. More specifically, the security of the authentication mechanism should be checked, the effectiveness of the application firewall must be validated, the security of the authorization process must be checked, auditing mechanisms must function properly, etc. Furthermore, patch management must be applied, so that all servers and the parts of the security infrastructure (firewall, RADIUS server) are kept up to date by applying all necessary security patches, in order to fix any emerging vulnerabilities of the community infrastructure. Finally, application security should be periodically confirmed and programming faults in the applications running on the web and application servers must be eliminated.

A periodic check of security might lead to changes to the overall access and behavioral policy of the community. This policy must also be reviewed at planned intervals, in order for it to remain effective.

Data protection requires a periodic backup in order to ensure the integrity of the medical data stored in the database. The community's data are backed up in an encrypted format and stored in backup tapes, which are kept in a physical secure off-site location (clause 7.7.7.2 in ISO/IEC 27799:2008). Finally, the disaster recovery plan must be tested periodically by using various disaster scenarios.

5.5.3 Increase Members' Trust

The success of a health-related virtual community is based on the frequency and quality of members' contribution (e.g., medical advices) and on the discreet use of patient sensitive data. Although, patients' identities can be concealed behind a virtual one, their health record is necessary for the doctor to provide a diagnosis. On the other side, patients should be confident that the identity of the doctor, who receives their data, is valid. This iterative negotiation process [44] assumes that both patient and doctor exchange digital credentials based on the access control policy of each part. Access restriction to sensitive information can be attached to these credentials upon members' discretion. The community administration authority or any other trusted institution (e.g., the hospital, medical center, ministry of health, etc.) will be the certificate authority (CA) in this process that guarantees anonymity and atomicity of members at the same time.

Finally, user information from the auditing server can be employed to support a reputation management application. Patients' or doctors' comments on another community member are recorded in the auditing server (Fig. 5.3, point 16). A reputation management application, in the application server (Fig. 5.3, point 12), will process data and provide each user with a reputation score for any community member based on the community reputation for this member and the direct trust toward this member.

5.5.4 *Physical Security*

Having adopted all these previously analyzed security mechanisms in the community's security infrastructure model, the community has achieved a sufficient level of logical security. By means of the security measures analyzed earlier, the community is protected from any attack that does not require physical presence.

However, the case should be considered where an attacker gains physical access to a server and launches an attack, such as a cold-boot attack against a server with encrypted data. In order to avoid such a scenario, physical security needs to be in place as well. Valuable IT equipment, according to ISO/IEC 27002:2005, "should be physically protected against malicious or accidental damage or loss, overheating, loss of mains power etc." Thus, the community's information systems should be protected by supply generators. Moreover, physical access to the information systems' room should be allowed only to authorize IT staff (administrators) or personnel accompanied by authorized IT staff and only with the combined use of access cards and access code. Furthermore, the hardware tokens needed to access the community servers' encrypted hard drives are also kept in a secure location, elsewhere than the community's IT room. Monitoring devices, security guards, and other security measures are advisable and subject to the importance of the application.

5.6 Legal Parameters

The following paragraphs present how data protection laws are applied to personal data or to cases where appropriate security measures are not implemented. Emphasis is given to medical data, since these are the data being processed inside a healthcare community. First, the legal and regulatory framework is presented. The framework applies to medical data, whether this data resides in EU, in the United States, or is subject to international transfers. Then the potential legal consequences are illustrated by means of a paradigm, which is based on the assumption that the proposed virtual community operates in Greece. This paradigm presents how the Greek Data Protection Law (Law 2472/1997) can be employed in favor of the community.

5.6.1 Legal and Regulatory Framework

The opt-out policy adopted by the US Government defines that companies cannot collect consumer's data if the consumer asks for it. Concerning medical information, US laws [48] assume total confidentiality in several issues (i.e., abortions, contraception, or psychological diseases) but delegate decisions to the state laws in others.

European Union has adopted an opt-in model for all personal data, which assumes that all personal information is classified until their owner grants access on them [15]. According to the EC directive on the protection of individuals with regard to the processing of personal data and on the free movement of such data (95/46/EC), only health professionals can access medical information and are responsible for protecting confidentiality. According to the Recommendation (97) 5 [16], medical data can be collected without user consent, only for preventing a real danger or in the case of a criminal offense. Moreover, if the law provides for this, data may be collected and processed in order to preserve vital interests of the data subject or of a third person. In the case of genetic data, this includes the members of the data subject's genetic line.

The Greek Data Protection Law (Law 2472/1997) is in accordance to the European Data Protection Directive (95/46/EC). Article 2 paragraph b states that medical data are sensitive data. Article 4 states that in order for personal data to be lawfully processed the entire data process needs to be analog to the dedicated purpose. Article 6 defines that the "data controller"[3] needs to notify the Hellenic Data Protection Authority (HDPA) on processing personal data and describes in short what this notification should include. Article 7 paragraph 1d allows the processing of medical data, subsequent to the HDPA's permission, by persons that professionally provide health services and are subject to the duty of confidentiality or to a

[3] The term data controller is analyzed in detail in Opinion 1/2010 of Article 29 Working Party [3] (Working Party that was set up under Article 29 of EU Data Protection Directive) on the concepts of "controller" and "processor." This opinion is available on http://ec.europa.eu/justice_home/fsj/privacy/workinggroup/wpdocs/2010_en.htm (Last accessed on June 4, 2010). According to Article 2 paragraph d' of the EU Data Protection Directive, the term "data controller" "shall mean the natural or legal person, public authority, agency or any other body which alone or jointly with others determines the purposes and means of the processing of personal data." The same definition for the term "data controller" is given in ISO 22857:2004 (Terms and Definitions, paragraph 3.3).

Code of Deontology. This processing is allowed under the condition that it is necessary for medical prevention, diagnosis, care, or management of health care services. With the amendment of the law in 2006 (Law 3471/2006) [31], Article 7A paragraph 2d adds some exemptions to the previous-mentioned article deriving some data controllers from the notification and permission process. However, these exemptions do not include legal entities and organizations providing medical services, as well as data controllers that collect and processes medical data as part of a telemedicine project or in order to provide medical services through a computer network. Lastly, Article 10 paragraph 3 states clearly that the data controller needs to take appropriate security measures in order to protect privacy of sensitive data. The HDPA requires a security policy, a security plan, a Code of Deontology, a risk analysis document, and a secure destruction policy. In the case of a virtual healthcare community, if it operates in Greece, it will abide to general sanctions of Greek Law and to the Greek Data Protection Law (Law 2472/1997) and the Greek Medical Code of Deontology (Law 3418/2005 [30]) in particular.

In general, data controllers can follow during the transfer of personal health information (PHI) the ISO/CD 22857:2004 standard, which provides guidelines on data protection to facilitate transborder flows of PHI. This specialized ISO standard does not in any case replace national legislations on data protection, while "*in cases, where a multilateral treaty between a number of countries has been agreed (e.g. the EU Data Protection Directive), the terms of that treaty will take precedence*" [19]. As far as Greece is concerned, international transfer of medical data is governed by Article 9 of the Greek Data Protection Law (Law 2472/1997) and is not allowed outside the EU without certain prerequisites. For every cross-border exchange of medical data, the competent Data Protection Authority must be notified. The authority must examine the specific national rules and determine whether the data transfer is allowed or not. Possible legal issues that might arise could involve improper use of patient data, selling data to insurance companies, and use of medical data for other than the notified purpose. In case of illegal processing of data, if the data controller resides in Greece, then he is subject to penal, civil, and administrative sanctions according to Articles 21–23 of Greek Data Protection Law (Law 2472/1997). Most EU national laws assume similar penalties.

5.6.2 Application of Greek Data Protection Law to a Virtual Healthcare Community

Supposing that the proposed virtual community resides in Greece, it will abide to several laws, with Greek Data Protection Law being the most significant. The community, being a data controller for sensitive medical data, does not belong to the exemptions of Article 7A paragraph 1d, as explained earlier, because it collects and processes medical data in order to provide telemedicine services. Thus, the data administrator of the community is obliged to notify the HDPA on processing sensitive medical data and request permission for this process. The notification process is depicted in Fig. 5.4.

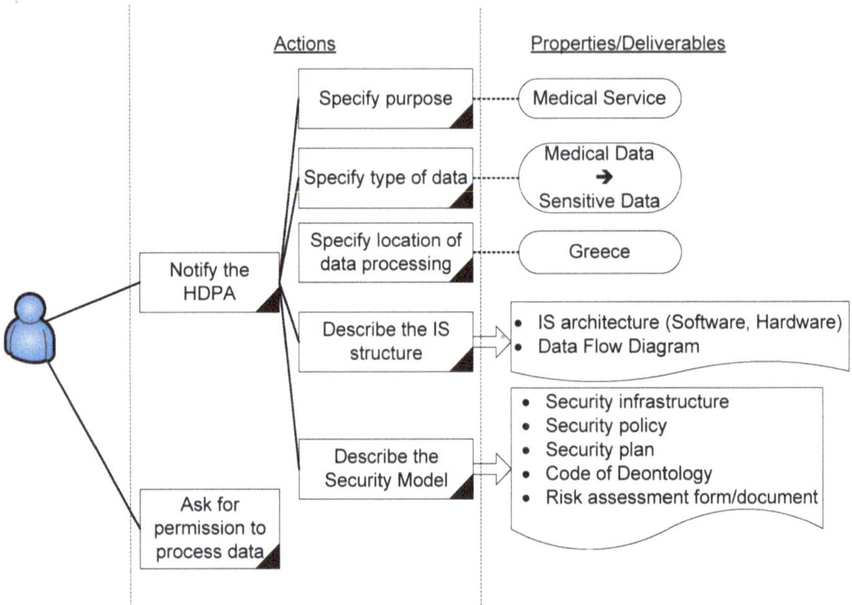

Fig. 5.4 The HDPA notification process

The administrator(s) of the community must notify the HDPA that they process medical data, which are sensitive data, for the purpose of providing medical services, and that they reside in Greece. The administrators must also inform the HDPA on the architecture of their information system and the data flow in it. Finally, they should submit a detailed security report, which contains the security infrastructure of the community, the security policy, the security plan, the Code of Deontology, and the latest performed risk assessment. They can also optionally submit their secure destruction policy document, which is not obligatory in the HDPA notification process. With all these completed, the data controller (i.e., the virtual community operating authority) has completed its notification submission and waits for it to be examined and approved.

In Fig. 5.5, the HDPA notification examination process is depicted. The HDPA auditors examine the type of data processing and the type of processed data; they check the community purpose and examine the information systems and the security model of the community portal. If something is missing, they ask for clarifications or even modifications of the original process in an iterative process that improves information security and enhances the achieved level of data protection. If everything is ok, the permission to process data is granted to the community administrators. If the administrators deny or do not manage to comply with the HDPA requirements, then the permission to process data is denied.

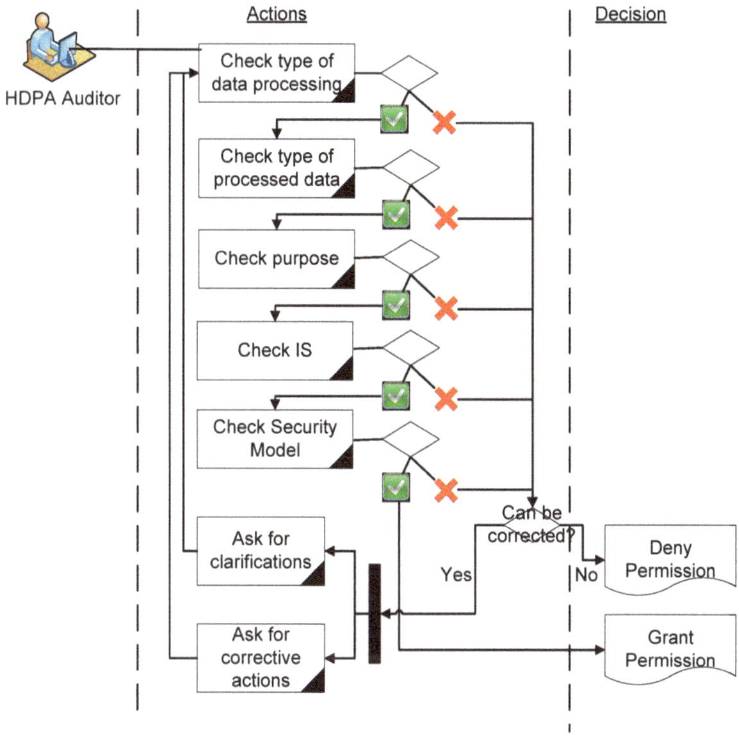

Fig. 5.5 The HDPA notification examination process

5.7 Usage Scenarios

As explained in Sect. 5.3, the development of a secure solution for virtual healthcare communities comprises design, implementation, assessment, and redesign steps is an iterative process. In the following paragraphs, we present several usage scenarios, which aim to expose the vulnerabilities of the model and provide future community developers with a set of test cases for the evaluation of their implementations. Each scenario contains a case description, a summary of the community assets which are on risk, a list of the security mechanisms that will be activated, and a reference to real-world incidents that justifies the importance of each case. The security risks usually apply either on the network [33] or on the application level [38]. A holistic security plan also considers attacks "from the inside" of the community [2]. Strictly defined policies and careful auditing will prevent security violations and will provide useful "tracking" evidence in case of internal attacks or information leaks.

5.7.1 Scenario 1: Unauthorized Access

5.7.1.1 Description

Typically the motive behind a hacking attack to the virtual medical community information systems is the hacker's interest to prove worthy of gaining access to system and to explore a protected computer system. In a typical scenario, the hacker scans the network of the virtual community and tries to enumerate the community's information infrastructure in order to gather as much data possible concerning the target network. After that, the hacker proceeds with vulnerability scanning aiming to identify open ports and running services that can be exploited and used as points of entry to the system. At the final step, the hacker uses various attacks methods, which aim to exploit identified system vulnerabilities in order to gain access to the community systems. The hacker's ultimate goal is to gain administrative access to an important system server (i.e., the database, the application, or the web server), practice on it, and subsequently use it to gain access to even more systems.

5.7.1.2 Critical Points

In order to keep the hacker as far from the community servers as possible, it is important to strengthen the fortification of the community infrastructure focusing on the "outside perimeter." The perimeter of the healthcare community comprises the proxy server, where the authentication takes place; the firewall; and the wireless access points. These systems must be properly configured in order to prevent unauthenticated user access.

5.7.1.3 Security Mechanisms Being Activated

The proposed architecture uses authentication tokens, in order to control access. The token mechanism allows encryption of the traffic by combining a user controlled section (i.e., the token that generates the OTP password) and a user ID. The potential hacker has to find a way to hijack the encrypted session by exploiting a vulnerability of the authentication mechanism, in order to gain access to the system. Using the proxy as the single point of entry introduces a single point of failure, but if set up correctly (with on time patch management), the only danger exists in zero-day exploits.

A second defensive obstacle for the hacker, who manages to hijack the session, will be the firewall, which will identify potential illegitimate traffic and block the attack. The key here is to constantly update the firewall and properly set up the access rules in order to prevent potential breaches. Applying state-of-the-art encryption (e.g., WPA2 with long random passwords or passphrases and the 802.1x protocol), the possibility of a hacker setting a fake access point and gathering enough traffic to hijack a session is reduced. Lastly, securing the computer systems of the community members limits the possibility of a "Trojan Horse" or "worm" attack that will open a backdoor to the community.

5.7.1.4 Real-World Incident

On February 2006, the University of Washington Medical Center reports an intrusion incident,[4] during which hackers gained access for almost 18 months to more than 200 computers, housing medical and business records. The breach occurred because someone failed to install security patches. The solution was to remove the breached computers from the network and wipe clean their hard drives. As a final step, a commercial intrusion-alert system was installed in all machines.

5.7.2 Scenario 2: Information Stealing

5.7.2.1 Description

Another potential threat is a skillful internal or external user, who steals sensitive information in order to perform fraud, identity theft, etc., and achieve personal profit. In the simplest case, an individual internal user, who has physical access to the system, can copy data in a portable drive (user A in Fig. 5.6).

A different information stealing attack can be performed in a web application using SQL injection. In this scenario, the attacker takes advantage of input validation vulnerabilities, queries the database with specially crafted SQL inputs that draw illegitimate information from the database (user B in Fig. 5.6).

Another frequent incident is hardware theft or accidental loss of hardware (i.e., laptops, portable storage devices, or backup media) which results in loss of medical information (user C in Fig. 5.6).

5.7.2.2 Critical Points

The critical point in the first scenario is the protection of data stored inside the community's servers. Since the attacker has already managed to infiltrate the first layer (enter the community perimeter) by means of physical presence, he/she should not be able to retrieve and store any sensitive medical data in a portable drive. The second scenario mainly targets the vulnerabilities of the data exchange applications and mainly refers to the validation of user input. The third scenario

---

[4] DataLoss database report of incident 224 [cited June 4, 2010]. Available from http://datalossdb.org/incidents/224-hacker-gains-opportunity-to-view-patient-medical-records

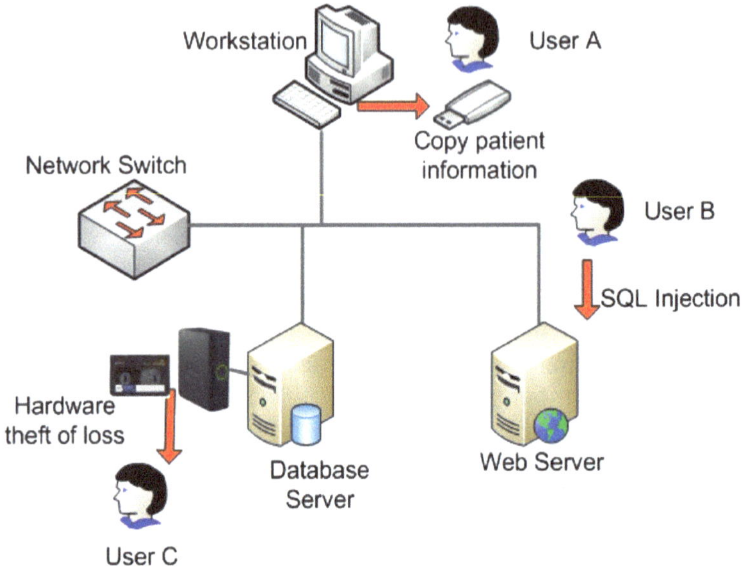

Fig. 5.6 Information stealing

exploits vulnerabilities in the physical layer (e.g., the potential absence of an access control system protecting the IT room) as well as the logical layer (e.g., the existence of unencrypted hard drives containing sensitive data).

5.7.2.3 Security Mechanisms Being Activated

In the first scenario, having an endpoint security solution in place, the community is able to block or control access to portable media devices by its users. Thus, the attacker either cannot use a portable media device in the first place or cannot copy any sensitive data to a portable drive, since the endpoint security solution policy prohibits it. Either way such an attacker is not able to steal any data from the community.

In the second scenario, using specialized input filtering modules and a web application firewall in the presentation layer to perform input filtering by methods such as web attack signatures, identification of SQL injection characters, and dynamic profiling of usual data traffic is the first layer of defense against information stealing attacks such as SQL injection. Authorization at the application server level adds an extra obstacle to illegal data access, in case that the malicious user input has not been identified by the web application firewall.

In the third scenario, encrypting the server's hard drives and keeping the hardware tokens needed to read them in a separate location harden the attacker from stealing a server hard drive containing sensible data. The same applies to backup tapes, which are encrypted and thus effectively useless to an attacker. Additionally, the existence of physical security measures (access card systems, access codes, security cards, etc.) makes it even harder to access the community's IT room or steal a backup tape from its physically secure storage location.

5.7.2.4 Real-World Incident

On February 2009, St. Anthony Central Hospital in Denver reported that for 18 months, an employee was stealing records by means of a USB drive (as many as 20 records per week) and used them to make fake driver's licenses and counterfeit Social Security cards.[5]

The Royal Bolton Hospital reported on January 2008 the theft of a computer that contained the private details of 350 chest patients.[6] The hospital contacted all patients to inform them of the theft, but insisted that all information is data-protected and cannot be accessed by anyone other than the relevant hospital staff. In order to improve security, the hospital recalled all its computers and laptops so that vital security software can be installed, which will encrypt patients' details. Additionally, encryption software was installed on all memory sticks and pen drives. Finally, all information was planned to be transferred to a central server and hosted in a secure storage network – rather than on individual hard drives.

5.7.3 *Scenario 3: Fake Identity*

5.7.3.1 Description

In this case, someone infiltrates the system with a fake identity in order to perform fraud. When the attacker pretends to be a doctor, wrong consultation may be provided to the patients. When pretending to be a patient, then wrong information will be collected.

5.7.3.2 Critical Points

The critical point is to certify the doctor's or patient's identity by using proper authentication methods. Additionally, in case of an identity theft, auditing must be in place, in order to prove the fraudulent activity and prevent and undo any damage.

---

[5] DataLoss database report of incident 2143 [cited June 4, 2010]. Available from http://datalossdb.org/incidents/2143-employee-steals-patients-medical-records-for-counterfeiter

[6] DataLoss database report of incident 1935 [cited June 4, 2010]. Available from http://datalossdb.org/incidents/1935-laptop-containing-the-personal-details-of-about-200-cancer-patients-stolen

5.7.3.3 Security Mechanisms Being Activated

The use of tokens as an authentication method along with its registration on a certification authority hinders the possibility of a malicious user entering the community with fraudulent purposes. Additionally, content moderators can function as a second certification authority, preventing the fraudulent users' actions and protecting users from deception. Auditing mechanisms can give an audit trail to the imitator. Finally, reputation mechanisms can increase members' awareness on faulty consultation and fraud.

5.7.3.4 Real-World Incident

The DataLoss Database and the World Privacy Forum report several incidents on identity theft (e.g., [13]), which resulted in fraudulent social security numbers and abuse of insurance company benefits. The motive behind a fake or stolen medical identity is to obtain medical services, goods, or money by falsifying claims for medical services and falsifying medical records to support those claims.

However, the danger can be even greater, when the theft is discovered during the course of a medical emergency. In this case, the medical profile is distorted by several false entries added by the criminal. This was the case of a Florida woman who discovered that someone impersonating her had caused false entries to be placed in her medical file as reported by the Federal Trade Commission [17]. In the case of a virtual community, the threat of fake identities is bigger, since patients may not have personal contact with their doctors.

5.7.4 Scenario 4: Provide Fictional Patient Data

5.7.4.1 Description

This attack aims in modifying patient data in the *database*, or infiltrating the mobile sensor network and *transmitting* invalid data.

The attacker (MITM – Attacker in Fig. 5.7) gains physical access to the community's premises and sets up a Man in the Middle (MITM) machine and uses it to intercept traffic and steal sensitive medical data. In a first step, the attacker sets up a sniffer and listens to ARP packets. The attacker's initial objective is to learn the IP and MAC addresses of the two communicating parties (Workstation X, Workstation Y, in Fig. 5.7). Workstation X sends an ARP request message to Workstation Y asking the MAC address of Workstation Y. Workstation Y replies with an ARP reply message. The attacker sniffs both messages and subsequently sends a forged ARP reply message (Arp Attack 1, Fig. 5.7) to the requestor's machine (Workstation X) saying "I own the IP you have requested. My MAC address is '00-0G-7E-3T-4C-98.'" Workstation X will gladly update its ARP table with the new one that it has just

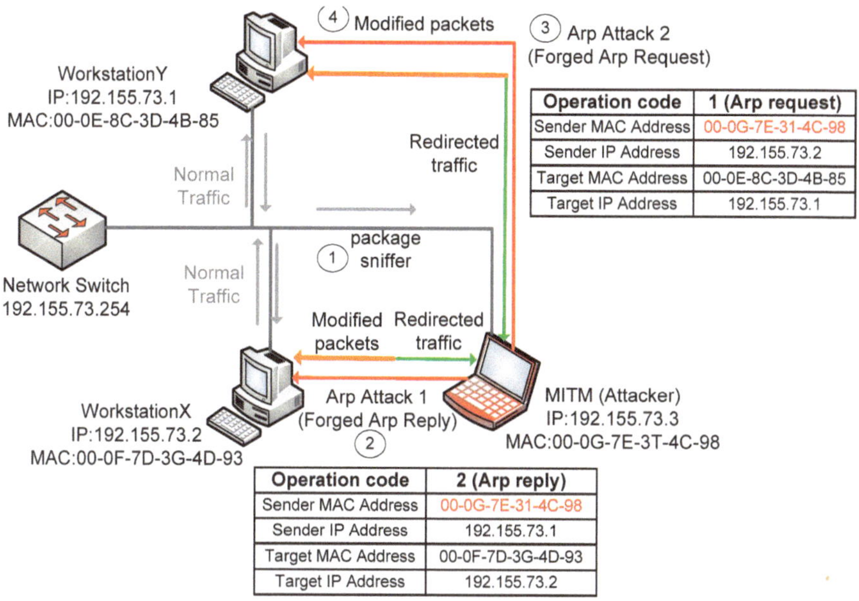

Fig. 5.7 A tampering man in the middle attack

received. At the same time, the attacker sends a forged ARP request message to Workstation Y (Arp Attack 2, Fig. 5.7) saying that he owns the IP address of Workstation X. As a consequence, all packets pass through the MITM machine and can be processed illegitimately. The attacker is able to intercept all packets exchanged, alter the medical data in transit, and delete information from the database.

5.7.4.2 Critical Points

In the MITM scenario, the critical point is the protection of the community network's infrastructure. Even if the attacker succeeds in gaining physical access to a community's network port, he must not be able to gain actual network access. Even if the attacker manages to obtain an actual network IP address, he must not be able to intercept or alter legitimate traffic.

5.7.4.3 Security Mechanisms Being Activated

Several mechanisms are activated in the first level in order to confront the MITM attack. The first step is having employed physical security measures to deter the malicious attacker from gaining access to an actual network port. Even if the attacker obtains the latter, his presence in the network will be audited by the community's auditing mechanisms. Since the community's network infrastructure is carefully configured, having possibly static routes configured in respect to critical systems, the attacker will not be able to fool any user that the MITM is a critical application server. If the attacker manages to infiltrate by means of a MITM attack into the communication between two legitimate users, the intercepted traffic will be gibberish, since the traffic is encrypted by means of tokens. In case that all before-mentioned measures fail, backup and transaction auditing mechanisms will allow the detection of data corruption or modification and will assist IT administrators to rollback data in a previous stable state.

5.7.4.4 Real-World Incident

Although MITM attacks mainly target banks, one should expect such attacks in a medical community. The aim of these attacks is to steal passwords, pin, social security numbers, etc. A typical example is the exploit found on SiteKey, a security control used by several web banking applications, which allowed criminals to imitate the original web site and steal data from clients.[7] In a more recent example, Kevin Mitnick set up a Man in The Middle Server that intercepted his call to the IVR of Washington Mutual Bank and managed to steal his account number and four digits of his social security number.[8]

5.7.5 Scenario 5: System Attack

5.7.5.1 Description

The attack aims to block the smooth operation of the system, in order to obfuscate the community (e.g., in a DDOS attack). "A DDOS attack disrupts or completely denies service to legitimate users, networks, systems, or other resources. The intent of such an attack is usually malicious and often takes little skill because the requisite tools are readily available" [34]. DDOS attacks are usually performed through a large number of PCs, infected by Trojan Horses or Rootkits, which constitute a botnet network. The attacker (bot herder) remotely controls the PCs and orchestrates the attack which aims to bring down the entire network. The PCs usually belong to unsuspected users, who are unaware that their computers are infected.

---

[7] First live SiteKey exploit seen in operation (30/10/2007) [cited June 4, 2010]. Available from http://cr-labs.com/publications/SiteKeyExploit-20071030–1.pdf

[8] Former Hacker Tackles IVR and Voice Biometric Security [cited June 4, 2010]. Available from http://www.speechtechmag.com/Articles/Editorial/FYI/Former-Hacker-Tackles-IVR-and-Voice-Biometric-Security-50358.aspx

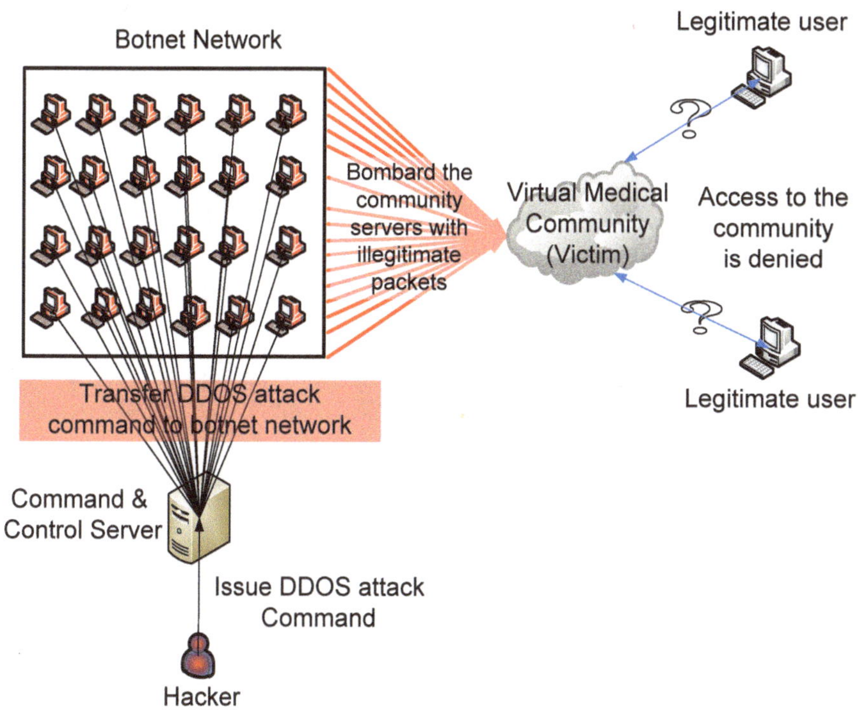

Fig. 5.8 A botnet attack against the virtual community

In such a scenario, as depicted in Fig. 5.8, the attacker logs into his Command and Control Center and transfers a distributed denial of service attack command to his botnet network. The zombie PCs of the botnet network bombard the community's information systems with illegitimate packets. Even if a single exploitable vulnerability exists, the attack will succeed, and legitimate users will not be able to access the community's services.

5.7.5.2 Critical Points

The attacks mainly target the application server layer, and the designer's aim should be to confront these attacks on the proxy server or the firewall, so that the functionality of the community cannot be impaired. A single vulnerability can be enough to run the system down so a disaster recovery plan should always be ready. In the attack shown in Fig. 5.8, the attacking botnet network aims to bring down the users' points of entry and usage, namely, the authentication proxy, the web server, or the application server (designated targets depicted with red arrows in Fig. 5.9).

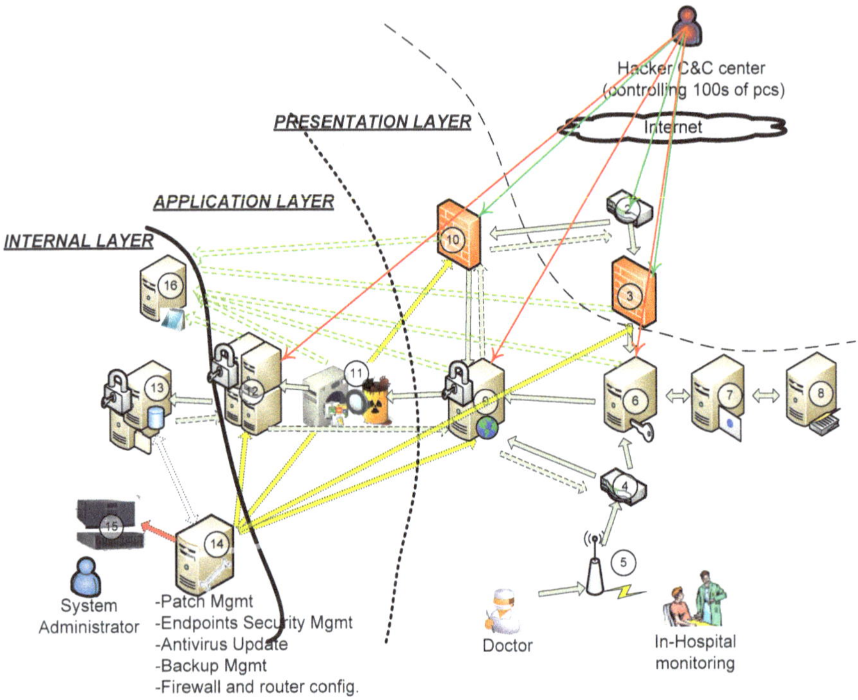

Fig. 5.9 The security infrastructure of the virtual community responds to a botnet attack

5.7.5.3 Security Mechanisms Being Activated

The first step in securing the application server is to harden the application firewall by using the latest attack signatures for update. For the attacks that cannot be detected, it is necessary that the firewall and the other network devices are set up correctly to deal with packets arriving at closed ports, with illegitimate packets, etc. Several techniques, such as network ingress filtering and use of BGP to block DOS attacks (see [41, 42]), are tools that administrators can use, in order to fortify their systems. Applying these techniques might cause legitimate traffic to be blocked also; thus, the decision to apply them must be taken carefully.

The second step is to set up a patch management suite that operates in a regular basis, in order to limit system's vulnerabilities, which can be exploited in a DDOS attack. Lastly, in case of a zero-day exploit, a disaster recovery plan must be able to function properly, in order to bring the soonest possible the community systems back to normal working state.

In the attack shown in Fig. 5.7, once the DDOS attack is launched, the community's defenses are activated, and the firewalls block the attack based on their proper configuration and their patching state (dashed green arrows in Fig. 5.9). This means that the employed patch management suite also plays a role (yellow arrows in

Fig. 5.9). If the attack is not blocked and the community goes down, the damage needs to be assessed and maintained, while the community must get back online (thick red arrow in Fig. 5.9). All these will be achieved based on the community's disaster recovery plan. The attack, successful or not, will be logged in the auditing server (dashed yellow arrows in Fig. 5.9).

5.7.5.4 Real-World Incident

In July 2008, an attack was started against several governmental, healthcare, and business web sites worldwide [9]. The attack was performed by bots infected by a malware and compromised by Asprox toolkit attack. The bots originated from over 1,000 unique web site domains including web sites of respectable organizations, governmental institutes, healthcare organizations (such as nhs.uk, samedical.org), etc. The attack toolkit is designed to inject a script into legitimate webpages. The malicious script exploits several vulnerabilities on the victim's machine in order to heighten the chances for successful exploitation: MDAC Vulnerability, QuickTime Rtsp Vulnerability, and AOL SuperBuddy ActiveX Control Code Execution Vulnerability. The successful execution of the script resulted in the downloading and execution of a Trojan Horse on the victim's machine.

The remedy to an attack of this type is to apply all the available patches in a daily basis and perform daily scans for malware and Trojans on all computers in the network. Patches may include configuration guidelines for firewalls and routers that may block illegitimate traffic.

5.7.6 Scenario 6: Malware

5.7.6.1 Description

This kind of incident scenario involves a computer system, whether a server system or a user PC, being infected by a malicious program (malware). The effects of any malware depend mainly on its payload which defines the type of infection (worm, Trojan Horse, Rootkit, spyware, adware, etc.) the infected system suffers from. The most dangerous infections are the ones the system cannot even see (Rootkits), the ones that come disguised as useful programs (Trojan Horses), and the ones that not only cause damage but spread also across the network to machines suffering of the same security hole (worms). A Trojan Horse can be used to steal medical data, a Rootkit can be used to control whole computer systems causing damage that cannot be calculated, while worms can cause a lot of damage by not only infecting a single computer system but also damaging similar systems effectively, wracking havoc among users, and disrupting entire systems with notorious examples: the Morris Worm, the Slammer Worm, etc. [50].

5.7.6.2 Critical Points

The backbone of the community's infrastructure (servers) as well as the end user's equipment might be the target of this attack. The attacker depending on the payload of the virus used will aim to exploit a single vulnerability preferably by using a zero-day exploit virus. The attacker could aim to steal information by means of a Trojan Horse or render the database server, for example, unavailable by using a worm, or control the RADIUS server by infecting it with a Rootkit.

5.7.6.3 Security Mechanisms Being Activated

The first step to guard against malware attacks is to have antivirus suites in place that protect both critical systems such as servers and end-users' systems, namely, members' systems. These antivirus suites must be kept up to date by frequently applying updates. This is performed, as designed, in the proposed security infrastructure for the community.

The second step is to have a properly configured patch management suite in place that operates in a regular basis, in order to limit system's vulnerabilities, which can be exploited by a malware through appropriate exploits. Lastly, in case of a zero-day exploit, a disaster recovery plan must be able to function properly, in order to bring the soonest possible the community systems back to normal working state.

5.7.6.4 Real-World Incident

On May 2009, the Alberta Health Services (AHS) network in Edmonton has reported that a virus has infected 150 of their computers for a 2 weeks period.[9] The virus, which was previously unknown to the AHS antivirus software vendors, captured lab results, diagnostic imaging reports, and whatever else was on a computer screen and then transmitted the information to an external web site. Once the virus was detected, AHS worked quickly to remove the virus and take necessary steps to reinforce antivirus protection.

5.7.7 Scenario 7: Social Engineering

5.7.7.1 Description

In this incident scenario, a malicious outsider gains access to an organization's infrastructure by manipulating people working in the organization in a way that they happily reveal information which is otherwise confidential, such as Social Security

[9] DataLoss database report of incident 2174 [cited June 4, 2010]. Available from http://datalossdb.org/incidents/2174-personal-health-information-of-11–582-stolen-by-virus

Number and password. Such an attack could come from anywhere. For example, a person posing as a technician might call and persuade a user to reveal his password as part of a security maintenance procedure.

5.7.7.2 Critical Points

This kind of attack scenario aims mainly at the human factor. In order for a social engineer to be successful, he must be able to access physically or electronically a user of the community that has something useful to divulge, such as passwords and sensitive data. In the case of the proposed virtual community, targeted items could be means of authentication and data related to end users or doctors.

5.7.7.3 Security Mechanisms Being Activated

The use of tokens as an authentication method along with its registration on a certification authority hinders the possibility of a malicious user obtaining a password through a social engineering attack. The attacker would have to convince the user to hand on his e-token device as the log-in procedure requires something the user has (e-token) and something a user knows (password). The e-token device adds an extra authentication layer, as an attacker who learns something a user knows (password) is still denied access to the community's systems. Additionally, even if a social engineer manages to enter the site and tries to convince users to hand on sensitive data, content moderators can function as a second certification authority, preventing the fraudulent users' actions and protecting users from deception. Auditing mechanisms can give an audit trail to the social engineer. The existence of an overall access and behavior policy educates the user and prevents him from being an easy prey to social engineering attacks. Finally, physical security measures deter any attacker from entering the community's IT room unaccompanied and gaining physical access to sensitive data.

5.7.7.4 Real-World Incident

On May 2009, a security consultant working in Siemens targeted a client that provides financial services [40]. His goal was to establish what level of access to information he could gain by means of social engineering. Without using any special equipment, he walked into the company's premises, established a base in a meeting room, and managed to access various company's premises, with most indicative the company's data room, IT, and telecoms network. He also managed to obtain usernames and passwords from 17 out of 20 company's employees by posing as a member of an IT department. He even managed to assess the working state of the company's CCTV circuit and bring a second consultant into the company's premises.

5.8 Discussion and Conclusions

This chapter presented a security-enabled architecture for a virtual healthcare community. The architecture is associated with a risk management model, which is based on the identification and protection of the community assets. In this community, patients have web access to the community services and provide their medical data using wireless sensor devices and/or web browsers, and doctors access community services either remotely or from inside the hospital and share their expertise with patients and other practitioners.

The design of a secure and trustful community is a difficult though interesting task, which should be preferably performed by following standardized procedures. In this direction, this chapter capitalizes on widely accepted security standards (the ISO 27000 family of standards) and provides a roadmap for developing a secure solution.

In this dynamic environment, new applications are added, thus opening new exploits, creating new threats and new attack forms. Security and trust management requires careful handling of all the aforementioned issues and continuous maintenance of the community infrastructure. In this work, we presented the details of the application of the risk management model in a healthcare community and several security violation incidents, in healthcare and other sectors, which illustrate the various security mechanisms and validate our security model.

In addition to the security model, the risk management model, and the scenario-based evaluation, we presented a study on the legal implications of security violation incidents and introduced the process followed by the Hellenic Data Protection Authority for preventing and handling violators.

The next steps of this work comprise the prototype implementation of the security model for a healthcare community and an evaluation that will cover all possible attack scenarios.

References

1. Akyildiz, I. F., Su, W., Sankarasubramaniam, Y., & Cayirci, E. (2002). Wireless sensor networks: A survey. *Computer Networks, 38*(4), 393–422.
2. Apostolakis, I., Chryssanthou, A., & Varlamis, I. (2009). A holistic perspective of security in health related virtual communities. In A. Lazakidou & K. Siassiakos (Eds.), *Handbook of research on distributed medical informatics and E-health* (pp. 367–381). Hershey, PA: IGI Global.
3. Article 29 Data Protection Working Party. (2010, February). Opinion 1/2010 on the concepts of "controller" and "processor". Brussels, Belgium.
4. Becker, M. Y., Fournet, C., & Gordon, A. D. (2007, July 6–8). Design and semantics of a decentralized authorization language. In *Proceedings of the 20th IEEE Computer Security Foundations Symposium (CSF 07), Venice, Italy* (pp. 3–15). Washington, DC: IEEE Computer Society.

5. Becker, M. Y., & Sewell, P. (2004, June 28–30). Cassandra: Flexible trust management applied to electronic health records. In *Proceedings of the 17th IEEE Workshop on Computer Security Foundations; Asilomar Conference Center, CA, USA, 2004* (pp. 139–154). Washington, DC: IEEE.
6. Blaze, M., Kannan, S., Lee, I., Sokolsky, O., Smith, J. M., Keromytis, A. D., et al. (2009, February). Dynamic trust management. *IEEE Computer Magazine*, *42*(2), 44–52.
7. Chryssanthou, A., Latsiou, C., & Varlamis, I. (2009, June 9–13). Security and trust in virtual healthcare communities. In *Proceedings of the 2nd International Conference on Pervasive Technologies Related to Assistive Environments (PETRA 09), Corfu, Greece* (pp. 1–8). New York: ACM Press.
8. Curtis, D. W., Pino, E. J., Bailey, J. M., Shih, E. I., Waterman, J., Vinterbo, S. A., et al. (2008). SMART – An integrated, wireless system for monitoring unattended patients. *Journal of the American Medical Informatics Association, 15*(1), 44–53.
9. Cyberinsecure.com. (2008, July 18). *Asprox botnet mass attack hits governmental, healthcare, and top business websites* [cited 2010 June 4]. Retrieved July 30, 2010, from http://cyberinsecure.com/asprox-botnet-mass-attack-hits-governmental-healthcare-and-top-business-websites/
10. DataLoss Database. (2010, June). *Open security foundation; c2005–2010*. Available from http://datalossdb.org
11. Demiris, G. (2005). Virtual communities in health care. In B. Silverman, A. Jain, A. Ichalkaranje, & L. Jain (Eds.), *Intelligent paradigms for healthcare enterprises* (Germany-studies in fuzziness and soft computing, Vol. 184, pp. 121–137). Berlin/Heidelberg: Springer.
12. Demiris, G., Parker, O. D., Fleming, D., & Edison, K. (2004). Hospice staff attitudes towards telehospice. *The American Journal of Hospice & Palliative Care, 21*(5), 343–348.
13. Dixon P (2006, March 3). *Medical identity theft: The information crime that can kill you* [cited 2010 January 4]. The World Privacy Forum. First report in a series [Internet]. Cardiff by the Sea, CA, USA: World Privacy Forum. Retrieved May 22, 2011, from http://www.worldprivacyforum.org/pdf/wpf_medicalidtheft2006.pdf
14. Ebner, W., Leimeister, J. M., & Krcmar, H. (2004, January 5–8). Trust in virtual healthcare communities: Design and implementation of trust-enabling functionalities. In *Proceedings of the 37th Hawaii International Conference on System Sciences (HICSS 04) – Track 7, Big Island, Hawaii* (p. 70182). Washington, DC: IEEE.
15. European Council. (1995). Directive 95/46/EC on the protection of individuals with regard to the processing of personal data and on the free movement of such data. *Official Journal of the European Communities, 38*(281), 31.
16. European Council. (1997). *Explanatory memorandum to recommendation (97) 5 on the protection of medical data*. Strasbourg, France: Council of Europe.
17. Federal Trade Commission. (2000). *Identity Theft Victim Assistance Workshop*. Washington, DC: Federal Trade Commission; c2000–2010 [cited 2010 June 4]. Retrieved June 4, 2011, from http://www.ftc.gov/bcp/workshops/idtheft/
18. Hitrustalliance.net. (2009). *Frisco, TX: Health Information Trust Alliance* [updated 2010; cited 2010 June 4]. Available from https://www.hitrustcentral.net/
19. ISO/CD. (2005). *ISO/CD 22857:2004: Health informatics – Guidelines on data protection to facilitate trans-border flows of personal health information*. Geneva, Switzerland: ISO/CD.
20. ISO/IEC. (2005). *ISO/IEC 27001:2005: Information technology – Security techniques – Information security management systems – Requirements*. Geneva, Switzerland: ISO/IEC.
21. ISO/IEC. (2005). *ISO/IEC 27002:2005: Information technology – Security techniques – Code of practice for information security management*. Geneva, Switzerland: ISO/IEC.
22. ISO/IEC. (2008). *ISO/IEC 27005:2008: Information technology – Security techniques – Information security risk management*. Geneva, Switzerland: ISO/IEC.
23. ISO/IEC. (2008). *ISO/IEC 27799:2008: Health informatics –Information security management in health using ISO/IEC 27002*. Geneva, Switzerland: ISO/IEC.

24. Jones, V. M., van Halteren, A. T., Dokovski, N. T., Koprinkov, G., Peuscher, J., Bults, R., et al. (2006). Mobihealth: Mobile services for health professionals. In R. S. H. Istepanian, S. Laxminarayan, & C. S. Pattichis (Eds.), *M-health emerging mobile health systems* (pp. 237–246). New York: Springer.
25. Kaplan, D. (2009, March 2). Group unveils first-of-its-kind standard to secure patient data. *SC Magazine, NEWS*. Retrieved March 4, 2009, from http://www.scmagazineus.com/group-unveils-first-of-its-kind-standard-to-secure-patient-data/article/128168/
26. Kui, M., Yue, W., Xu, Z., Xiaochun, X., & Gengdu, Z. (2005, September 21–23). A trust management model for virtual communities. In *Proceedings of the 5th International Conference on Computer and Information Technology (CIT 05), Shanghai, China* (pp. 741–745). Washington, DC: IEEE.
27. Kyriacou, E., Pavlopoulos, S., Berler, A., Neophytou, M., Bourka, A., & Georgoulas, A. (2003). Multipurpose health care telemedicine systems with mobile communication link support. *Biomedical Engineering Online, 2*, 7.
28. Laleci, G. B., Dogac, A., Olduz, M., Tasyurt, I., Yuksel, M., & Okcan, A. (2008). SAPHIRE: A multi-agent system for remote healthcare monitoring through computerized clinical guidelines. In R. Annicchiarico, U. Cortés, & C. Urdiales (Eds.), *Agent technology and e-health* (Whitestein series in software agent technologies and autonomic computing, pp. 25–44). Basel, Switzerland: Birkhäuser.
29. Law 2472/1997: Protection of individuals from personal data processing, Pub. L. No. 2472, Greece (1997).
30. Law 3418/2005: Medical code of deontology, Pub. L. No. 3418, Greece (2005).
31. Law 3471/2006: Protection of personal data and privacy in the telecommunications sector – Amendment of Law 2472/1997, Pub. L. No 3471, Greece (2006).
32. Lorincz, K., Malan, D. J., Fulford-Jones, T. R. F., Nawoj, A., Clavel, A., Shnayder, V., et al. (2004). Sensor networks for emergency response: Challenges and opportunities. *IEEE Pervasive Computing, 3*(4), 16–23.
33. Maji, A. K., Mukhoty, A., Majumdar, A. K., Mukhopadhyay, J., Sural, S., Paul, S., et al. (2008, January 29). Security analysis and implementation of web-based telemedicine services with a four-tier-architecture. *Proceedings of the 2nd International Workshop on Connectivity, Mobility and Patients' Comfort (CMPC), Tampere, Finland* (pp. 46–54). New York: ACM.
34. McClure, S., Scambray, J., & Kurtz, G. (2003). *Hacking exposed: Network security secrets and solutions* (4th ed.). Berkeley, CA: McGraw-Hill/Osborne.
35. Mondy, J., & Torresi, M. (2008). CIGNA creating a virtual health care community. *CIGNA website, News Releases*. Retrieved June 4, 2010, from http://newsroom.cigna.com/article_display.cfm?article_id=925
36. Mufti, M., Agouridis, D., Din, S., & Mukhtar, A. (2009, June 9–13). Ubiquitous wireless infrastructure for elderly care. In *Proceedings of the 2nd International Conference on Pervasive Technologies Related to Assistive Environments (PETRA 09), Corfu, Greece* (pp. 1–5). New York: ACM Press.
37. Ng, H. S., Sim, M. L., & Tan, C. M. (2006). Security issues of wireless sensor networks in healthcare applications. *BT Technology Journal, 24*(2), 138–144.
38. Orrin, S. (2004). *The twelve most common application level hack attacks*. Watchfire Corporation Whitepaper. Retrieved June 4, 2010, from http://www.emedia.co.uk/FM/GetFile.aspx?id=58740
39. Parducci, B., Lockhart, H., Levinson, R., & McRae, M. (2005). *eXtensible Access Control Markup Language (XACML) Version 2.0 core specification*. Billerica, MA: OASIS. Retrieved from www.oasis-open.org/committees/xacml/
40. Raywood, D. (2009, May 6). Social engineering attack allowed consultant to access company's data room and steal passwords. *SC Magazine, NEWS*. Retrieved June 4, 2010, from http://www.scmagazineuk.com/Social-engineering-attack-allowed-consultant-to-access-companys-data-room-and-steal-passwords/article/136278

41. *RFC2267 – Network ingress filtering. Defeating denial of service attacks which employ IP source address spoofing*. (2010). Available from Internet Engineering Task Force website. Retrieved January 2, 2004, from http://www.ietf.org/rfc/rfc2267.txt
42. *RFC3882 – Configuring BGP to block denial-of-service attacks*. (2010). Available from Internet Engineering Task Force website. Fremont, CA. Retrieved June 4, 2010, from http://www.ietf.org/rfc/rfc3882.txt
43. Schopp, L. H., Hales, J. W., Quetsch, J. L., Hauan, M. J., & Brown, G. D. (2004). Design of a peer-to-peer telerehabilitation model. *Telemedicine Journal and e-Health, 10*(2), 243–251.
44. Seamons, K., Winslett, M., Yu, T., Yu, L., & Jarvis, R. (2003). Protecting privacy during on-line trust negotiation. In R. Dingledine & P. Syverson (Eds.), *LNCS 2482: Proceedings of the 2nd Workshop on Privacy Enhancing Technologies (PET 2002), April 14–15, 2002, San Francisco, USA* (pp. 129–143). Berlin: Springer.
45. Stanberry, B. (1998). The legal and ethical aspects of telemedicine: Data protection, security and European law. *Journal of Telemedicine and Telecare, 4*(1), 18–24.
46. Stefanov, H., Bien, Z., & Won-Chul, B. (2004). The smart house for older persons and persons with physical disabilities: Structure, technology arrangements, and perspectives. *IEEE Transactions on Neural Systems and Rehabilitation Engineering, 12*(2), 228–250.
47. U.S. Congress. (1996) Health Insurance Portability and Accountability Act, USA. Pub. L No. 104-191, 110 Stat. 1936.
48. US Department of Health and Human Services, Office for Civil Rights. (2003). *Standards for privacy of individually identifiable health information*. Washington, DC: US Department of Health and Human Services.
49. Varlamis, I., & Apostolakis, I. (2010). Self-supportive virtual communities. *International Journal on Web Based Communities, 6*(1), 43–61. doi:10.1504/IJWBC.2010.030016.
50. Vlachos, V., Spinellis, D., & Androutsellis-Theotokis, S. (2009, September 23–25). Biological aspects of computer virology. In A. P. Sideridis & C. Z. Patrikakis (Eds.), *Proceedings of the 3rd International Conference on e-Democracy, Athens, Greece* (pp. 202–219). Berlin: Springer.
51. Wang, X., Lao, G., DeMartini, T., Reddy, H., Nguyen, M., & Valenzuela, E. (2002, November 22). XrML – eXtensible rights markup language. In *Proceedings of ACM Workshop on XML Security (XMLSEC '02); Fairfax, VA* (pp. 71–79). New York: ACM.
52. Warren, S., Lebak, J., Yao, J., Creekmore, J., Milenkovic, A., & Jovanov, E. (2005, September 1–4). Interoperability and security in wireless body area network infrastructures. In *Proceedings of the 27th Annual International Conference of Engineering in Medicine and Biology Society (IEEE-EMBS), Shanghai, China, 4,* 3837–3840.

Chapter 6
Cybernationalism: Terrorism, Political Activism, and National Identity Creation in Virtual Communities and Social Media

Matthew F. Palmer

Department of Comparative and International Education, Lehigh University, Bethlehem, PA, USA, mfp210@gmail.com

Abstract Virtual communities allow for intensely homophilous groups to have a meeting place that would otherwise be impossible in the spatial world. Subsequently, the ability to develop social capital among groups that have traditionally been unable to recruit and mobilize is transformed by the growing access to web communication. The resulting communities are especially influential in groups centered on political or nationalist participation. This chapter will focus on three popular types of cybernationalism (terrorism, political activism, and ethnic-identity production) as it relates to social media and virtual communities. It will explore how social media and virtual community participation is conducive to the spreading of nationalism crucial to the developments of social movements.

Keywords Social media • Social networks • Terrorism • Activism • Nationalism

6.1 Introduction

Only a month prior to penning this chapter, Norway became crippled by the deadliest terrorist attack in their nation's history. First by an explosion in the nation's capital and then by a gunman's murderous rampage through a youth's summer camp, the handful of hours were marked with horror and massacre. Ultimately, near 100 people lost their lives. Police soon delved into the terrorist's past and recent movements, uncovering memorabilia, statements, and personal belongings from the terrorist's residence. Among the most telling of these aims were the seizure of a computer and the examining of the terrorist's web activity. It showed the terrorist was active among chat rooms, web forums, and social media devoted to right-wing nationalism and the rebuffing of multiculturalism. He had authored a 1,500-plus page manifesto, all of which abhorred the political initiatives of the state to increase diversity and provide refuge to foreigners, primarily those of Muslim emigration. Reviewing the texts and statements, authorities concluded the man is an ultra-right-wing nationalist

A.A. Lazakidou (ed.), *Virtual Communities, Social Networks and Collaboration*, Annals of Information Systems 15, DOI 10.1007/978-1-4614-3634-8_6,

believing that a rampage would halt the growth of Islam that was ultimately acting as a cancer to European society.

Understanding the impetus for terror has been undertaken by myriads of academic disciplines. Responsibility for this type of act has been given to a broadly inclusive maxim ranging from fully constructivist in nature to more biological foundations. While much attention has been given to alleviating the *reason* for attacks, what remains largely neglected is the development of an applied understanding of both *why* and *how* such acts are committed. Throughout history, there have been egregious attacks of terror toward individuals, groups, and states. They have been committed by the delusional and the sane, the proletariat and the bourgeoisie, and the ecclesiastical and the secular. The only scenario in which significant overlap has not been achieved is the use of the Internet. The martyrs of prior centuries did not meet through an online forum much like the members of Weather Underground did not "like" one another on Facebook before their urban mobilization. The actions that occurred in Norway were no doubt horrific, but they were not the first instance of mass violence in the history of the human. The only stark novelty in the attack was the extent to which the cyberworld was included as a basis for radicalization, mobilization, and action. This event serves to remind us of our newborn epoch of technology, where individuals cease to operate solely within their immediate environment, and instead, live pluralistically between the ambient society and the cyber society. Subsequently, we are required to investigate this allure to complement a substantial knowledge of the social human. It is through a symbiosis of social and cyber theory that proves most appropriate in our analysis of the Norwegian tragedy. As we shall also see, such a synthesis is not limited solely to acts of terror, but to a broader scope of social change.

First, however, it is essential to define our working terminology for the purpose of this chapter. Although in other scholarly works one will hear different labels being applied to groups in a manner inconsistent with this chapter, a slight clustering of terminology will be employed henceforth. Loosely defined and for the bounds of this chapter, we define virtual communities as "social aggregates" that have transferred from the spatial communities to the cyber [72]. Such a label fits well within the grand scheme of the web with which we are interested. Rheingold's [71] influence, however, has morphed with the advent of social media and more traditional methods of web interaction, and pragmatically, the two operate very differently from one another. However, they are apt to fall under the same umbrella in this chapter because the focus is not the aspects of *how* the interaction occurs, but instead, *why* it occurs. From this perspective, the divide between what constitutes a "virtual community" and "social media" is eroded, and henceforth, we shall refer to the two as one in the same. It is noted and understood that explicit differences separate the two in how they are accessed, developed, and controlled. However, this chapter is concerned with the abstract qualities that allure people to finding human reciprocity on the web regardless of what particular space or structure it inhabits, and as such, this chapter is not as concerned with stringent differentiation unless otherwise stated.

Specifically, the focus of this chapter is that of why the Internet is conducive to the spread of nationalism and social change, whether in the form of mainstream political maneuvering, oppositional activism, or even violent terrorism. Continuing with the definition of terms, we must detail the nomenclature specific to the scholarship of nationalism. When referring to a nation, we do so differently than as if we were referring to a state. The former centers around the ethnic bond that groups people, while the latter points to the categorization of peoples based on political action or autonomy. Unless there is a politically active state that is *explicitly* comprised of a homogenous ethnicity, there is no constitution of a nation-state. Thus, our definition requires a strict separation between referring to the ethnic bond of a nation and the political sovereignty of the state. Nationalism, on the other hand, is more forgiving a term and articulates the seemingly irrational behavior of individuals or collectives in support of the state or the nation. It is the instance of the Norwegian terrorist as he attempted to purge his state of cultural infection, the civil rights movements that protested for progressive civic construction, and even the emotional speech given by a politician to his colleagues and constituents.

The chapter is structured to begin with a heavy emphasis on elucidating a nationalism-based framework as it is applied to cyberspace, an idea that has yet to adequately broach the study of the web. Subsequently, the majority of this chapter will focus on laying the foundation for a theoretical interpretation of why virtual communities act as miniature nationalist congregations. While a complete exegesis of nationalism is beyond the boundaries of this chapter, it is no doubt essential to briefly review nationalist theory and its spatial applications. After these principles of scholarship with cyber-participation theory, the chapter will then shift to empirically evidencing the theoretical framework.

6.2 A Brief Review of Nationalism and Its Implication for Web Participation

Our overarching aim is to understand why the sociocognitive foundations of nationalism and civic participation do not differ substantively from those responsible for the allure of web community participation. As we shall see, the underlying premise of what drives nationalist fervor is strikingly similar to what motivates people to take part in virtual communities. Hereafter we shall use *cybernationalism* as a term that bundles the two. The assertion of similarity does not suggest, however, the declaration of a cybernation that grants the rights and privileges of a spatial one. Rather, it explores the notion that being a *netizen* is an act reminiscent of substate nationalism, and that such participation imbues the user with emotions of appreciable overlap.

Beginning with the spatial application, nationalism as an emotive catalyst has been analyzed most thoroughly with respect the individual-state or individual-nation dyad. From such scholarship is two primary offerings (essentialist and constructivist) and tangential critiques to explain nationalist behavior [8, 24, 46], though a central convergence remains "the need for nationalists to be able to tell a particular type of story about the nation and its importance, a story that resonates emotively with people, that glorifies the nation, [and] that is easily transmitted and absorbed" [8]. A primordialist approach advances the concept that the nation arises from a clustering of culturally homogenous individuals that, in addition to sharing common kinship, might have unique, regionalized ethnobiological qualities [38, 80, 96]. Peoples united through common beliefs or practices eventually morphed into groups that would assert political will in addition to cultural. Looking elsewhere another sphere, a more postmodern analysis suggests nationalism comes only after the formation of a state, and that without the social invention of a nation, the psychological drivers of it would be absent [3, 39, 49]. Both Anderson [3] and Gellner [39] suggest economic changes were the driving catalyst of nation formation. The most important takeaway from both is that nationalist behavior arises from, according to arguments, either a socially constructed framework or an emotive response embedded in the human body.

The dichotomy of nationalist theory is again reaffirmed in the microlevel examination of the national citizen. Thus, by analyzing individual action, we can extrapolate and better inform our theoretical basis for cybernationalist stratification. For example, is the populace emotively bonded through industry [39, 49] or through the mystical roles of unification, such as the symbols, rituals, and shared beliefs [12, 22, 81]? Fiscal linkage will produce different behaviors than ethnic bonds with respect to cyber-participation. What has become clear throughout researching this chapter is that the individual seeks virtual community participation mostly for ideological reciprocity and collective identity [20, 51, 53, 61, 65, 69, 71, 75, 76, 88, 94, 95, 101, 104]. Members of web forums and users of social media do not generally convene for the purpose of defending means of production or centers of wealth. Rather, they do so for the proverbial sense of belonging and community [62, 71, 97, 98]. This harkens Smith's [81] definition of an *ethnie*, a group with a "collective proper name, a myth of common ancestry, shared historical memories, one or more differentiating elements of common culture, an association with a specific 'homeland', and a sense of solidarity for significant sectors of the population" [81, p. 12].

Describing web community members through such a framework is extremely appropriate for it highlights the mystical and intellectual bond shared among the community. The nationalist content of the web mirrors what has been produced in the spatial world that centers on Smith's previously mentioned definitions [81]. Most important for the study of cybernationalism, using *ethnie* as our nomenclature does not mandate a spatial tethering to a geographical territory, but only demands an allegorical connection. It does not require that a group of people impose sovereign will and autonomy over an expanse, but only that they celebrate a unity through metaphysical linkage. Subsequently, we find describing *netizens* through terms associated with an ethnie provides us with an illustrious working definition of web-based communities, and later discussion will further explore such implications.

Now, we shall continue to explore the notion of territory as it is central to both camps of nationalist theory. Modernist critique argues that nationalist identity came only after economic exploitation of territory and the regionalism that spawned from the growth of commerce [3]. Ownership of resources and production belies this approach and focuses heavily on the shift from agrarian to industrial economies as a basis for nationalist behavior. An essentialist, on the other hand, points to the emblematic aspects of territory as a basis for common ancestry. Myths, legends, and rituals are borne from geographical hallmarks [50, 80, 84]. The prominent hunter gains mythical status within one tribe as a deft angler is praised in another, and only on specific terrain will national legends reach storied levels. Would one hold the same regard for the American General George Washington if his iconic passage was pictured over a flowery springtime meadow instead of the iceberg-laden river? It is the idea that landscape serves as the happenstance origin of nations, peoples, and myths that become central to a more evolutionary-minded approach to nationalism.

The above generalization of the American historical icon illustrates the bond our between our subconscious and a physical territory, and the social construction of landscape, and subsequently, the creation of a border. Whether politically or geographically defined, the border was of great significance to the ethnie [15, 23, 25, 57, 87, 88, 103]. It marked a sphere of influence and control and began separating the "us" and the "them." The earliest clan, for instance, just happened to find themselves together and in the same location as a result of extrinsic factors. Through a shared struggle, shared resources, and shared hardships, this geographical "sameness" eventually morphed into loosely defined "political sameness." The uniqueness of the land translated directly into the uniqueness of the people. Ironically, the defining characteristics of geographical and political borders are reaffirmed in both perspectives of nationalist development. The underlying quality of "separateness" and distinction is a key constant in nationalism [10, 22, 34, 42, 48, 53, 105, 106].

Although we may define *netizens* through nationalist terms, we must, obviously, be careful not to assert that cyber communities are authentic political states. We cannot suggest a Facebook group holds international legitimacy, and we cannot propose that a web forum should issue travel passports. There are no inherent civic benefits to online "citizenry." As such, it might seem at first glance either trivial or capricious to frame web interaction in nationalist terminology. But while the tangible by-products of citizenship are absent, the emotive response to web participation is exceedingly powerful to the user. The emotional and social connection a majority of the world shares with the web has rapidly increased even in just a few years [17, 18, 36, 40, 63, 68, 72, 97, 99, 100]. The Web 2.0 has become enmeshed in a great proportion of the world's livelihood [40, 63], and subsequently, it is no longer possible to suggest a person has an online persona distinct from his or her spatial one. Behavior and intent observed in the spatial world is likely to parallel their cyber counterparts. It is this reason why explaining Internet community participation through a nationalist framework will offer a better understanding not just of web interaction but in spatial encounters as well. The Internet has such a tremendous power in augmenting and facilitating the spread of nationalism, arguably more so than any previous methods of telecommunication.

However, this argument becomes null if we are unable to liken nationalist participation with cyber-participation. Of which, the first priority is to conclude *netizens* engage virtual communities in the same sense as they do the nation, the state, or the substate ethnic group. Spatial ethnies reproduce culture in order to reaffirm their unique identity [12, 22, 50, 80–84], and it is precisely this concept of cultural maintenance that merits further analysis. Whether through economic interaction, the process of sharing information and news, or military conquest, interaction between cultures and peoples is inherent to the premise of nationalism. The entire notion rests on the idea that different nations share different characteristics. Had the world been given to us in total homogeneity, there would be no foreign culture to demonize and no culture of one's own to exalt! There is an inherent pride in belonging to a culture [58, 79], and with such pride comes the urge of testimony [106]. The rest of the world must know the achievements and prowess of one's own people! Constructivist interpretations place economic interaction at the forefront of this idea [3, 39, 49] while a primordialist approach looks to the sharing and celebrating of ethno-symbolic cultural idiosyncrasies as the platform [24, 25, 50, 57, 84]. Whatever the case, it remains certain that national identity is something developed through defining an "us" and a "them."

6.2.1 Cultural Production, Maintenance, and the Overlap of Methods Between the Spatial and Cyber

In order for nationalism to be produced and maintained through the web, there must be a method for the distinction of the "us" and the "them" with respect to web communities. This idea of sameness and exclusion that is central to nationalist feeling is certainly prominent in web interaction and is the result of both differences in infrastructure as well as the social construction of space and identity. As we begin our analysis, it is best to continue our discussion of space and boundaries. The Internet has been hailed as the equalizer of economies and a mechanism for empowering anyone with access to broadband. However, there is a great amount of similarity between spatial borders and their *sociospatial* counterparts [23, 32, 36, 44, 57, 60, 67]. There are no oceans in cyberspace that restrict trade or access to other regions, but this does not mean there are no social constructions of limitation that alter the way in which nationalism is transferred throughout the web.

The idea of separateness has been key to observing the growth of national distinctiveness throughout history, and even in interaction spurred through economic advancement, consequential cultural exchange is an inherent by-product of cultural engagement. For example, the desire for "exotic" goods from faraway lands pushed the conquistadors to global travel for the same reason modern China has flocked to natural resource-rich African nations. Advances in infrastructure related to increases in opportunities for broad and far-reaching travel enabled individuals to inject themselves into other nations [3]. As the global social network was permeated, individual networks morphed. Migration expanded the social networks of once homogenous towns, and it continues to have a sizeable effect on local and global cultural and networks of information sharing. Subsequently, it has had a similar effect on the concept of national similarity and uniqueness.

A pragmatic answer to explain how information diffuses across small and large networks is found in the study of social network theories. In order to examine the spread of nationalist ideology compared to nations and virtual communities, we must explore the basic methods in which information is shared between people and groups. Mark Granovetter [41] details how ideological diffusion among networks that are not defined solely through "strong" ties (relationships with a high degree of contact frequency and interpersonal reciprocity) but interspersed with "weak ties" (ones that act more as acquaintances or low-intensity relationships) is more thorough than strong tie-only networks. The concept asserts that an individual's immediate network will consist mostly of strong ties that communicate often, and through frequent interaction, the information disseminates very quickly within the network. However, networks of only strong ties will greatly stifle information transmission, for eventually nobody will have anyone to share anything among. In order for the information to reach the greatest number of individual actors, it must be able to jump from network to network. A simplistic example would be that of an office rumor shared between the workers on a specific floor in a building. They might gossip among themselves, but if they are contained, the information will eventually become antiquated. Everyone will know about the rumor, and it will cease to be in conversation. However, if a clerk from another floor stops by for chatter, he or she might become privy to the information and return to his or her floor of origin and share it among a different network. That clerk is responsible for doubling the amount of individuals that become aware of a piece of information merely by acting as a conduit between two networks.

Social network theories continue to be overlooked in the study of nationalism but are very compelling reasons for its spread. Let us switch the above example of an office with a broader one of a culturally homogenous town. As human migration grows, a handful of young foreigners enter the town in search of prosperity. These foreigners assimilate into the town and develop relationships with the inhabitants where the daily exchange between the local population and the foreigners is laced additionally with cultural exchange. The foreigners might share events from their community of origin, and the local population might offer news from their families a few towns away. We now see the exchange of ideas through a hub caused by societal migration, with ideas now disseminated trans-community (or, expanding upon the example, trans-regionally and transnationally). In order for information, including nationalist rhetoric and sentiment, to be shared most prolifically, there must be a number of individuals or beings that act as travelers between social networks. Subsequently, the most efficient to extinguish the spread of nationalist ideology is to suppress the interaction of networks with their linking weak ties. A reoccurring theme in nationalist scholarship has been that of creating the proverbial "us" and "them," and we have shown that such occurs only through interaction. One cannot breed the idea of separateness from "the other" if that other has yet to be seen or heard.

Yet, cyberspace is peculiar when looking at how individuals use networks to create the distinctive "us" and "them." Ideological diffusion of ideas is not dependent upon the frequency or intensity of online relationships. This is evidenced anecdotally in social media and real-time information sharing environments. Users do not have to spatially know an individual or entity in order to acquire information from them. When a Twitter member "follows" another entity, the relationship that defined tie strength in the spatial world is rendered obsolete in the cyberworld. Because the liminal barriers of interaction are largely removed, weak and strong ties are developed with greater speed. A mere mouse-click separates one from being aloof to being informed in real time. It is this premise that allows YouTube videos to become "viral" and for news stories to be shared quickly and easily. Whereas nations are composed by geographical origin and barriers, virtual communities are founded upon user homophily and shared interests [11, 13, 16, 19, 33, 47, 51, 62, 66, 91]. Subsequently, we see the development of information hubs that serve as rallying points from which people receive information. Similar minds come to similar producers of news and events and, subsequently, interact with other like-minded users, even if solely through osmosis.

This becomes especially important to consider with respect to cybernationalism because this method of cyber-demography and communication allows for a greater diffusion of nationalist rhetoric at much shorter time intervals. As opposed to hearing about rallies or political events after they happen, social media and electronic communications allow for community members (local, global, and ethnic) to be aware while the event is taking place. It is the difference between recapping historic events and being participatory, and the cognitive effects of this interaction are qualitatively different than that of the newspaper era. Political charisma that becomes vital to the flourishing of social movements becomes transferrable to infinitely more networks via the web.

It is not just in the acceptance of new ideology where cyberspace facilitates the spread of nationalism but also through the protection and reproduction of current culture. Content-wise there are certainly web pages and forums devoted to the overt production of cultural nationalism [1, 6, 7, 59, 76, 95]. Yet the majority of cultural reproduction takes place more subversively, similar to the banal nationalism that subconsciously contributes to the preservation of nationalist culture. Ambient nationalism as seen in the Internet is nearly subliminal and ubiquitous. In defining the Internet broadly, ambient nationalism describes very well the understated nature of the nationalist composition of the Internet and, subsequently, offers an insight into the power of virtual community participation.

Constant reinforcement of belonging is the basis for both nationalism and web participation. Nationalist sentiment is celebrated and glorified among the in-group of participants [34, 35, 46, 58, 79, 93, 106], and such national distinction is a method that differentiates and places highly the culture of one's own. Without this loosely defined concept of national introspection and reflection, the sentiment might wilt. Collective identity is reproduced from collective participation, and we see nationalist identity propagated through the application of daily rituals [12]. In the spatial world, the spectrum of these rituals can range from the daily reaffirming of national allegiance in the form of a pledge or an ornate annual celebration. It can be done quickly or require laborious hours of preparation. Most importantly, however, is the act of a group celebrating the mythical identity of a nation. In theory, and usually practice, these rituals hold a specific uniqueness to the celebratory culture.

The American celebration of independence might mimic the holidays of other nations in that it marks the annual time of which to celebrate political sovereignty; however, the cultural icons that are revered are inimitable. National uniqueness is not limited to observed holidays but is replicated throughout a myriad of other daily occurrences, such as the recitation of a pledge or even the subtle act of placing small flags on government correspondence.

The spatial world does not hold a monopoly over this method of cultural reproduction. The uniqueness of cultural belonging is both overtly rampant and subliminal in cyberspace [1, 4, 6, 36, 53, 76]. It might be seen through a regionalized ending on a site's uniform resource locator (URL). It could be in the form of national colors embedded into patriotic media. Some governments are even conducting political business solely through the web, and even the electronic submission of a parking violation penalty could be viewed as an act of political engagement. This is merely one of many "lines" that are blurred that previously served to starkly separate actions conducted in the spatial world and actions conducted in cyberspace. As such, it is naïve to think that a website's national demeanor is not crucial to one's engagement with it, much like the broken English of a traveler, the gender segregation customs of the Arab world, or the banalities of mealtime protocol in rural Africa that have a substantial impact on interpersonal behavior.

This example highlights the notion of socially constructed culture as a catalyst for the stratification of online participation. Websites of certain content cater to specific users, but also, websites of certain cultural accessibility further host a precise group of visitors. Despite the advances of technology in translating language, the social colloquialism and dialectical nuances are still present to regionalize language. Though the newspaper is digitized, for instance, it has failed to shed the diction, the verbiage, and even the center of focus that betrays its localized anonymity. If an entire electronic newspaper focuses on the events from a specific setting, it simultaneously highlights the gaze of the nation, much like routine focusing on a particular celebrity eventually defines the desires of the populace. Individuals in news tend to represent the nation to other cultures [12], and thus the digitizing of news and the ubiquity of access has allowed the virtual world to reproduce nationalism in this method. While embracing the idea of unrestrictive access leading to the erosion of local ties, we have neglected to question whether the routine interaction with web news has really served to be a routine interaction with another "them." Is not the defining of others another vocabulary for defining what "we" are not? The Internet, then, more frequently informs the *netizen* of what constitutes "us" and what defines "them."

Language has been essential to the construction of local and national identity since the inception of nationalism [2–4, 15, 53–55, 60]. Anderson's [3] critique of "print capitalism" is well known for articulating the effects of language and economy on the development of nations. Much like the linguistic differences of early industrial nations prompted nationalist segregation, the language of cyberspace has consequences on the development of a nationalist cyber-identity. The homogenization of the Internet language has been documented and is a reflection of Anderson's [3] assertion on how the death of minority languages is a casualty of economic spread.

Language has become more than only a barrier to information access. Its effects on web archival, the documenting, and the preservation of language have arguably offset the Internet's segregation-related consequences. The advances in infrastructure have given rise to a surge in access to historical or sparsely spoken language. Creating a weblog (blog) or social media group is often done without expense, but it can serve as at least a semipermanent host to a language near cultural extinction. Diasporan social media and listservs, for example, can retain the linguistic variations of a tribal or regional language [77, 89, 94]. Members are not forced to completely neglect the ethnic means of communication just because the local merchant does not stock the preferred language. We have seen the languages of African, Eurasian, and of Middle Eastern descent assert subnational identities by using the Internet as a linguistic museum. The web can safeguard biblical dialects and can be used as a visual "yearbook" to document the morphing of language throughout the years [45]. It can highlight the difference between the language of heritage and that used for daily communication, the latter of which is crucial to the reproduction of culture and nationalism [12, 50].

Not only do passing "tweets" and "posts" become immortal on the Internet, but also entire web pages containing translations and instruction of "dead" languages are available freely. The Internet provides a virtual linguistic museum, offering access to obsolete languages that once required contact with libraries or fluent oral speakers. Historical documents have become nearly open source and oftentimes available to browse online. That we are able to preserve and consult our linguistic antiquity is a hallmark of web-based nationalism. We are able to preserve and display the documents that led to our modern governments. The American Declaration of Independence hangs proverbially in cyberspace, and the average citizen has free access to the verbiage and content. The Web 2.0 is a quintessential archival of manifestos and state documents and charismatic political mantra. Hearing a lecture or visiting a museum is a temporal activity, but having media saved on the web or on one's personal computer creates an environment of ever-possible reference and review. Despite the common assertion that the Internet has created homogenized, supranational identities and modes of communication, the sharing of nationalism has, to the contrary, grown.

There is something more fundamental than language, however, that aids in the creation of nationalism and geospatially linked identities. Language is inherently spatial and denoting of locality. It signifies from which terra firma the speaker hails and links that person with a specific iconic origin. Language and dialect outs the speaker with regard to what cultural stereotype they represent. Inborn with territory is the idea of geographical hallmarks, physical borders, and the socially constructed spaces that further distinguish the "us" and the "them" [8, 32, 37, 43, 54, 61, 63, 67, 87, 103]. The fruits of the landscape, the agrarian beauty, or the imposing mountain facades have been the muse for artisans and poets to glorify their specific homeland [3, 39, 84]. It then seems counterintuitive to suggest nationalism is rampant on the web if there is no such land that exists to produce the rhetoric. However, what is most important about territory in nationalism is that it remains imagined and emblematic. An individual thousands of miles removed from a dominant political border would be unlikely to *directly* engage with it, yet it can be visualized internally as something which sets the faraway boundaries of what "our" nation owns. Natural landmarks are among the distinctive properties of nations that produce nationally specific culture. Eurasian mountain ranges, vast deserts, and ecologically diverse jungle canopies set apart regions from one another. The Internet, while being unable to tangibly support a physical landscape, is very well suited to the preservation of the idealized recreation of a nation's tract of earth. The hardship that marked the winters of Valley Forge in the history of the United States becomes reproduced through stories or media and is shared throughout the web, not unlike the oral transmission of history that marked our tribal origins. Just as well, the Internet acts as a repository for the sharing of iconic media of current geopolitical locations. Videos and photographs of social protests, the tragic results of terrorist activity, or the olive branch of international aid can be captured and passed along in real time. Again, the *netizen* is able to be a part of social change from a distance and, thus, become intertwined into the history of both the land and the actions of the nation involved. Metaphoric landscape, as well, is the foundation for the idea of a shared struggle and a shared past [3, 80, 83, 84]. The toil specific to an ancestry on a particular plot of land creates a sense of cultural individualism, further highlighting the resulting separateness of cultures.

With respect to cyber-mobilization and nationalism, there is an amplified emotion of the latter when one feels his or her homeland is under attack or duress [58, 79]. The product of this synthesis is a coming together of people to rally behind the sanctity and protection of a shared mythical past. Subsequently, in addition to preserving the iconic pastoral landscapes of nations, the Internet serves as a medium that portrays the struggle, hardship, and oppression that provides emotive catalysts toward nationalism. The same photographs of political rallies suggested previously also paint the picture of individuals coming together in order to safeguard national ideals. This can be used to show a nation in peril because of government oppression or ineptness. The "plight" of peoples is an essential component to nationalist media and is one shared gratuitously throughout the web. Photos and video taken during wartime or kinetic military action are shared on popular social media sites, and the premise of a nation or national ideal under attack is shared in real time.

6.3 Observing Nationalism in the Structure of the Web

It may seem at first that a proper analysis of web-based nationalism would highlight the content of web forums, online chat rooms, or social media sites or the growing concern that social media is contributing to spatial social protest and violence [5, 29, 90]. Yet, our development of a theoretical framework has not been so much as *what* is shared via the web, but instead the method in which cyberspace is conducive to the diffusion of nationalism. It is not the manifesto that is a novel concept, but rather, it is the way in which it is distributed from mind to mind. Cyberspace has not *created* nationalism. It has not *radicalized* the individual or the nation. Merely, it is in the very construction of the Internet where the symbiosis of spatial and cybernationalism is found.

Throughout the research of this chapter, it was shown that three types of nationalists were catered to through either nationalist content or the way in which the web is structured: the sovereign-ethnic nationalist, the activist, and the terrorist. The foremost scenario centers on reproducing emblematic signifiers of the state. This first instance observes the manufacturing of agreed-upon symbols of unification and their diffusion across web networks both domestically and via the diaspora, with the specific focus being the icons representative of the nation's superior presence and history. This differs in the next scenario, which instead offers a national counter-culture. Whereas the former is pro-nation, the latter is pro-*change* of the nation. This category most often includes oppositional civic participation and peaceful political activism. Lastly, the Internet has become a haven for violent oppositional groups that are bonded through nationalist, separatist, ethno-nationalist, or religious nationalist ideology. The overarching commonality of this last description is the clandestine use of the web to recruit members, to proliferate ideology, and even to mobilize members toward violence. The remainder of this chapter will focus on the different qualities of cyberspace that promote unique venues of nationalist participation.

6.3.1 The Effects of Language on Web Participation and e-Nationalism

The commercializing of language is not limited to Anderson's [3] critique of modernity and nationalism, and the idea of "print capitalism" has morphed and been kept vibrant in cyberspace. The salience of language creates ripples in the cultural, economic, political, and social consequences of virtual group membership and participation. As stated, inherent in the idea of language is that of regionalization, and, typically, there is a geopolitical connotation to language. The offshoot of linguistic individualism eventually becomes the social construction of borders and the creation of "different" cultures and places. In cyberspace, verbiage and diction is the accent of a writer. In building national cohesion, case studies have proven the significant role that dialectical fluency and its reproduction has had in the shaping of nationalist discourse [2, 4, 53, 55, 59, 89, 94]. The sharing of region-specific language among the in-group serves not only to strengthen their bond of "sameness" but also to anoint the language as timeless. Making permanent a minority-spoken language fortifies it against cultural demise, and subsequently, the Internet is a fantastic conduit for such preservation. The language of the group becomes a barometer to categorize and define it [3, 12, 50, 55, 94].

In addition to language producing cultural revival and safeguard, it also is the cause of cyber-stratification and its inhibition. Unlike nations and ethnies borne from geographical similarity, virtual communities stem from the free congregation of ideological homophily [13, 62, 91]. As the similar minds meet and exchange text, they share the buzzwords and pop culture that distinguishes the group. The keywords that are shared among the members become what defines them to the impersonal search engines and web crawlers that bring the group to other users, and eventually, no matter how illustrious and diversely vibrant a group, the virtual community becomes reduced to archival labeling. The advent of the search engine has unintentionally mandated that web communities become "searchable" and defined, and the inherent labeling of communication is central to the concept of "us" and "them" distinction in nationalism. Reductionist rhetoric has been a hallmark of nationalist groups since their advent, and here, the Internet not just facilitates the narrowing of group definition, but its very structure requires it.

The economic ramifications are equally sizable and match the theoretical observances of Anderson's [3] idea of "print capitalism." Though the web has become host to language preserved through weblogs (blogs) and social media, the lingua franca of commerce has yet to become as diverse. A critical interpretation might go so far as to suggest it is the economic production of for-profit web archivists (Google, Yahoo!, etc.) that has created a financially nationalist monopoly on who defines the "us" and the "who." In order to even begin searching for a web-based cultural group, the hypothetical diasporan must first log on to an intermediary to crawl the web. The implications this has on the electronic transfer of commerce and wealth could be very substantial, although at this time only limited research has been directed toward such an understanding.

6.3.2 *Banality, Rituals, and the Emblematic Structure of the Web*

The economic and pragmatic aspects of language would be void, though, if it were not for the mystical component of language which allows the "irrational" facets of nationalism to exist [22]. The control of wealth via the web is not enough to promote solely a modernist interpretation of the web's importance, for this interpretation lacks the ability to explain emotive actions that have crossed from the Internet environment to the physical world that are not related to economic prosperity. Purely constructivist interpretations of web nationalism would not explain the suicide bomber recruited through web forums or the activist that is moved by the sharing of counterculture media. Exploring the banality of the Internet in creating ritual, sharing myths and ideology, and promoting idealized links to history and territory complements the preceding analysis by offering an explanation of how culture is manufactured and reproduced.

Billig [12] uses examples of daily minutia that reinforces nationalism such as the pledging of allegiance before school or the subliminal effects of flag display. His assertion is that nationalism is commonplace and ordinary, and the inherent ubiquity adds to its transmission. Web spaces function similarly through all spectrums of nationalist sharing. In addition to signifying the category of a web space, the URL anchors the produced content geopolitically. Billig [12] confirms that the content produced in news or popular culture invariably becomes a figurehead for the population broadly. We see this reaffirmed by the ritual of web participation with respect to where one travels on the web. For instance, an individual traveling only to .ru-ending web addresses will have a nationally biased diffusion of web information. Web forums offer colloquial variations in language and reinforce the uniqueness of, further requiring participants to ritualize engagement. Chinese military websites have created military-esque ranks to further specialize engagement and increase nationalist participation [107]. The semantic associations of text become iconic. The common language becomes the basis for a pattern of sharing, with virtual community groups behaving like spatial nationalists, which "base their appease for support and messages to the public in identarian terms" [27, p. 33].

The insertion of subliminal textual uniqueness is evidenced additionally in other forms of media. Media serves to offer a physical linkage to an event or collective emotion, and this can be overt, such as the sharing of media captured from philanthropic, oppressive, or violent acts, or the subversive, such as the embedding of watermarks into images spread by jihadi terrorist groups. The emotive effects of seeing and hearing various media are harnessed by state organizations and terrorist groups alike. In either case, web media is crucial for bridging the imagined world of cyberspace to the dimensional world where politics and conflict reside. There is a significant difference in reading a web participant textually detail accounts of government oppression in Chechnya, for example, and of seeing a YouTube video tangibly evidence the same story. The effect on legitimacy is reinforced, and the user is given "proof" that conversation describes nonfiction. State web spaces offer videos of their soldiers providing humanitarian aid, activists host video of rallies and charisma, and violent groups offer evidence of battlefield success to bolster a potentially recruitable audience.

The ability to share media at speeds previously unimaginable is a substantial invention that aids the spread of nationalism. Social media has played a role in shaping the recent riots in London and the political demonstrations in the Arab Spring. There is a unique ability for the Internet to share media and information in real time, something impossible through previous news sharing technologies. Hearing and seeing events while they occur adds the sense of immediacy that could not have been harnessed in prior eras. Propaganda distributed through print news describes the aftereffects of national attacks, but pictures on Twitter show the nation while in *immediate* peril. Oftentimes the content itself will be similar to nationalist rhetoric of previous era, though it becomes doubly emotive through because of its cyber-insertion.

Nationalists have long since been stirred by sentiment that pits the homeland in peril or suggests it is becoming impure. The idea of cultural suicide pushes the nationalist to embrace fundamentalist views of territory and culture, as if by providing a reformed and conservative alternative will counter the alleged backwash of modernity. The Internet, then, is rife with video and pictures that highlight oppressive actions. Jihadi websites publish videos of women raped by "infidel" soldiers. Activists distribute media documenting the abuses of animals in testing facilities. Political pundits create social media pages that highlight the political choices of their opponents that, depending on the source, range from political heroism to acts just shy of treason. Social media sites facilitate rapid sharing and advanced graphical software allows for changes in the original media to further suit the needs of framing. The result is a sincerely emotional sentiment that pains the nationalist, regardless of veracity, and is legitimized because it is tangible. 9/11 conspiracy theorists have used three-dimensional reenactments to garner support for something that has been widely proven false [30, 85], and governments have used media to portray their actions as philanthropic when they might be otherwise. The immediacy of this, again, contributes to the snap-emotive response. The power of visualizing overrides the sense of reason, a phenomenon quite apropos to Connor's [22] description of the irrationality of nationalism.

Lastly, the pragmatic consequences of the Internet can be significantly troubling. For clandestine or terrorist groups that require more discretion for hosting and distributing violent rhetoric, the Internet has become the modus operandi for inexpensive and widely reaching communication and planning [1, 6, 21, 70, 86, 92, 96, 102]. Terrorists have used the Internet to spread a nationalist message to otherwise foreign users. Media created in support of ethno-nationalist terrorism is embedded with the reductionist symbols associated with nationalism. They are distributed freely and gratuitously yet remain linked to an entity of hate. Manuals and training materials act as things to both indoctrinate into the rituals of the group and to teach the most basic skills of weaponry and explosives. There is a constant focus and an overarching goal that remains omnipresent.

Yet, the creation of culture aimed at political change is not required to be violent in nature or intention. The power of the web has been harnessed by activists in attempts to draw more political capital into their sphere of mobile activists. Nongovernmental organizations use the web to promote a facade and to inexpensively create an aura about them [14, 28, 73, 74, 106], and grassroots political organizations have used listservs and electronic word-of-mouth to spread the organizational aspects of protesting and campaigning [5, 31, 52, 56, 64, 78]. Activism has also developed into a trans- and supranational aspect, with the web developing global and international identities of charitable or activist organizations and offering them an economic foothold in the international chain of commerce [5, 9, 26, 28, 73, 74]. Social change is additionally fostered through local political action that can be organized by the web and social media, evidenced recently in the United Kingdom's surge in "flash mobs" and rioters allegedly rebelling for social change [29, 90].

6.4 Conclusion and Recommendations for Further Exploration

In summation, it is essential to acknowledge the allure of virtual participation does not rest solely through a psychological interpretation. Much as web content is diverse and seemingly ever morphing, analysis of why we choose to participate in web communities so fervently must be examined from nontraditional facets. Using scholarship developed for interpreting actions in the spatial realm is becoming more and more accepted for use in the cyber because we are seeing less and less distinction between the worlds. Yet, for how much the academic field proclaims to know about Internet involvement, we are still very much in our infancy of understanding. So, too, is the Internet in its earliest developmental stages with respect to its capability. As the "digital divide" lessens and technology becomes, if one can imagine it, truly commonplace and mundane, the individual user will conduct more business, explore more social opportunities, and grow intellectually, all through the primary use of the electronic intermediary. The epistemological consequences of such interaction have only been skimmed by academics, and there is still a vast amount of scholarship that is available for intellectual first dibs.

What is evident, however, is the extent to which our virtual communities shape our spatial environment. We can no longer assume that because there is no physical touch between the virtual world and the inhabited one that there is an impassable divide. Pundits and politicians have suggested recent social change is the result of virtual participation alone and the by-product of a completely novel human emotion ushered in via the Web 2.0. As we have seen, there is little difference of engagement between sharing stories by typing on mobile technologies and the oral transmission found among campfires of iconic pastoral ancestry. Whether a spear or a rifle, a horse or a plane, or parchment or the Internet, in the end, there is one constant, and such is what we should strive to examine.

References

1. Adams, J., & Roscigno, V. J. (2005). White supremacists, oppositional culture and the World Wide Web. *Social Forces, 84*(2), 759–778.
2. Aghvami, M. (2009). *Persian bloggers: Exile, nostalgia, and diasporic nationalism* (pp. 1–61). Toronto, ON, Canada: Ryerson University.
3. Anderson, B. (2006). *Imagined communities: Reflections on the origin and spread of nationalism* (New ed., p. 240). London/New York: Verso.
4. Anyefru, E. (2008). Cyber-nationalism: The imagined Anglophone Cameroon community in cyberspace. *African Identities, 6*(3), 253–274.
5. Ayres, J. M. (1999). From the streets to the internet: The cyber-diffusion of contention. *The Annals of the American Academy of Political and Social Science, 566*, 132–143.
6. Back, L. (2001). Aryans reading Adorno: Cyber-culture and twenty-first century racism. *Ethnic and Racial Studies, 25*(4), 628–651. doi:10.1080/01419870220136664.
7. Bakker, P. (2001, February). *New nationalism: The internet crusade*. Presented at the International Studies Association Annual Convention, Chicago, pp. 1–22.
8. Bell, D. S. A. (2003). Mythscapes: Memory, mythology, and national identity. *The British Journal of Sociology, 54*(1), 63–81.
9. Bennett, W. L. (2003). New media power: The internet and global activism. In N. Couldry & J. Curran (Eds.), *Contesting media power: Alternative media in a networked world* (p. 319). Lanham, MD: Rowman & Littlefield.
10. Berdún, M. M. G. I. (1999). *Nations without states: Political communities in a global age* (p. 216). Malden, MA: Blackwell.
11. Best, S. J., & Krueger, B. S. (2006). Online interactions and social capital: Distinguishing between new and existing ties. *Social Science Computer Review, 24*(4), 395–410. doi:10.1177/0894439306286855.
12. Billig, M. (1995). *Banal nationalism* (p. 200). London/Thousand Oaks, CA: Sage.
13. Bisgin, H., Agarwal, N., & Xu, X. (2010, August–September). Investigating homophily in online social networks. In *2010 IEEE/ACM International Conference on Web Intelligence-Intelligent Agent Technology (WI-IAT)* (pp. 533–536). Washington, DC: IEEE. doi:10.1109/WI-IAT.2010.61.

14. Blood, R. (2000). Activism and the internet: From e-mail to new political movement. *Journal of Communication Management, 5*(2), 1–11.
15. Brewer, M. B., & Gardner, W. (1996). Who is this "we?" Levels of collective identity and self representations. *Journal of Personality and Social Psychology, 71*(1), 83–93.
16. Cairncross, F. (1997). *The death of distance: How the communications revolution will change our lives* (p. 303). Boston, MA: Harvard Business Press.
17. Castells, M. (1997). *The power of identity* (p. 461). Malden, MA: Wiley-Blackwell.
18. Castells, M. (2009). *The rise of the network society* (p. 656). Malden, MA: Blackwell.
19. Centola, D., Gonzalez-Avella, J. C., Eguiluz, V. M., & San Miguel, M. (2007). Homophily, cultural drift, and the co-evolution of cultural groups. *Journal of Conflict Resolution, 51*(6), 905–929. doi:10.1177/0022002707307632.
20. Cheong, P. H., & Gong, J. (2010). Cyber vigilantism, transmedia collective intelligence, and civic participation. *Chinese Journal of Communication, 3*(4), 471–487.
21. Coll, S., & Glasser, S. B. (2005, August 9). Terrorists turn to the Web as base of operations. *The Washington Post.* Retrieved June 5, 2011, from www.washingtonpost.com
22. Connor, W. (1994). *Ethnonationalism: The quest for understanding* (p. 234). Princeton, NJ: Princeton University Press.
23. Conversi, D. (1999). Nationalism, boundaries, and violence. *Millennium: Journal of International Studies, 28*(3), 553–584.
24. Conversi, D. (2006). Mapping the field: Theories of nationalism and the ethnosymbolic approach. In A. S. Leoussi & S. E. Grosby (Eds.), *Nationalism and ethnosymbolism: History, culture and ethnicity in the formation of nations.* Edinburgh, UK: Edinburgh University Press.
25. Conversi, D. (2010). Globalization, ethnic conflict, and nationalism. In B. Turner (Ed.), *Handbook of globalization studies* (pp. 346–366). London: Routledge/Taylor & Francis.
26. Danitz, T., & Strobel, W. (1999). The internet's impact on activism: The case of Burma. *Studies in Conflict & Terrorism, 22*(3), 257–269. doi:10.1080/105761099265766.
27. Dartnell, M. Y. (2006). *Insurgency online: Web activism and global conflict.* Toronto, Canada: University of Toronto Press.
28. Deibert, R. J. (2000). International plug 'n play? Citizen activism, the internet, and global public policy. *International Studies Perspectives, 1*, 255–272.
29. Dodds, P., & Satter, R. G. (2011). *Social media used to spread Britain's riots.* London: Associated Press. Retrieved August 9, 2011, from https://ezproxy.lib.lehigh.edu/login?url=http://hosted.ap.org/dynamic/stories/E/EU_BRITAIN_RECIPE_FOR_RIOTS?SITE=AP&SECTION=HOME&TEMPLATE=DEFAULT&CTIME=2011-08-09-18-45-59
30. Dunbar, D., & Reagan, B. (2006). *Debunking 9/11 myths: Why conspiracy theories can't stand up to the facts* (p. 170). New York: Hearst.
31. Elin, L. (2003). The radicalization of Zeke Spier: How the internet contributes to civic engagement and new forms of social capital. In M. McCaughey & M. Ayers (Eds.), *Cyberactivism: Online activism in theory and practice* (pp. 97–117). New York: Taylor & Francis.
32. Elkins, D. J. (1997). Globalization, telecommunication, and virtual ethnic communities. *International Political Science Review/Revue internationale de science politique, 18*(2), 139–152.
33. Ellison, N., Steinfield, C., & Lampe, C. (2006, June). *Spatially bounded online social networks and social capital: The role of Facebook.* Presented at the Annual Conference of the International Communication Association, Dresden, Germany.
34. Eriksen, T. H. (1993). *Ethnicity and nationalism* (p. 140). London/Sterling, VA: Pluto Press.
35. Eriksen, T. H. (1994). Nationalism, Mauritian style: Cultural unity and ethnic diversity. *Comparative Studies in Society and History, 36*(3), 549–574.
36. Eriksen, T. H. (2007). Nationalism and the internet. *Nations and Nationalism, 13*(1), 1–17.
37. Freeman, L. C. (1992). Filling in the blanks: A theory of cognitive categories and the structure of social affiliation. *Social Psychology Quarterly, 55*(2), 118–127.

38. Geertz, C. (2000). *The interpretation of cultures (Basic Books Classics)* (p. 480). New York: Basic Books.
39. Gellner, E., & Breuilly, J. (2008). *Nations and nationalism* (p. 152). Ithaca, NY: Cornell University Press.
40. Gotved, S. (2006). Time and space in cyber social reality. *New Media & Society, 8*(3), 467–4 86. doi:10.1177/1461444806064484.
41. Granovetter, M. S. (1973). The strength of weak ties. *The American Journal of Sociology, 78*(6), 1360–1380.
42. Greenfeld, L. (2006). *Nationalism and the mind: Essays on modern culture* (p. 228). Oxford, England: Oneworld.
43. Gupta, A., & Ferguson, J. (1992). Beyond "culture": Space, identity, and the politics of difference. *Cultural Anthropology, 7*(1), 6–23.
44. Halavais, A. (2000). National borders on the World Wide Web. *New Media & Society, 2*(1), 7–28.
45. Hanson, F. A. (2007). *The trouble with culture: How computers are calming the culture wars* (p. 192). Albany, NY: State University of New York Press.
46. Hardin, R. (1995). Self-interest, group identity. In A. Breton (Ed.), *Nationalism and rationality* (pp. 14–42). Cambridge, England: Cambridge University Press.
47. Haythornthwaite, C. (2002). Strong, weak, and latent ties and the impact of new media. *The Information Society, 18*(1), 385–401. doi:10.1080/01972240290108l9.
48. Herb, G. H., & Kaplan, D. H. (1999). *Nested identities: Nationalism, territory, and scale* (p. 343). Lanham, MD: Rowman & Littlefield.
49. Hobsbawm, E. J. (1990). *Nations and nationalism since 1780: Programme, myth, reality* (p. 191). Cambridge, England: Cambridge University Press.
50. Hosking, G. A., & Schöpflin, G. (1997). *Myths and nationhood* (p. 214). New York: Routledge.
51. Huang, Y., Shen, C., Williams, D., & Contractor, N. (2009). Virtually there: Exploring proximity and homophily in a virtual world. In *International Conference on Computational Science and Engineering, Vancouver, BC, Canada* (pp. 354–359). Washington, DC: IEEE.
52. Jacobs, D. (2005). Internet activism and the democratic emergency in the U.S. *Ephemera, 5*(1), 68–77.
53. Jones, A. (2008). *Cyber-extended identity among 1.5 and 2nd generation female Armenian immigrant high school students: A segmented assimilation* (pp. 1–116). Los Angeles: University of Southern California.
54. Jones, R., & Desforges, L. (2003). Localities and the reproduction of Welsh nationalism. *Political Geography, 22*, 271–292.
55. Kadende-Kaiser, R. M. (2000). Interpreting language and cultural discourse: Internet communication among Burundians in the diaspora. *Africa Today, 47*(2), 120–148.
56. Kahn, R., & Kellner, D. (2004). New media and internet activism: From the "battle of Seattle" to blogging. *New Media & Society, 6*(1), 87–95. doi:10.1177/1461444804039908.
57. Kaufmann, E., & Conversi, D. (2007). Ethnic and nationalist mobilisation. In J. Tournon & A. Guelke (Eds.), *Ethnic groups and politics: Recent analytical developments* (Vol. 14, pp. 1–47). Berlin, Germany: VS-Verlag. Retrieved from http://www.pacte.cnrs.fr/Recherche/RC14/1-1-Kaufmann-_Conversi_draft3.pdf
58. Kecmanović, D. (1996). *The mass psychology of ethnonationalism* (p. 244). New York: Plenum.
59. Kuntsman, A. (2010). Webs of hate in diasporic cyberspaces: The Gaza war in the Russian-language blogosphere. *Media, War & Conflict, 3*(3), 299–313.
60. Lee, S.-J., & 2. (2006). The assertive nationalism of South Korean youth: Cultural dynamism and political activism. *SAIS Review, XXVI*, 123–132. doi:10.1353/sais.2006.0036.
61. Levine, D. M. (2004). Reconfiguring the Ethiopian nation in a global era. *International Journal of Ethiopian Studies, 1*(2), 1–16.
62. McPherson, M., Smith-Lovin, L., & Cook, J. M. (2001). Birds of a feather: Homophily in social networks. *Annual Review of Sociology, 27*(4), 415–444.

63. Mitra, A., & Schwartz, R. L. (2001). From cyber space to cybernetic space: Rethinking the relationship between real and virtual spaces. *Journal of Computer-Mediated Communication, 7*(1), 1–23.
64. Nah, S., Veenstra, A. S., & Shah, D. V. (2006). The internet and anti-war activism: A case study of information, expression, and action. *Journal of Computer-Mediated Communication, 12*(1), 230–247. doi:10.1111/j.1083-6101.2006.00323.x.
65. Navarrete, A. C., & Huerta, E. (2006). Building virtual bridges to home: The use of the internet by transnational communities of immigrants. *International Journal of Communications Law & Policy, 11*, 1–20.
66. Newman, L., & Dale, A. (2007). Homophily and agency: Creating effective sustainable development networks. *Environment, Development and Sustainability, 9*(1), 79–90. doi:10.1007/s10668-005-9004-5.
67. Newman, D., & Paasi, A. (1998). Fences and neighbours in the postmodern world: Boundary narratives in political geography. *Progress in Human Geography, 22*(2), 186–207.
68. O'Reilly, T. (2007). What is Web 2.0: Communications & strategies, design patterns and business models for the next generation of software. *Communications and Strategies, 65*, 17–37.
69. Odutola, K. A. (2010). *The cyber-framing of the Nigerian nationhood: Diaspora and the imagined nation* (pp. 1–276). Newark: Rutgers, the State University of New Jersey.
70. Qin, J., Zhou, Y., Reid, E., Lai, G., & Chen, H. (2007). Analyzing terror campaigns on the internet: Technical sophistication, content richness, and Web interactivity. *International Journal of Human Computer Studies, 65*(1), 71–84. doi:10.1016/j.ijhcs.2006.08.012.
71. Rheingold, H. (2000). *The virtual community: Homesteading on the electronic frontier* (p. 447). Cambridge, MA: The MIT Press.
72. Riva, G., & Galimberti, C. (1997). The psychology of cyberspace: A socio-cognitive framework to computer-mediated communication. *New Ideas in Psychology, 15*(2), 141–158.
73. Rodgers, J. (2003). *Spatializing international politics: Analysing activism on the internet.* London: Routledge.
74. Rutherford, K. R. (2000). Internet activism: NGOs and the Mine Ban Treaty. *The International Journal on Grey Literature, 1*(3), 99–105.
75. Sasada, H. (2006). Youth and nationalism in Japan. *SAIS Review, 26*(2), 109–122. doi:10.1353/sais.2006.0044.
76. Saunders, R. A. (2004). Nationality: Cyber-Russian. *Russia in Global Affairs, 2*(4), 156–166.
77. Saunders, R. A. (2006). Denationalized digerati in the virtual near abroad: The internet's paradoxical impact on national identity among minority Russians. *Global Media and Communication, 2*(1), 43–69. doi:10.1177/1742766506061816.
78. Schwartz, E. (2002). NetActivism 2001: How citizens use the internet. In S. Hick & J. G. McNutt (Eds.), *Advocacy, activism, and the internet: Community organization and social policy* (p. 241). Chicago: Lyceum Books.
79. Searle-White, J. (2001). *The psychology of nationalism* (p. 169). New York: Palgrave Macmillan.
80. Smith, A. D. (1981). *The ethnic revival* (p. 240). Cambridge, England/New York: Cambridge University Press.
81. Smith, A. D. (1991). *National identity (ethnonationalism in comparative perspective)* (p. 226). Reno: University of Nevada Press.
82. Smith, A. D. (1992). National identity and the idea of European unity. *International Affairs (Royal Institute of International Affairs 1944-), 68*, 55–76.
83. Smith, A. D. (1996). *Nations and nationalism in a global era* (p. 211). Cambridge, England: Polity Press.
84. Smith, A. D. (2001). *Nationalism: Theory, ideology, history* (p. 182). Malden, MA: Polity.
85. Stempel, C., Hargrove, T., & Stempel, G. H., III. (2007). Media use, social structure, and belief in 9/11 conspiracy theories. *J&MC Quarterly, 84*(2), 353–372.

86. Stenersen, A. (2008). The internet: A virtual training camp? *Terrorism and Political Violence, 20*(2), 215–233.
87. Takei, M. (1998). Collective memory as the key to national and ethnic identity: The case of Cambodia. *Nationalism and Ethnic Politics, 4*(3), 59–78. Retrieved from http://dx.doi.org/10.1080/13537119808428538
88. Tambiah, S. J. (2000). Transnational movements, diaspora, and multiple modernities. *Daedalus, 129*(1), 163–194.
89. Teik, K. B. (2010). *Cyber-networks, physical coalitions and missing links: Imagining and realizing dissent in Malaysia 1998–2008* (pp. 1–29). Chiba, Japan: Institute of Developing Economies.
90. *The Guardian*. (2011, August 8). *London riots – Live blog*. Retrieved August 8, 2011, from https://ezproxy.lib.lehigh.edu/login?url=http://www.guardian.co.uk/uk/series/london-riots-live
91. Thelwall, M. (2009). Homophily in MySpace. *Journal of the American Society for Information Science and Technology, 60*(2), 219–231. doi:10.1002/asi.20978.
92. Thomas, T. L. (2003). Al Qaeda and the internet: The danger of "cyberplanning". *Parameters, 33*(1), 112–122.
93. Tomlinson, J. (2003). Globalization and cultural identity. In D. Held & A. McGrew (Eds.), *The global*. Cambridge: Polity Press.
94. Tynes, R. (2007). Nation-building and the diaspora on Leonenet: A case study of Sierra Leone in cyberspace. *New Media Society, 9*(3), 497–518. doi:10.1177/1461444807076980.
95. Vidanage, H. R. (2004). Cyber cafes in Sri Lanka: Tamil virtual communities. *Economic and Political Weekly, 39*(36), 3988–3991.
96. Weimann, G. (2004). *www.terror.net: How modern terrorism uses the Internet* (Special report, pp. 1–13). Washington, DC: United States Institute of Peace.
97. Wellman, B. (2001). Physical place and cyberplace: The rise of personalized networking. *International Journal of Urban and Regional Research, 25*(2), 227–252.
98. Wellman, B., Boase, J., & Chen, W. (2002). The networked nature of community: Online and offline. *IT & Society, 1*(1), 151–165.
99. Wellman, B., & Haythornthwaite, C. A. (2002). *The internet in everyday life* (p. 588). Malden, MA: Wiley-Blackwell.
100. Wellman, B., Quan-Haase, A., Boase, J., & Chen, W. (2002b, October). Examining the internet in everyday life. In *Euricom Conference on e-Democracy* (pp. 1–18). Nijmegen, the Netherlands.
101. Wheeler, D. (2000). New media, globalization, and Kuwaiti national identity. *Middle East Journal, 54*(3), 432–444.
102. Whine, M. (1999). Cyberspace: A new medium for communication, command, and control by extremists. *Studies in Conflict & Terrorism, 22*(3), 231–245. doi:10.1080/105761099265748.
103. Williams, C., & Smith, A. D. (1984). The national construction of social space. *Progress in Human Geography, 7*(4), 502–518.
104. Wilson, S. M., & Peterson, L. C. (2002). The anthropology of online communities. *Annual Review of Anthropology, 31*(1), 449–467. doi:10.1146/annurev.anthro.31.040402.085436.
105. Winland, D. (2002). The politics of desire and disdain: Croatian identity between "home" and "homeland". *American Ethnologist, 29*(3), 693–718. Retrieved from http://www.jstor.org/stable/3805469
106. Yang, G. (2009). Online activism. *Journal of Democracy, 20*(3), 33–36. doi:10.1353/jod.0.0094.
107. Zhou, Z. Y. (2005). Informed nationalism: Military websites in Chinese cyberspace. *Journal of Contemporary China, 14*(44), 543–562.

Chapter 7
E-Government and Data Protection in the Public Sector

Mary Lampri

Data Processing and Automation Division, Supreme Council for Civil Personnel Selection, Pouliou Str. 6, GR-11523 Athens, Greece, mlampri@asep.gr

Abstract Legal and regulatory requirements and client expectations regarding management and retention of personal, financial, and other business information are greater than ever. As sensitive data is increasingly shared within organizations and across organizational boundaries, it requires persistent protection from interception and viewing by unauthorized parties. Data encryption technologies are one means of achieving this protection. In addition, organizations must ensure that their document management systems and practices can safeguard personal information contained in documents throughout their life cycle. The Internet and computer networking means that there is a need for new security measures and policies to reduce the threats and challenges inherent from these new technologies and software applications and network devices. The security aspects of public sector information systems are important as the respective systems are often part of critical infrastructures or deal with personal or sensitive data.

Keywords E-Government • Data protection • Information security • Public sector

7.1 Introduction

In the past three decades, information and communications technology (ICT) has helped to transform the global economy and enable private enterprises and governments to achieve unprecedented results. Greater productivity, more efficient internal processes, and new ways of collaborating within organizations and with partners and customers are helping companies of all sizes to compete more effectively in fast-paced global markets. Governments are also taking advantage of these advances to operate more efficiently and deliver services more effectively to citizens.

The massive and rapid flow of personal information over the Internet has played a key role in this transformation by supporting intelligent data analysis, expanded sales

A.A. Lazakidou (ed.), *Virtual Communities, Social Networks and Collaboration*, Annals of Information Systems 15, DOI 10.1007/978-1-4614-3634-8_7,

and service channels, and more innovative approaches to addressing organizational challenges. Yet as organizations handle growing volumes of personal data and use it in an increasing variety of ways, they also face more compliance requirements and a greater responsibility to adequately protect the privacy and integrity of this data.

Many consumers, business leaders, government policymakers, and privacy advocates are calling for more effective policies, processes, and technologies to protect and manage the personal information entrusted to organizations. These organizations must balance the desire to optimize the flow, utility, and value of this information with the responsibility to safeguard it from loss, theft, and misuse.

The Internet and computer networking means that there is a need for new security measures and policies to reduce the threats and challenges inherent from these new technologies and software applications and network devices. Information, network equipment, transmission media, computer systems, and servers are subject to threats. Determining the exact requirements for security for a given organization is essential for implementing the proper security measures. Such measures are designed to protect information systems from security breaches.

The main purpose of information security is to protect and safeguard the organizations' assets from threats. "For many organizations, information and the technology that supports it represent the organization's most valuable assets" [9]. The information security attacks of an organization's assets have high cost impact, loss of customer confidence, and negative business reputation. An organization must analyze its assets and the threats these assets face from either inside attacks or outside attacks.

7.2 Information Systems Security Measures

Security measures and countermeasures are implanted to protect organizations from different security attacks. To guarantee the security requirements of a given organization, it is essential to be able to evaluate the current security demands of an organization as well as the measures taken to achieve such requirements.

Security weaknesses cause a negative impact on organizations such as financial loss, reputations, and loss of customer confidence [11]. The intention of implementing security measures, controls, and policies is to guard information security objectives and information assets. Information security objectives, which are confidentiality, integrity, and availability, are the main concern in categorizing information security level [4, 10, 13].

Organizations are required to take appropriate security measures based on their requirements. Security measures can be grouped into three major groups: physical, personal, and network security measures. Each group employs several means for security protection. Within each group, security measures can be further classified into measures aimed at securing the confidentiality, integrity, and availability of the data and system. Banks, on the other hand, have high demand for data confidentiality.

Hence, the measures required to protect confidentiality are essential for banks. In essence, an organization may have different security requirements for information security objectives. Similarly, an organization may have different security requirements at different times [2].

7.3 Information Security Threat and Vulnerability

Vulnerability is the weakness of information and information systems which can lead to attacks, harm, modification, destruction, disclosure, interruption, and interception [2]:

1. *Destruction*: occurs when information, hardware, and software are destroyed due to malicious intention.
2. *Disclosure*: occurs when unauthorized users have access to information or information systems and disclose the confidential information. Unauthorized disclosure has a serious impact on maintaining security and privacy of the system.
3. *Modification*: occurs when unauthorized users change the information held in computer and server systems.
4. *Interruption*: occurs when a computer network becomes unavailable for access. An example is the denial of service.
5. *Interception*: occurs when unauthorized users copy information that resides in a computer system or while the data is in transmission mode.

All organizations having information systems, Web sites, intranet, and Internet are subject to a number of security threats. Organizations are facing an increase of varieties of security threats. As risk level grows and the need for organizational compliance in this field increases, information systems security becomes more important to an organization's overall business approach.

Mitigating vulnerability by deploying measures to reduce security breaches, monitoring news about the new vulnerabilities, developing new risk assessment, deploying new technologies, and employee training can mitigate new threats and protect an organizational asset. The importance of understanding the impact of an organization's security threats is facilitating an organization more efficiently to measure the security risk. The nature of threats to information security has changed due to the hackers' and crackers' sophistication. Organizations must investigate the information systems vulnerability [2].

7.4 Public Sector Information Security

In most countries, the public sector performs numerous critical functions for their economic and social life and development and sets the legislation, the rules, and the whole framework for all economic and social activities. Public sector also includes the armed forces, the police, the social security, the emergency services, the legislative and judicial authorities, and numerous independent oversight authorities, all of them being of critical importance for the whole economic and social activity. Additionally, in some countries, there are public organizations (public sector enterprises) providing services and goods, which are considered essential for strategic reasons, and therefore fall under the state umbrella. This category can be very wide and can include banks, hospitals, research institutes, educational establishments, state-owned lotteries, energy, telecommunications, and transport organizations, as well as industries processing critical raw materials, handling nuclear power, and defense equipment manufacturers. Public sector organizations have increasingly relied on the use of information systems for collecting, processing, and analyzing data, in order to support their functions [12].

Security is more than a principle or a right. If implemented properly, security is a way of life. It protects basic values that underpin our culture and liberties.

Security involves more than *just IT.* Holistic security is about physical security, disaster preparedness, emergency response, and critical infrastructure protection. Security requires multilevel cooperation and coordination of military, law enforcement, and subject matter experts. Security touches auditors, facilities managers, and maintenance workers.

Security management begins with the adoption of security policies that have legitimacy within the enterprise. Security policies come from a process that builds consensus among many key stakeholders. This includes elected officials and other policymakers as well as end users, government employees, and citizens. Security policies should embody standard practices that everyone in the organization must follow. These standard practices include an understanding of specific outcomes or goals the enterprise is committed to achieve. These goals are critical to security planning and critical to assessments about how well the organization protects its assets.

Five key qualities should be considered when decisions are made about system goals and their effectiveness [8]. The system must have (see Fig. 7.1):

- Potential for change
- High availability
- High usability
- Adequate performance
- Reliable security (i.e., trustworthiness)

Each of these five qualities must be in balance. For example, security affects system availability, and it can also degrade performance and usability. It is a trade-off. As systems become more difficult to access, the usability of the system will decrease. Security also adds overhead to the system, which in turn adversely affects performance. The trade-offs require an understanding of risks, user/stakeholder needs, current costs, staff skills, and the business demands for each system. These business demands, which can be categorized by attribute, are the key. They drive total cost of ownership and determine staffing skills required to balance the trade-offs. Figure 7.2 presents key factors related to each attribute.

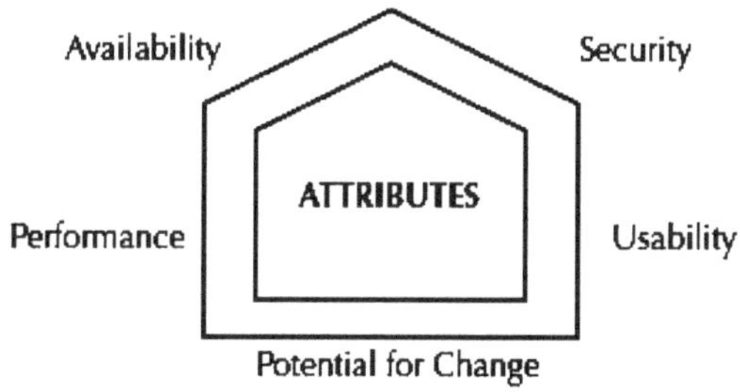

Fig. 7.1 System architecture qualities [8]

Availability	Usability	Performance	Security
Reliable components Error detection Fault tolerance Repair Preventive maintenance Distribution, installation, and activation	User testing and evaluation Requirements capture and analysis Ergonomics Consistent user interface Support services, training, and documentation	System predictability Comparability and benchmarks Manageability, control, and monitoring	Confidentiality Integrity Availability to authorized users Accountability Non-repudiation

Fig. 7.2 Business demand attributes

These attributes flow through the business, application, information, and technical architectures. They permeate the subarchitectures that describe information technology from different perspectives—from the point of view of the application developer, end user, service provider, and IT manager. Many specialists are involved, and their perspectives are critical to system integrity, reliability, and, ultimately, performance. Again, security, a key architectural component, is about people and how well they are able to blend perspectives and talents.

Security is a tough business. It is intellectually challenging and emotionally draining. It is simply wrong to place the burden of security solely on the shoulders of security officers, technologists, and IT executives. Security is a shared responsibility across the entire enterprise, to include subject matter experts, functional users, and oversight professionals.

Secure organizations are built on a culture that is open, resource sharing, and focused. Secure organizations do not happen by accident. For security to be effective, governments should teach all their employees control standards and build the standard practices into their planning and measuring processes. They should provide clear feedback through audit reports and metrics to confirm that security is properly practiced. Good security comes from a highly trained and motivated workforce.

7.5 Information Systems Security in the Greek Public Sector

Greek public sector organizations have only a basic level of information systems security awareness and adopt mostly basic information systems security measures, such as backup copies, recovery procedures, security zones, and firewall systems. Most of them have a special interest in digital data confidentiality, probably because the ISs of many public sector organizations contain personal and sensitive data. However, only a small percentage of them have developed a systematic, complete, and integrated approach toward the security of their IS, such as an information systems security plan and an information systems security policy. In addition, only a small percentage of them have established systematic procedures for information systems internal audit. The importance of proper training and generally the importance of the human factor for achieving high levels of information systems security is often underestimated [12].

7.6 E-Government 2.0

E-government can be defined as government use of information technologies in order to communicate externally in the public sector (with citizens and businesses) and internally (with other government departments) [5–7, 16]. Ebrahim and Irani [5] gives measures for the level of e-government development.

Despite spending enormous amounts on Web-based initiatives, government agencies often fail to meet users' needs online. By employing new governance models, investing in Web capabilities, and embracing user participation, agencies can raise the effectiveness of their online presence.

Early breakthroughs in e-government—the use of information and communications technologies to provide and improve public sector services, transactions, and interactions—have enabled government organizations to deliver better service and improve effectiveness and efficiency. In many countries, more than 70% of taxpayers now file taxes electronically, for example, and many other transactions—ranging from renewing drivers' licenses and paying parking tickets to managing government benefits—can be conducted online. Employees within government agencies also use the Internet routinely to manage internal processes, such as human resources and travel.

However, despite the continued allocation of enormous resources, progress on the e-government front appears to have plateau over the past few years. Many new e-government initiatives have neither generated the anticipated interest among users nor enabled clear gains in operational efficiency. In the face of unprecedented fiscal constraints, as well as users' heightened expectations based on the integration of the Internet into their daily life and work, it is imperative that the public sector refines its approach to e-government to ensure that these initiatives achieve maximum impact.

Three obstacles have, however, limited the impact of e-government efforts: ineffective governance, lack of Web-related capabilities, and reluctance to allow user participation in the creation of applications and content.

7.7 Information Privacy and Data Protection in the Public Sector

As the collection and use of personal information in digital form become increasingly prevalent, widely publicized security and data breaches and growing public concerns about identity theft threaten to curtail the growth of online commerce and services. Governments and organizations that fall short in effectively managing and protecting users' personal information face considerable risks—including damage to their reputation, penalties and sanctions, lost market share, and needless expense.

A holistic approach to data governance begins with an understanding of the information life cycle—the collection, updating, processing, and eventual deletion of personal information—and the adoption of a technology framework that enables governments and organizations to set controls which safeguard individuals' privacy.

To encourage businesses and organizations to take a holistic approach to data governance, governments can set an example by embracing these principles and practices themselves. Governments can also help protect citizens by working with industry to adopt effective standards and policies on data retention, reduce the risk to users' privacy that comes with unneeded and long-term storage of personal information, and take appropriate action when breaches do occur. Comprehensive data breach notification legislation is another important step that can help keep citizens informed of serious risks to their online identity and financial information as well as strengthen consumer confidence in online commerce and services.

For the past decade, the public sector has been driven by the need to develop electronic forms of "government," from information provision through to citizen management. This has caused a huge investment in e-business services and the data collection practices many of these systems create, rely on, or interact with—locally or as part of an extended network of services provision and/or providers.

A substantial part of the e-government investment is the management of the data that now drives e-gov itself; this falls under the framework for information assurance (IA). Information assurance is a policy and guidance framework through which electronic government progresses—everything from the development, procurement, provision, and maintenance of governmental (both central and local) services. Information assurance drives to implement policies and tools to enable and assure the availability, integrity, and confidentiality of e-government services, having particular focus upon identity registration, enrollment, and authentication processes, which underpin access to these services. Information assurance also aims to protect, and offer integrity for, private information of citizens and organizations—and hopefully promotes trust between service providers and citizens in the provision and delivery of a better form of government.

7.8 The Role of Government in Data Governance

Data governance is the application of policies and processes within an organization in order to maximize the value of data, manage what data is collected, and determine how it is used to advance the organization's goals. Storing data, especially personal information, involves risks that must be appropriately managed through data governance policies and processes. The organization's policies and processes also must address compliance requirements, including the many statutes and regulations that surround data, especially in regulated industries such as the financial and health sectors. Mandatory data retention periods are one example of such requirements.

Data governance, although not a new concept, is gaining renewed interest as organizations grapple with privacy concerns. With growing volumes of personal information to manage, enterprises and governments must balance their goals for using this data to add value to their organization with demands from citizens and policymakers for more accountability and better protections.

Governments are uniquely positioned to shape and advance the adoption and implementation of data governance within organizations—and ultimately enhance the privacy protections of their citizens—through thoughtful and precise policy positions and legislation, including the following:

- *Adopt data governance policies and processes.* By adopting data governance policies and processes, governments can demonstrate a commitment to data governance and learn practical lessons about implementation that can be used to form the basis of future policy positions and legislation.
- *Promote data governance.* Governments can use their unique position to promote data governance through academic programs, public-private partnerships, government-sponsored publications, and conferences. The insights that governments gain by adopting data governance, when shared freely, are often the most valuable tool in promoting data governance.
- *Implement effective data retention requirements.* Governments and organizations of all sizes are quickly becoming overwhelmed by the amount of data that they are required to process and store in the course of performing routine business. This problem can be exacerbated by overly broad data retention legislation. Governments can seek a balance between the societal benefits of data retention, including security and law enforcement, and the risks to privacy that come with long data retention periods.
- *Pass comprehensive data breach notification legislation at the federal level.* Citizens should be informed when their personal information held by governments or organizations is lost or stolen, especially if there is a high likelihood that the information will be used fraudulently or to commit identity theft. Legislation should help balance the rights of citizens to be fully informed with a broader need to limit breach notification to situations where there is a tangible risk of harm. Needless and excessive notification of breaches can decrease consumer

confidence in the ICT industry as well as reduce the likelihood that individuals will take proactive steps to protect themselves when they are truly at risk. Federal legislation, aligned with similar laws in other countries, will promote consistency across jurisdictions, simplifying compliance for organizations.

7.9 Determining Key Factors in E-Government Information Systems Security

Prior to e-government, records and information were stored mainly on paper in files, filing cabinets, and vaults. Paper documents have a degree of separation between the client and the flow, storage, and retrieval of documents. Manual record management systems have established procedures to process and transfer documents through the system. These documents could also be tracked transparently through the organization; hence, if tampered with, the changes would be clearly evident. The security measures required to protect them focused mainly on the physical protection of the document and restricting permissions for people to physically access the records. They were written into policies and procedures and updated over many years. Although the documents could be copied, the paper type, the color, and the size would be difficult to match with or replace the original. Also, copying documents is traditionally a relatively slow process. This provided for documents a completely different degree of security to that of intranet or Internet-based systems, which have the capability for immediately downloading information, giving the client (end user) the ability to copy and retransmit this information in nanoseconds. This vulnerability exists for any organization, whether private or public, that has a Web presence.

In general, IS security (ISS) is the effective implementation of policies to ensure the confidentiality, availability, and integrity of information and assets to protect from theft, tampering, manipulation, or corruption. IS security has previously concentrated on confidentiality of information stored electronically. The rapid growth in the volume of such information and the uptake of e-commerce within organizations have heightened the need for increased security to protect the privacy of this information and prevent fraudulent activities.

The objective of information security is to preserve an organization's information assets and the business processes they support in the context of:

- Confidentiality—ensuring that information is only available to the people and systems authorized to receive it. Information may be confidential for many reasons including privacy, commercial, or political.
- Integrity—ensuring that information is only changed by people and systems authorized to make changes to it.
- Availability—ensuring that information and information processing systems are available when information is required.

7.10 E-Government Security in Developing Countries

The concept of an e-government system is to provide access to government services anywhere at any time over open networks. This leads to issues of security and privacy in the management of the information systems. Managing such issues in the public sector has different emphases than in the private sector. The broader e-government approach is sociotechnical by nature, involving people and processes as well as technologies; hence, particularly in transitional countries, the social culture and characteristics of the country are factors in successful e-government development.

The majority of ICT management standards and best-practice guidelines have been developed by technologically leading countries. The management of e-government security assurance is a relatively recent focus with which even technologically leading countries have unresolved issues. For countries which are still developing technologically, e-government security management has added issues, mostly to do with environmental factors which differentiate them from the implicit assumptions of leading countries.

Legislation and laws should provide the basis for ensuring an adequate level of compliance to international regulations and laws as well as giving internal direction. Many developing countries have yet to consider adopting adequate legislation related to information security management, laws that criminalize cyber attacks and enable police to adequately investigate and prosecute such activities [15]. In addition, many do not have privacy or network security laws or regulations which could be used to take action against the misuse of ICT resources [1, 3, 14].

This implies that many developing countries are not only limited in taking action against intruders targeting their information assets but also against intruders who might use their country's information network as a base to perform illegal activities globally. This type of activity is a major issue in the information age. This presents another potential fundamental difference between developing countries and developed countries in terms of the existence and absence of the necessary regulations and laws to ensure a higher level of compliance.

7.11 Conclusions

Security measures, countermeasures, policies, procedures, and guidelines are implemented in organizations to maintain the desired level of information security level. As a result, organizations will be able to secure their information security objectives. Organizations are struggling against security attacks. Implementing the most appropriate security measures in organizations assists organizations to protect their information's assets and reduce security vulnerabilities. Defining information security levels enables organizations to implement proper security measures. Implementing security measures helps organizations to decrease possible damage and loss due to security attacks.

Important actions for governments include adopting policy positions and passing legislation in support of data governance, adopting data governance practices themselves and promoting their use, supporting information card technology to enable interoperable identity and access controls, implementing effective data retention requirements, and passing comprehensive data breach notification legislation.

References

1. Aljifri, H. A., Pons, A., & Collins, D. (2003). Global e-commerce: A framework for understanding and overcoming the trust barrier. *Information Management & Computer Security, 11*(3), 130–138.
2. Alshboul, A. (2010). Information systems security measures and countermeasures: Protecting organizational assets from malicious attacks. *IBIMA Publishing Communications of the IBIMA, 2010*(486878), 1–9.
3. Bakari, J. K., Tarimo, C. N., Yngstrom, L., & Magnisson, C. (2005, July). State of ICT security management in the institutions of higher learning in developing countries: Tanzania case study. In *Computers & Security Proceedings of the Fifth IEEE International Conference on Advanced Learning Technologies (ICALT 05)*. Washington, DC: IEEE Computer Society.
4. Chen, C. C., Shaw, R. S., & Yang, S. C. (2006). Mitigating information security risks by increasing user awareness: A case study of information security awareness system. *Information Technology, Learning, and Performance Journal, 24*, 1–14.
5. Ebrahim, Z., & Irani, Z. (2005). E-government adoption: Architecture and barriers. *Business Process Management Journal, 11*(5), 589–611.
6. Gilbert, D., Balestrini, P., & Littleboy, D. (2004). Barriers and benefits in the adoption of e-government. *The International Journal of Public Sector Management, 17*(4/5), 286.
7. Heeks, R. (2006). *Implementing and managing eGoverment*. London: Sage.
8. Heiman, D. (2002). *Public-sector information security: A call to action for public-sector CIOs*. National Association of State Chief Information Officers (NASCIO), USA.
9. John, L. W. (2000). COBIT: A methodology for managing and controlling information and information technology risks and vulnerabilities. *Journal of Information Systems, 14*, 21–25.
10. Johnson, M. E. (2008). Information risk of inadvertent disclosure: An analysis of file sharing risk in the financial chain. *Journal of Management Information Systems, 25*(2), 97–123.
11. Kumar, R. L., Park, S., & Subramaniam, C. (2008). Understanding the value of countermeasures portfolios in information systems security. *Journal of Management Information Systems, 25*, 241–279.
12. Loukis, E., & Spinellis, D. (2001). Information systems security in the Greek public sector. *Information Management & Computer Security, 9*(1), 21–31.
13. Nyanchama, M. (2005). Enterprise vulnerability management and its role in information security management. *Information Systems Security, 14*, 29–56.
14. Shalhoub, Z. K. (2006). Trust, privacy, and security in electronic business: The case of the GCC countries. *Information Management & Computer Security, 14*(3), 270–283.
15. United Nations. (2005). *Information economy report 2005*. Available from http://www.unctad.org/ecommerce/
16. World Bank. (2011). *Definition of e-government*. Retrieved February 7, 2011, from http://go.worldbank.org/M1JHE0Z280

Chapter 8
Building SCIENAR, a Virtual Community of Artists and Scientists: Usability Testing for the System Improvement

Iole Alfano, Manuela Carini, and Lorella Gabriele

University of Calabria, Cosenza, Italy, alfano.iole@unical.it; carini@unical.it; lgabriele@unical.it

Abstract In recent years, the rapid expansion of new technologies fostered the development of new models for online group aggregation, such as virtual communities, social networks, and collaboration tools. This chapter provides an overview about the development of the SCIENAR Virtual Community, a social network capable of strengthening the role of the "artistic-scientific" community in the production of new science and new art. In particular, the key role played by the usability evaluation has been highlighted through the implementation of a product suitable to different final users in order to bring out potentialities and eventual critical areas.

Keywords Virtual community development • Usability • Human-computer interaction • USER-CENTERED DESIGN

8.1 Introduction

Nowadays, new information and communication technologies have allowed a wide variety of people to easily share interests and manage, exchange, and disseminate knowledge and information. Communication tools, such as Virtual Communities (VCs), are used for different purposes in different fields, such as educative and commercial areas. In particular, SCIENAR Virtual Community (VC) has been developed within the framework of the European project SCIENAR – Scientific Scenarios and Art (http://www.scienar.eu/main). The central idea of SCIENAR consists of developing and building three emblematic scenarios closely related to three different historical ages, in which the interaction between Mathematics and Arts is deep. In particular, the scenarios refer to the following: the birth of Mathematics in the antiquity – arithmetic and geometry; Development of Mathematics from Renaissance to the 1900: perspective and symmetry; and mathematics in the twentieth century: curvature, motion, relativity, and chaos. SCIENAR aimed to implement a social

A.A. Lazakidou (ed.), *Virtual Communities, Social Networks and Collaboration*, Annals of Information Systems 15, DOI 10.1007/978-1-4614-3634-8_8,

network capable of strengthening the role of the "artistic-scientific" community in the production of new science and new art. This objective can be achieved by promoting synergies and collaborations between the different users involved in the large field of research of Arts and Science [1].

The SCIENAR VC provides a simple and efficient interface useful to navigate through networks of scientists and artists, allowing users to discover easily many examples of the close connection existing between arts and science.

After developing the first prototype of the SCIENAR VC, we evaluated the usability in order to bring out potentialities and eventual critical areas.

In this chapter, we provide an overview about the developing process adopted to create and to improve SCIENAR VC. Particular attention is given to illustrate some perspectives for future works. The paper is organized as follows: Sect. 8.2 reviews the literature on the definitions of virtual communities, their application in different scientific fields, and the key role played by the usability evaluation in developing a usable product. In Sect. 8.3, we illustrate the structure of the SCIENAR VC prototype. Finally, Sect. 8.4 deals with the usability study carried out to individuate problems and strong points of the developed VC.

8.2 Background

The advent of always more powerful web applications and the rapid expansion of new technologies favored the arising of new models concerning online group aggregation. According to Maslow [21], the social needs of belonging, which includes the desire to have friends, to be accepted by others, to receive friendships and affection, and to be part of a group, are identified as psychological needs and set among the "fundamental" and "superior" needs. Consequently, communities, virtual communities, social networks, and collaboration tools arise from the primary human need to join and feel aggregated with other people, promoting a new type of interaction between groups and integrating computer technologies and the web, with the aim to be part of a social space [10, 22, 27].

A social network represents a social structure made by people, as friends or family, that share same virtual environment and same technology, forming a recognizable group joined by organizational constraints, common interests (i.e., linguistic, religious, and economic), goals, and values, but not necessarily a common geographic location. According to different researches [4, 13, 14, 16, 17, 32, 33], a VC is characterized by the creation and manipulation of shared spaces, communication, clear positions of responsibility, online interaction, and constant check on the quality of offered services/information; and the individual skills are available for the benefit of whole group. These relationships usually begin from "contents," sharing users' personal information, affiliations, needs, and aspirations. Any exchange of value among participants includes exchanging profile information, sharing general information, registering for an event, a clear and shared sense of belonging, broad communication and engagement, resources (tools), openness, curiosity, and imagination [6, 8, 9, 28].

Virtual communities have been object of researches since their dawning. Some of these define them as a technology supported on a computer and mediated by the cyberspace; their activities are enabled by information technology, while contents or topics are affected by the evolution of relationships among participants [15, 17]. In fact, they reflect the complex interactions that characterize the society and the human behavior.

The practice of using VCs as a source of information has been recently adopted in different fields, like education [5, 29, 34, 36], science and arts communication [1], software development [2], consumer behavior [18, 37], and the health field [7]. Since they are characterized by low cost and time efficiency [11], they are also used for information exchange, social relationships, and entertainment.

In an increasingly networked society with a need for global and flexible ways of professional interactions, VCs can fill collaborative gaps in traditional, hierarchical organizations [3, 35].

The development and success of VCs are constrained by its usability and sociability. In recent years, many researches [12, 23, 25, 26] have shown how usability evaluation represents a quality attribute of any interactive software system. In fact, the central focus of a usability evaluation is to ensure that software products are characterized by learnability, low error rate, rapid execution of tasks, easiness to remember the basic instruction, and high user satisfaction. ISO 9241 defined usability as the capability of any device to be easily used by a user in order to achieve the task for which it is designed. The key role of usability evaluation arises from the need of different companies to improve their competitiveness and business performance. Since 1992, Shneiderman [31] highlighted that the usability analysis provides important guidelines for the designers in the development processes of any product. Mahdjoub et al. [20] stress that, during the design process, engineers often underestimate some factors such as ergonomics. Hence, many products have not been designed to respond to the really end-user expectations, including their usability needs. Salvo et al. [29] emphasize how the process of redesigning can represent a challenge because it is less expensive to carry out usability testing to achieve valuable feedback and to better adapt a system to user needs. Sanchez-Franco and Rondan-Cataluña [30] underline how the usability of a virtual community should be a key issue in the marketing strategy of any business operating in online environment. Moreover, they emphasize how users are often captured by perceptions of visual aesthetics and usability of the website; hence, the success goes through the users' experiences and their emotions.

In their study, Tickle et al. [32] identify the following four factors that play a key role in the successful development of a VC: culture, technology, resources, and community functionalities. Furthermore, Paredes and Martins [24] underline how successful virtual interactive environments should have adaptable contents according to user's hardware and software capabilities in order to promote user's participation.

Summing up, although many products are designed for a wide variety of users, they are often complex and unsuitable. Hence, in implementing SCIENAR VC, an interactive design process has been carried out involving final users in the designing process through a usability evaluation.

8.3 An Overview on SCIENAR Virtual Community

SCIENAR Virtual Community has been created using Joomla!, an open source Content Management System (CMS). Over the last few years, thanks to the stability, prerogatives, and functionalities of Joomla!, it has been successfully used both for amateur and business purposes at different levels. Moreover, our development team created new modules that allow a high level of interactivity in the virtual community. Three types of users have been foreseen: administrator, user, and visitor. The administrator can access all features of the platform, including those of the "back end," in order to supervise and to manage the CMS. User can access all features provided by the "front end" and contribute to the production of contents; finally, the visitor is authorized only to publish contents and features that do not require user authentication through login credentials (username and password).

The layout (Fig. 8.1) of the site is organized in three columns which display the interactive modules and the menu on the left and right sides, with the central one showing the contents. All the contents, which describe the three scenarios, are organized into categories containing one or more subcategories. The "leaf nodes" of the database are represented by record cards that can be generated by experts and inexperts, but they are published only after a check of an authorized user group, that is, the scientific committee. The scientific committee is a group of users, with username and password, that can access their personal homepage and insert scientific contents; access the resource area; download and upload documents, audio, and video; add new web links; and enable some users to watch movies (WebTV – chat). In the VC, a collection of resources, documents, and tools related to the topics of arts and sciences are present, and any user can access the platform contents without login. Briefly, any web surfer can access the following sections: *Project* (link to the official website of the SCIENAR project where it is possible to find information on the aims of the project, the consortium, events, and publications produced under the same project); *Artists* (this section shows a list of artists, representative of the three scenarios, inserted in the database. These artist's cards contain a brief biography of each artist, some useful links, and artworks connected to the scenario); *Galleries* (this is a collection of art galleries in which users can search and view the galleries that take care of exhibitions and events related to the theme of science and arts); *Artworks* (includes a series of artworks linked to the scenarios. In this way, each artist can make all his works visible and accessible and, at the same time, can visualize artworks of other artists, thus stimulating the creativity and the invention of new artifacts); *Cross Paths* (a series of results obtained with cross searches on specific topics, thanks to indexing processes by the keywords); *Virtual Labs* (is characterized by the organization of interactive laboratories aimed, mainly, to a better understanding

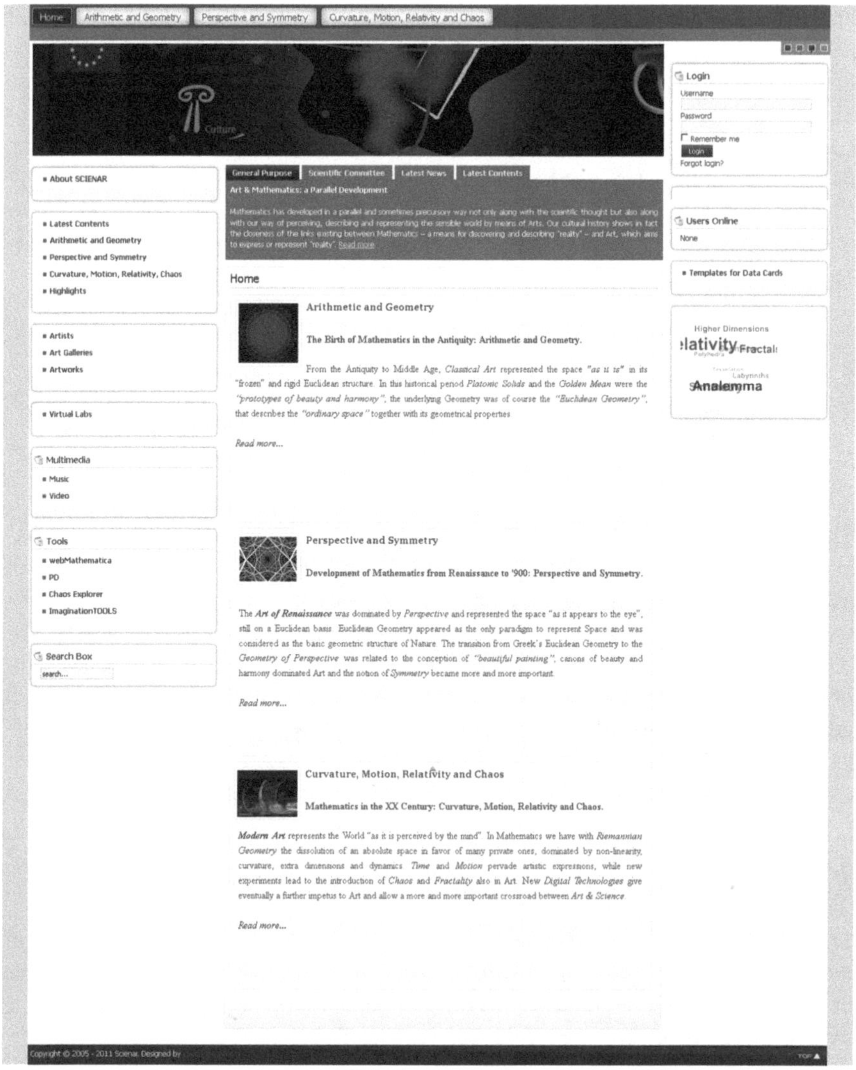

Fig. 8.1 Homepage screenshot of SCIENAR VC

of science, to create new ways to communicate information to the public, and to improve scientific teaching and artistic concepts). Furthermore, the use and application of new technologies for the exploration of new areas of research and for the creation of artistic products/scientific innovations is encouraged and promoted. In particular, the laboratories aim to visualize science to better communicate it; visualize science to better teach it; use digital technologies as a mean to explore the interplay between science and arts; and produce new art and/or new science. For each laboratory and purpose, exemplifying multimedia applications are presented: *Tools* (user can access a range of digital tools and software, view different examples of their application, and get suggestions for developing new ideas and creation of new artworks); *Latest News* (it shows the latest news concerning national and international events as well as publications related to science and art fields, and the SCIENAR project – conferences, seminars, workshops – but also exhibitions of art and multimedia installations); *Web links*; *WebTV*; and *Chat* (the enabled users can only watch movies proposed by the scientific committee).

Each scenario and their contents can be an inspiration source for artist and/or scientist for further artwork creation and useful for knowledge diffusion and dissemination of innovative approaches and results.

8.4 Research Design

8.4.1 Aim of the Study

The main objective of this research is the evaluation of usability of SCIENAR VC in order to develop a system that is easy to use and friendly for different groups of users and to improve and to stimulate creative activities of researchers and media artists involved in the project.

Through usability test, problems will be identified and the most appropriate solutions will be evaluated in order to solve the functional limitations. Hence, the final goal of this work is to ensure that SCIENAR VC will be fully usable by experts (artists and scientists) and novice users (unskilled users).

8.4.2 Subjects

The sample consisted of 30 subjects (13 male and 17 female). Due to the nature of the website, half of them are artists or scientists and they are recruited from the SCIENAR scientific committee, a group of scientific experts that supervised the work project. Unskilled users make up the remaining half.

8.4.3 Materials

After a specific survey of existing literature on usability testing, it was considered appropriate to adopt the questionnaire for User Interface Satisfaction (USE), created and validated by Lund [19]. This tool is composed of two parts: the first one foresees that the researcher identifies a list of tasks that the user should carry out while navigating the system, while the second part is a questionnaire. This one was made up of 33 closed questions to which users answer using a seven-point Likert scale in order to know user's personal opinion on virtual community.

Four characteristics were investigated to measure the system usability:

1. *Utility*. It explores the utility perceived by the user regarding the website contents.
2. *Ease of use*. It surveys what measure it is easy to navigate the website and assesses the capacity of the tools to stimulate interaction.
3. *Ease of learning*. It reviews what measure the organization's website permits an easy and quick learning.
4. *Satisfaction*. The measure of satisfaction describes the perceived utility of users and the level of comfort that they express while navigating the website.

The last three questions, in open form, were fundamental to acquire the personal opinion of participants about the usability of the system.

8.4.4 Procedure

At the beginning of the session, all participants were informed of the research aim; they were asked to complete the tasks and to fill the questionnaire. During the task execution, a researcher recorded the start time and the end time of the test (close to each task). Taking into account the aim of the research, the following tasks were defined:

Task 1. Open the browser, access the website http://www.scienar.eu/network, go to the menu "Cross Path", choose the link "Perspective and Symmetry", and see the description "Mosaics".

Task 2. Go to the menu "Artists", try for "Gianni Colombo", and read the description.

Task 3. Register yourself to the website from the section "Login".

Task 4. Access the Login area using the following data: Username is "Usertest" and password "passwordtest". Access the "Template for Data Cards" menu, click on the link "Living Artist", fulfill the card with your data, and click on "Submit" to send it to the administrator.

Task 5. Access the Tools menu, open the link Chaos Explorer, read the description of the software, and download the software.

Task 6. Access WebTV section, click on the link, see the video, then close the window.

Task 7. Access Multimedia menu, click on the Music link, choose the "Roots and Routes" CD-ROM, and listen to "Quattro Isole Italiane" musical excerpt.

Task 8. Access the Multimedia menu, click on the Images link, and find the "Land-Art Inspired By Solar Clocks" image.

Task 9. Access to the "Artworks" menu, find the "CYSP I" artwork, and read the description.

Task 10. From the Login area, log out.

All subjects were settled down in front of a workstation consisting of a PC connected to a 17-in. monitor running Microsoft® Windows XP and a web browser Microsoft® Internet Explorer®.

Subsequent to filling the demographic survey (name, age, gender, artist, or no), each subject carried out the tasks individually and without any time limitation.

After each task completion, the subject had to indicate its own level of competence, associated with the request activity, and to describe any errors or problems encountered during the execution of the same task.

Only after having completed the execution of all assigned tasks did the researcher deliver to each subject the questionnaire in order to evaluate the usability of the website. The researcher, who monitored the activities, did not assist the subject with any help or support.

The obtained results were loaded on grills provided in Excel, while the descriptive statistics were compiled using SPSS software.

8.5 Findings and Discussion

Thirty subjects participated in the study and a total of 30 valid questionnaires have been collected and analyzed. Taking into account the focus of SCIENAR VC, we used a sample composed by artists and unskilled users. Half of the sample was composed by artists, while the other half by unskilled users. 40% of the sample was less than 18 years old, 43% were aged between 18 and 25, while 17%, between 26 and 35. Moreover, 43% was male and 57% was female. All the participants successfully completed task 1 (Open the browser, access to the website http://www.scienar.eu/network, go to the menu "Cross Path", choose the link "Perspective and Symmetry", and see the description "Mosaics"), task 2 (Go to the menu "Artists", try for "Gianni Colombo", and read the description), task 3 (Register yourself to the website from the section "Login"), task 4 (Access to the Login area using the following data: Username is "Usertest" and password "passwordtest". Access to the "Template for Data Cards" menu, click on the link "Living Artist", fulfill the card with your data, and click on "Submit" to send it to the administrator), task 5 (Access to the Tools menu, open the link Chaos Explorer, read the description of the software, and download the software), task 6 (Access to WebTV section, clicking on the link, see the video, then close the window), and task 8 (Access to the Multimedia menu, click on the Images link, and find the "Land-Art Inspired By Solar Clocks" image). Only 60% of the participants were able to complete correctly task 7 that required access to Multimedia menu, click on the Music link, choose the "Roots and Routes" CD-ROM, and listen to "Quattro Isole Italiane" musical excerpt. Task 9 (Access the "Artworks" menu, find the "CYSP I" artwork, and read the description) was completed by 90% of the subjects, while 80% was able to perform task 10 (From the Login area, log out) (Fig. 8.2).

Task completion time was recorded for each participant. Figure 8.3 represents the average time for each task and shows that some tasks were more difficult to complete than others. Task 4, which required access to the Login area using the data

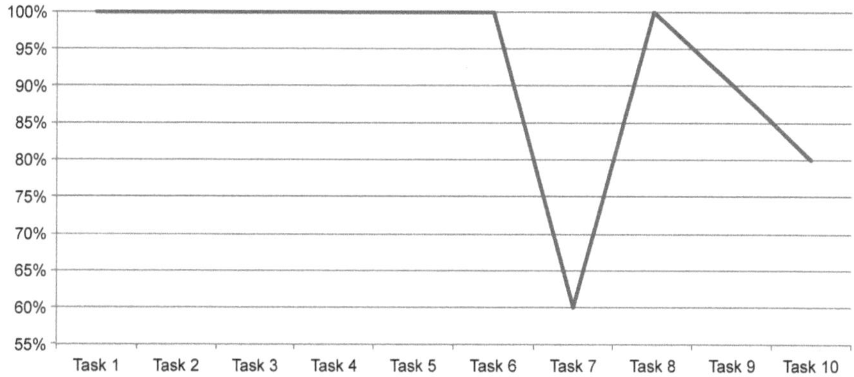

Fig. 8.2 Completion rates for each task performed

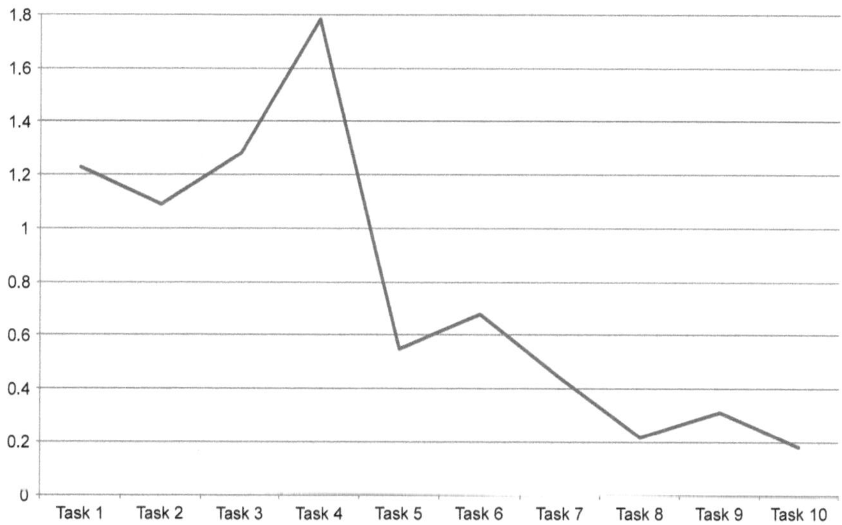

Fig. 8.3 Average time completion of the performed tasks

supplied by the researcher, showed the highest average time (AT = 1.78) for completion. After logging in, the user had to search and access the "Template for Data Cards" menu, select the link "Living Artist", and fulfill the template with its data, finally clicking on "Submit" to send it to the administrator.

The tasks that registered the highest completion times were task 1 (AT = 1.23), which is foreseen to open the browser, access the SCIENAR Virtual Community website, and explore a menu; task 2 (AT = 1.09) which is foreseen to find "Gianni Colombo" in the "Artists" menu and to read his biography; and task 3 (AT = 1.28) which foresees the user registration in the section "Login".

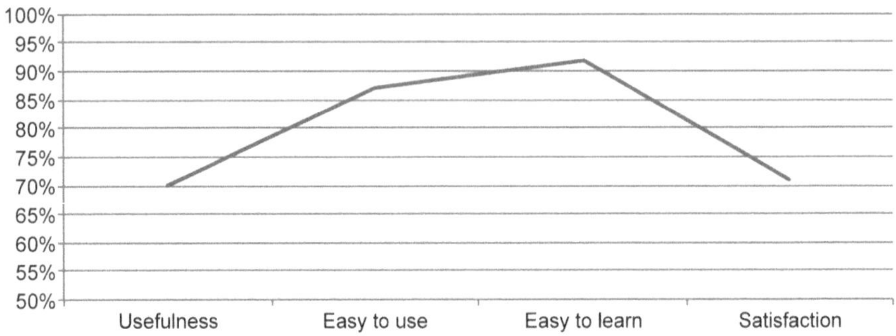

Fig. 8.4 Agree ratings on the SCIENAR Virtual Community

The other tasks were completed in less than a minute: task 5 (AT=0.55) that required access to the "Tools" menu, opening the link Chaos Explorer, reading the description of the software, and downloading the software; task 6 (AT=0.68) that required access to WebTV section, clicking on the link, seeing the video, and then closing the window; task 7 (AT=0.44) which required finding a particular musical excerpt within a series of submenu; task 8 (AT=0.22) that required access to the Multimedia menu, clicking on the "Images" link, and finding the "Land-Art Inspired By Solar Clocks" image; task 9 (AT=0.31) that required access to the "Artworks" menu, finding the "CYSP I" artwork, and reading the description; and finally task 10 (AT=0.18) that required logging out.

Participants rated the site considering four overall measures that include usefulness, ease of use, ease of learning, and satisfaction. They used a seven-point Likert scale with measures ranging from "strongly disagree" to "strongly agree" with intermediate values. Since agree ratings are represented by the two measures "agree" and "strongly agree," the percentage of "agree" (Fig. 8.4) was calculated taking into account only these measures.

Almost all of the subjects agreed with the four measures, ranging from 70% to 92%. In particular, 92% of participants state that the community interface is "ease of learning," while 87% of subjects think that it is "ease of use." Moreover, some users expressed their satisfaction in navigating the system (71%), finding it useful to achieve the objective (70%).

Comparing the collected data separately for artists and unskilled users, we can see some differences. Due to the SCIENAR Virtual Community purpose, artists are more satisfied than unskilled users. In fact, as shown in Fig. 8.5, many artists (74.20%) state that the community is useful to achieve their objectives, improving their work. Among the unskilled users, 65.80% assessed the usefulness of the community. As regards the "ease of use" aspect, the majority of interviewed artists (92.10%) think that their goal can be achieved in an easy way by using the SCIENAR Virtual Community, while only the 29.70% of unskilled users agree. Moreover, almost all artists (95%) and unskilled users (88.30%) believe that the Virtual

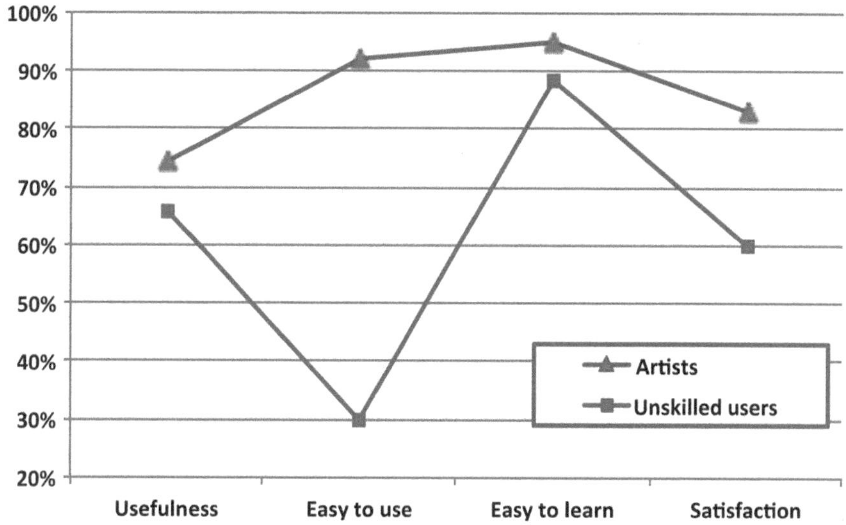

Fig. 8.5 Agree ratings on the SCIENAR Virtual Community for artist and unskilled users

Community interface is "ease of learning." Finally, concerning the satisfaction category, after their interaction with the system, 82.90% of artists and 60% of unskilled users are satisfied. Despite the community was born for artist and scientist needs, these results demonstrate that this virtual space can stimulate the interest of unskilled users, bringing them closer to the world of science and arts.

The above results agree with the task completion and the spent time. In fact, unskilled users completed 90% of the proposed tasks, spending more time ($M = 0.86$) than artists who completed 96% of tasks, spending an average time of 0.69 min. However, both categories have shown some difficulties in completion of task 7 (Access Multimedia menu, click on the Music link, choose the "Roots and Routes" CD-ROM, and listen to "Quattro Isole Italiane" musical excerpt) and task 10 (From the Login area, log out), although the percentage of completion for artists (67%) is higher than unskilled users (53%). Task 10 was completed by 67% of unskilled users and by 93% of artists. Finally, task 9 (Access to the "Artworks" menu, find the "CYSP I" artwork, and read the description) was completed by all artists and by only 80% of unskilled users (Fig. 8.6).

Upon completion of the tasks, all participants provided feedback for what they liked most and least about the SCIENAR Virtual Community and recommendations for improving it. A large percentage of participants showed positive opinions in regard to the interface and the accessibility of sections. In fact, someone said "Most of the links are where you expect it to be," "It is clear and facilitates to find information," and "It is divided properly and simply." Almost all the users appreciated the graphics of SCIENAR Virtual Community, in particular, the pleasing use of colors for layout and the attractive icons. Some said that the community is original, new,

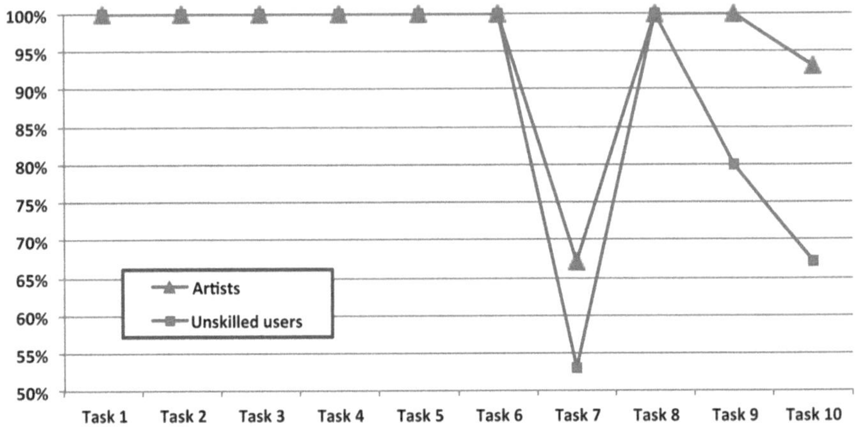

Fig. 8.6 Completion rates for each task performed by artist and unskilled users

and creative. Concerning the content present in the community, a few of the subjects appreciated their organization in sections and a large percentage liked many of the images concerning arts in science. In particular, they found excellent the speed in loading pages, although it is a prototype.

Moreover, exploring the resources (texts, videos, images) included on the community, somebody stated that "It offers the opportunity to learn new forms of art" and "It provides useful examples, to which one can refer to." Among the things participants liked least, there was the fact that the list of artists present in the site is not in alphabetical order: this implied that during the completion of Task 2 (Go to the menu "Artists", try for "Gianni Colombo", and read the description), they took longer to identify the name. As regards the graphics, a little percentage thinks that the website is shortly attractive and the graphics is too simple. Among unskilled users, some of them claim that the community "is not immediately clear what that is for" and point out it is scarcely intuitive. These comments can be related to the fact that they are not experts of the sector of arts and science, and for this reason, they need more time in founding specific contents. Finally, all the subjects reported the lack of an alternative language than English.

8.6 Conclusion and Future Trends

In this work, we presented and discussed the key role of usability evaluation in the developing process of any technological product and, in particular, of the method used in implementing SCIENAR Virtual Community. The main objective of SCIENAR Virtual Community is to strengthen the role of the "artistic-scientific" community in the production of new science and new art. This latter objective can be achieved by promoting synergies and collaborations between the different protagonists involved in the large field of research of arts and science.

We administered the USE questionnaire [19] to collect important information as regards strong points and limitations of the system in order to highlight problems and errors. The evaluation of usability involved a sample composed by users belonging to arts/science field (named artists) and unskilled users. From the analysis of the results, we observed that the artists had less difficulty than unskilled users, evaluating the VC as more useful, interesting, and easy to use and to learn. Moreover, all participants provided interesting feedback for what they liked most and least about the website and recommendations for improving the website.

The comparison between the feedback given by the general users and artists provided new insights about the organization of SCIENAR VC both from an aesthetical point of view and for the contents.

Further research efforts will be focused on improving the VC, taking into account the obtained feedback and recommendations given by the sample of the research. Implementing the recommendations and continuing to work with users will ensure a user-centered website.

Acknowledgment We are especially thankful to Professor Pietro Pantano (project coordinator of SCIENAR) and to Professor Eleonora Bilotta (in charge of the Usability Action of SCIENAR Project).

References

1. Alfano, I., Carini, M., Gabriele, L., & Naccarato, G. (2010). SCIENAR virtual community: A useful tool to promote the synergies among artists and scientists. *International Journal of Online Engineering, 6*(2), 8–13. doi:10.3991/ijoe.v6i2.1293.
2. Barcellini, F., Détienne, F., Burkhardt, J. M., & Sack, W. (2008). A socio-cognitive analysis of online design discussions in an open source software community. *Interacting with Computers, 20*, 141–165.
3. De Moor, A., & Weigand, H. (2007). Formalizing the evolution of virtual communities. *Information Systems, 32*, 223–247.
4. Dõgan, G., Van Assena, M. A. L. M., Van de Rijt, A., & Buskens, V. (2009). The stability of exchange networks. *Social Networks, 31*, 118–125.
5. Effken, J. A., Boyle, J. S., & Isenberg, M. A. (2008). Creating a virtual research community: The University of Arizona PhD program. *Journal of Professional Nursing, 24*(4), 246–253. doi:10.1016/j.profnurs.2007.06.024.
6. Füller, J., Bartl, M., Ernst, H., & Mühlbacher, H. (2006). Community based innovation: How to integrate members of virtual communities into new product development. *Electronic Commerce Research, 6*, 57–73. doi:10.1007/s10660-006-5988-7.
7. Hanten, G., Cook, L., Orsten, K., Chapman, S. B., Li, X., Wilde, E. A., et al. (2011). Effects of traumatic brain injury on a virtual reality social problem solving task and relations to cortical thickness in adolescence. *Neuropsychologia, 49*, 486–497.
8. Hemetsberger, A. (2002). Fostering cooperation on the Internet, social exchange processes in innovative virtual consumer communities. In S. M. Broniarczyk & K. Nakamoto (Eds.), *Advances in Consumer Research* (Vol. 29, pp. 354–356). Valdosta, GA: Association for Consumer Research.

9. Hsu, M. H., Ju, T. L., Yen, C. H., & Chang, C. M. (2007). Knowledge sharing behavior in virtual communities: The relationship between trust, self-efficacy, and outcome expectations. *International Journal of Human Computer Studies, 65*, 153–169. doi:10.1016/j.ijhcs.2006.09.003.
10. Hummel, J., & Lechner, U. (2002, January). *Social profiles of virtual communities*. Paper presented at HICSS'02 35th Annual Hawaii International Conference on System Sciences, Big Island, HI (Vol. 7, p. 172b). doi:ieeecomputersociety.org/10.1109/HICSS.2002.994154
11. Illum, S. F., Ivanov, S. H., & Liang, Y. (2010). Using virtual communities in tourism research. *Tourism Management, 31*, 335–340.
12. Ipri, T., Yunkin, M., & Brown, J. M. (2009). Usability as a method for assessing discovery. *Information Technology and Libraries, 28*(4), 181–183.
13. Kim, J., Song, J., & Jones, D. R. (2011). The cognitive selection framework for knowledge acquisition strategies in virtual communities. *International Journal of Information Management, 31*, 111–120.
14. Kloos, B. (2005). Community science: Creating an alternative place to stand? *American Journal of Community Psychology, 35*(3–4), 259–267.
15. Lee, F., Vogel, D., & Limayem, M. (2002). Virtual community informatics: What we know and what we need to know? In R. H. Sprague (Ed.), Paper presented at *35th Hawaii International Conference on System Sciences* (pp. 2863–2872). Los Alamitos, CA: IEEE Computer Society Press.
16. Lin, H. (2008). Determinants of successful virtual communities: Contributions from system characteristics and social factors. *Information Management, 45*, 522–527.
17. Lin, F., Lin, S., & Huang, T. (2008). Knowledge sharing and creation in a teachers' professional virtual community. *Computers in Education, 50*, 742–756.
18. Lu, Y., Zhao, L., & Wang, B. (2010). From virtual community members to C2C e-commerce buyers: Trust in virtual communities and its effect on consumers' purchase intention. *Electronic Commerce Research and Applications, 9*, 346–360.
19. Lund, A. M. (2001). Measuring usability with the USE questionnaire. *STC Usability SIG Newsletter, 8*(2). Retrieved June, 2011, from http://stcsig.org/usability/newsletter/0110_measuring_with_use.html
20. Mahdjoub, M., Monticolo, D., Gomes, S., & Sagot, J. C. (2010). A collaborative design for usability approach supported by virtual reality and a multi-agent system embedded in a PLM environment. *CAD Computer Aided Design, 42*, 402–413.
21. Maslow, A. H. (1982). *Motivazione e personalità*. Roma: Armando.
22. Memmi, D. (2006). The nature of virtual communities. *AI & Society, 20*(3), 288–300. doi:10.1007/s00146-005-0020-7.
23. Nielsen, J. (2000). Why you only need to test with 5 users. *Jakob Nielson's Alertbox*. Retrieved October 21, 2000, from http://useit.com/alertbox/20000319.html
24. Paredes, H., & Martins, M. F. (2011). Social interaction regulation in virtual web environments using the social theatres model. *Journal of Network and Computer Applications*. doi:10.1016/j.jnca.2011.02.009.
25. Preece, J. (2000). *Online communities: Designing usability and supporting sociability*. Chichester, England: John Wiley and Sons.
26. Preece, J. (2001). Sociability and usability: Twenty years of chatting online. *Behavior and Information Technology Journal, 20*(5), 347–356.
27. Romm, C., Pliskin, N., & Clarke, R. (1997). Virtual communities and society: Toward an integrative three phase model. *International Journal of Information Management, 17*(4), 261–270.
28. Rheingold, H. (2000). *The virtual community: Homesteading on the electronic frontier*. Cambridge, MA: MIT Press.
29. Salvo, M. J., Ren, J., Brizee, H. A., & Conard-Salvo, T. S. (2009). Usability research in the writing Lab: Sustaining discourse and pedagogy. *Computers and Composition, 26*, 107–121.

30. Sanchez-Franco, M. J., & Rondan-Cataluña, F. J. (2010). Virtual travel communities and customer loyalty: Customer purchase involvement and web site design. *Electronic Commerce Research and Applications, 9*, 171–182.
31. Shneiderman, B. (1992). *Designing the users interface: Strategies for effective human-computer interaction*. London: Addison-Wesley Longman.
32. Tickle, M., Adebanjo, D., & Michaelides, Z. (2011). Developmental approaches to B2B virtual communities. *Technovation, 31*, 296–308.
33. Toivonen, R., Kovanen, L., Kivelaa, M., Onnela, J. P., Saramaki, J., & Kaski, K. (2009). A comparative study of social network models: Network evolution models and nodal attribute models. *Social Networks, 31*(4), 240–254.
34. Tomai, M., Rosa, V., Mebane, M. E., D'Acunti, A., Benedetti, M., & Francescato, D. (2010). Virtual communities in schools as tools to promote social capital with high schools students. *Computers in Education, 54*, 265–274.
35. Toral, S. L., Martínez-Torres, M. R., & Barrero, F. (2010). Analysis of virtual communities supporting OSS projects using social network analysis. *Information and Software Technology, 52*, 296–303.
36. Wachter, R. M., Gupta, J. N. D., & Quaddus, M. A. (2000). IT takes a village: Virtual communities in support of education. *International Journal of Information Management, 20*, 473–489.
37. Wu, J., Chen, Y., & Chung, Y. (2010). Trust factors influencing virtual community members: A study of transaction communities. *Journal of Business Research, 63*, 1025–1032.

Chapter 9
User-Generated Content for Location-Based Services: A Review

Lee Fueng Yap, Masahiro Bessho, Noboru Koshizuka, and Ken Sakamura

Interfaculty Initiative in Information Studies, The University of Tokyo, 7-3–1 Hongo, Bunyo-ku, Tokyo 113-0033, Japan, lfyap@sakamura-lab.org; besshy@sakamura-lab.org; koshizuka@sakamura-lab.org; ken@sakamura-lab.org

Abstract User-generated content (UGC) has become one of the important elements in today's Internet world. The proliferation of UGC has prompted many efforts to develop useful services using this freely available information. One of the domains of interest is in the field of location-based services (LBS). In this chapter, we present a review of LBS that leverage UGC. We illustrate the differences between conventional LBS and LBS that use UGC in order to highlight the implications of using UGC in LBS. In order to analyze how UGC has been used in LBS, a collection of existing UGC-based LBS have been identified and divided into two groups. It was found that some of the current systems were modeled under the assumption that most of the UGC contributors were honest in providing updates to the systems. However, this does not always correspond to the reality. Hence, the three fundamental requirements for successful UGC-based LBS deployments are discussed in this chapter. These requirements are information trust, user's privacy protection, and information classification. The state-of-the-art solutions for fulfilling these requirements are listed and discussed. We strongly believe that the quality of UGC used by the system, the protection of contributor's privacy, and the system's response time are basic requirements for successful UGC-based LBS.

Keywords User-generated content • Volunteered geographic information • Location-based services

9.1 Introduction

User-generated content (UGC) also known as the consumer-generated media (CGM) is digital information created by the Internet user through the World Wide Web for the use of others. Popular examples of UGC are reviews, videos, photos, blogs, microblogs, news feeds, and podcasts. UGC has gained overwhelming popularity in the recent years. According to a 2009 survey by eMarketer.com carried out in the

A.A. Lazakidou (ed.), *Virtual Communities, Social Networks and Collaboration*, Annals of Information Systems 15, DOI 10.1007/978-1-4614-3634-8_9,

United States [1], there were nearly 116 million UGC consumers and 82.5 million UGC contributors in 2008. These figures are expected to climb significantly to 155 million UGC consumers and 115 million UGC contributors by year 2013.

There are several factors that contribute to the widespread use of UGC. First, it is due to the ubiquitous use of mobile communication devices, such as smartphones and tablet personal computers. Furthermore, the reduction of data transmission cost has enabled these devices to be always connected to the networks. Another substantial factor is the introduction of Web 2.0 platform in the last decade [2, 3]. Prominent examples of such platforms are the social networking sites, photos sharing sites, and product reviews sites, which promote collaborative exchange of information among the users. Web 2.0 platforms have significantly transformed the information publishing landscape of the Internet as it has enabled novice users to create and share information easily and quickly with other Internet users, which was once an exclusive privilege for technically skilled users [4].

Figure 9.1 shows the timeline of applications that generate UGC since the 1990s. One of the interesting trends observed after year 2006 is the inclusion of geographic data into the UGC. UGC embedded with geographic data such as Global Positioning System (GPS) coordinates or place names has been regarded as volunteered geographic information (VGI) [5]. For ease of discussion, all UGC that contains geographic data will be addressed as VGI in this chapter.

The ubiquitous adoption of mobile devices integrated with GPS and the deployment of Wi-Fi positioning system have provided a mean to support the calculation and estimation of the mobile device's geographic position in real time. Another crucial factor that contributes to the proliferation of VGI is the deployment of Web applications, which enable users to add in geographic data to UGC. The process of adding geographic data to UGC is normally known as geotagging. Popular examples of these applications are Flickr [6] and Picasa [7]. Moreover, the reusability of digital map services such as Google Maps [8] and OpenStreetMap [9] within Web-based applications has further encouraged users to create more VGI as VGI can be used or reused for creating useful location-based services (LBS), such as restaurant recommendation system. In fact, it has been recognized that the additional geographic data encapsulated in UGC has great potential for creating new, innovative, and cost-effective LBS [10, 11].

However, LBS that use VGI are considered rather new and more convoluted compared to conventional LBS due to the nature of VGI, which is extremely dynamic, lacking of consistency, and hard to regulate. Moreover, unlike the conventional model of LBS, where boundaries between the service provider and users are well defined, the VGI-based LBS enable collaborations from the users. With this model, the users have also become the content producers. Another interesting phenomenon demonstrated by the new form of LBS is the tendency of deploying cross-service in the form of mashups, for example, offering location-based restaurant recommendation service to users of mobile social network service by using VGI garnered from the mobile social network service. It is therefore challenging to employ these resources for enhancing or creating reliable services. Since not much

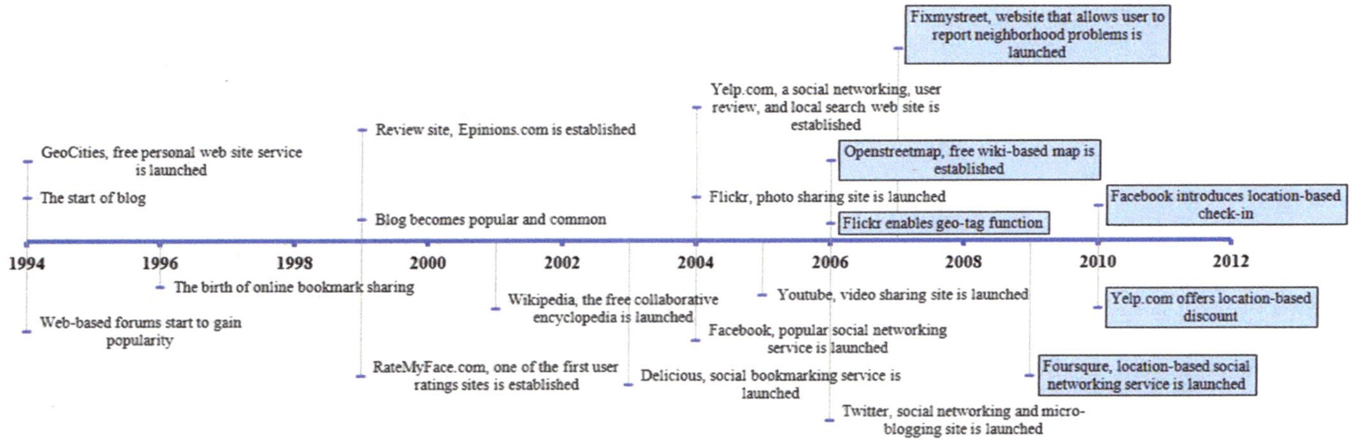

Fig. 9.1 Timeline of applications that generate UGC

research has been conducted to investigate the landscape of this nascent field, this chapter aims to provide a holistic view of how UGC has been used in LBS.

This chapter is structured into various sections. Section 9.2 discusses the differences between conventional LBS and VGI-based LBS. This section also explains the implications of using UGC/VGI in LBS. Section 9.3 dissects different types of VGI-based LBS to understand how UGC/VGI has been used. The common problems faced by these applications are also explained. Section 9.4 lists the three general requirements of VGI-based LBS, namely, information trust, user's privacy protection, and information classification. This section also analyzes how to deploy current techniques used in UGC to fulfill the identified requirements for VGI-based LBS. Section 9.5 concludes this review.

9.2 Conventional Location-Based Services and VGI-Based Location-Based Services

The development of ubiquitous computing and various wireless network technologies has enabled the proliferation of LBS. LBS are defined as services which are triggered based on the location of the user who is making the request [12]. Some prominent examples of LBS are emergency caller location tracking service, information and entertainment-seeking services, and advertising services [13]. These LBS implementations are normally one-way service, where information is sent from the service provider to the user.

However, in the recent years, the nature of LBS has slowly transformed. LBS have enabled the user to contribute real-time information to the service based on the user's current location. Popular usage models of this kind include Foursquare's location-based check-in [14], Twitter's location-based news feed submission [15], Waze's real-time traffic monitoring system [16], disaster warning system based on Twitter [17], and various emergency management systems [18, 19]. This revolution has brought VGI into LBS. The VGI used in the LBS can be any digital media ranging from photos, videos, to microblogs tagged with geographic information such as GPS coordinates or name of the location.

A recent news article from ABI Research, Inc., indicates that the users of car navigation system participated actively in enhancing the service's map using UGC [20]. This result implies that users are willing to contribute towards making better services through the use of UGC. The advantages of using UGC/VGI in LBS are the ability to get the latest information from a large number of sources and disseminate this information at a very high speed. This feature is particularly important when the coverage areas supported by the LBS are large. It will be costly to send dedicated personnel to collect all the required real-time data. With the use of VGI, the LBS can be enriched with additional and dynamic information uploaded by geographically dispersed users. Hence, VGI can be considered as an effective and economical solution for the service providers.

However, with the introduction of VGI to LBS, the landscapes of conventional LBS have slowly transformed. The use of VGI in LBS has caused some significant

Table 9.1 Comparison of conventional LBS with VGI-based LBS

	Conventional LBS	VGI-based LBS
Information source	Service provider	Service provider and users
Information delivery	Static	Dynamic and collaborative
Information trust	The trust level is high as information is normally provided by the service provider solely	The trust level is dependent on the users' inputs and the service provider's monitoring
Information verification process	Service provider normally verifies the information before publication	Service provider, users, or trusted third parties take part in verifying the trust of the submitted information
User privacy	Protected by service provider	Dependent on the policy and implementation of the service
Information classification system	Defined by the service provider	Dependent on the source and implementation of the service

implications to both the service providers and users. The indentified implications are as follows:

- The trust relationship among the user, service provider, and the contributor of VGI has become complicated.
- The quality, reliability, and credibility of the uploaded information become less clear than before.
- The information verification process has become more convoluted and time-consuming as more parties are involved in updating the contents of LBS.
- The privacy of the user becomes an issue when the user discloses more personal information than before.
- The volume of information increases drastically and hence complicates the information classification system of LBS.

Table 9.1 compared the differences of conventional LBS and VGI-based LBS. Although it seems that using VGI in LBS has done more harm than good, there are still a lot of LBS that leverage on VGI. In the next section, we will discuss different types of LBS that use VGI. These LBS can be broadly classified into two categories. We will dissect and discuss each type of the VGI-based LBS.

9.3 Type of VGI-Based LBS

In general, all UGC/VGI-based LBS can be broadly classified into two categories, as shown in Fig. 9.2. The classification is based two criteria, namely, the purposes of the UGC/VGI and the sources of the UGC/VGI.

- *LBS that use VGI generated by services' users (type 1)* – Such LBS include navigation system that encourages its user to update the maps, inserting personal comments on a place or reviewing a hotel suggested by the LBS and so on.

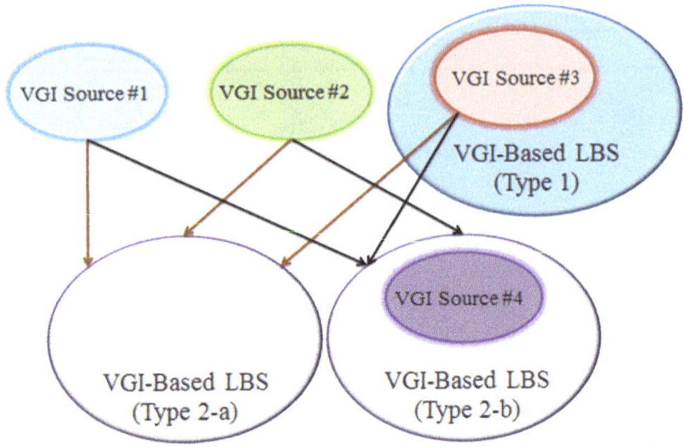

Fig. 9.2 Classification of VGI-based LBS

These types of LBS depend solely on VGI generated internally. The main purpose of the VGI is to enhance the service by delivering up-to-date information to its users.

- *LBS that use VGI collected from one or more services (type 2)* – Such LBS focus on deriving new services from UGC/VGI generated from other services. For example, providing location-based disaster warning services by leveraging UGC/VGI collected from location-based social networking services and photo sharing sites. The contributors of UGC/VGI are generally unaware of how their information is used in the new services. Depending on the service implementation, type 2 VGI-based LBS can depend solely on external sources of UGC/VGI *(type 2-a)* or rely on both external and internal sources *(type 2-b)*, as shown in Fig. 9.2. Type 2 VGI-based LBS are generally more popular than type 1 VGI-based LBS, and it is sometimes regarded as mashup application.

9.3.1 VGI for Enhancing Existing LBS

In this section, we examine some of the existing type 1 VGI-based LBS. The VGI used in the LBS are collected from its users. Generally, the contributors are explicitly informed on how the submitted VGI will be used by the LBS.

In 2007, Holone et al. [21] have developed a prototype for pedestrian navigation system that uses UGC. The main feature of the system is to use UGC to help users with different needs to do route planning. Users are divided into three groups, namely, wheelchair users, parents with baby strollers, and normal users. Users from all groups are given the opportunity to rate and give feedback with regard to the accessibility on the suggested route so that better routes can be generated for other users of the same group. This work has demonstrated the benefits and potential of UGC in pedestrian navigation system.

In [22], the authors proposed a system that uses UGC/VGI to assist wheelchair users and their care workers in doing route planning. By using GPS-enabled mobile terminals installed with custom-built application, the wheelchair users and their care workers report problems faced by them as they traverse a city center to reach their destination. Images, audio comments, and questionnaires related to the reported problem are captured and uploaded to the server that hosted the service in real time. Other users can access all the UGC/VGI uploaded by the contributor from Web-based map. The map is designed with layered approach, where different layers of data can be added on top of each other to achieve a better understanding. The community-based route planning system relied on a group of trusted and dedicated users to make the system more usable.

Another location-based service that makes use of UGC/VGI is the Map Share service offered by TomTom [23]. The Map Share service allows users to make instant corrections to their map directly via dedicated device. The corrections made by the TomTom community are shared among other Map Share users. The changes that can be made by the users include reverse traffic direction, edit street name, add missing point of interest, edit speed limit, and so on. To moderate the quality of the map edited by its users, TomTom takes the responsibility in verifying all the submitted changes. Verified version is then distributed to all the Map Share's community. Since the validation carried out by TomTom's moderators might take some time to complete, user can choose to receive real-time updates from a specific group of users. The TomTom Map Share service is an example of commercialized LBS that leverage on VGI.

FixMyStreet [24] is a community project launch in February 2007 by the United Kingdom government. This project aims to provide the citizens a platform for reporting, viewing, or discussing problems related to public infrastructures. This project has enabled direct communication between local council and the citizens. Users can submit descriptions, photos, and videos embedded with location information when reporting the problem. The submitted information is mapped to digital map for better illustration. All reported problems are accessible to any users. The users can add in new UGC or VGI to better describe any existing problem. This project has demonstrated the benefits of using citizens as sensor to report local problems.

Google crisis response system [25] provides an information portal that helps users to locate critical information such as emergency alerts and news updates during natural disasters and humanitarian crises. Although most of its content is managed by the Google team, the system accepts UGC/VGI contributed by people who are at the disaster area so that up-to-date information can be shared with other victims. Example UGC/VGI contributed by the local people includes water and food distribution information. The collected UGC/VGI is plotted on Google Maps, providing LBS to the users of the system.

9.3.2 VGI for Creating New LBS

In this section, we look at some of the examples that use UGC/VGI garnered from other services to create new LBS.

In [26], the authors designed a location-based service system that collects VGI with temporal information from the Web and geographic information system (GIS) data obtained from remote sensors to describe moving phenomenon, such as hurricanes, flooding, and global warming that happened at a particular location over a period of time. The sources of the VGI come from mobile blogs, photo galleries, social network services, and news feeds. The collected VGI and remote sensors data are integrated and processed by the moving phenomenon engine of the system. By using a specially designed visualization tool, the system enables user to perform queries on a particular moving phenomena by sending arbitrary spatial-temporal geometry to the moving phenomenon engine. The return results are presented in three-dimensional view of space-time. No new UGC/VGI is produced; this system illustrates how multiple sources of UGC/VGI can be used to create a new location-based service.

The authors in [27] designed a social mobile platform for tourist application that facilitates user to automatically receive automated voice-based descriptions on a tourist spot when he/she walks near to the designated location. The voice-based descriptions are collected from another location-aware system known as the Murmur. These voice-based descriptions are UGC created by the locals who are staying close to the tourist spot. The descriptions contain personal experiences and feeling regarding the tourist spot. The system also enables user to record new voice-based descriptions for the visited spots. The newly generated VGI is stored at the message repository and is made available to other users. Furthermore, user can also upload photographs, videos, reviews for restaurants, and suggested routes for enhancing the service. This system has demonstrated the reuse UGC/VGI from other services and the creation of new VGI to enhance the location-based service.

Geotagging has become a common way to structure photos in photo sharing services like Flickr and Picasa. In [28], the authors developed an augmented reality prototype that leverages public geotagged photos collected from Flickr to create a 3D space linked to real-world coordinates using the mobile phone. By pointing the mobile phone at an object, the display of the mobile phone shows all photos downloaded from Flickr which are related to the object in 3D formats. The system was designed for browsing VGI in situ, in an augmented reality view. By filtering out the VGI, the user can view only the photos that were created during a specific period or content created by his/her friends. The system also provides a map and satellite image of a place, which allows the user to look at the neighboring geotagged photos and videos. No new UGC/VGI is generated from this system.

In [29], the authors proposed a system that extracts restaurants and food reviews information from pool of blogs to create a location-based recommendation system. With the extracted information, the system provides location-based restaurant recommendation service to users who are at close proximity with the nearby restaurants. The name of restaurants and their respective signature dishes are displayed on the application's map. The users of the application can also access all the reviews regarding the restaurant via the application's interface. By reusing the blog entries and reviews from the Web, this location-based service offers recommendation service to people who are not familiar with the particular place.

Twitter has recently become one of the most popular microblogging and social networking service [30]. It has enabled users to broadcast information almost instantly to their social network. De Longueville Bertrand et al. [31] have recently performed an analysis on how to use the Twitter message also known as tweets as a source of spatial-temporal information for forest fire incident in France. Although the results suggested that only a small number of the gathered tweets contain accurate geographic information, the authors claimed that with wider penetration of smartphones, it could make tweets with geographic information more accurate and abundant in the near future. About 31% of the gathered tweets are secondary source obtained from other mediums such as blogs, chats, and other UGC/VGI. This work demonstrates that location-based social networking services such as the Twitter can be a rich source for VGI-based LBS.

Ushahidi project [32] is an open-source software that provides a platform to aggregate UGC/VGI from various sources in the Internet such as news feeds, videos, e-mails, and SMS to create new LBS. The collected data can be plotted on digital maps such as the Google Maps to provide interactive visualization. The Ushahidi software has been adopted in many crises happened in the world since 2007; one of the recent examples is the Japan Recovery Map [33] which aims to provide useful location-based information to the victims of Great East Japan Earthquake.

9.3.3 The Problems

Some of the models and systems described in this section are modeled under the assumption that most of the UGC/VGI used in the LBS are contributed by users who are honest. This assumption can be an analogy to the early days of the Internet which based on a belief in the essential goodness of users, and there was little anticipation of the subversive phenomena of spam, viruses, and denial of service attacks that now pervade the network [5]. It might seem that the problem of systems abuse is not a major issue for LBS that relaying on UGC/VGI as for now. However, this assumption cannot be left unattended. This is because as the numbers of VGI-based LBS increases and more important LBS are designed with VGI, more mechanisms should be implemented to assure the usability of the systems. From the analysis on previous VGI-based LBS, it seems that the following requirements should be taken into considerations:

- A pool of active users who contribute honest and high-quality VGI
- A system that can filter out poor-quality VGI in order to uphold the quality of the service
- A system that accepts feedbacks from users regarding the UGC/VGI used in the LBS
- A system that protects UGC/VGI contributors' privacy
- A systematic VGI classification system that can locate suitable VGI in a timely manner

It can be summarized that the quality of VGI-based LBS depends heavily on the trust of the VGI used by the services, particularly for LBS that rely mainly on VGI for their content. If large amount of false and poor-quality VGI is used in the LBS, data pollution will occur. This might affect the normal function of the LBS. The second problem that needs to be tackled is user's privacy concern. The contributor's privacy needs to be protected when he shares information with others. Another prominent problem faced by VGI-based LBS is information overloading, where the system is unable to process a large amount of VGI contributed by the users in real time. Therefore, VGI-based LBS need information classification system that can locate suitable VGI in a timely manner and clean up outdated and irrelevant VGI without disturbing the functionality of the LBS.

In the next section, these three requirements for creating reliable VGI-based LBS are discussed.

9.4 The Requirements for VGI-Based LBS

As pointed out in Sect. 9.3, the basic requirements for VGI-based LBS are information trust, user's privacy protection, and information classification. Since the research in UGC/VGI is relatively mature, we examine how the state-of-the-art techniques in UGC can be used for fulfilling each of the three requirements suggested for VGI-based LBS.

9.4.1 Information Trust

The service providers of LBS should play pivotal role in assuring the trust of the UGC/VGI used in their systems. This is very crucial if the LBS rely on UGC/VGI from multiple external sources, such as geotagged photos collected from photo sharing Web sites and news feeds gathered from location-based social network. The LBS service providers need to be very careful when choosing the source. Moreover, users of the LBS should also be given opportunities to regulate the quality of the UGC/VGI used in the LBS.

The main motivation behind the efforts of assuring the trust of UGC/VGI is to ensure the quality of the service. Efforts from all the stakeholders, namely, UGC/VGI contributors, UGC/VGI consumers, and LBS service providers, are needed. There are several ways to increase the trust of UGC/VGI; the techniques are listed as follows:

1. *Trusted third party* – In this implementation, the trusted third party known as the localization certificate authority is contacted when a VGI has just been created [10]. The current location of the VGI contributor is cross-checked with the geographic information embedded in the VGI in order to prevent location spoofing

attack. After confirming the VGI, VGI contributor receives a certificate from the trusted third party. The certificate binds the VGI contributor' location with the hash of the VGI. This certificate can be used to proof the location information embedded in the VGI, increasing the trust of the VGI. This technique aims to create trusted VGI with verification from trusted third party.

2. *Hardware protection* – To prevent the users from fabricating VGI, such as falsifying location information or altering photo taken by the camera, authors in [34] have designed an architecture that relies on the trusted platform module (TPM) to create trusted VGI. The use of TPM in the design prevents malicious software resides in the capturing device from interfering with the VGI generation. Each generated VGI is embedded with time-stamp information and signed with the private key of the TPM device. When user shares this trusted VGI, the signature of the VGI is verified before it is used; this makes submitting falsified VGI harder. This is another way to generate trusted VGI.
3. *Filtering by VGI-based LBS service provider* – Moderation can be used to maintain the trust of the VGI used in the LBS. TomTom's Map Share system [23] adopts this method in managing the VGI contributed by its users. Although this implementation requires a lot of efforts, in terms of man power and cost, it helps to maintain the quality of the service. Furthermore, the VGI provided by the users can help to narrow down the work scope of the LBS personnel, such that they only need to perform verification at places where modifications were reported instead of traveling the whole area supported by the LBS to identify changes. However, this technique is not suitable for systems which interests of service provider might conflict with the users. The moderators' actions to remove any VGI could be dubious.
4. *Verified account* – Verified account is a security feature provided by Twitter [35] to a limited number of its users. The main function of this account is to limit confusion and making easier for other users to identify authenticated account. Since the virtual identity of a verified account holder is linked to his the real-life identity, it is thus assumed that tweets and VGI gathered from verified accounts are usually trustworthy because dishonest contents will affect the reputation of the account holders in the real world. This technique pushes the responsibility of generating trusted VGI to the contributors.
5. *Ranking/status* – This method is usually implemented in a close community system, where the UGC/VGI contributors are being assigned title or rank according to the criteria set by the service provider. Essentially, the ranking/status approach is built based on reputation model, which represents the history of past interactions happening between members of one community. There are several algorithms used in defining the title or rank of a user. For example, Amazon.com [36] uses positive feedbacks from other users, the number of contributed UGC, and the recentness of the contributed UGC with higher weight for more recent contributions to determine the title or rank of the users. In this method, the quality of a UGC is directly linked to the status or rank of its contributor. UGC/VGI contributed by reputable users is generally more reliable. This mechanism has some similarity with verified account method because the

is associated. For example, the tag "wedding" might have several hypernyms such as "party," "marriage," and "ritual." During the content creation stage, the user can select one or more of the hypernyms to describe the tag. Furthermore, if none of the predefined hypernym represents the UGC's contributor intended meaning, new hypenym can be added in to the system. According to the authors, the proposed semantic tagging system can lead to more accurate content classification because it can return all content that matches the search keyword plus all content associated with tags that are hyponyms of the search keyword. As a result, this increases the efficient of the search results.

3. *Information filtering portal* – The SwiftRiver Sweeper [45] is an application developed for Ushahidi platform [32] to aggregate and classify real-time feeds from Twitter, e-mail, SMS, and the Web before the UGC/VGI is to be used for creating new services. The application enables service providers of VGI-based LBS to view all the contents collected by the Sweeper in charts format. They can also select only to view content received from a particular channel, view content rated as accurate, or view content assigned with certain veracity value. The veracity value ranges from 1 to100, and the value is assigned by other users to represent the truthfulness of a particular UGC/VGI. This value is defined by River ID, which is another application by SwiftRiver. River ID is still an under development project at the time of this writing. Other useful functions provided by Sweeper include automatic deletion of duplicate UGC and autotagging of UGC. Sweeper can help in filtering out poor-quality UGC and organize the information into categories so that more efficient services can be deployed in a timely fashion.

9.5 Conclusion

In conclusion, the evolution of various enabling technologies such as the proliferation of wireless networking technologies, widespread use of mobile devices, and adoption of Web 2.0 has transformed the traditional usages and deployments of LBS. The users of LBS are now no longer mere consumers but also playing the role of content producers. As a result, the content updates for these LBS have become more dynamic. Furthermore, communication between the LBS service provider and the users has become more interactive. There are many LBS that leverage UGC/VGI to enhance or create new services. The most common UGC/VGI used in LBS is photos, news feeds from social network sites, videos, and blogs. It is foreseen that the mobile social network services will be one of the most important sources for future VGI-based LBS. In fact, it is anticipated that VGI-based LBS and mobile social networking services might be integrated seamlessly, making the border between these two services disappears gradually.

The basic requirements for VGI-based LBS implementation outlined in this chapter are information trust, user's privacy protection, and information classification. Information trust can be regarded as the most crucial element for high-quality VGI-based LBS. Privacy protection is another important requirement because without proper privacy protection to the VGI contributors, they will be reluctant to share more information in the future. Finally, proper information classification system can reduce the time to search for appropriate VGI, thus making the VGI-based LBS more useable.

Although all these requirements are important for successful deployment of VGI-based LBS, the service providers should consider balancing service usability with protection mechanisms, as comprehensive protections typically require costly implementation. Furthermore, the degree of protection for each requirement is also very much dependent on the needs and genre of the LBS. For example, the requirements for disaster warning LBS will need more stringent protection in information trust compared to contributor's privacy protection because high level of trusted information is needed to protect the lives and assets of the involved individuals. Moreover, natural disaster warning LBS are normally available for a short time period only; the number of VGI contributed to the LBS by a particular individual is usually not enough for tracking and profiling attacks. In the case of navigation-based LBS, the contributor's privacy protection is important because his daily life patterns can be tracked by the LBS if he/she uses the LBS over a long period of time, making him/her susceptible to tracking and profiling attacks. In short, the priority of requirement changes according to applications' needs. Studies and efforts are needed when designing, developing, and implementing LBS that leverage UGC/VGI. The ultimate goal should be creating secure and privacy-sensitive VGI-based LBS that can benefit UGC/VGI contributors, users, and service providers of VGI-based LBS.

This chapter has looked at the basic requirements for using UGC/VGI in LBS. There are still many issues regarding reusing UGC/VGI for other application domains, common to LBS that are not covered in this chapter. Some prominent issues include infringement of copyright and the liability of the service provider when the use of poor-quality UGC/VGI in the service causes unexpected problems to the users. Hence, application designers and developers need to be extra careful when designing VGI-based applications.

References

1. Verna, P. (2009). *A spotlight on UGC participants*. eMarketer.com. http://www.emarketer.com/Article.aspx?R=1006914. Accessed 17 July 2011.
2. Flanagin, A. J., & Metzger, M. J. (2008). The credibility of volunteered geographic information. *GeoJournal, 72*, 137–148. doi:10.1007/s10708-008-9188-y.
3. O'Reilly, T. (2005). *What is Web 2.0 design patterns and business models for the next generation of software*. http://oreilly.com/web2/archive/what-is-web-20.html. Accessed 17 July 2011.
4. John, K., Nigel, D., & Chandra, N. (2008). User-generated content. *IEEE Pervasive Computing, 7*(4), 10–11. doi:10.1109/MPRV.2008.85.
5. Goodchild, M. F. (2007). Citizens as sensors: The world of volunteered geography. *GeoJournal, 69*(4), 211–221. doi:10.1007/s10708-007-9111-y.
6. Flickr. http://www.flickr.com/. Accessed 17 July 2011.

7. Picasa. http://picasa.google.com/. Accessed 17 July 2011.
8. Google Maps API Family. http://code.google.com/apis/maps/index.html. Accessed 17 July 2011.
9. Open Street Map Project. http://www.openstreetmap.org/. Accessed 17 July 2011.
10. Lenders, V., Koukoumidism, E., Zhang, P., & Martonosi, M. (2008). Location-based trust for mobile user-generated content: applications, challenges and implementations. In *Proceedings of the 9th Workshop on Mobile Computing Systems and Applications*. New York: ACM. doi:10.1145/1411759.1411775.
11. Saroiu, S., & Wolman, A. (2009). Enabling new mobile applications with location proofs. In *Proceedings of the 10th Workshop on Mobile Computing Systems and Applications*. New York: ACM. doi:10.1145/1514411.1514414.
12. Unni, R., & Harmon, R. (2003, July). Location-based services: Models for strategy development in M-commerce. In *International Conference on Management of Engineering and Technology, 2003, PICMET '03* (pp. 416–424), Portland, OR. doi:10.1109/PICMET.2003.1222821.
13. Zhang, W., Cui, X., Li, D. F., Yuan, D. B., & Wang, M. R. (2010, June) The location privacy protection research in location-based service. In *18th International Conference on Geoinformatics*, (pp. 1–4), Beijing, China. doi:10.1109/GEOINFORMATICS.2010.5568118.
14. Foursquare. https://foursquare.com/. Accessed 9 June 2011.
15. Twitter. http://twitter.com/. Accessed 9 June 2011.
16. Waze.com. http://www.waze.com/. Accessed 9 June 2011.
17. Huges, A. L., & Palen, L. (2009). Twitter adoption and use in mass convergence and emergency events. *International Journal of Emergency Management, 6*(3/4), 248–260. doi:10.1504/IJEM.2009.031564.
18. Prentice, S., & Huffman, E. (2008) *Social media's new role in emergency management*. http://www.inl.gov/technicalpublications/Documents/3931947.pdf. Accessed 9 June 2011.
19. Gulf of Mexico Oil Spill. http://www.esri.com/services/disaster-response/gulf-oil-spill-2010/index.html. Accessed 9 June 2011.
20. ABI Research. (2008). *User-generated content will be a key component of maps, navigation, and location-based services* [News Article]. London: ABI Research. http://www.abiresearch.com/press/2834-User-Generated+Content+Will+Be+a+Key+Component+of+Maps,+Navigation,+and+Location-Based+Services. Accessed 9 June 2011.
21. Holone, H., Misund, G., & Holmstedt, H. (2007, September). Users are doing it for themselves: Pedestrian navigation with user generated content. In *1st International Conference on Next Generation Mobile Applications, Services and Technologies, 2007* (pp. 91–99), Cardiff, England. doi:10.1109/NGMAST.2007.4343406.
22. Rashid, O., Dunabr, A., Fisher, S., & Rutherford, J. (2010, June) Users helping users: User generated content to assist wheelchair users in an urban environment. In *Ninth International Conference on Mobile Business and 2010 Ninth Global Mobility Roundtable (ICMB-GMR)* (pp. 213–219), Athens, Greece. doi:10.1109/ICMB-GMR.2010.73.
23. Tom Tom Mapshare. http://www.tomtom.com/page/mapshare/. Accessed 9 June 2011.
24. Fix my street. http://www.fixmystreet.com/. Accessed 9 June 2011.
25. Google crisis response system. http://www.google.co.jp/intl/ja/crisisresponse/japanquake2011.html. Accessed 7 August 2011.
26. Kim, K. S., Zettsu, K., Kidawara, Y., & Kiyoki, Y. (2009). Moving phenomenon: Aggregation and analysis of geotime-tagged contents on the web. *Web and Wireless Geographical Information Systems., 5886*, 7–24. doi:10.1007/978-3-642-10601-9_2.
27. Freyne, J., Brennan, A. J., Smyth, B., Byrne, D., Smeaton, A. F., & Jones, G. J. F. (2009, August). Automated murmurs: The social mobile tourist application. In *International Conference on Computational Science and Engineering, (CSE '09)* (pp. 1021–1026), Vancouver, BC, Canada. doi:10.1109/CSE.2009.348.
28. Belimpasakis, P., Selonen, P., & Yu, Y. (2010). Bringing user-generated content from internet services to mobile augmented reality clients. In *Cloud-Mobile Convergence for Virtual Reality Workshop (CMCVR)*, (pp. 14–17), Waltham, MA. doi:10.1109/CMCVR.2010.5560611.

29. Shih, C. C., Peng, T. C., & Lai, W. S. (2009, November). Mining the blogosphere to generate local cuisine hotspots for mobile map service. In *Fourth International Conference on Digital Information Management, ICDIM 2009*, (pp. 151–154), Ann Arbor, MI. doi:10.1109/ICDIM.2009.5356785.
30. Krishnamurthy, B., Gill, P., & Arlitt, M. (2008). A few chirps about twitter. In *Proceedings of the First Workshop on Online Social Networks* (pp. 19–24). New York: ACM. doi:10.1145/1397735.1397741.
31. Longueville, B. D., Smith, R. S., & Luraschi, G. (2009). OMG, from here, I can see the flames!: A use case of mining location based social networks to acquire spatio-temporal data on forest fires. In *Proceedings of the 2009 International Workshop on Location Based Social Networks* (pp. 73–80). New York: ACM. doi:10.1145/1629890.1629907.
32. The Ushahidi Project. http://www.ushahidi.com/. Accessed 3 August 2011.
33. The Japan Recovery Map. http://www.sinsai.info/ushahidi/. Accessed 3 August 2011.
34. Saroiu, S., & Wolman, A. (2010). I am a sensor, and I approve this message. In *Proceedings of the Eleventh Workshop on Mobile Computing Systems & Applications*. New York: ACM. doi:10.1145/1734583.1734593.
35. Twitter Help Center-About Verified Account. http://support.twitter.com/articles/119135-about-verified-accounts. Accessed 3 August 2011.
36. Amazon.com. http://www.amazon.com/gp/customer-reviews/guidelines/top-reviewers.html. Accessed 11 August 2011.
37. Schlieder, C., & Yanenko, O. (2010). Spatio-temporal proximity and social distance: A confirmation framework for social reporting. In *Proceedings of the 2nd ACM SIGSPATIAL International Workshop on Location Based Social Networks* (pp. 60–67). New York: ACM. doi:10.1145/1867699.1867711.
38. Deuze, M., Bruns, A., & Neuberger, C. (2007). Preparing for an age of participatory news. *Journalism Practice, 1*(3), 322–338. doi:10.1080/17512780701504864.
39. Yu, H., Kaminsky, M., Gibbons, B. P., & Flaxman, A. (2006). Sybilguard: Defending against sybil attacks via social networks. In *Conference on Applications, Technologies, Architectures, and Protocols for Computer Communications, Pisa, Italy* (pp. 267–278). New York: ACM. doi:10.1145/1159913.1159945.
40. Yang, Y. F., Sun, Y. L., Kay, S., & Yang, Q. (2009). Defending online reputation systems against collaborative unfair raters through signal modeling and trust. In *Proceedings of the 24th ACM Symposium on Applied Computing, Honolulu, HI*. New York: ACM. doi:10.1145/1529282.1529575.
41. Trusted Computing Group. (2003). *Trusted Computing Platform Alliance (TCPA) main specification version 1.1b*. http://www.trustedcomputinggroup.org/files/resource_files/64795356–1D09–3519-ADAB12F595B5FCDF/TCPA_Main_TCG_Architecture_v1_1b.pdf. Accessed 11 August 2011.
42. Facebook. https://www.facebook.com/help/?page=419. Accessed 11 August 2011.
43. Dattolo, A., Ferrara, F., &Tasso, C. (2010, May). The role of tags for recommendation: A survey. In *Conference on Human System Interactions (HSI)*, (pp. 548–555), Rzeszow, Poland. doi:10.1109/HSI.2010.5514515.
44. Hope, G., Wang, T. G., & Barkataki, S. (2007). Convergence of web 2.0 and semantic web: a semantic tagging and searching system for creating and searching Blogs. In *Proceedings of the International Conference on Semantic Computing, Washington, DC, USA* (pp. 201–208). New York: ACM. doi:10.1109/ICSC.2007.27.
45. Swift River. http://ushahidi.com/products/swiftriver-platform. Accessed 11 August 2011.

Chapter 10
Generating Social Awareness Through Social Network Sites

Penelopi Alexandrou

Kingston University, London, UK, p.alexandrou@kingston.ac.uk

Abstract Generating social awareness suggests the ability to provide information and experiences to people that allows them to acknowledge some form of injustice or inequality. Social awareness has three variations: acquired, awakened and expanded. This study aims to identify whether social network sites and, in this particular case, Facebook are able to act as the vessel that transfers this knowledge to its users around the world, generating social awareness on issues that users were previously unaware of or did not support.

In an attempt to move away from political topics, the example of a social campaign selected was one of cultural heritage – the Greek people's campaign for the transfer (or repatriation) of the Parthenon Sculptures, currently on exhibit at the British Museum in London, back to the Acropolis of Athens where a new museum for this purpose was completed in 2009.

The online ethnographic approach included observation and content analysis of material from a Facebook Group, Cause and Page in both 2009 and 2011 as well as interviews of members of each of these sites for both time periods. While Greek interviewees were aware of the campaign, the majority of non-Greek interviewees were new to the campaign, their support (or in one case, lack thereof) generated through Facebook. The interviews and content on the sites suggest that two of the three forms of social awareness can be generated through Facebook, while at the same time Facebook maintains the status of a virtual public sphere of access to information and discussion where opinions can be shaped and a forum, its users believe, has the power to mobilize change.

Keywords Social network sites • Facebook • Social awareness • Parthenon sculptures

A.A. Lazakidou (ed.), *Virtual Communities, Social Networks and Collaboration*, Annals of Information Systems 15, DOI 10.1007/978-1-4614-3634-8_10,

10.1 Introduction

Scholarly research into the effects of the Internet has revealed that the Internet is not only a tool for casual interaction but can rather take the role of a democratic public sphere, where people can voice out concerns they otherwise were unable to do and where people can generate awareness over various social issues [49]. Castells [8] goes further and coins the term *network society* to characterize the way society currently operates globally; social networks have always been adjusted as part of society through the ages because they provide the primary human necessity of communication. In comparison to other social structures such as the government, church or school, the power of social networks was limited within a community. He argues that with the integration of new technologies, including the Internet and thus the development of virtual social networks or online communities, these limitations have been lifted, and it is in fact through these networks that information and power now flow. Social networks are a norm in all societies, and therefore *network society* is inclusive of all societies in the world.

Social network sites (SNS) such as Facebook, LinkedIn, and Bebo differ from other online communities in that their focus is the ability of users to maintain social ties with people that already belong to one of their social networks although the ties between these people may not be particularly strong ([6], p. 211).

The social network site Facebook has gone through a series of transformations to convert it from the university student-focused site of its humble beginnings to one of the most popular sites around the world. The transformation of Facebook has led to an addition of features and an increase of its applications; aside from a mode of communicating with friends or acquaintances on an international level, Facebook is a forum where friends can play games and share pictures and stories. Facebook has also developed into a forum where people seek to generate social awareness.

In the 2008 US presidential campaign, both Democratic Party candidates, Hilary Clinton and Barack Obama, were very 'web active,' maintaining profiles on social networks such as Facebook with direct links to their campaign websites. The Republican candidate John McCain was often criticized for not taking enough advantage of these media outlets for his campaign [34, 44, 51]. In addition, Facebook is said to have played a part in the 2011 political uprising in Egypt, with news reports from as early as 2008 reporting on the tracking down and arrest of citizens that were using Facebook to organize anti-government movements [57].

This chapter aims to analyze and discuss how a social network site, such as Facebook, can generate social awareness on issues and topics *beyond* the political sphere. This will be done with the use of empirical data from a study carried out that documents the campaign that was launched on Facebook in favour of the request by the Greek people to relocate (or repatriate) the Parthenon Sculptures, currently on exhibit at the British Museum in London, UK, back to the new museum at the Acropolis of Athens. This particular campaign was selected as it can also discuss the ability of Facebook and social network sites to generate awareness on a cross-cultural level, for long withstanding issues that are not directly political in nature and are met with contradicting views.

This chapter will initially provide a lucid definition of the term social awareness and its various forms, as well as what 'to generate social awareness' thus entails, before it seeks to review relevant literature that acts as a foundation for the conceptual development of the study. It will then present the selected methodology of online ethnography and how it can be applied to determining generating social awareness, followed by the analysis of findings and the discussion of relevance of these results, their limitations and variation from analysis of political issues.

10.2 Social Awareness

Research for this study determined that civic engagement, citizenship, social consciousness and their variations were terms used by authors to define similar, if not identical, ideas included in the understanding of social awareness. It was therefore necessary to clarify these terms in order to locate their limitations and, after consideration of the alternatives, provide a redefined definition of social awareness.

10.2.1 Social Consciousness

In *A Theoretical Model of Social Consciousness* (2005), Giddings sums up social consciousness to mean 'how people position themselves in relation to social injustice and social action' (p. 233). She goes on to elaborate on three variations of social consciousness: acquired, awakened and expanded social consciousness respectively employing the term 'awareness' to equate and define 'consciousness'.

Acquired social consciousness is the acceptance of current social conditions as fixed without criticism or a perceived necessity for change. While this position is often considered to be held by people unaware of the social injustice around them, people who do in fact recognize some form of inequality or unfairness may also choose to maintain acquired social consciousness. This choice is the result of the current social structure of power relations being so deeply embedded into the people's reality that it is perceived natural to the extent that any injustice or privilege people experience is not identified as such but, rather, as deserving to them. The system is not challenged for any bias as people choose to physically or psychologically withdraw from any action ([30], pp. 224, 228–229, 233).

Awakened social consciousness is reactive acknowledgement of social injustice and inequalities that exist in the traditional social structure. People in this position have either experienced some form of bias or prejudice or have witnessed other groups being treated unjustly, initiating their reaction to challenge the social system that persists and present alternatives. These people are loyal and determined to their cause and use various resources to promote it ([30], pp. 227, 230–231, 234).

Much like awakened social consciousness, expanded social consciousness is the acknowledgement of inequalities of the current social system, yet unlike the former, people who hold this position are not reactive in their resistance; people are critical and selective in their actions and attempt to act from within the system and not in opposition to it. These people do not make the cause personal and can continuously change their form of resistance based on situational context. Due to this careful selection of action, people are able to expand on the methods in which they can challenge the current social systems, developing new ones ([30], pp. 227, 232, 234–235).

Giddings [30] supports that a person can maintain all three variations of social consciousness concurrently. Moreover, maintaining social consciousness on a particular form of injustice does not suggest social consciousness on other inequalities or bias that may exist within that system, although evidence has proven that once a person has become sensitive to the notion that there is prejudice within the system, that person is more likely to question a traditional position on a social issue. Language, and as an extension the media, is considered a key contributor of information that can develop people's understanding of reality and generate some form of social consciousness.

Therefore, determining the generation of social consciousness through the use of social network sites, as required for this case study, is according to Giddings [30] based on the display of varying characteristics that can in turn divide social consciousness into three subcategories.

10.2.2 Civic Engagement and Citizenship

The notion of civic engagement and citizenship is closely tied to the practice of politics in democratic societies and involves the participation and interest of citizens in the actions of the state for their community. Citizenship does not only include legal benefits and rights within a society but is also a 'form of social agency' ([13], p. 8) or civic engagement. Once a person recognizes that they belong to a social group, the problems or issues of that social group are understood to affect that person as well. Based on the knowledge, motivation and values they maintain, citizens make critical decisions that determine whether or not to take action and what form of action that would, as they perceive it, improve the quality of life of their community or social group ([16], p. vi; [12], p. xxvi). In addition to the aforementioned, which Norris [46] refers to as political knowledge and political participation, she supports that civic engagement also requires trust in the (political) system within the community and its representatives since lack of this trust would discourage any action to improve the community.

If equating civic engagement or citizenship with the perceived notion of social awareness for this case study, characteristics of social awareness are therefore more specialized than those identified by the model provided by Giddings [30].

10.2.3 Social Awareness Defined

As mentioned above, the term 'awareness' is used to define 'consciousness'. Awareness and consciousness are in fact interchangeable; awareness means to be conscious of something, which in turn means to be aware or know something. Consciousness is perhaps more closely associated with a psychological state of mind. On the other hand, awareness denotes the same condition with less relation to psychology embedded in the term. Nevertheless, both adequately address the same situation.

Citizenship and civic engagement correspond more to the expanded social consciousness described by Giddings [30] within a political setting; both require critical thought and decision-making based on knowledge in order to *act* rather than *react* within the social system. The objective of this case study is to determine whether social network sites generate social awareness. The use of civic engagement or citizenship would therefore converge the term into defining a particular form of social awareness, whereas the intention of the research is to first determine if *any* social awareness can be generated and then proceed to categorize it.

In addition, Giddings' three forms of social consciousness introduced should not be misinterpreted as levels of social consciousness; if a person displays acquired social consciousness, this does not mean they are more or less aware of a social issue than a person who displays expanded social consciousness. The difference lies in the way they perceive the problem and the process that they believe is ideal to resolve it.

Considering the above terms, the concept of social awareness is consistent with that of Giddings' social consciousness. Social awareness refers to the individual's outlook or attitude on the realization of a social bias or grievance as well as their opinion on whether any action is required and would be successful in an attempt to amend this grievance. Paradoxically what Giddings fails to expand upon is what the term 'social' includes. The term 'social' refers to everything related to the makeup of a community or society – its politics, history, culture, heritage, property and everything that together constructs the identity of the people and society as a whole. Giddings' case study is concerned with the unequal treatment of people with different ethnic backgrounds in a diverse society that continues to maintain a mainstream culture. Social inequalities or unfair treatment may not just occur on a personal or individual level but may occur through what people regard as an attack on their heritage, culture or property.

10.3 Relevant Literature

10.3.1 Virtual Social Networks

Research into social networks and communities was traditionally bound within a physical environment, but with the advancement of transportation and communication technology, these boundaries have shifted as researchers now consider human mobility and virtual social networks. The transportation infrastructure and the invention of the Internet have altered society's social organization; people who are miles apart can interact with each other on a daily basis, forming strong relationship bonds, an impossible venture in the past. The ability to travel reinforced these relationships with face to face interaction. Qualitative research studies conducted independently by both Hornsby [37] and Bakardjieva [4] are two examples of research that identified the reasons people include Internet use in their daily routine as the need for some form of social interaction without the limitations of distance; people with dispersed social networks due to relocation seek to maintain social ties, people who feel socially isolated due to physical, financial or psychological constrains seek support and friendship, and finally people who lack mental stimulus in their life due to an unchallenging employment or lack of employment wish to engage in stimulating interaction.

10.3.2 Effects on Media

Media outlets and business firms are able to combine forces with other outlets around the world with the goal to reach either a global or a more exclusive dispersed audience. At the same time, there is a shift from mass media outlets to 'new media' or independent outlets found online created by people with no affiliation to large media groups who use the Internet to distribute a message to the rest of the world. The interactive feature of the Internet allows the rest of the world to respond and discuss these messages and make individual judgments on their relevance and validity ([8], pp. 12–13).

In effect, users have created a virtual space, a virtual public sphere where users can debate openly online over various topics, which will then lead to them engaging in 'citizen participation' [46] within society. Public spheres act as a resource of information and knowledge of facts that are beyond the reach of an organized physical society (e.g. city, nation) ([42], p. 18). The use of the Internet as a public sphere has been proven most effective with younger Internet users. For younger Internet users, concern is whether others, particularly politicians, are actually listening to them. The Internet allows them to have a voice, to raise awareness of their own opinions but also to become informed of other positions [14].

The ideal democracy portrayed by the creation of virtual public spheres is challenged when considering access to the Internet is not uniform for all people around the world. This therefore means that the diffusion of information and ideas is also unevenly distributed, hence not quite as democratic ([47], p. 13). Moreover, there is indication that censorship or control of content is implemented. Views that contest power or threaten those highly invested in the Internet are blocked. Chinese authorities block topics such as 'democracy' or 'Tibet' ([50], p. 118) and more recently 'Egypt' [36]. The Iranian government blocked social network sites such as Facebook just prior to the 2009 June elections [11]. Following protests challenging the authenticity of the results in favour of the incumbent government, more international websites were blocked [45], a situation replicated by the government officials in Egypt and Tunisia in the spring of 2011, following civilian mobilization and protest against the ruling regimes [31]. Various business associations have lobbied for the imposition of a global copyright enforcement ([50], p. 119).

10.3.3 Social Network Sites

Social Network Sites (SNS) are

> web-based services that allow individuals to (1) construct a public or semi-public profile within a bounded system, (2) articulate a list of other users with whom they share a connection and (3) view and traverse their list of connections and those made by others within the system ([6], p. 211).

When joining an SNS, people are prompted to create a profile, where they are asked a number of questions describing various personal characteristics (e.g. name, gender, hobbies, religious or political views) that are compiled and made visible within the network. People can then search for people who belong to their social networks and request to include them in their personal network; the primary difference of SNS with other online communities where networks are not necessarily created with people the user already maintains social ties. Profile content and mode of interaction vary between each SNS. Once a profile is created, the names or full profiles of members of a person's social network are viewable by the other members of that person's social network or the whole network, access depending on the design and privacy settings of each SNS. Viewing contacts that belong to other social networks provides an opportunity to recognize more people that can be added to one's own personal social network, increasing the number of contacts one can interact with. In addition, each SNS has developed their site to include features such as the ability to share online videos extracted from other websites, share music, personalize the appearance of profiles, and play online games. Regardless of the attributes that make each SNS distinct from the other and more appealing to SNS users, the main incentive to join an SNS continues to be the ability to interact, albeit loosely, with one's extended social network ([6], pp. 211, 213).

10.3.4 Facebook

Facebook is an SNS created in 2004 by a Harvard University student Mark Zuckerberg and was initially called 'The Facebook'. It was meant solely for use as a social network for Harvard University students. Within a few months however, the site was adjusted and introduced to over 30 universities. By 2005, The Facebook enjoyed membership of students from most universities of the United States and Canada, changed its name to 'Facebook' and officially became a company. Gradually, Facebook enabled membership to high school students, followed by company employees and eventually in mid-2006 to all Internet users around the globe. In 2007, it saw a staggering increase of membership of over 50 million users with an estimated one million people joining every week. Recent estimates are roughly at over 750 active users with 70% of its users located outside of the United States, with India and Brazil representing two of its fastest growing markers [1, 20, 21].

As with other SNS, the main goal of Facebook users is to interact with people of their social network or their friends. A user can select privacy settings that determine who can view their own list of *friends* and their profile [27]. Communication is possible through private messages, through public messages on users' *Wall*s (a feature of a Facebook profile that allows messaging and posting of news and videos for others to see and comment on), through concurrent conversations with friends logged on to Facebook at the same time or through status updates where users inform their friends their current circumstances or thoughts [26].

Development of Facebook saw the addition of a number of features that go beyond simple communications. Online games and activities; sharing of photographs; the creation of groups and specialized profiles to promote events, products, social causes or people; daily horoscopes and virtual gift giving are but a few of these added features [22].

10.3.4.1 Facebook Research

The popularity of Facebook and the loyalty displayed by its users have intrigued a number of scholars from various disciplines including psychology, sociology, anthropology, computer science and business. Business and marketing experts were quick to realize the commercial potential of Facebook resulting in high investment, purchase offers,[1] while social science lagged slightly behind in realizing the significance of Facebook in society. Nevertheless, there is an increasing amount of research and projects that examine the attributes of Facebook from the varying perspectives of these disciplines.

While reviewing social science Facebook literature, the reoccurring topics of research were user privacy, trust and vulnerability with respect to personal information sharing,[2] sociability and social ties,[3] and political participation and activity.

Research on social awareness and Facebook has proved to be limited or rather focused on political campaigns and activities. The earliest research on political awareness determined that the creation of a Facebook Page or profile for a political candidate aspires to connect with the younger voting demographic which is also the demographic with the lowest voting turnout during most elections. The younger

[1] Examples include Rosenbush [53], Delaney et al. [15], and Rosenbush [52].

[2] Examples include Jones and Soltren [39], Cain et al. [7], Fogel and Nehmad [29], Taraszow et al. [55], and Wang et al. [56].

[3] Examples include Ellison et al. [17], Kleck et al. [40], Zywica [58], and Papacharissi and Mendelson [48].

demographic has shifted to new online media more so than any other demographic in society that enables one-to-one interaction or interactivity. A political candidate with a Facebook Page that is frequently updated and that contains more personal information about the candidate as a way to appear more personable and approachable to the users but also includes political facts and links to more information is a candidate who shows interest in the young voters and their preferences ([33], p. 21). Candidate websites with strictly political content and no possibility of interactivity have been met with less enthusiasm by younger age groups because their need to be heard is not met [43].

The debate over the effects of Facebook on election campaigns and voter turnout is continuously examined to this day as are the effects of Facebook and other social media on political change and uprising as seen in the spring of 2011 with the uprising in Egypt whose success was attributed to the use of social media outlets such as Facebook that enabled the spread of the message and organize and mobilize the anti-government groups and campaigns [3, 31]. A recent paper suggested that the shutdown of Internet access as a result of the numerous anti-government groups and campaigns organized online was in fact what mobilized the population, what one can infer as social media indirectly affecting political change [32].

Political participation and civic uprising are examples of expanded and awakened social awareness. This is however in the context of politics. This case study is an attempt to introduce a different social topic that is not directly related to political campaigns as an example in order to determine whether Facebook can generate the variations of social awareness on other issues.

10.4 Research Question and Objectives

The main purpose of Facebook is maintaining social relationships at a physical distance, yet certain features and applications have been developed that make it possible to express and promote concern for social issues to Facebook members. The aim of this research is to address the question of whether social network sites such as Facebook can generate social awareness, the knowledge and understanding of a social inequality that can be manifested in three forms: acquired, awakened and expanded social awareness. Based on the outlook, a person displays action that he or she believes would best amend this inequality. Does use of Facebook, therefore, enable its users to obtain information and knowledge on a particular social issue or concern? Can awareness be generated for a topic that is not directly related or concerned with political campaigns and debates? If so, which forms of awareness can Facebook generate? How do these users act or react? Is membership on Facebook a form of action or reaction? Is Facebook another example of a virtual public sphere where issues can be discussed and debated by people who feel strongly about them but live far apart? Is it also a medium where information on topics can reach users for the first time and generate support, passion or some form of awareness over these topics?

10.5 Methodology

10.5.1 Online Ethnography

Ethnography is a method primarily associated with the discipline of anthropology and traditionally denotes the study of different cultures in remote places. It involves an in-depth study of social life, where the researcher is required to observe various social conditions and interactions during a set amount of time. Ethnography has been adopted by various social sciences to study cultures and social issues of not just remote cultures but any culture. This is due to the suitability of ethnography in researching the intricate notions of culture and social life. Greater access and interaction among cultures has further modified the ethnographic method to focus on particular aspects of the culture rather than a culture as a whole. This way, particular research questions are addressed ([35], pp. 41–42).

Online ethnography, also termed 'netnography', is an adaptation of traditional ethnographic methods for the study of 'cultures and communities emerging through computer mediated communications and uses information publicly available in online forums' ([41], p. 130). According to Kozinets [41], conducting a successful netnography requires the development of an 'entrée' and the collection and analysis of data that do not disregard a set of ethical guidelines. While his own research focuses on consumer behaviour in a marketing setting, he acknowledges that online ethnography can be applied to various disciplines interested in determining and understanding people's needs and influences.

10.5.1.1 The Entrée

An entrée is preliminary research conducted in order to locate appropriate forums or sites that contain data significant to the questions and interests a researcher wishes to explore. Personal interest in social awareness and fascination over Facebook popularity and usage were the initial foundations for developing this study. Knowledge of the Facebook site led to a prompt identification of Facebook sites that would provide relevant data for social awareness. Facebook Pages, Facebook Groups and the independent application of Causes are the three sites accessible within Facebook that allow users to promote a social issue or concern. They are also the key sites where social awareness generation could be studied. In addition, each of these sites includes different features that make them distinct from one another.

Since a number of social issues were available to be examined, it was necessary to focus on one social issue that was not directly related to politics since another goal of this study was to embark on new Facebook research not related to political campaigns. During this preliminary research, there was a coincidental invitation to join a Facebook Cause in favour of the return of the Parthenon Sculptures from the British Museum in London to the new Acropolis Museum recently completed in Athens. This provided an ideal social cause that could serve as the focus for the study. It is rightfully a social issue since the Parthenon Sculptures were removed from the Acropolis of Athens, one of the most important symbols of ancient Greek heritage. However, the artefacts remain in the British Museum which has also presented arguments in favour of keeping the artefacts in their possession, arguments that have also found great support. This study will review Facebook Pages, Groups and Causes promoting the request for the return of the Parthenon Sculptures and how they generate social awareness not only among the Greeks themselves but also to the international Facebook population.

Kozinets [41] suggests that selection of an ideal forum is based on a reasonable amount of membership and on the availability of relevant information. For the particular social cause in addition to high membership, it was also necessary to select a Facebook Page, Cause and Group where information available was primarily in the English language, an indication that the site favours membership not exclusive to Greek speakers but to the international Facebook members.

10.5.1.2 Data Collection and Analysis

Data collection for an online ethnography is a multi-method affair. According to the research questions, a researcher needs to determine the way relevant data can be collected. Nevertheless, participant observation is a characteristic approach for any ethnography. In the case of participant observation, a researcher observes social interactions and may choose to participate at some level. Based on these observations, a researcher can then make certain inferences about the culture. In an online ethnography, the traditional 'fieldwork' is substituted with 'deskwork' where a researcher collects data found on websites rather than while in the 'field' within the community in question ([54], p. 84).

Participant observation in an online ethnography collects data in two forms. The first is a duplication of relevant data directly from the website, while the second is observations of the researcher about the computer-mediated interactions on the site. The participant factor for this study will in fact be limited since the objectives of the study do not require that the researcher gets involved in any computer-mediated interaction.

Conducting interviews is another form of data collection, popular in ethnography, which can collect personal accounts that can further reinforce general observations. For this case study, in addition to the participant observation, semi-structured interviews will be conducted with 12 individuals, a reasonable number for a case study of this size. Since there are three sites where social awareness can in theory be generated, four people will be selected from each site. There is a personal assumption made that Greek members of these sites are more likely to be aware of the social issue prior to Facebook, and therefore, two of the four people from each site will be Greek, while the other non-Greek to determine whether this assumption is valid. In addition, although initial social awareness may already have been generated before Facebook membership, it might be interesting to see whether Facebook has provided further information on the topic even to the Greek members that have shifted their social awareness from one form to another.

Semi-structured interviews are preferred because meeting with the interviewee is likely to occur only once. Questions and topics that the researcher wants to address are predetermined, yet the researcher also provides an atmosphere where the interviewee can further expand on their responses in directions that the researcher may not have considered yet may prove beneficial to the study ([5], p. 212). Ideally, the interviews will take place face-to-face or at least through the technology of software such as Skype, which allows face-to-face interaction mediated through a camera and a microphone. While face-to-face interaction may not favour anonymity of the interviewee, it may enhance intimacy between the interviewee and the researcher who are in fact strangers ([38], p. 26). That way, the interviewee may feel more comfortable answering questions if they can in turn see a researcher with a friendly disposition.

10.5.1.3 Analysis

The analysis of the text is based on the logic of content analysis. The research questions and objectives have already been set. Once the data has been collected or located, the content of the site will be analyzed based on the objectives of the study. In the case of these Facebook sites, it is necessary to consider the presence of static and dynamic qualities. The layout and other features that can be used to promote social awareness are static, yet the ability to upload new items and to engage in discussion suggests that the forums are dynamic and information is added and removed continuously. It was therefore necessary to review material that was posted during a set period of time; the first period was material entered from January 2009 to August 2009, the year the Acropolis Museum was completed, and the second period was material posted from January 2011 to August 2011. Six people were interviewed in 2009 while an additional six in 2011.

The content of these sites is coded and divided into particular themes and topics related to the research objectives ([2], p. 467). Unlike grounded theory, the themes are developed prior to content analysis and do not develop during data collection, although certain modifications may occur ([28], p. 276). A main theme of the analysis focuses on the discussions or opinions posted by various members that may indicate the generation of some form of social awareness. This theme is then broken down to sub-themes based on predetermined categories such as the form of social awareness. Finally, the semi-structured interviews will also be analyzed to determine whether responses obtained correspond to the results of content analysis conducted on the sites and whether they can provide additional information relevant to the research objectives.

10.5.2 Ethics

The main ethical debate with respect to the Internet and computer-mediated communication is what can be classified as public and what as private ([41], p. 134).

Facebook membership is open to anyone who has an e-mail address, and unless access is restricted by the creators of Facebook Groups, all discussions and content can be viewed by every member of Facebook [27]. Therefore, it is possible to deduce that this information is public. Nevertheless, a researcher must be considerate and respectful of people's opinions and views and not manipulate their power to distort facts for the benefit of their research ([41], p. 135).

For this study, there is no participation in the Facebook sites by the researcher to avoid the possibility of directing data to obtain more desirable results. Furthermore, any discussions analyzed are done without reference to names. Finally, interviewees are informed of the objectives of the research and guaranteed anonymity and respect of their views and opinions.

10.5.3 Limitations

Traditional ethnography has always met criticism by scholars who use quantitative research methods for its lack of objectivity and procedure with which to validate research results for accuracy. It can be argued, however, that not all research questions and interests can be answered with calculations and statistics. Ethnography is unique in its ability to provide an in-depth study that considers multifaceted properties of social interactions ([35], p. 41).

Nevertheless, focus on member discussions and opinions and use of semi-structured interviews suggest that there will be extensive use of data that is not generated by the researcher but rather by the members themselves and thus more accurate. The task of the researcher is to 'cautiously' interpret the data (Douglas, 1976, pp. 124–125, cited in [28], p. 276).

10.6 Analysis of Findings

10.6.1 The Return of the Parthenon Sculptures Argument

The Facebook sites reviewed are in support of the return of the Parthenon Sculptures, often referred to as Parthenon Marbles and less so as Elgin Marbles. According to the sample sites, at the start of the nineteenth century, Lord Elgin, the British ambassador to the Ottoman Empire at the time, had purchased the sculptures from the Ottoman authorities governing Athens, for personal display back in Britain. Due to bankruptcy, Lord Elgin was forced to sell the sculptures to the British Museum where they were put on exhibit and where they can be found to this day. At the time of extraction, the sculptures were part of the Acropolis structure and required workers to remove them. There are reports that suggest both the removal process and the transfer to Britain had damaged the sculptures. Accounts of the significance the Greeks placed on these sculptures date back to the uprisings against the Ottoman

Empire where Greek troops chose to surrender rather than endanger the Acropolis when shots were fired too close to the structure.

While sentiments in support of the return have been expressed as far back as 1816, it was not until the 1980s that the Greek government began to actively and officially pursue their return. A main argument of the British Museum was that the Greeks had no place that could preserve the sculptures from the polluted air of Athens. However, recently, the new Acropolis Museum was completed, an attempt by the Greek government to provide an adequate home for the sculptures within metres from their original location.

The British government continues to refuse the Greek government's official request maintaining that their keeping at the British Museum enables a more international public to learn about ancient Greek heritage and history as part of a more 'worldly perspective' rather than just a Greek perspective. The Greek government and other supporters however assert that the return of the sculptures to Athens is a significant return of cultural heritage and a human right.[4]

There are a number of points that can of course be expanded and disputed depending on which position people uphold. The sites are in no way meant to be unbiased or objective; they are in favour of the return of the Parthenon Sculptures to Athens as there are sites in favour of their stay at the British Museum.

10.6.1.1 Site Design

The selected Facebook Group, *Demanding the Return of the Parthenon Marbles to their Rightful Place*[5] with 88,261 current members down from 93,107 in 2009; Facebook Page, *Repatriation of the Parthenon Marbles*[6] with 8,700 Likes up from 6,429 Fans in 2009; and Facebook Cause, *Repatriation of the Parthenon Marbles*[7] with 56,631 members up from 53, 357 in 2009, were selected for analysis.

While the layout of the three sites differs somewhat, all three sites include a *Wall* or *Current Activity* area where members are able to discuss the issue and post material that expresses their opinion on the issue. In addition, each site provides a mission statement or information with some background facts on the issue and photos of the Acropolis and other ancient statues and sculptures.

The differences between the Group and Page are less evident than that of the Cause as Facebook Causes is a third-party application available on Facebook. The

[4] The background provided is an amalgamation of the facts made available to Facebook users on the sites by the site administrators and not the members in order to provide a clear idea of the position the sites maintain.

[5] *Demanding the return of the Parthenon marbles to their rightful place* [18].

[6] *Repatriation of the Parthenon marbles* [19].

[7] *Repatriation of the Pathenon marbles* [51] (previously http://apps.facebook.com/causes/14926?m=3f1cca43 [9]).

main difference between Groups and Pages is in fact the privacy settings that enable Groups to remain private among friends or *open* to the general public, while Pages are public and should be run by official representatives of what the Page is presenting to the broader Facebook audience [23–25]. Nevertheless, because Groups is one of the oldest applications on Facebook, it maintains the most members although it is the only site of the three that has shown a decline in both membership and discussion posts, perhaps because the members have opted to use Pages or Causes for more exposure of their opinions to the public.

The Cause site is directed to causes.com, a website whose mission statement states,

> We're focused on ambitious projects and believe that each day we come to work, we're making the world a better place. We proudly go one step further than not doing evil; we're doing good [10].

It, therefore, focuses on the impact of each site for the particular cause with access to information such as member names (removed from Groups and Pages), members who recruit most members to join and members who have raised funds or donated to the cause, although in the given case it is not applicable, and therefore, the numbers are low, while it also graphs on membership through time. The number of members is then categorized into various levels. With 56,631 members, the cause is currently at level 15, the Rally level, i.e. the number of supporters is equivalent to the number of people that would rally for a cause.

10.6.2 Findings

10.6.2.1 Walls and Discussions

In all three sites, the *Discussions* were less popular venues than the main *Wall* posts for any form of commentary. Irrelevant material was minimal, with the Group displaying the most amount of irrelevant advertising (sale of electronics, mobile telephones, etc.) while the Cause the least, but also the least amount of overall commentary. Although the *Discussions* venue is meant for the initiation of linear discussion or debate, it seems that the main *Wall* is preferred due to the central positioning that enables easier access for reading and posting material.

Common topics were identified in all three sites which ranged from short statements of support to additional historical facts or accounts pertaining to the Parthenon Sculptures, news articles and videos. The Page application allows for comments or media posting that is made by the Page administrator to appear on Fans' newsfeeds, which keeps the topic present in people's minds. At times, the language used by certain members is Greek, although the setup of the sites is primarily English. Use of harsh language and insults towards the opposing stance was also quite frequent but usually met with requests by other members to show greater respect.

Virtual Public Sphere

Interpretation and understanding of data vary with each person. Members may support the return of the Parthenon Sculptures but are often critical of different aspects of the process initiating debates and validating the notion that Facebook is in fact a virtual public sphere. Political affiliations come into play when laying blame for the lack of success on this ongoing issue, historical enthusiasts argue over the labelling of Lord Elgin as a thief of cultural heritage or a lover of antiquity that wanted to remove the sculptures as a safeguard, and people forward petitions in support for the cause while others argue the inefficiency and promote alternative approaches.

In addition, members engage in debates over the actual support of the return of the Parthenon Sculptures; since viewing the commentary it is clear that some members are in fact opposed to this idea,

> […] There is no way that they should be removed from the British Museum as without both Lord Elgin and without the British Museum, there would now be almost no ancient Greek statuary in existence[…] –F.G. (Group)[8]

This highlights the need people have for public spheres and for their opinions to be heard.

10.6.2.2 Generating Social Awareness

As noted in the above descriptions of each site, membership numbers are quite high. However, within the material analyzed for the two designated time periods, there was only one occasion where a person literally voiced out on a *Wall* that they had never heard of the debate over the Parthenon Sculptures prior to Facebook, but have since become avid supporters, direct evidence of social awareness generation. What must also be considered is the observation also mentioned above which suggests that based on the number of comments and discussions in every site versus membership numbers, the majority of members do not participate in commentary or discussions to verbalize their support or any other stance.

The interviews were able to provide evidence of Facebook generating social awareness since four of the non-Greek interviewees were not aware of the debate prior to Facebook and neither was one Greek. If the interviewees are representative of a certain percentage of the members, then Facebook also generates expanded social awareness. The interviews also proved generation of awakened social awareness, which is seen in Facebook comments as well.

[8] While one can argue that Facebook content is public, out of respect, the comments will not be followed by the full names of those who commented, but just the initials, the same discretion exercised on the interviewees.

Expanded Social Awareness

First-Hand Expanded Social Awareness

Three of the 12 interviewees displayed first-hand expanded social awareness, three non-Greeks: P.M., a nutritionist from Australia; J.K., an auditor from the United Kingdom; and G.T., an educator from the United States. All were unaware of the debate and developed different positions on the matter, nevertheless positions triggered by the Facebook invitation.

P.M. had never heard of the issue in the past and was invited to the Cause by a Greek friend. Going through the information available in the Cause site, she decided to join and supports the return of the Parthenon Sculptures:

> P.M.: It's given me new insight…it's a big thing and the more people know, the greater the pressure on the UK to have them returned hopefully sooner rather than later.

Asked whether she believed being a member of a Cause on Facebook would be effective,

> P.M.: Well, that's the objective of Causes isn't it? Definitely time will tell if Facebook can make an impact, but I think we can gradually see it happening every day. It's become part of our lives so someone is going to take notice … just hope that it's sooner rather than later.

G.T. was invited to the Cause by a colleague and found the material available on the site compelling,

> G.T.: Other countries are returning artefacts to their point of origin, I don't see why the UK should be any different and I think their position is in fact weakening. The British public seems to lean in favour for their return as well!

J.K. had visited the British Museum in London and saw the display of the Parthenon Sculptures, yet he was not aware of the running debate. Unlike P.M., however, his response to the invitation was in fact to further research the position of the British Museum and other media outlets so he can know both sides of the debate. While acknowledging that the arguments may have been expressed by other people in the Group, he chose to do his own personal research and concluded that he does not agree with the permanent return of the Parthenon Sculptures, but perhaps for their loan.

> J.K.: I think it is a great privilege to be able to see the Parthenon Marbles at the British Museum. Granted it is not British history, but it is important for us (British) to know about the history of other places. Plus, so many people from around the world come to the BM, so there's no doubt that history is still passed on and I think that in the end that's what is really important.

He remained a member of the Group because of his partial support and the fact that he enjoyed reading different opinions on the matter. He has since come to question his opinion based on a claim made by another member of the Group that there is evidence the sculptures are not properly maintained at the British Museum:

> J.K.: Another few members commented that the way the Marbles are cared for is somewhat negligent on the BM's part. I am curious to know more about that. That's a troubling thought; something that would make me think twice about where I stand…If the Greek museum can care for them better then maybe it is time…

According to Giddings' [30] expanded social awareness, both positions displayed social awareness. Both spent time to research an issue they had not known about and chose to support it. J.K. was particularly critical and sought other forms of media (perhaps driven to some extent by the need to defend the official position held by his home country, which is in opposition to the one held by the Group) although ultimately was greatly affected by the arguments on Facebook.

Expanded Social Awareness by Association

A.W. is an architect from the United States who through the years has developed an interest in lobbying on behalf of social or environmental concerns. He is a firm supporter of the return of indigenous remains and artefacts back to the indigenous people from which they originated. He had joined Facebook sites in support of this position, and it was through these sites that he learned of the Parthenon Marbles debate. He then voluntarily searched for sites in support of the return of the Parthenon Marbles. For A.W., the argument in favour of the return of indigenous artefacts extends to the Greeks and any other culture in this situation:

> A.W.: This issue affects anyone with a 19th century museum carrying items removed during the 'exploration of the world' by the west and the cultures that have lost important artefacts…it calls into question what the function and responsibility of the museum is in a globalised society with cheap travel and sophisticated telecommunications.

A.W., therefore, already held an opinion on the return of artefacts to indigenous tribes and found similarities in the plea for the return of the Parthenon Marbles. He also believes that being a fan of a Facebook Page is a form of lobbying for the cause and a space where various input on the matter can become readily available to the public.

The choice of A.W. to become a member of a Facebook Page and to view it as a form of action is representative of a person with expanded social awareness. While Facebook did not generate his general awareness on ownerships of artefacts as heritage, Facebook did generate expanded social awareness on the specific case of the Parthenon Marbles, thus expanded social awareness by association. Based on this rationale, it is possible that references of other social issues within the sites in support of the return of the sculptures could generate expanded social awareness by association for other existing debates. Moreover, this extension of support corresponds with Giddings' observation that people who display social awareness over an issue are more likely to sense and understand another concern.

Presence of Expanded Social Awareness

Interviewee M.K. from Lamia, Greece, was familiar with the request for the repatriation of the Parthenon Sculptures, but when interviewed, she expressed how she thought that Facebook activity in these Pages and Groups was necessary to impose pressure on the British Museum and government.

> M.K: To use Facebook means that you are using any media available to voice your demands and I urge people to do the same…don't just join a Group with like-minded people though… become Friends with the British Museum and voice your demands to them.

In this case, although we do not see Facebook generating awareness in her case, we see expanded social awareness in effect.

Awakened Social Awareness

The key difference between expanded social awareness and awakened social awareness is *action* versus *reaction*. While people displaying expanded social awareness believe that joining a site, which favours the return of the sculptures, is a form of participation that would favour the cause, awakened social awareness is in search for alternatives to obtain this return, using Facebook as an outlet.

A topic that has appeared on the *Wall* of all three sites studied is that of 'No Marbles, no Flame'. It is a relatively new movement that promotes an ultimatum approach rather than a request to the British government: either the British Museum returns the sculptures, or the Olympic Flame will not be handed over to the 2012 Olympic Summer Games host city, London. The logic behind this movement is that since both the Olympic Games and the Parthenon Sculptures originate from Greece, the Olympic Flame should not be allowed to be transferred to the Olympic Games of 2012 in London unless the sculptures are returned. The Olympic Flame holds symbolic significance at the games. Traditionally, the Olympic Flame is lit at the site of the ancient Olympic Games in Olympia, Greece, and is then transferred to the modern host city where an opening ceremony culminates with the lighting of the flame to mark the commencement of the games. It would therefore cause great upset if the flame was not present. Whether the Greek people or government has any legal power to actually engage in such an act however is questionable since the Olympic Games are an international organization not run by Greece.

The responses from members of these sites vary. Some, including M.F. who specifically comments on the topic in her interview, do not agree with this approach.

> M.F.: […] I don't think that this is the way to get the message across. It's almost like a threat, a threatening compromise, but it shouldn't be […]

Others have in fact expressed their support. The YouTube video uploaded by the administrator of the Facebook Page titled 'No Marbles, No Flame'[9] has 52 Likes and comments from Greeks and non-Greeks in favour of the idea, including the simply put,

> No marbles, no flame. I like that idea. –C.M. (Page)

This reaction to the unsuccessful attempts of the Greek government to bring back the structures is in fact representative of awakened social awareness. The comment above implies that perhaps this person did not know of this alternative. Also, it is likely that some of the 52 Likes and others that did not respond to it at all had not known either, yet approve of this idea. Therefore, Facebook can generate awakened social awareness.

G.L. claims that her lack of interest in Greek politics is the reason that she could not recollect the Parthenon Sculptures debate. After being invited to the Group, she also saw that others had expressed this position, and she has since supported it,

[9] To see the video: http://www.youtube.com/watch?v=LqC2EMIDec4&feature=player_embedded

joining other Groups created to solely promote this ideology, generating her awakened social awareness,

> G.L.: I saw someone post a comment about this. I thought finally, a good idea! If a Greek person like myself could forget this existed, then that's bad that I forgot, but have we done enough to keep it in focus all the time?[…] A request will not make anything happen. We shouldn't have to request if it's rightfully ours, right? Too much waiting around as always. Eventually someone has to say 'hello, we mean business' and we need to get the world to listen!

Acquired Social Awareness

The final form of social awareness suggested by Giddings is that of acquired social awareness. In this case, if a person perceives some injustice, then they believe that nothing can or should be done about it. The sites were not able to determine whether Facebook generates this form of awareness, although it does validate its presence. One Greek member's comment on the Facebook Group translates,

> There is no real point in arguing about this guys, it's good to hope, but realistically this won't happen –L.V. (Page)

I.S. from Athens and G.D. from Piraeus and currently residing in the UK also present acquired social awareness since although they support the idea of their return, they truthfully do not believe it will be to any avail,

> I.S.: I don't think this (the return) will happen ever. It is a good idea, I like it, I really do, but I simply don't think it can happen and I haven't been convinced otherwise.

> G.D: We know that the British Museum will not let them go and legally, I have reviewed the laws in the UK, there is no legal way to get them back. I am a supporter of this cause that's why I took the time to see the legal side of it and honestly, unless they have a change of heart and just hand them over, I do not think we have a chance.

10.6.2.3 Silent Support

Interviewee M.F. called attention to how taking part in discussions or making comments is not the only indication of true support or commitment by the members; a marketing assistant working in Athens, M.F., was well aware of this issue prior to joining the Facebook Cause. She does not find it necessary however to discuss the topic with other members because for her, support is shown by simply being a *member* of the Cause.

> M.F.: […]me being a member shows my support[…] Numbers are important[…] if it is organized and it is a reasonable case, then it will affect it because people, the right people, the officials will eventually see how many people support it.

Social awareness is not generated in the case of M.F., but she informs us that her choice to join the Cause was in fact selective since she wanted to join an organized cause that would efficiently promote this social concern in order for it to be taken seriously.

Most members do not comment or discuss their position on the sites; the Facebook Page has the additional feature to add a 'Like' on something as a way to show support without having to verbalize it, and Causes tracks the number of people each person has recruited to show a person's contribution. If a certain percentage of members think like M.F., then their membership is evidence of their support for this cause.

The three additional interviewees – I.F. from Thessaloniki, Greece, and two non-Greeks, B.D. from Serbia, and F.S. from Italy – share this opinion:

> I.F.: They have my support, I am there, but it isn't necessary for me to repeat what is already said. I am aware of the problem, but I do not receive the information first, so I give others my voice and they have my **support**.
>
> B.D.: I am familiar with the issue and I think that keeping up to date and being a fan of the Page shows my support.
>
> F.S: I made a comment on the Group when I first joined, to say that you have my support, Greece, but I don't get involved. I think numbers speak for themselves and if I am called to sign a petition now and again, I do.

10.7 Discussion

The analysis of the data collection concluded that social awareness can in fact be generated with the use of Facebook. More precisely, there is direct evidence that supports the presence and generation of expanded and awakened social awareness but only the presence and not generation of acquired social awareness. One can, however, assume that because membership consists of a number of people with various opinions on the matter, it is possible that Facebook could also generate acquired social awareness, and a relevant limitation of this study is in fact the size of the sample group interviewed; ideally, a larger sample could provide a wider perspective on the issue at hand and perhaps lead to a trend of similar responses that would validate the interviewee positions. However, in the case of acquired social awareness, this may still prove difficult to detect since acquired social awareness is in *inaction*.

Furthermore, the analysis determined that even Facebook sites that express obvious support over a specific topic such as the return of the Parthenon Marbles can be converted into a virtual public sphere. Commentary is not just limited to support and internal debates over the most effective support of this cause; members include users who are in fact opposed to the return but are in search of a space where they can express their opinions and discuss with the opposition.

With respect to the differences between this study and studies carried out that focus on political campaigns and activity, it is clear that awareness has not resulted in uprisings and demonstrations; in reality, it is not an issue that affects the daily lives of citizens as political issues do, nor does it affect their opinions on who to vote or if they should vote, especially since supporters do not reside in the same country.

Nonetheless, this does not suggest that generating social awareness will not at some point make an impact for the campaign.

What must be noted, however, is the growth of support for this cause; while membership in two of the three sites has increased, the rate of growth in 2011 is considerably lower than in 2009 as is the amount of discussion and material posted on the sites. This can be due to the fact that in 2009, the completion of the new Acropolis museum gave a push for a long withstanding debate to resurface, and while petitions and support is maintained, there is concern that after 2 years the cause is losing steam since the position of the British Museum or British government has not been affected. Furthermore, like political issues, events can change the degree of motivation for action; since the new Acropolis museum is in fact less new every day and thus less newsworthy, coupled with the current political and economic problems in Greece has shifted focus on other issues and thus shifted support, which is something motivators and site administrators should always consider. Nevertheless, generating social awareness on Facebook continues to take place.

10.8 Conclusion

This case study was an attempt to determine, with data collected directly from the social network site Facebook and a small group of interviewees, whether social awareness can develop as a result of Facebook use for an issue not directly related to politics.

Facebook offers its members three application options or sites that can promote support for various topics, which include the Page application, the Cause application and the Group application. Data analysis concluded that social awareness over the return (or repatriation) of the Parthenon Sculptures can in fact be generated; although as expected the majority of Greek interviewees were already familiar with the cause, the majority of non-Greek interviewees had not been aware of the existing debate even though two had in fact visited the sculptures at the British Museum. The design of Facebook to function as a social media tool enabled the use of friends to form connections that inform people about topics they would have never heard of otherwise.

It is not quite clear the impact Facebook or social network sites will play on issues less critical to its users than the political fate of a nation and its people but complex enough to require the cooperation and action of more than one nation and resolution of conflicting perspectives. In the case of the Parthenon Sculptures, the campaign has been ongoing for decades, and it has now entered the age of network society, the expected step to keep the campaign alive.

Acknowledgements I would like to thank Dr. Alessia Cogo at the University of Southampton (previously University of Surrey) who, as my supervisor, supported the research that resulted in the completion of my thesis of which this chapter is an extension.

References

1. Ahmad, A. (2011). Social network sites and its popularity. *International Journal of Research and Reviews in Computer Science, 2*(2), 522–526.
2. Alexander, V. D. (2008). Analyzing visual materials. In N. Gilbert (Ed.), *Researching social life* (3rd ed., pp. 462–481). London: Sage.
3. Attia, A. M., Aziz, N., Friedman, B., & Elhusseiny, M. F. (2011). Commentary: The impact of social networking tools on political change in Egypt's "Revolution 2.0". *Electronic Commerce Research and Applications, 10*(4), 369–374.
4. Bakardjieva, M. (2005). *Internet society: The internet in everyday life*. Thousand Oaks, CA: Sage.
5. Bernard, H. R. (2006). Interviewing: Unstructured and semi-structured. In H. R. Bernard (Ed.), *Research methods in anthropology: Qualitative and quantitative approaches* (4th ed., pp. 210–250). Walnut Creek, CA: AltaMira Press.
6. Boyd, D. M., & Ellison, N. (2007). Social network sites: History and scholarship. *Journal of Computer-Mediated Communication, 13*(1), 210–230.
7. Cain, J., Scott, D., & Akers, P. (2009). Pharmacy students' Facebook activity and opinions regarding accountability and e-professionalism. *American Journal of Pharmaceutical Education, 73*(6), 104.
8. Castells, M. (2006). The network society: From knowledge to policy. In M. Castells & G. Cardoso (Eds.), *The network society: From knowledge to policy* (pp. 3–21). Washington, DC: Johns Hopkins Center for Transatlantic Relations.
9. *Causes on Facebook: Repatriation of the Parthenon Marbles*. (n.d.). Retrieved August 30, 2009, from Facebook: http://apps.facebook.com/causes/14926?m=3f1cca43
10. *causes.com: Anyone can change the world*. (2011). Retrieved July 11, 2011, from causes.com: Anyone can change the world: http://www.causes.com/about
11. CNN.com. (2009, May 23). *Report: Iran blocks Facebook ahead of presidential election*. Retrieved July 10, 2009, from CNN.com: http://edition.cnn.com/2009/WORLD/meast/05/23/iran.elections.facebook/index.html
12. Colby, A., & Ehlrich, T. (2000). Introduction: Higher education and the development of civic responsibility. In T. Ehlrich (Ed.), *Civic responsibility and higher education* (pp. xxi–xliii). Phoenix, AZ: Oryx Press.
13. Dahlgren, P. (2007). Introduction: Youth, civic engagement and learning via new media. In P. Dahlgren (Ed.), *Young citizens and new media: Learning for democratic participation* (pp. 1–18). New York: Routledge.
14. Dahlgren, P., & Olsson, T. (2007). From public sphere to civic culture: Young citizen's internet use. In R. Butsch (Ed.), *Media and public spheres* (pp. 198–209). New York: Palgrave Macmillan.
15. Delaney, K. J., Buckman, R., & Guth, R. A. (2006, September 21). Facebook, riding a web trend, flirts with a big-money deal. *The Wall Street Journal, 248*(69), p. A1.
16. Ehlrich, T. (2000). Preface. In T. Ehlrich (Ed.), *Civic responsibility and higher education* (pp. v–x). Phoenix, AZ: Oryx Press.
17. Ellison, N. B., Steinfeld, C., & Lampe, C. (2007). The benefits of Facebook "friends": Social capital and college students' use of online social network sites. *Journal of Computer-Mediated Communication, 12*, 1143–1168.
18. Facebook. (n.d.). *Demanding the return of the Parthenon marbles to their rightful place*. Retrieved August 22/30, 2009/2011, from Facebook: https://www.facebook.com/group.php?gid=2234360214
19. Facebook. (2009). *Repatriation of the Parthenon marbles*. Retrieved August 30, 2009/2011, from Facebook: https://www.facebook.com/ParthenonSculptures
20. Facebook. (2011a). *Statistics*. Retrieved June 2011, from Facebook: https://www.facebook.com/press/info.php?statistics

21. Facebook. (2011b). *Timeline*. Retrieved July 16, 2011, from https://www.facebook.com/press/info.php?timeline
22. Facebook Help Center. (2011a). *Application basics*. Retrieved July 16, 2011, from Facebook: https://www.facebook.com/help?page=1095
23. Facebook Help Center. (2011b). *Chat*. Retrieved July 16, 2011, from Facebook: https://www.facebook.com/help?topic=chatclient
24. Facebook Help Center. (2011c). *Facebook help center – Frequent answers and questions*. Retrieved July 16, 2011, from Facebook: https://www.facebook.com/help/search/?q=Groups+and+Pages
25. Facebook Help Center. (2011d). *Messages – Facebook help center*. Retrieved June 16, 2011, from Facebook: https://www.facebook.com/help/?topic=messages_and_inbox
26. Facebook Help Center. (2011e). *Wall: How to use the Wall feature and Wall privacy – Facebook help center*. Retrieved July 16, 2011, from Facebook: https://www.facebook.com/help?page=820
27. Facebook Help Center. (2011f). *Data use policy*. Retrieved June 2011, from https://www.facebook.com/full_data_use_policy
28. Fielding, N. (2008). Ethnography. In N. Gilbert (Ed.), *Researching social life* (3rd ed., pp. 266–284). London: Sage.
29. Fogel, J., & Nehmad, E. (2009). Internet social network communities: Risk taking, trust, and privacy concerns. *Computers in Human Behaviour, 25*(1), 153–160.
30. Giddings, L. S. (2005). A theoretical model of social consciousness. *Advances in Nursing Science, 28*(3), 224–239.
31. Harb, Z. (2011, May). Arab revolutions and the social media effect. *M/C Journal*. Retrieved June 2011, from http://journal.media-culture.org.au/index.php/mcjournal/article/view/364
32. Hassanpour, N. (2011). Media disruption exacerbates revolutionary unrest: Evidence from Mubarak's natural experiment. In F. H. Honig (Ed.), *American Political Science Association (APSA)* (p. 43), Washington, DC.
33. Hayes, R. (2008). Providing what they want and need on their own turf: Social networking, the Web and young voters. In *unCONVENTIONal* (pp. 1–26). San Diego, CA: NCA 94th Annual Convention 2008.
34. Hill, S. (2009, April 8). World Wide Webbed: The Obama campaign's masterful use of the internet. *Social Europe Journal, 4*(2). Retrieved June 3, 2009, from http://www.social-europe.eu/2009/04/world-wide-webbed-the-obama-campaign%e2%80%99s-masterful-use-of-the-internet/
35. Hine, C. (2000). *Virtual ethnography*. London: Sage.
36. Ho, S. (2011, January 31). *China blocks some internet reports on Egypt protests*. Retrieved June 2011, from Voice of America: http://www.voanews.com/english/news/China-Blocks-Some-Internet-Reports-on-Egypt-Protests-114925514.html
37. Hornsby, A. M. (2004). Surfing the net for community: A Durkheimian analysis of electronic gatherings. In P. Kivisto (Ed.), *Illuminating social life* (3rd ed., pp. 59–91). London: Pine Forge Press.
38. Johnson, A. N. (2005). Internet behavior and the design of virtual methods. In C. Hine (Ed.), *Virtual methods: Issues in social research on the internet* (pp. 21–34). Oxford, UK: Sage.
39. Jones, H., & Soltren, J.-H. (2005). *Facebook threats to privacy*. Cambridge, MA: MIT.
40. Kleck, C. A., Reese, A. C., Behnken, D. Z., & Sundar, S. S. (2007). *The company you keep and the image you project: Putting your best face forward in online social networks. Creating communication: Content, control, critique*. Paper presented at the 57th Annual Conference of the International Communication Association, San Francisco, CA, pp. 1–30.
41. Kozinets, R. V. (2006). Netnography 2.0. In R. W. Belk (Ed.), *Handbook of qualitative research methods in marketing* (pp. 129–142). Cheltenham, UK: Edward Elgar Publishing.
42. Lee, S., & Chib, A. (2007). *Finding the missing links: A social networks framework for community development*. Communicating Worldviews: Faith-Intellect-Ethics, Paper presented at the 93rd Annual NCA Convention, Chicago, pp. 1–35.

43. Livingstone, S. (2007). Interactivity and participation on the internet: Young people's response the civic sphere. In P. Dahlgren (Ed.), *Young citizens and new media: Learning for democratic participation* (pp. 103–124). New York: Routledge.
44. McKeever, C. (2008). *Obama and Hillary use Twitter for social networking*. Retrieved March 10, 2009, from OpenSourceMarketer: http://opensourcemarketer.com/obama-and-hillary-use-twitter-for-social-networking/
45. Niosi, M. (2009, June 13). *Lights turned off on media after elections*. Retrieved July 12, 2009, from France24.com: http://www.france24.com/en/20090613-lights-turned-off-media-after-elections-iran-youtube-facebook-censorship
46. Norris, P. (2003). *Digital divide: Civic engagement, information poverty and the internet worldwide*. Cambridge, UK: Cambridge University Press.
47. Papacharissi, Z. (2002). The virtual sphere: The internet as a public sphere. *New Media & Society, 4*(1), 9–27.
48. Papacharissi, Z., & Mendelson, A. (2011). Toward a new(er) sociability: Uses, gratifications and social capital on Facebook. In S. Papathanassopoulos (Ed.), *Media perspectives for the 21st century* (pp. 212–230). Oxon, UK: Routledge.
49. Quily, P. (2008, November 5). *Barack Obama Vs. John McCain social media and search engine scorecard*. Retrieved March 10, 2009, from Adult ADD Strengths: http://adultaddstrengths.com/2008/11/05/obama-vs-mccain-social-media/
50. Ray, L. (2007). *Globalization and everyday life*. New York: Routledge.
51. *Repatriation of the Parthenon marbles: causes.com*. (2011). Retrieved June 30, 2011, from causes.com: Anyone can change the world: http://www.causes.com/causes/14926-repatriation-of-the-parthenon-marbles
52. Rosenbush, S. (2009, March 11). Facebook's on the block. *BusinessWeekOnline*, Retrieved March 11, 2009, from http://www.businessweek.com/technology/content/mar2006/tc20060327_215976.htm
53. Rosenbush, S. (2009, March 11). Facebook's changing fortunes. *BusinessWeek Online*. Retrieved March 11, 2009, from http://www.businessweek.com/technology/content/oct2006/tc20061031_832999.htm
54. Rutter, J., & Smith, G. W. (2005). Ethnographic presence in a nebulous setting. In C. Hine (Ed.), *Virtual methods: Issues in social research on the internet* (pp. 81–92). Oxford, UK: Berg.
55. Taraszow, T., Aristodemou, E., Shitta, G., Laouris, Y., & Arsoy, A. (2010). Disclosure of personal and contact information by young people in social networking sites: An analysis using Facebook™ profiles as an example. *International Journal of Media and Cultural Politics, 6*(1), 81–101.
56. Wang, Y., Norrice, G., & Cranor, L. (2011). Who is concerned about what? A study of American, Chinese and Indian users' privacy concerns on social network sites. In J. McCune, B. Balacheff, A. Perrig, A.-R. Sadeghi, A. Sasse, & Y. Beres (Eds.), *Trust and trustworthy computing* (Vol. 6740, pp. 146–153). Berlin/Heidelberg: Springer.
57. Wolman, D. (2008, October 20). Cairo activists use Facebook to rattle regime. *Wired*.
58. Zywica, J. (2008). The faces of Facebookers: Investigating social enhancement and social compensation hypotheses; predicting Facebook and offline popularity from sociability and self-esteem and mapping the meanings of popularity with semantic networks. *Journal of Computer-Mediated Communication, 14*, 1–34.

Chapter 11
Markov Random Field and Social Networks

Stelios Zimeras

Department of Statistics and Actuarial-Financial Mathematics, University of the Aegean, G.R. 83200 Karlovassi, Samos, Greece, zimste@aegean.gr

Abstract A Markov random field (MRF) is composed of 2D or 3D Markov chains providing spatial homogeneity in some sense. Markov random fields are reviewed and investigated as models of that kind of models. In a matter of graphs, spatial interactions between nodes defining local conditionals in regions denote Markov networks. These models are the set of sites, with a certain probability structure to the possible labeling of those sites.

Physical properties of the neighbors could be explained by partial differential equation (PDE) inside the potential function introducing PDE-MRF models. In Bayesian analysis, they have been used to describe the local characteristics of the spatial interaction between sites introducing Bayesian networks. A social network is a social structure constructing nodes, which are connected by one or more specific types of interdependency. When the nodes are explained by conditional probability modeling between them, in that case a connection between MRF and social networks could be established, to identify the local connectivity.

In this work, spatial behavior of the MRF models in nonrectangular lattice would be investigated. MRF models called PDE-MRF models are introduced based on the total variation of the region, considering smoothness assumptions. Finally, the Markov assumptions to deal with social network models are generalized and are discussed; some classes of estimations have been introduced using the Gibbs sampler.

Keywords Markov random fields • Autoexponential model • Social networks • Gibbs sampler • Partial differential equations • Mean field

A.A. Lazakidou (ed.), *Virtual Communities, Social Networks and Collaboration*, Annals of Information Systems 15, DOI 10.1007/978-1-4614-3634-8_11,

11.1 Introduction

Stochastic models and statistical methods have been successfully applied in Bayesian modeling and Markov networks. As network may be defined as a homogeneous graph region with connections between nodes under irregular lattice system. Spatial variations over the subparts of the graph network introduce conditional probabilities between nodes.

In that point of view, connectivity between different nodes must be introduced leading us to spatial connectivity between levels' regions. Spatial connectivity includes neighborhood structure between regions, where investigation of that structure includes modeling of the spatial homogeneity. The last could be illustrated by using spatial modeling techniques (like spatial autocorrelation, partition functions, and multilevel models). Spatial investigation involves stochastic modeling especially in cases where the incomplete data involves hidden information. Stochasticity could be introduced as the randomness of our data.

So incompleteness (hidden information) leads us to the meaning of stochasticity where incomplete information could be explained (and modeled) by adding particular functions, which explain a large amount of information introducing a new modeling.

The Bayesian approach to reconstruction in spatial processes involves the modeling of prior information as local characteristics of the spatial process, introducing Markov random field [5, 17]. The prior component usually involves unknown prior parameters which control the influence of the prior distribution. In many applications, appropriate values for these parameters will be found by *trial and error*; in other cases, a fully Bayesian approach will be adopted and the prior parameters estimated in the same way as other model parameters. However, in all these cases, it is expected that the procedures depend *smoothly* on the prior parameters and that there is a unique relationship between the parameters and different types of behavior of the process introducing influence of partial differential operators (PDE-MRF models). Models based on Markov random fields can be used to extract statistical information about the structure of real-world phenomena which could be represented in some sense as textures [14]; Cross and Jain [8], Qian and Titterington [22], and Ranngarajan and Chellappa [23] used these models to generate texture images from the autobinomial model, and Spitzer [26] investigated the Markov random field models defining general properties using the definitions of random fields and Gibbs random fields.

Social network analysis is the study of social relations among a set of social nodes (defined as actors). Network analysis takes the global relation of social structures based on the spatial variability between patterns of relationships derived from individual connectivity.

Relational data, such as social networks, can be modeled as a pairwise Markov random field (MRF) [27]. In particular, each actor's attribute in the social network is a random variable in the MRF, and each actor-actor link is considered as a pairwise dependency between two random variables. Inference on the MRF can be used for classification of the missing attributes in the data. To the best of our knowledge, MRFs which use the dependencies coming not only from the observed friendship links but also from the observed affiliations have not been applied to classification tasks in social networks. Yet, the affiliation network structure provides rich dependencies which go beyond pairwise.

A particular subclass of Markov random fields is the automodels, introduced in [5] and further studied in [2, 6, 8, 31, 33]. In practice, estimates using Bayesian methods cannot be computed analytically. For this reason, Monte Carlo algorithms can be used to generate samples from the posterior distribution and parameter estimates calculated from this sample. The fundamental idea is to use an algorithm, which generates a discrete time Markov chain converging to the desired distribution. The most common algorithms include the Gibbs sampler [11] and the Metropolis–Hasting algorithm [16, 17]. Applications of these methods cover a wide range of areas including detection of lesions in medical imaging [3], astronomy [24], medical biology [9, 33], and medical imaging in SPECT [4, 12, 29, 31, 33]. In this work, spatial behavior of the MRF models in nonrectangular lattice would be investigated, concentrating on the first-order neighborhood structures. New MRF models called PDE-MRF models are introduced based on the total variation of the region, considering smoothness assumptions. Finally, the Markov assumptions to deal with these kind of social network models are generalized and are discussed; some classes of estimations have been introduced using the Gibbs sampler.

11.2 Markov Random Fields Modeling

Markov random fields (MRFs) are popular for modeling regions (uniform or nonuniform). They are able to express a region based on the local spatial characteristics. These models assume that the intensity of each node depends on the intensities of only the neighborhood. Theoretically, this assumption forms a homogeneous region. The most important characteristic of these models is that the global representation of the region can be formed as a stochastic propagation of interactions defining a local neighborhood structure. In this section, basic definitions and notations are given, which were introduced by Aykroyd et al. [2], Besag [5, 6] and Cross and Jain [8]. The reader is directed to these papers for further details.

Markov random field (MRF) theory enables the modeling of contextual dependencies between a set of sites S. These sites might be pixels in an image or individuals in a social network. Suppose that we have a two-dimensional space, S, which has been partitioned into n nodes, labeled by the integers $\Lambda_i = \{1, 2, \ldots, n\}$ defined as state space. Each node variable can be discrete (finite or infinite) or continuous. We refer to the possible values of the node variable as intensities. A lattice is a set of sites or nodes in a graph. A region with m rows and n columns can be represented as an $m \times n$ rectangular lattice, where each site corresponds to a node in the graph.

An $m \times n$ lattice is written as a set of indices: $S = \{(i,j) | 1 \leq i \leq m, 1 \leq j \leq n\}$ or using a single index as: $S = \{i | 1 \leq i \leq m \times n\}$. Denote the sites of a lattice S, with a variable

X_i at each site $i \in S$. Let X_i be a random variable assigned to a node x_i and $\mathbf{X}=\{X_i, i\in S\}$ be a random variable vector for a region; then an intensity $\mathbf{x}=\{x_i, i\in S\}$, with $x_i \in \Lambda_i$, can be assumed as a realization of $\mathbf{X}$, such as $X_i=x_i$, $x_i \in \Lambda_i \subset \mathrm{R}$, $\forall\, i\in S$. The function $p(x_i|\ldots)$ denotes the conditional probability distribution (or density function) of X_i given the other arguments. The configuration space for the variable $\boldsymbol{x}$ is denoted by Ω with: $\Omega = \prod_{i\in S}\Lambda_i$. For simplicity, each node of the finite lattice can take colors from the set $\Lambda=\{0, 1, 2,\ldots, c-1\}$. A region is modeled by defining each node in the graph as a random variable $\{X_i, i\in S\}$ and the gray level associated with the node equal to the value x_i. Let $p(\mathbf{X}=\mathbf{x})$ be the joint probability density (jpd) measure on Ω with $p(\mathbf{X}=\mathbf{x})>0$ $\forall \mathbf{x}\in \Omega$. Besag [5] proved that the jpd $p(\mathbf{X}=\mathbf{x})$ is uniquely determined by its local conditional probability density function $p(x_i \mid x_j, j\neq i) = p(X_i = x_i \mid X_j = x_j, j\neq i)$, $i\in S$, $\mathbf{x}\in \Omega$. To define a Markov random field, a neighborhood structure N is needed, which defines the range of interaction from one node to another. A neighborhood system $N=\{N_i, \forall\, i\in S\}$ is a collection of subsets of S for which (1) $i\notin N_i$ (a site is not part of its neighborhood) and (2) $j \in N_i \Leftrightarrow i \in N_j$ (i is in the neighborhood of j if and only if j is in the neighborhood of i). In general, $\forall\, s\in S$: $s=(i,j)$, an nth-order homogeneous neighborhood system could be defined as $N^n = \left\{N_{(i,j)} : (i,j)\in S\right\}$ and $N^n_{(i,j)} = \left\{(k,l)\in S : (k-i)^2 + (l-j)^2 \leq n\right\}$.

For a regular lattice, the set of neighbors of i is defined as the set of sites within a radius of $\sqrt{r}$ from i, $N_i = \left\{j\in S \mid \left[\operatorname{dist}(j-i)\right]^2 \leq r, j\neq i\right\}$, where dist($i$,$j$) denotes the Euclidean distance between i and j and r takes an integer value. Obviously, sites near the boundary have fewer neighbors than interior ones (free boundary condition). Furthermore, $N^0 \equiv S$ for all $n\geq 0$: $N^n \subset N^{n+1}$. Considering conditional probabilities on lattices, site j is said to be a neighbor of site i ($\neq j$) if and only if the functional form of the conditional probability distribution of X_i given all other node values depends upon x_j [6]. The form of neighbors for each site can be defined as $p(x_i \mid x_1, x_2,\ldots, x_{i-1}, x_{i+1},\ldots, x_n) = p(x_i \mid x_{\partial i})$, where ∂i is the set of nodes which are neighbors of site i and $x_{\partial i}$ the set of values of nodes which are neighbors of node x_i. The usual neighborhood system in region analysis defines the first-order neighbors of a node as the four nodes sharing a side with the given node (Fig. 11.1). Higher order neighbors are defined in an analogous manner.

A clique C is a subset of S for which every pair of sites is neighbors. Single node is also considering cliques. The set of all cliques on a lattice is called C. Cliques are important when considering the equivalence between MRFs and the Gibbs distribution. Figure 11.2 illustrates the set of cliques for the first-order or nearest-neighbor system with forms $\{(i, j)\}$, $\{(i-1, j), (i, j)\}$, $\{(i, j-1), (i, j)\}$ (Fig. 11.2).

Let S^n denote the lattice points in n-dimensional space, not necessarily finite. For two points, x_i and x_j in S^n, $\mid x_i - x_j \mid$ is the Euclidean distance between

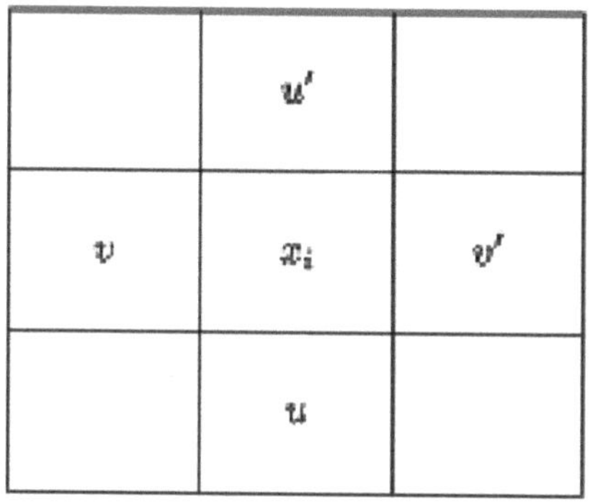

Fig. 11.1 First-order neighbors

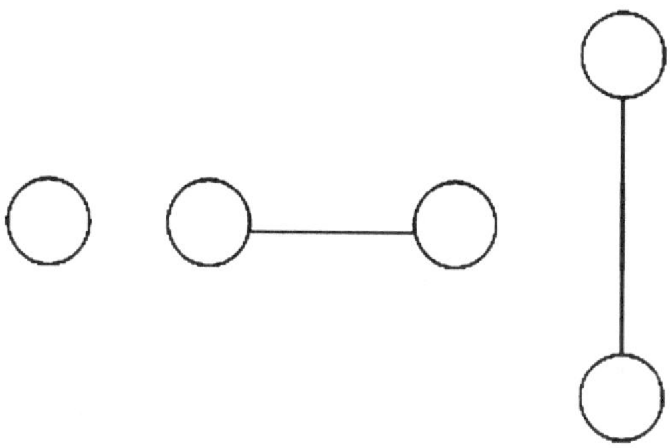

Fig. 11.2 Clique type for first-order neighbors system

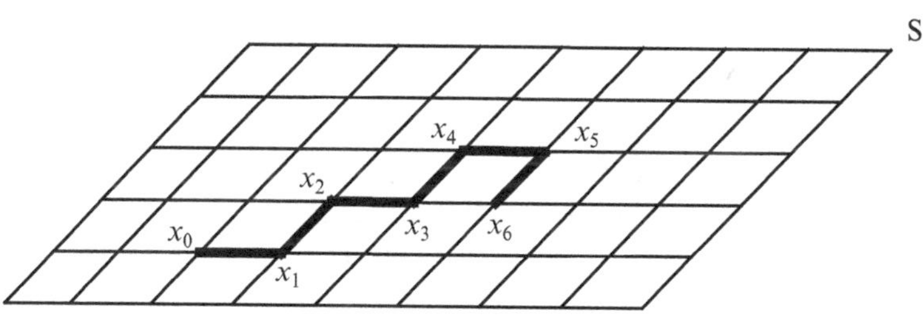

Fig. 11.3 Graphical presentation of a path in a 2D space

x_i and x_j. A finite subset S$\subset$ S^n is called a domain if it is connected, that is, if x_i, $x_j \in$ S implies the existence of the path $_? x_i = x_0, x_1, x_2, \ldots, x_{n-1}, x_n = x_j$ such that all $x_i \in$ S and $|\; x_i - x_{i+1} \;| = 1$. For example, let n be the space dimension with $n=2$. So S^2 is a 2D space and denotes a path with $x_0 = x_1, x_2, x_3, x_4, x_5 = x_6$ (Fig. 11.3).

Note that the condition $|\; x_i - x_{i+1} \;| = 1$ means that the distance between x_i and x_{i+1} is only 1 unit. The boundary ∂S of a domain S consists of all x_j

$\in S^n$-S, which have one or more neighbors in S (x_i and x_j are *neighbors* if $|x_i - x_j| = 1$). If Ω is the configuration space, *X* is the collection of all subsets of Ω, and *P* is a probability measure of *F*, then the triple (Ω, *X*, *P*) is called a random field (rf) on *S* [26]. A random field, with respect to a neighborhood structure, is a Markov random field if the joint probability density on the set of all possible intensity values **x** satisfies the following properties: (1) $p(\mathbf{X})>0$ for all **X**, and (2) *p*(all nodes in the lattice except x_i)=$p(X_i|$ neighbors of x_i). According to the Hammersley-Clifford theorem [5, 6, 18], an MRF can equivalently be characterized by a Gibbs distribution. Two assumptions are very important following Hammersley-Clifford theorem. Firstly, suppose that there are only a finite number of values available at each site. Secondly, assume that the value zero is available at each site. From the factorization theorem is defined that for all the possible realizations, the positivity condition occurred, that is, Ω={**x**: pr(**x**)>0}. From the Hammersley-Clifford theorem, it is seen that a positive Gibbs field is a positive Markov random field and uniquely determined by its local characteristics. Hence, sampling from such field by updating the values of a single vertex according to some specified algorithm only requires knowledge of the values of the neighbors. The definition of Markov random fields stated that the probability measure must fulfill the local Markov property. This is not a restriction for the equivalence between local and global Markov property since it is considered the following theorem. Thus the joint probability is given by $p(x)=\frac{1}{Z}\exp\{-U(\mathbf{x})\}$, where *Z* is the normalized constant or partition function and *U*(*x*) is the energy function with form $U(\mathbf{x})=\sum_{c\in C}V_c(\mathbf{x})$ with the summation that is over the local clique potentials set $V_c(\mathbf{x})$ over all possible cliques C [11] (Fig. 11.4).

An rf (Ω, *X*, *P*) on *S* is a Gibbs random field (Grf) if *P* is defined by the Gibbs form *p*(*x*) [26]. Configurations of low energies are the more likely, whereas high energies correspond to low probabilities. A function *U* from $S^n \, x \, S^n$ to *R* is called a symmetric, homogeneous, nearest-neighbor pair potential function if for all $x_i, x_j \in S^n$: (1) $U(x_i, x_j)=U(x_j, x_i)$(symmetry), (2) $U(x_i, x_j)=U(0, x_i - x_j)$ (homogeneity), and (3) $U(x_i, x_j)=0$ if $|x_i - x_j|>1$ (nearest-neighbor property). We make the additional assumption that the MRF is homogeneous; that is, the potential function is the same for all cliques. This property gives rise to translation invariance of an MRF model. Without loss of generality, we assume that the maximal cliques in the MRF are square patches of a fixed size; other, nonsquare, neighborhoods could be used. Configurations of low energies are the more likely, whereas high energies correspond to low probabilities. The interaction structure induced by the factorized form ($p(x)=\prod_{c\in C} f_c(x_c)$, where $f_c(x_c)$ depends only on the variable subset $x_c=\{x_i, i\in c\}$ and $\prod_{c\in C} f_c(x_c)$ is summable over Ω) presented by an independent graph: the independence graph associated with the factorization is the undirected graph G=[*E*,*S*] with vertex set *S*={1,2,…,*n*} and edge set *E* defined as:

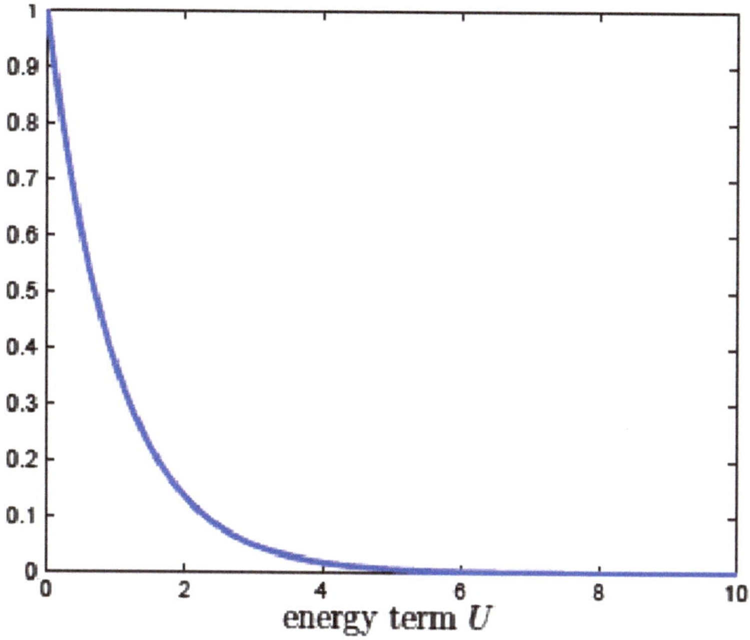

Fig. 11.4 Graphical presentation for energy $U(x)$

$\{i,j\} \in E \Leftrightarrow \exists c \in C : \{i,j\} \subset c$. As a consequence of the definition, any subset c is either a singleton or composed of mutually neighboring sites: C is a set of cliques for G. On a finite graph, any nearest-neighbor potential induces an MRF (for infinite graph, the case holds when $\sum_x \exp\left[-\sum_{c \in C} V_c(\mathbf{x})\right] < \infty$). If $G=[E,S]$ is a graph, two vertices i and j are neighbors if $(i,j) \in S$. Figure 11.5 represents an independent graph associated with partitions.

Energy function $U(x)$ can be written in terms of clique potentials which accounts for the contribution to the energy from the cliques:

$$U(\mathbf{x}) = \sum_{c \in C} V_C(x_c) = \sum_{1 \le i \le S} x_i G_i(x_i) + \sum_{i \le i < j} \sum_{\le S} x_i x_j G_{i,j}(x_i, x_j)$$

where $G_i(.)$ are arbitrary functions. The above models are called *automodels* [5, 32]. Considering the energy function expression, one may also deduce results on the energy form by assuming that the conditional probabilities are defined by the exponential family, using the following assumption [5]: the probability structure only depends on contributions from sites taken either singularly or in pairs, and the conditional probability distribution is a member of the regular exponential family of distributions.

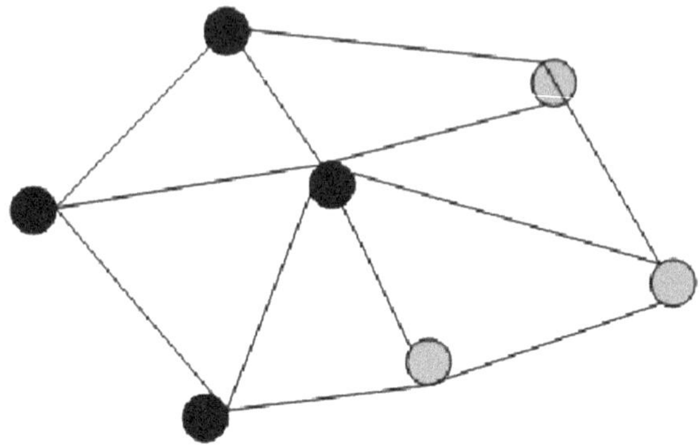

Fig. 11.5 Independent graph associated to a region partition

11.3 PDE-Markov Random Field Models

Physical properties of the neighbors direct us to the assumption of smoothness and homogeneity implementing various Markov random field models as prior models. The statistical methodology allows us to analyze priors that allow moderate discontinuities in the regions. Smoothness constraints are often expressed as the prior probability, or as energy function $U(x)$ measuring the effectiveness of the smoothness assumption in x. For spatial MRFs, the smoothness prior often involves derivates. Then, the potential at a point has the form of $\left[f^{(n)}(x)\right]^2$, where n determines the number of sites involved in the cliques (e.g., $n=1$ corresponds the pair-site smoothness potential) [30]. Therefore, the prior energy could be expressed as $U(x)=\int\left[f'(x)\right]^2\mathrm{d}x$. Based on the consideration of smoothness-prior assumption for regions, a suitable form of energy function can be considered explained by partial differential equation (PDE) inside the potential function. Modification of the smoothness assumption could be introduced using total variation of the region. The total variation function was first introduced into image analysis by Li [19], where it recognizes an important vision feature in image analysis, the *edges*. The total variation of a function f, denoted by TV (f), is defined as $\mathrm{TV}(f)=\int\left|\nabla f(x)\right|\mathrm{d}x$. The problem to solve is thus the following: $\min\int\left|\nabla f(x)\right|\mathrm{d}x$. A function is said to have bounded variation if $\mathrm{TV}(f)<\infty$. The TV prior is defined as $p(x)\approx\exp\{-U(x)\}\approx\exp\{-\mathrm{TV}(f)\}$. If it is assumed that $u-u^*$ (or $v-v^*$) is spatially changing, then interaction between neighboring nodes may be approximated by first-order differential operator with the general form: $V_{\mathrm{pde}}=\int_{c\in C}\left[f_1\frac{\partial X}{\partial u}+f_2\frac{\partial X}{\partial v}\right]\mathrm{d}u\mathrm{d}v$, where f_1 and f_2 are proposed functions, X is the random variable vector for an region, and the partial derivatives calculate the interaction between neighboring nodes.

The mean field theory investigates the influence of the intensity x_i in the calculation of the expectation which can be approximated by the influence of $\langle x_i\rangle$. By definition, the expectation of the intensity can be calculated by

$< x_i > = \sum_{x_i} x_i p(\mathbf{x}) = \frac{1}{Z}\sum_{x_i} x_i \exp\{-U(\mathbf{x})\}$. Zhang [30] suggests that the mean field approximation of the above form can be given by $< x_i > = \frac{1}{Z}\sum_{x_i} x_i \exp\{-U^{MF}(\mathbf{x})\}$, where influence of the field can be approximated by the mean of the neighbors. Mean field theory concerns the evaluation of the mean field **<x>** over the above distribution. Justification for the mean field estimates in optimization problems stems from the fact that the mean field represents the minimum variance Bayes estimator for **x**. In order to find the mean field at x_i, one needs the mean field at the neighbors of x_i. Therefore, the mean field is usually computed by iterative procedures. Recalling the pseudolikelihood method [6, 31], for every automodel the conditional expectation of a node given its neighbors is proportional to the model parameter $E[x_i \mid x_{\partial i}]$. So it is reasonable to replace the value of each neighbor by its conditional expectation (mean field theory [7, 21]).

11.4 Social Networks

Social network analysis (SNA) combines the study of relations and patterns of communication within social groups. In SNA, a social group is modeled as a graph composed of nodes and edges. The nodes in the graph represent social actors and the links the relationship between them. A graph consisting of n nodes and m edges is defined as $G=[V,E]$, where $V_{i,}\ i=1,\ldots,n$ is the set of nodes and $E_j,\ j=1,\ldots m$ is a set of links or edges. Graphs where the edges do not have an associated direction are undirected graphs.

Conditional independence statements about X: $\{X_{A_i} \perp X_{B_i} \mid X_{C_i}\}$. A definition of social group is based on the concept of a clique (Fig. 11.6). The cliques are useful to study small social networks.

The main goal in social networks is to investigate diagrammatical spatial interaction between nodes applying probabilistic modeling techniques. Statistical modeling of social networks is implemented based on MRF [10] and exponential random graphical models (ERGMs) [1, 28]. Spatial interaction between neighboring nodes (indicating cliques) defines homogeneous regions without spatial variability.

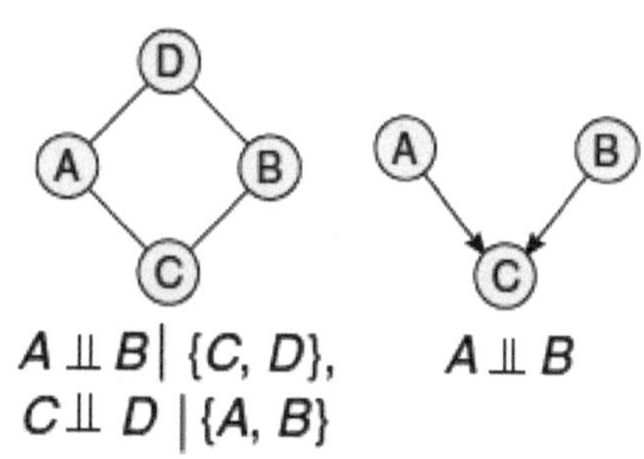

Fig. 11.6 Undirected graphs with conditional independence

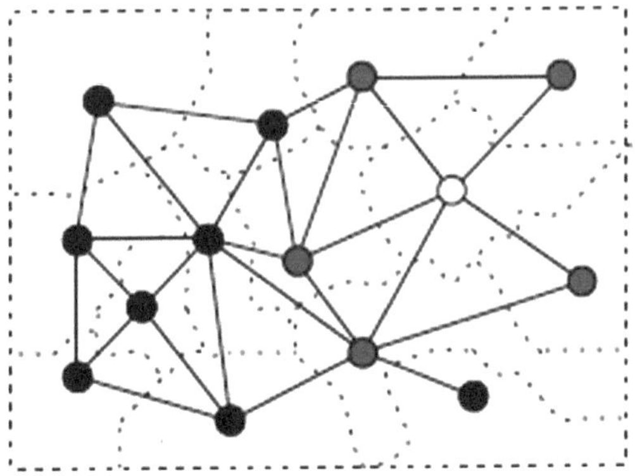

Fig. 11.7 Irregular MRF social network

In social networks, MRF models could be defined as conditional Markov networks with exact conditions as MRF models. Figure 11.7 illustrates a nonregular lattice social system.

11.5 MCMC Estimation

Due to the complexity of the solution, simulation realizations of the spatial process could be introduced. Since the configuration space is extremely large (for a binary $N \times N$ MRF, there are 2^M possible states where $M = N^2$, which, for N of the order of 100, is $2^{10000} \approx 10^{3010}$). Markov chain Monte Carlo methods have been studied by various researchers as an alternative to exact probability computation. The general goal is to implement an algorithm which is operating by generating a Markov chain of regions $X^1, X^2 \ldots X^N$ which converges to a region $\mathbf{x} \in \Omega$ such that $\lim_{n\to\infty} p\left(X^n = x \mid X^1 = x^1\right) = p(x)$, $\forall \mathbf{x} \in \Omega$ [25]. Then realizations of the Markov chain form a pseudosample from the required distribution. In particular, our interest is concentrated on the distribution $p(x)$ using a particular realization $X^1, X^2 \ldots X^N$ on the Markov chain with transition probability $p(x \to x')$. Typically asymptotic results include $X^t \xrightarrow[t\to\infty]{d} X \sim p(x)$; $\frac{1}{t}\sum_{i=1}^{t} f(x^i) \xrightarrow[t\to\infty]{} E_p\{f(x)\}$, where the expectation $E_p\{f(x)\}$ is to be estimated. The corresponding empirical average will be used, namely, $\overline{f}_N = \frac{1}{N}\sum_{t+1}^{N} f\left(x^{(t)}\right)$. This Markov chain is assumed to be time homogeneous. After a sufficient long burn-in period (m iterations), the sequence will gradually converge to a unique stationary distribution $p(x)$. This is an ergodic average [20]. Convergence to the required expectation is ensured by the ergodic theorem. The Gibbs sampler [11], a particular MCMC method, is an iterative process for simulating a sample from a specified probability distribution. At each iteration, the value of only one node can change. Although the sequence in which the nodes are visited is arbitrary, it is common to visit them in order 1,2,…,*n*. The Gibbs sample is a general method for producing samples from a distribution. It is particularly useful when the distribution being sampled is a Gibbs distribution, and the resulting samples form a Markov random field. Let X_s be a finite dimensional random field that takes on values in a discrete and finite set Ω for all $s \in S$. If we assume that the distribution of X is strictly positive, then without loss of generality we know that the distribution of X can be written in the form $p(x) = \frac{1}{Z}\exp\{-U(\mathbf{x})\}$. The marginal distribution of a node can be written as $p(x_s \mid x_i, i \neq s) = \frac{\exp\{-U(x_s \mid x_i, i \neq s)\}}{\sum_{x_s' \in \Omega} \exp\{-U(x_s' \mid x_i, i \neq s)\}}$.

We can generate samples from the distribution of $p(x)$ by using the following Gibbs sampler algorithm:

1. Start with configuration $\mathbf{x}$.
2. Choose a node i.
3. Replace x_i by a value sampled from the conditional distribution of X_i given the values of the neighbors.
4. If not stop then go to 2.

This iterative scheme is continued to produce a sequence $(X^0, X^1, \ldots, X^t)$, which is realization of a Markov chain with transition probabilities from x^t to x^{t+1} given by $p(x^t \to x^{t+1}) = \prod_{l=1}^{n} p(x_l \mid x_j^{t+1}, j < l, x_l^t, j > t)$. After an initial transient period, a realization from the required probability distribution has occurred. In practice, it is important to monitor convergence to the equilibrium distribution. For a discussion of convergence, see [13, 15].

11.6 Conclusions

Stochastic models and statistical approaches have been successfully applied in various areas of social networks. The main task is the choice of an appropriate model as the prior and estimation of model parameters. MRF models could be applied to investigate the spatial connectivity between nodes.

Because of the complexity of the problems, direct estimation cannot be used. For that reason, estimates can be generated from Monte Carlo Markov chain methods based on samples from the posterior (or the prior) distributions. The most commonly used algorithms include the Gibbs sampler and the Metropolis-Hastings. Social networks are MRF models where the lattice system is nonuniform, and connectivity between sites is replayed by the connectivity between nodes (explaining social groups) using undirected graphs.

In this work, we analyze the connection between MRF models and social networks via undirected graphs. Conditional independence between neighbor nodes was explained, considering spatial variability of the regions (which it is defined by the cliques of the graph). Finally, estimation of the MRF models could be achieved by using MCMC techniques like the Gibbs sampler.

References

1. Anderson, C., Wasserman, S., & Crouch, B. (1999). A $p*$ primer: Logit models for social networks. *Social Networks, 21*, 37–66.
2. Aykroyd, R., Haigh, J. G. B., & Zimeras, S. (1996). Unexpected spatial patterns in exponential family auto-models. *Graphical Models and Image Processing, 58*, 452–463.
3. Aykroyd, R. G., & Green, P. J. (1991). Global and local priors and the location of lesions using gamma-camera imagery. *Philosophical Transactions of the Royal Society Series A, 337*, 323–342.
4. Aykroyd, R. G., & Zimeras, S. (1999). Inhomogeneous prior models for image reconstruction. *Journal of American Statistical Association (JASA), 94*(447), 934–946.
5. Besag, J. (1974). Spatial interaction and the statistical analysis of lattice systems (with discussion). *Journal of the Royal Statistical Society: Series B, 36*, 192–236.
6. Besag, J. (1986). On the statistical analysis of dirty pictures (with discussion). *Journal of the Royal Statistical Society: Series B, 48*, 259–302.
7. Chandler, D. (1978). *Introduction to modern statistical mechanics*. New York: Oxford University Press.
8. Cross, G. R., & Jain, A. K. (1983). Markov random field texture models. *IEEE Transactions on Pattern Analysis and Machine Intelligence, 5*(1), 25–39.
9. Diggle, P. J. (1983). *Statistical analysis of spatial pattern point*. London: Academic Press.
10. Frank, O., & Strauss, D. (1986). Markov graphs. *Journal of the American Statistical Association, 81*, 832–842.
11. Geman, S., & Geman, D. (1984). Stochastic relaxation, Gibbs distributions, and Bayesian restoration of images. *IEEE Transactions on Pattern Analysis and Machine Intelligence, 6*, 721–741.
12. Green, P. J. (1990). Bayesian reconstructions from emission tomography data using a modified EM algorithm. *IEEE Transactions on Medical Imaging, 9*, 84–93.
13. Green, P. J., & Han, X. L. (1992). Metropolis methods, Gaussian proposals and antithetic variables. *Lecture Notes in Statistics, 74*, 142–164.
14. Haindl, M. (1991). Texture synthesis. *CWI Quarterly, 4*, 305–331.
15. Hamersley, J. A., & Clifford, P. (1971). *Markov fields on finite graphs and lattices*. Unpublished work.
16. Hastings, W. K. (1970). Monte Carlo simulation methods using Markov chains, and their applications. *Biometrika, 57*, 97–109.
17. Ising, E. (1925). Beitrag zur Theorie des Ferromagnetismus. *Zeitschrift für Physik, 31*, 253–258.
18. Kindermann, R., & Snell, J. L. (1980). *Markov random fields and their applications*. Providence, RI: American Mathematical Society.
19. Li, S. (1995). *Markov random fields in computer vision*. New York: Springer.
20. Metropolis, N., Rosenbluth, A., Rosenbluth, M., Teller, A., & Teller, E. (1953). Equations of state calculations by fast computing machines. *Journal of Chemical Physics, 21*, 1087–1091.
21. Poston, T., & Stewart, I. (1978). *Catastrophe theory and its applications*. London: Pitman.
22. Qian, W., & Titterington, D. M. (1991). Multidimensional Markov chain model for image texture. *Journal of the Royal Statistical Society: Series B, 53*, 661–674.

23. Ranngarajan, A., & Chellappa, R. (1995). Markov random fields models in image processing. In M. Arbib (Ed.), *The handbook of brain theory and neural networks* (pp. 564–567). Cambridge, MA: MIT Press.
24. Ripley, B. D., & Sutherland, A. I. (1990). Finding spiral structures in images of galaxies. *Philosophical Transactions of the Royal Society Series A, 332*, 477–485.
25. Smith, A. F. M., & Robert, G. O. (1993). Bayesian computation via the Gibbs sampler and related Markov chain Monte Carlo methods. *Journal of the Royal Statistical Society: Series B, 55*, 3–23.
26. Spitzer, F. (1971). Markov random fields and Gibbs ensembles. *The American Mathematical Monthly, 78*, 142–154.
27. Taskar, B., Abbeel, P., & Koller, D. (2002, August). Discriminative probabilistic models for relational data. In *Proceedings of the 18th conference on uncertainty in artificial intelligence* (pp. 485–492). San Francisco: Morgan Kaufmann.
28. Wasserman, S., & Pattison, P. (1996). Logit models and logistic regression for social networks: I. An introduction to Markov graphs and p*. *Psychometrika, 61*, 401–425.
29. Weir, I. S. (1993). *Statistical modeling and reconstructions in single photons emission computed tomography*. Ph.D. thesis, Bristol University, Bristol, UK.
30. Zhang, J. (1992). The mean field theory in EM procedures for Markov random fields. *IEEE Transactions on Signal Processing, 40*(10), 2570–2583.
31. Zimeras, S. (1997). *Statistical models in medical image analysis*. Ph.D. thesis, Leeds University, Leeds, UK.
32. Zimeras, S. (2006). Simulating texture patterns using auto-logistic models. *WSEAS Transactions on Systems, 5*(10), 2269–2276.
33. Zimeras, S., & Georgiakodis, F. (2005). Bayesian models for medical image biology using Monte Carlo Markov chain techniques. *Mathematical and Computer Modeling, 42*(2005), 759–768.

Chapter 12
Mobile Communities – Current Status and Challenges

Volkmar Schau[1], **Kathrin Kirchner**[1], **Christian Stolcis**[2], **Christian Erfurth**[3], **Gerald Eichler**[4], **and Wilhelm R. Rossak**[1]

[1] Friedrich Schiller University of Jena, Jena, Germany, volkmar.schau@uni-jena.de; kathrin.kirchner@uni-jena.de; wilhelm.rossak@uni-jena.de
[2] Navimatix GmbH, Jena, Germany, christian.stolcis@navimatix.de
[3] University of Applied Sciences Jena, Jena, Germany, christian.erfurth@fh-jena.de
[4] Telekom Innovation Laboratories, Darmstadt, Germany, gerald.eichler@telekom.de

Abstract The current progress in mobile and collaborative technologies (MCT) has the potential to radically change the shape and practice of daily living. The combined use of integrated sensors, networks, and smartphones can fill in the information access gap existing between stationary and mobile workplaces. Moreover, mobile technology can have a positive impact by removing barriers related to geographical and temporal constraints. Among the most important issues that need to be considered are adequate hardware, adaptive communication infrastructures, appropriate software services, location and context awareness, as well as user profiling and interaction. So far, in most cases, only isolated aspects of community systems, for example, technological aspects or services, have been discussed in the literature. In this chapter, we will aim to provide an integrated overview of different technological as well as some social approaches to realize community systems and identify common components.

Keywords Mobile community • Mobile collaboration • Location awareness • Context awareness

12.1 Introduction

We are presently in the middle of a global telecommunication revolution. A powerful confluence of technological, economic, and social forces is leading to rapid change in the capabilities, price, and performance of telecommunication services. Technological forces are driving intense innovation and the convergence of voice, video, and data communications [21]. Current progress in mobile and collaborative technologies (MCT) has the potential to radically change the shape and practice of daily living. The combined use of integrated sensors, networks, and smart mobile

A.A. Lazakidou (ed.), *Virtual Communities, Social Networks and Collaboration*, Annals of Information Systems 15, DOI 10.1007/978-1-4614-3634-8_12,

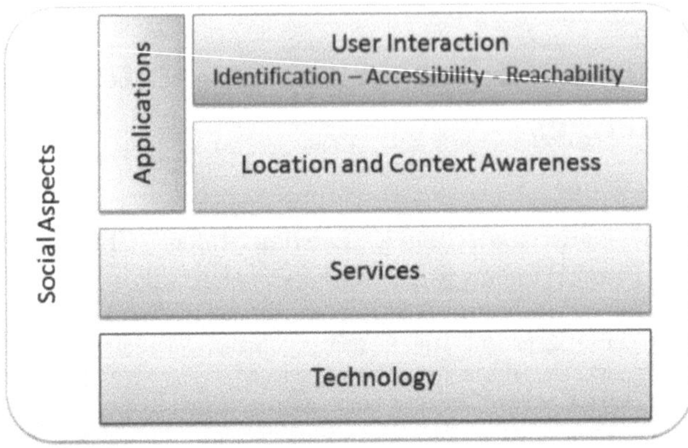

Fig. 12.1 Different aspects of mobile community systems

handheld devices can fill in the information access gap that existed between stationary and mobile workplaces.

While descriptions of innovative mobile collaboration and visions of future scenarios abound in literature, the specific meaning of "mobility" and the related types of mobility, including their direct impact on the usage of handheld devices, remain mostly unclear. Thus, we first provide our definition of mobility types, based on a short review of available literature. *Traveling*, *hiking*, and *visiting* were seen as three ways to qualify the essence of mobility. *Traveling* is defined as "the process of going from one place to another in a vehicle." For example, a journey from one city to another could belong to this category of mobility. *Hiking* refers to a form of "extensive local mobility" where an individual may spend considerable time walking around [20] in a fairly restricted area. Finally, *visiting* refers to stopping by at some location and spending time there [28]. In all of these (user-centered) types of mobility, MCT is enabled by a common set of features, as shown in Fig. 12.1, as a layered generic framework.

This chapter will give an overview of the state of the art and identify future challenges for each of these features (see Fig. 12.1). It is structured as follows: In Sect. 12.2, we present an overview of current technologies and platforms for mobile collaboration. Section 12.3 discusses social aspects, whereas Sect. 12.4 focuses on services and applications. A wide view on location and context awareness is provided in Sect. 12.5. Section 12.6 concludes, summarizes, and provides a brief discussion of future challenges.

12.2 Technology and Platforms

The power of technological development and the strength of different applications for structured community interaction determine the future of mobile collaboration. Mobile collaboration apps have been developed in parallel to the development of wireless technologies. However, it will finally be the concrete capabilities of mobile devices that determine the level of innovation, mobile collaboration and community development can achieve. Today, mobile devices offer already a rich set of features. They are now capable to provide special ring tones, games, music, calendars, calculators, and cameras [34] as well as sensors.

This is a major step forward since AT&T offered the first mobile telephone service in 1946 through the public telephone system. It required a manual search of an open radio channel for starting a phone call. The user was linked to a mobile operator, who dialed the call over the public telephone system. In this arrangement, controlled by a talk button, only one party was able to speak at a given time. This was called a "semi-duplex" radio connection [21]. In 1964, AT&T improved mobile telephone services by offering automatic dialing and channel searching, as well as a "duplex" connection [21].

12.2.1 Device Development

Today, most devices have plenty of capabilities to send and receive data. Moreover, a camera phone provides the customer with the capability to make and immediately publish pictures, even to make video calls. On the other hand, the personal digital assistant (PDA) was developed from the desire to carry a handheld version of computer features, like contacts, data sets, and documents. This topic revolves around Palm, Inc., a pioneer in mobile and wireless Internet solutions. Palm believed that handheld computing is the next wave in individual productivity tools for the global workforce [21]. Today we know their prediction was true. It has been shown that mobile devices (smartphone, PDA, tablet, netbook) can be used as an effective means for data collection, storage and communication.

Research in mobiles devices found the following core issues: (1) *physical portability*, as the size of the device will affect the way the end user can carry along the device; (2) *display*, as enlarged color screens consume more power than simple ones; (3) *batteries*, as the need for mobile endurance is growing; and (4) *expansion,* as the ability to enhance the device with additional equipment [3] is regarded as crucial. Table 12.1 presents a differentiated view of involved devices today.

12.2.2 Mobile Network Development

Why have mobile devices become so popular over the last decade? The answer is simply their core asset – mobility [21]. Mobile computing does not only involve mobile devices which are designed to be carried around but also the mobile networks to which these computers are connected [12]. Mobile and wireless technologies are becoming increasingly pervasive. Wireless networks free users from the tethers that have bound them to their desk, enabling them to live and work in a more flexible and convenient way [21]. Mobile devices allow people to switch between

Table 12.1 Device features to support collaborative applications (Adapted from [11])

	Desktop PC	Notebook	Tablet	PDA	Smartphone
Data input capability	+++	+++	+++	−−	−−−
Multimedia support	+++	+++	+++	+	−
Memory capacity	+++	+++	+++	+	−
Storage capacity	+++	+++	+++	+	−−
Processing power	+++	+++	+++	+	−−
Screen size	+++	+++	+++	+	−
Battery power	−−−	+++	++	+	++
Wireless capability	−−−	+++	+++	+++	+++
Expansion support	+++	+	−	−−	−−−
Work while be transported (traveling or visiting)	−−−	+++	+++	++	++
Work while walking (wandering)	−−−	−−	++	+++	++
Wearability	−−−	+	++	+++	+++
Startup time	−−−	−−−	++	++	+++

mobile and corporate networks depending on availability. This ensures that people are always connected.

The communication support available in the user's environment conditions the type of mobile collaboration activities. So, mobile devices with WiFi communication capabilities are able to form networks in close proximity as a Mobile Ad hoc Network (MANET) [19] to support collaboration in scenarios where networking services are not readily available [1]. On the other hand, the type of mobility to be supported influences the type of work the user is able to do. Typically, wandering involves short and simple interactions between the user and the system [19] and requires basic communication support (network availability and bandwidth). By contrast, large bandwidth is usually required when traveling or visiting because the user is then able to carry out long and complex interactions with the system's support [11, 28].

Based on "computing and communication anytime, anywhere and over any device", two major industry road maps are converging today (Fig. 12.2): (1) analogue to 3G and (2) WiFi to WiMax and other mobile broadband wireless access (MBWA) proposed solutions along a computing-oriented road map. So far, these two wireless road maps have evolved nearly independently, driven by different application targets. Both cellular systems and PC-oriented wireless local area networks (WLANs) have seen three generations of deployment, and the fourth generation is already under development [6].

12.2.3 *Community and Collaboration*

Mobile collaborative and community applications require synchronous and asynchronous communication capabilities depending on the targeted activity. If asynchronous communication is required, every mobile computing device is able to provide

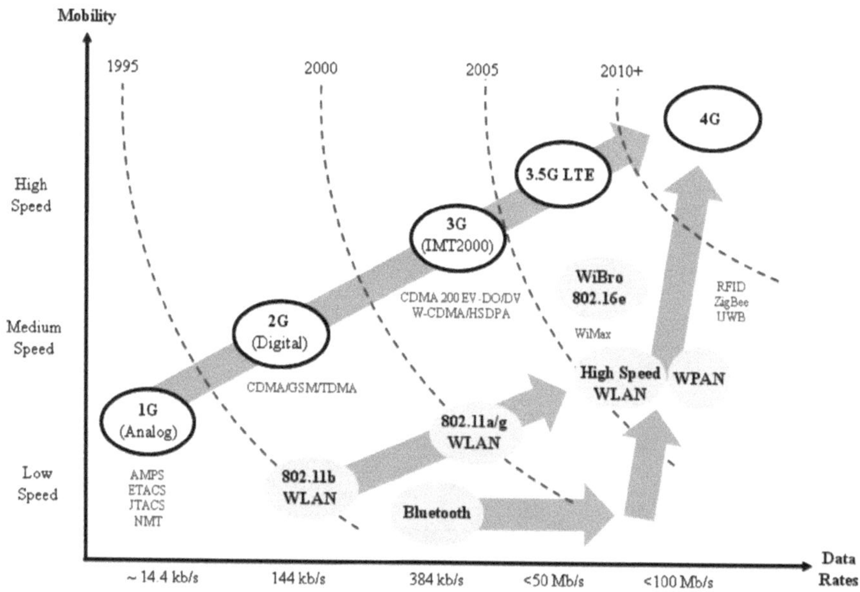

Fig. 12.2 Wireless technology road maps toward 4G (Adapted from B3G Conference 2005, Samsung)

such support based on minimal network availability. On the other hand, if synchronous communication is required, a permanent and stable communication service must be ensured [29]. Smartphones, supported by cellular networks, are typically the best option for synchronous communication because the network provides a physically nearly unlimited coverage range and good signal stability [22]. However, cellular networks only have a limited bandwidth. Another option providing synchronous communication is a WiFi communication infrastructure [19, 27]. Although the bandwidth is better than cellular networks, WiFi signal stability depends on the physical environment where it is deployed [1]. Furthermore, it has a limited coverage range [11, 22]. Thus, mobile computing networks are essential and define the setting and possible services that can be used, depending today mostly on available bandwidth and incurred cost. Till 2030 in Germany, an average mobile access data rate of 84 Mbps is expected [14]. Figure 12.3 gives an idea about the network rates of current and future mobile data services.

Mobile devices, which are inevitably used for distant communication, offer the potential platform for developing innovative collaboration services and a wide range of more traditional applications. Applications that were restricted to desktop computers have been successfully migrated to mobile devices in large numbers. In terms of direct user interaction, accessibility, reachability, and reliable identification are the cornerstones of future success (we cite here the XING network evolution from web desktop to mobile application). Accessibility as the capability of networking anytime and anywhere assumes that devices can easily be located (location) and

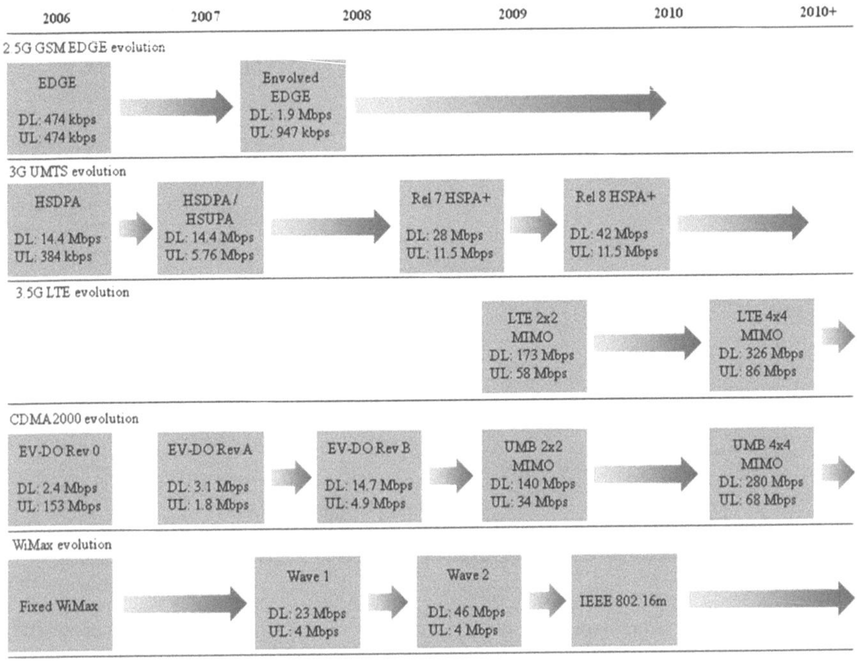

Fig. 12.3 Evolution of mobile data services (Adapted from Mobilizing unified communication and collaboration the dynamic enterprise, Alcatel-Lucent, USA)

people can connect to each other and collaborate (reachability). Localization offers completely new track and trace services [9]. Identification allows for instantaneous identification of an entity. Agile technologies like GPS, mobile device identification techniques, and network triangulation allow for services to zoom in and trigger additional matching activities, targeted on a narrowly defined physical location with high resolution. As these capabilities become more accessible, accurate, and available in real time, various service opportunities can be conceptualized [25].

12.3 Social Aspects of Mobile Collaboration

The technical capabilities of mobile devices provide the basis for the collaboration of mobile communities. A mobile community, as a social system, has a purpose that is achieved collectively. It is formed based on the needs of its members, whose loyalty is essential for trust generation which, in turn, is important for a successful community [17]: Mobile users want to profit from each other's knowledge while they are on the move. Therefore, community awareness has to be enabled in the mobile space. Different kinds of mobile communities exist [4], for example,

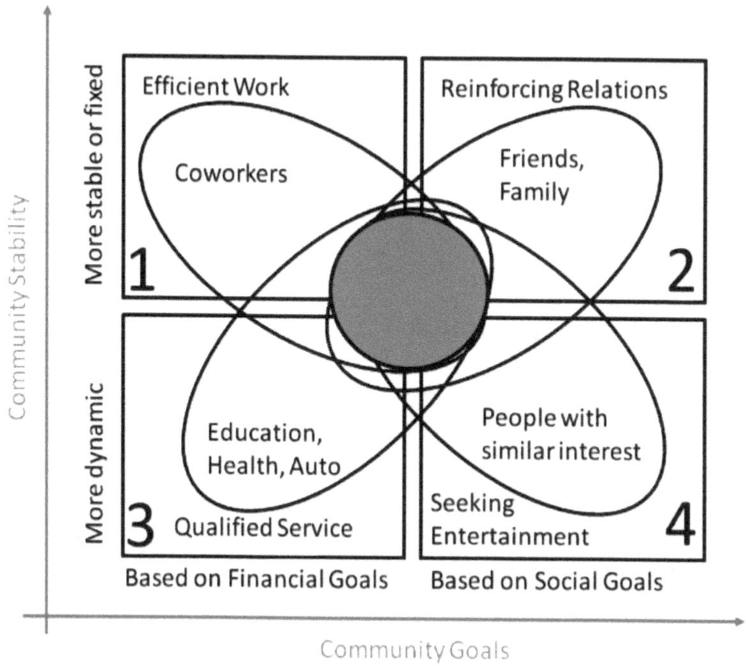

Fig. 12.4 Mobile communities (Adapted from [26])

discussion-oriented communities that are organized around particular interests; support communities that help each other in case of medical, financial, social, or other difficulties; and blogs and social network-based communities or other functional groupings, for example, for game playing, working together on projects, or trading.

Rhee and Lee [26] developed a mobile community model describing four types of communities (Fig. 12.4). They consider two dimensions – community goals and community stability. The aim of the community can be profit (in quadrants 1 and 3) or nonprofit (quadrants 2 and 4). Stability can be described as dynamic (3 and 4) or more stable (1 and 2). Most people are members of all four types of communities.

Mobile communities change the private and professional life of people that are involved. Examples are changing work habits and disappearing boundaries between work and personal life [14, 24], as demonstrated within the XING network. Company employees are flexible to work anytime and anywhere; they can be regarded as nomads [18]. In turn, private time and space becomes public. According to Ali-Hassan et al. [2], a mobile worker has fewer chances to meet colleagues in the office, thus reducing the potential for developing social relationships and common norms. On the other hand, people that participate in mobile communities can minimize their isolation. They are able to reach others more quickly in emergency situations and can keep better contact, so they feel safer and more secure [4].

A first wave of mobile use, centered on voice calls and SMS messages, was already followed by a second wave, centered on mobile-based applications and the mobile internet [8]. The definition of adoption rules for such a mobile service is, therefore, an important and commercially relevant question. Kargin et al. [16] surveyed users of mobile services and found that the content of a service is the most important factor for its use. Looking at social aspects, it is the influence of others that constitutes the major motivation for a person to start using a specific service.

12.4 Service and Application

Community systems usually deliver their features in form of services. This aspect is driven by technological evolution, for example, service-oriented patterns and architectures, and the need to realize a modular provisioning of end user features. Similar services can be found in many different systems, for example, chat, even though implementation details may vary. On a more abstract level, a community system can be regarded as a collection (selection) of a set of possibly already available applications or a special instantiation of more or less generic services. It is this selection that gives the system and its community a specific character.

Besides common services, like content management or interaction features, location-based or context-aware services become more and more important for mobile users. Nearly two in five social media users access services from their mobile phones [23]. Community systems try also to deliver services for covering social aspects like friendship, business contact support, or social networks. Social networking is the third most-used type of mobile application in the USA [23].

The terms service and application are often used as synonyms. However, in this context, there will be a clear differentiation. While an *application* should be a piece of software that is given to the user en bloc to run it on a physical device, *services* should be small generic parts that allow for the efficient construction of applications.

12.4.1 Mobile Collaboration Model

Mobile applications are typically more than plain client server interaction. They are often enriched by two things: (1) objects that represent any kind of contents and (2) communication aspects between users, often related to the objects of the application. The objects can be different types of distributed documents, which will usually be interrelated for a dedicated application purpose. For instance, a person can be represented as a profile.xml. Enriched by context information, triggers can be generated which invoke communication transactions, like search or deliver operations [29].

Using a graph, more abstract a vertex can be interpreted as *object*, while an edge is an *interaction* relation, as depicted in Fig. 12.5. The entire structure of the graph

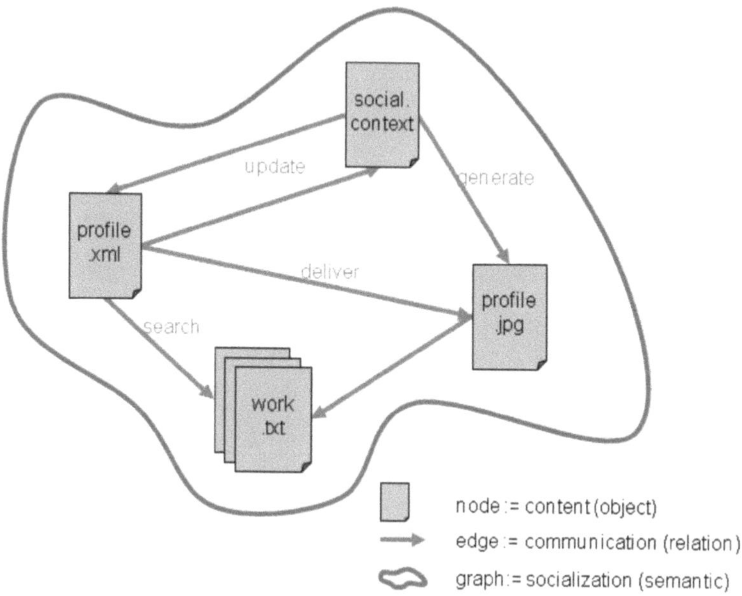

Fig. 12.5 Mobile collaboration model as a semantic graph

represents the *semantics* of the service, which, thus, supports a specific form of collaboration.

12.4.2 Service Clustering

Following the mobile community model, it would be natural to cluster services according to their purposes. With *semantic services*, *interaction services* and *object services* already three clusters are given. With *contextual services*, the special environmental character of mobile services is supported. The set of clusters is completed by *access services* to handle questions of permission and privacy. Figure 12.6 shows a selection of well-known basic services according to this classification.

The listed services are a collection that has typically different configurations and instantiations. A specific service of this collection might or might not be available in any concrete community system. Services within the cluster object services target the management of content or community members (users) in a community system. For instance, a search service in XING supports users to browse content or to find colleagues. An interaction service supports direct or indirect interaction between community members (or even anonymous users), for example, a chat. Semantic services allow enhanced features of a community system on the basis of available data, typically seen as a relation between content and users (objects).

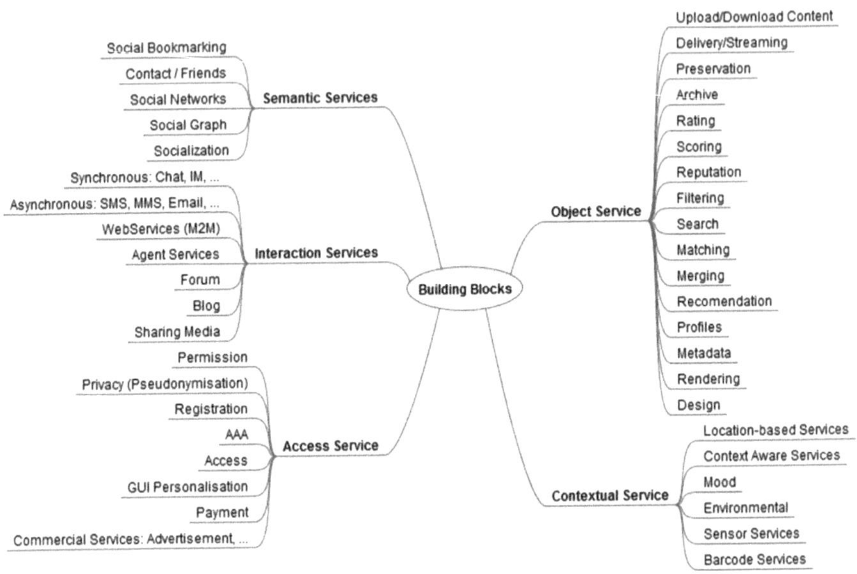

Fig. 12.6 Clustering of services

Access services cluster functions related to the correct and personalized usage of a community system. Location-based and context-aware services are examples for the enriched support of member mobility, for example, by taking dedicated environmental (sensor-) information into account and cross-referencing it with the end user's current mood, travel plans, or special needs.

12.4.3 *Analysis and Evaluation of Real Applications*

Services are the basic building blocks of any dedicated application and, thus, form an adequate means to compare them. Applying the above-identified five service clusters, we analyze XING, Twitter, Flickr, and last.fm (see Fig. 12.7).

The axis of the service clusters can objectively represent the number of exploited services. For getting a representative view, normalization against the number of possible services and their intensiveness of use would be required. In this example, a subjective view is preferred that builds on experience and service availability (depths).

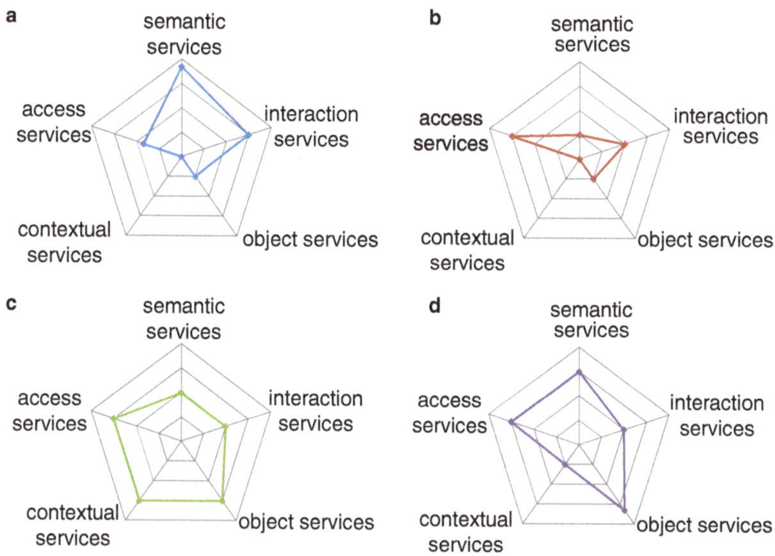

Fig. 12.7 Application analysis according service clusters. (**a**) XING, (**b**) Twitter, (**c**) Flickr, (**d**) last.fm

12.5 Location and Context Awareness

The word "*context*" can be generally defined as "that which surrounds, and gives meaning to something else" [35]. Since various areas of computer science have done research in this area for the past 20 years, many definitions where given to understand the concept in a computational environment. Schmidt et al. define context as "knowledge about the user's and IT device's state, including surroundings, situation, and to a less extent, location" [31]. Dey and Abowd [7] define context as "any information that can be used to characterize the situation of an entity. An entity is a person, place or object that is considered relevant for the interaction between a user and an application, including the user and applications themselves."

Besides these formal definitions, another way to describe context is enumerating examples of contexts (Fig. 12.8) [5]. Understanding the definitions of context, location, and context awareness is nothing more than using the available context information in computation for adapting user interfaces, applications, and the underlying computational data to the actual user environment and needs.

In fact, the use of context information represents the state of the art in many areas of computer-aided applications as, for example, user interfaces use context to adapt menus, user preferences, and dialogues, as well as menu status and arrangement. A quite new domain in using context awareness in computation is represented by mobile computing. As smartphones are representing a fast-growing market, new

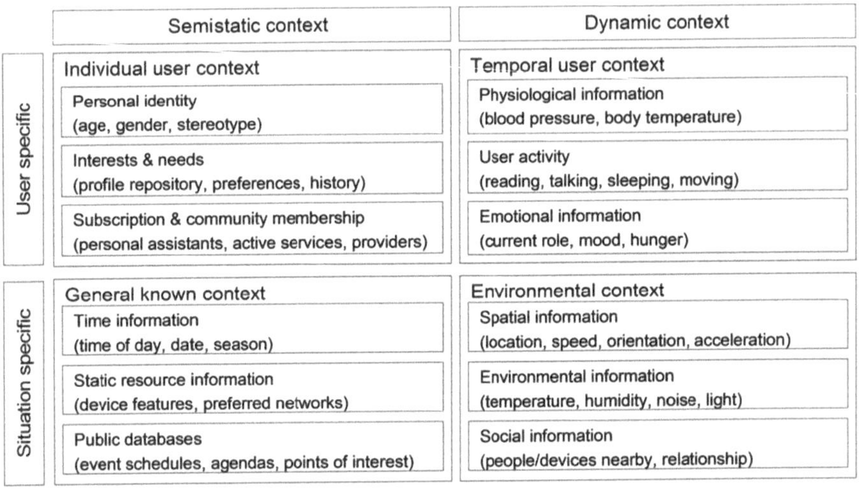

Fig. 12.8 Classification of context [10]

mobile applications, which take into account the characteristics and needs of these mobile devices, are crucial. Especially the limited display of such devices makes it necessary to provide the right information at the opportune moment.

12.5.1 Location and Context Awareness in Mobile Applications

Using information about the user's environment and context in mobile computing is not only necessary for creating appropriate applications for mobile devices but offers also new opportunities to create new kinds of mobile applications which have to deal with the constraints of mobile devices as limitations in communication, presentation, and interaction. But also because of the fact that in the domain of mobile applications the context is highly dynamic, the use of context awareness represents a very interesting paradigm in mobile applications.

But for all that, creating context-aware mobile applications imposes special demands on the used architecture. Less system resources, the unguaranteed network connection, and the need to save energy imply special restrictions to the subjacent architecture. As this is crucial for supporting context awareness on mobile devices, Hofer et al. [13] identified some requirements for an architecture supporting context awareness that are listed in Table 12.2.

12.5.2 Acquiring Context

The use of context information is crucial to provide adequate applications for smartphones. One of the most important things in mobile computation is to retrieve the context in order to being able to use this information in different applications.

Table 12.2 Requirements for an architecture that supports context awareness [13]

Lightweightness	The limited processing power and system resources have to be considered by the architecture
Extensibility	The architecture should support connections to remote sensors since it is not possible for a single device to sense all context information
Robustness	Due to possible connection restrictions of smartphones, the architecture has to be robust against disconnections of remote sensors
Meta-information	Besides the sensor information itself, the context model has to contain meta- information about the distance of the device to the sensor, its preciseness, etc., to be able to handle controversial information provided by the remote sensors
Context-sharing	Due to the fact that the sensed context is almost never complete because of limited capabilities of mobile devices and the goal of being mobile, the architecture should provide a mechanism to share the sensed context with other devices
Dynamism	As the context in mobile computing is highly dynamic and changes fast, the architecture has to take into account this fact, reacting in a dynamic and rapid way to context changes to adapt the application. So in addition to the above-mentioned points, we propose to extend the requirements with dynamism

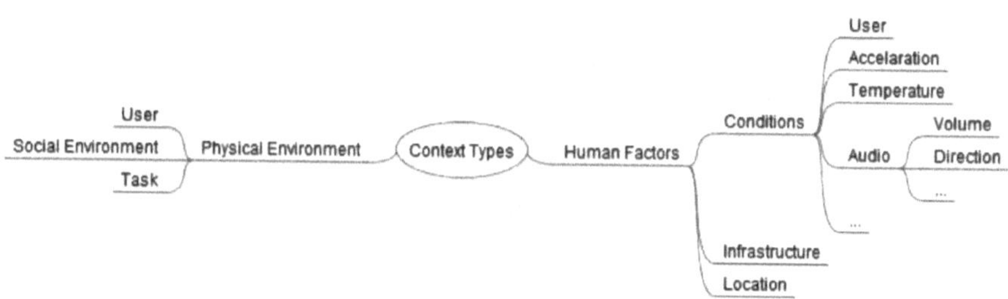

Fig. 12.9 Context classifications and subcategories

As context can be divided and partitioned into different types for the use in mobile application, Schmidt, Aidoo et al. [30] propose to distinguish two main aspects: human factors and physical environment (Fig. 12.9). Furthermore, each of these aspects (classifications) is divided into three subcategories which can again contain relevant features whose values determine context. The three categories related to human factors are information regarding the user (habits, emotional state, preferences, etc.), the user's social environment (social interaction, location of others, etc.), and the user's tasks (general goals, engaged tasks, etc.). The physical environment is structured into location (absolute position, relative position, position surrounding), infrastructure (surrounding resources for computation and communication), and physical conditions (noise, light, pressure, motion, etc.).

Acquiring this context information in mobile applications can be done in two different ways, explicitly and implicitly. Explicit context acquisition requires the user to specify the needed information, for example, the actual time zone for being able to use the appropriate time. Retrieving the context implicitly includes monitoring of the physical environment through various sensors, as well as tracking of conditions in user interaction. For example, imagine the XING mobile application in touch with a navigation system. For a proper route calculation, it requires the user to explicitly specify the destination and route preferences. For generating appropriate route guidance instructions, it retrieves implicitly the position through GPS and acceleration sensors.

12.5.3 Location and Context Awareness in Mobile Collaboration

Besides many benefits of mobile computing, the possibility to gain access to entertainment, information, and social communication from anywhere represents the principal advantage of mobile applications (mobile apps). Through the usage of context information, mobile apps can be further adapted to the actual user needs, enabling new application areas. One of these new areas is represented by mobile collaboration, which allows the user to collaborate with other users in order to achieve a collective goal. Collaboration in this environment is obtained by sending context information to other users and receiving in turn their context information, which results in an adapted behavior of the application and the user itself. For example, the knowledge of road conditions like accidents or aquaplaning on the route, detected by other users who already passed the mentioned position, could help the user and the navigation system to recalculate the route in order to avoid traffic congestion and other accidents.

The usage and interchange of context information defines a new kind of mobile application, allowing for different users to collaborate with each other to achieve a collective goal.

12.6 Summary, Trends, and Future Challenges

In this chapter, we provided an overview of different aspects of mobile community systems. Starting with technological aspects, we considered also social aspects, services, and applications, as well as aspects of location and context awareness.

Today, the core issue is that mobile collaboration opens the door to entirely new forms of pervasive data collection. The risks triggered by this kind of data collection are not always evident. Even to provide the option to manage data and application rights on an individual basis may not result in improved systems [33]. With the growing market of mobile applications and the usage of smartphones with different sensors, the collection of personal data will increase, nevertheless, often without being noticed by the user. The central issue in this case is not that the user does not know that data is collected; it is that this data usually leaves the personal vault immediately. Therefore, one of the biggest challenges resides in maintaining the privacy of users, for example, by letting them know what is happening to their personal data, how long an application retains their data, and whether the system will pass on any information to other parties. As with the "Fair Trade" label on food, Shilton [33] proposes to use a label for software applications to help users to identify and support systems that collect a minimum amount of personal data and do not pass that data on other parties. The question arises what providers are allowed to do with these data [32].

Another aspect is the concept of improved associative and context sensitive networking. For example, mobile shopping and entertainment, as typical community activities, will grow in the future and benefit strongly from sharing information about local shopping possibilities and products, including hints what other buyers have done in a similar situation in the same shop at wintertime, while snow starts to fall. The system will simply offer suggestions to its end user, based on location, past activities, current profile, a regional status, and a context-sensitive history of the shop and its shopper community.

The eCommerce community tries to target the "word of mouth" market, by focusing on "viral-marketing" strategies, where social networks and blogs transport commercial messages, hidden away in applications we trust to be noncommercial. How will we know if what we learn about our context and, possibly, the people that are currently in the same context is for real or just a commercial produced by an intelligent software that targets our profile? As we leave more traces in a mobile world, we are easier to profile.

The killer application of the future might be mobile dating. A user can create a profile and, based on his current position, can get information about people next to him/her that share the same interests and are open for a meeting. If we multiply that with the already named concerns regarding data handling and profiling, we come close to a situation where a specific "code of conduct" will have to go with a specific service, for the service provider as well as for the service user.

From a technical perspective, improved service clustering will allow for both, the analysis of existing applications and the efficient construction of new applications by selecting the appropriate building blocks. A new application may then be constructed on a logical level as a graph that names the selected services and possibly also helps to identify the missing ones, by comparing the new application with a number of typical patterns.

References

1. Aldunate, R., Ochoa, S., Pena-Mora, F., & Nussbaum, M. (2005). Robust mobile ad-hoc space for collaboration to support disaster relief efforts involving critical physical infrastructure. *ASCE Journal of Computing in Civil Engineering, American Society of Civil Engineers, 20*, 13–20.
2. Ali-Hassan, H., Nevo, D., & Nevo, S. (2010). Mobile collaboration: Exploring the role of social capital. *The Data Base for Advances in Information Systems, 41*(2), 9–24.
3. Ahsan, S., El-Hamalawi, A., Bouchlaghem, D., & Ahmad, S. (2007). *Mobile technologies for improved collaboration on construction sites*. Loughborough, England: Loughborough University.

4. Chayko, M. (2007). The portable community: Envisioning and examining mobile social connectedness. *International Journal of Web Based Communities, 3*(4), 373–385.
5. Chen, G., & Kotz, D. (2000) *A survey of context- aware mobile computing research* (Dartmouth Computer Science Technical Report No. TR2000–381). Department of Computer Science, Dartmouth College, UK.
6. Desoli, G., & Filippi, E. (2006). An outlook on the evolution of mobile terminals: from monolithic to modular multiradio, multiapplication platforms. *Circuits and Systems Magazine, IEEE, 6*, 17–29.
7. Dey, A. K., Abowd, G.D. (1999). *Towards a better understanding of context and context-awareness* (Technical Report No. GIT-GVU-99–22). College of Computing, Georgia Institute of Technology, Atlanta, GA.
8. Donner, J. (2009). Blurring livelihoods and lives: The social uses of mobile phones and socio-economic development. *Innovations, 4*(1), 91–101.
9. Eichler, G., & Böhm, A. (2006). Einheitliche Einzellokalisierung – Voraussetzung für Track & Trace Mehrwertdienste. *Praxis in der Kommunikationstechnik (PIK), 29*, 4–8.
10. Eichler, G., & Erfurth, C. (2006, June). Mobile and smart devices in a human community – The challenge of context-aware distributed networking, 6th I2CS 2006. In G. Eichler, P. G. Kropf, U. Lechner, P. Meesad, & H. Unger (Eds.), *10th International Conference on Innovative Internet Community Systems (I2CS) – Jubilee Edition 2010* (pp. 103–115). New York: ACM Press.
11. Guerrero, L., Ochoa, S., Pino, J., & Collazos, C. (2006). Selecting computing devices to support mobile collaboration. *Group Decision and Negotiation, 15*(3), 243–271.
12. Guerrero, L., Pio, J., Collazos, C., ,Inostroza A., & Ochoa, S. (2004). Mobile support for collaborative work. In G. Vreede, L. Guerrero, & G. Ravents (Ed.), *LNCS 3198 – X International Workshop on Groupware (CRIWG'04)* (pp. 363–375). Berlin/Heidelberg: Springer-Verlag.
13. Hofer, T., Schwinger, W., Pichler, M., Leonhartsberger, G., Altmann, J., & Retschitzegger, W. (2002, January). *Context awareness on mobile devices – The hydrogen approach*. Proceedings of the 36th Hawaii International Conference on System Sciences (HICSS'03), Big Island, HI.
14. IT Summit Germany. (2009). III. 2 Mobile broadband and mobile communication. In *Future of ICT and media – International Delphi study 2030* (pp. 132–139).
15. Jarvenpaa, S. L., & Lang, K. R. (2005). Managing the paradoxes of mobile technology. *Information Systems Management, 22*(4), 7–23.
16. Kargin, B., Basoglu, N., & Daim, T. (2009). Factors affecting the adoption of mobile services. *International Journal of Quality and Service Sciences, 2*(1), 29–52.
17. Kawash, J., El Morr, C., & Itani, M. (2007). A novel collaboration model for mobile virtual communities. *International Journal of Web Based Communities, 3*(4), 427–447.
18. Kleinrock, L. (2001). Breaking loose. *Communications of the ACM, 44*(9), 41–45.
19. Kortuem, G., Schneider, J., Preuitt, D., Thompson, T. G. C., Fickas, S., & Segall, Z. (2001, August). *When peer-to-peer comes face-to-face: collaborative peer-to-peer computing in mobile ad-hoc networks*. Proceedings of the First International Conference on Peer-to-Peer Computing, Linköping, Sweden. pp. 75–91.
20. Kristoffersen, S., & Ljunberg, F. (2000). From stationary to mobile work. In K. Braa, C. Sorenson, & E. Dahlbom (Eds.), *Planet internet* (pp. 137–156). Lund, Sweden: Studentliteratur.
21. Kumar, S., & Zahn, C. (2003). Mobile communications: evolution and impact on business operations. *Technovation, 23*(6), 515–520.
22. Malladi, R., & Agrawal, D. (2002). Current and future applications of mobile and wireless networks. *Communications of the ACM, 45*(10), 144–146.
23. Nielsen. (2011). *State of the media: social media report Q3*. Retrieved from http://blog.nielsen.com/nielsenwire/social/. Accessed 24 April 2012.
24. Prasopoulou, E., Pouloudi, A., & Panteli, N. (2006). Enacting new temporal boundaries: the role of mobile phones. *European Journal of Information Systems, 15*, 277–284.
25. Rao, B., & Minakakis, L. (2003). Mobile commerce opportunities and challenges: Evolution of mobile location-based services. *Communications of the ACM, 46*(12), 61–65.

26. Rhee, Y., & Lee, J. (2009). A model of mobile community: Designing user interfaces to support group interaction. *Interactions, 16*(6), 46–51.
27. Roth, J., & Unger, C. C. (2001). Using handheld devices in synchronous collaborative scenarios. *Personal and Ubiquitous Computing, 5*(4), 243–252.
28. Sarker, S., & Wells, J. D. (2003). Understanding mobile handheld device use and adoption. *Communications of the ACM – Mobile Computing Opportunities and Challenges, 46*(12), 35–40.
29. Schilitm, B., Adams, N., & Want, R. (1994) Context-aware computing applications. In *Proceedings of IEEE workshop on mobile computing systems and applications* (pp. 85–90), Santa Cruz, CA: IEEE Computer Society Press.
30. Schmidt, A, Aidoo, K. A., Takaluoma, A., Tuomela, U., Van Laerhoven, K., & Van de Velde, W. (1999) Advanced interaction in context. In *Proceedings of first international symposium on Handheld and Ubiquitous Computing, HUC'99* (pp. 89–101), Karlsruhe, Germany, Berlin/Heidelberg: Springer Verlag.
31. Schmidt, A., Beigl, M., & Gellersen, H.-W. (1999). There is more to context than location. *Computers and Graphics, 23*, 893–901.
32. Schön, S., Wieden-Bischof, D., Schneider, C., & Schumann, M. (2010). *Mobile Gemeinschaften: Erfolgreiche Beispiele aus den Bereichen Spielen, Lernen und Gesundheit*. Salzburg, Austria: Salzburg Research.
33. Shilton, K. (2009). Four billion little brothers? Privacy, mobile phones, and ubiquitous data collection. *Communications of the ACM, 52*(11), 48–53.
34. Shim, J. P., Varshney, U., Dekleva, S., & Knoerzer, G. (2006). Mobile and wireless networks: Services, evolution and issues. *International Journal of Mobile Communications, 4*(4), 405–417.
35. The Free On-line Dictionary of Computing. (2011). *Definition of the word "context"*. http://foldoc.org/context/. Accessed 15 Sep 2011.

Chapter 13
Social Networks in Environmental Epidemiology

Stelios Zimeras[1] **and S. Geronikolou**[2]

[1]Department of Statistics and Actuarial-Financial Mathematics, University of the Aegean, G.R. 83200 Karlovassi, Samos, Greece, zimste@aegean.gr
[2]Biomedical Research Foundation of Academy of Athens, 4 Soranou Efessiou Str, 11527 Athens, Greece, sgeronik@bioacademy.gr

Abstract Environmental epidemiology is the branch of epidemiology that pertains to the interaction of the disease with certain environmental factors. It studies hazards and conditions putative to pose imbalance to our health (disease, impairs, death), the burden of disease, the extent and limits of contamination, and the preventive steps that need to be taken.

A social network consists of a series of individuals or groups connected by links that represent some kind of relationship or interaction. The investigation of environmental social networks permits an evaluation of the influence that the connections between people have in the transmission of a given disease. The concept of neighborhood applied in social network analysis is illustrated based on graph theory, where adjacent points are nodes connected by a line and all the nodes that one point is connected with nearby nodes construct a neighborhood. In this chapter, a connection between social networks and epidemiology (especially in environmental and social aspect) would be introduced, introducing the spatial variability into the regional areas considering directional graphical models.

Keywords Social networks • Epidemics • Environmental epidemiology • Directional graphical models • Social epidemiology

13.1 Introduction

Evidence-based medicine is established on epidemiology results. In fact, epidemiology is the cornerstone method of public health research that helps inform for identifying risk factors for disease and determining optimal treatment approaches to clinical practice and for preventive medicine. Environmental epidemiology deals with environmental risk factor identifications and quantifications which they are effecting the social connectivity between regions. The last connections between regions or individuals introduce the idea of social networks.

A.A. Lazakidou (ed.), *Virtual Communities, Social Networks and Collaboration*, Annals of Information Systems 15, DOI 10.1007/978-1-4614-3634-8_13,

World Health Organization defines it as follows: "Epidemiology is the study of the distribution and determinants of health-related states or events (including disease), and the application of this study to the control of diseases and other health problems." Spreading diseases involves the meaning of stochastic modeling between regions.

Stochasticity is often introduced through stochastic functions (e.g., weather) or random effects in parameter values. Spatial connectivity includes neighborhood structure between regions, where investigation of that structure includes modeling of the spatial homogeneity. The last could be illustrated by using spatial modeling techniques (like spatial autocorrelation, partition functions, and multilevel models). Spatial investigation involves stochastic modeling, especially in cases where the incomplete data involves hidden information. Stochasticity could be introduced as the randomness of our data. So incompleteness (hide information) leads us to the meaning of stochasticity where incomplete information could be explained (and modeled) by adding particular functions, which explain a large amount of information introducing a new modeling.

The Bradford Hill criteria [6, 10, 11] are as follows: (1) strength of association (odds ratio), (2) consistency, (3) specificity, (4) temporal relationship (temporality) – not heuristic – factually necessary for cause to precede consequence, (5) biological gradient (dose–response relationship), (6) plausibility (biological plausibility), (7) coherence, (8) experiment (reversibility), and (9) analogy (consideration of alternate explanations).

Sensitivity analysis is often used as a model-testing tool to examine model behavior in terms of the most sensitive parameters. Sensitivity analysis is used to determine the importance of different parameters and components of the model on the output of the model. Given the large number of parameters involved in ecological models, the first step in uncertainty analysis is often to perform sensitivity analysis to identify the parameters that may have significant effects on model output. From the statistical modeling view, sensitivity analysis could be performed when the distribution of a specific system had been introduced (species).

13.2 Environmental Epidemiology

Social epidemiology has been defined as the branch of epidemiology that studies the social distribution and social determinants of health [3]. Different dimensions of the social structure may influence people's health at different time points. It is important to take account of the temporal and causal ordering of the various measures of social position and use methods that make explicit the various underlying causal pathways between different measures of social position and health. There are a number of such causal modeling methods being used in social epidemiological research [9]. Failure to take account of the different pathways between the social structure and health outcomes could result in biased results [21].

Table 13.1 Morbidity data in the Aegean: hospital entries (per 100,000 per county)

Nosological entity	Lesbos	Samos	Chios	Dodecanesos	Kyklades	National
						Total rate
Cancer	1.103	1.261	1.159	1.256	831	1.465
Cardiovascular diseases	1.563	**2.171**	1.497	1.359	843	1.748
Respiratory diseases	1.006	**1.439**	903	1.003	610	1.073
Digestive	1.246	**2.342**	1.366	1.216	936	1.418
Urinary	877	**1.168**	1.008	1.071	748	1.090
Gynecology	1.000	1.213	1.265	1.461	999	1.228
Poisonings and injuries	964	**1.580**	1.056	1.522	693	1.136
Others(ten nosol. entities)	3.225	**4.770**	1.883	3.640	2.096	3.816
Total	10.984	15.944	11.040	12.528	7.754	12.974

Source: Data of the Greek Ministry of Health
The bold figures highlight the categories where Samos had an increased morbidity

As an example, sociological epidemic in health, medical data for the Aegean and specifically for Samos islands, is introduced. In Table 13.1, morbidity rates per 100,000 people are shown for different Greek areas. The morbidity rates are substantially higher in Samos County than the other Aegean counties and the average of Greece for the majority of the diseases. The bold figures highlight the categories where Samos had an increased morbidity. Therefore, we reached a conclusion that cardiovascular disease is the main cause of mortality on the island.

Environmental epidemiology studies may be sound enough to widen or change the public health policy in one or more countries. Well-established studies, imputing certain contaminants or hazards for identified health impacts, recall Hill's criterion of consistency [23, 24].

Variability in ecological systems may result from spatial heterogeneity of environmental conditions or from randomness in interactions of different processes. Natural variability of data is a critical factor in social analysis because modeling only with average values can produce bias in predictions, especially for nonlinear models [17, 20]. Spatial variability in system attributes and driving variables need to be effectively incorporated into simulation modeling.

Model comparison can incorporate into model, especially when no data are available for model testing [2, 12, 15]. One model may be compared with another to identify the effectiveness of the estimation procedure as well as the success of the explanation of the real data (hierarchical analysis) [19]. The idea behind hierarchical modeling is the investigation of the complexity of the system using the appropriate model which explains better the real data [13].

Thacker et al. [22] created a seven-step "hazard-exposure-outcome" axis so as to describe the prerequisites for a valid linking outcome to be established. In other words, this algorithm is tracking the environmental agent variation or mixture or release (called "hazard" in environmental epidemiology jargon), his entering the human organism (called "exposure" to the same jargon), and putative or real health effect on it (called "health outcome").

Hazard data do not comprise individual measures and thus are not representative of such. Contaminant monitoring provides evidence about its existence but not on its impact on population. This kind of data is not appropriate for trend analysis and certainly cannot satisfy sampling or measure certainty: erroneous results may be difficult to detect.

In addition, problems usually concern misclassification of disease. They are based mainly on estimations rather than valid measurements [18]:

- The epidemiological aspect of relating a putative or approved hazard with certain health outcomes deals with more than one factor: epidemiology considers these covariates as necessary prerequisites for a feasible model to be fitted.
- The attempt to find possible associations between an environmental factor and a health outcome may comprise ecological bias. The most common problem to be faced is the proper statistical method for exposure evaluation.

Time clustering of a given health outcome helps identifying an environmental factor as hazard. Time and seasonal trends of a disease result from such cluster analyses. A sound paradigm of such studies have been those that identified high prevalence of deaths from summer heat waves. Hazard surveillance helps identify a trend and shape a descriptive surrounding of an environmental factor.

Ecologic studies identify the geographic coexistence of prevalence with a hazard. Correlations of exposure data with health outcome data describe the r correlation coefficient as measure for ascribing. Confounding, if not biased, results may occur by general aggregated calculations. Community interventions, health policies, lifestyle tendencies, and scientific hypotheses may profit from such correlations. Rarely prevailed health observations profit from Poisson regression analysis. On the contrary, survival analysis and binomial modeling are feasible for commonly prevailed observations. Case–control studies are treated with multiple logistic regression or survival analysis.

13.3 Social Networks

A social network consists of a series of individuals or groups connected by links that represent some kind of relationship or interaction [14]. The investigation of environmental social networks permits an evaluation of the influence that the connections between people have in the transmission of a given disease. The concept of neighborhood applied in social network analysis is illustrated based on graph theory, where adjacent points are nodes connected by a line and all the nodes that one point is connected with nearby nodes construct a neighborhood.

Social network analysis can also include other types of relationships for analysis, trying to identify the role these relationships play in the dynamics of infection by diseases. Graphical presentation of these relationships is defined as diseases map. Based on this explanation, two types of social network analysis are defined: the

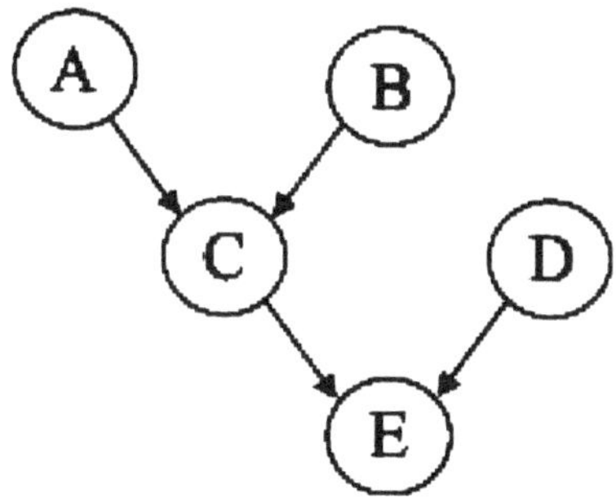

Fig. 13.1 Directed graph (DAG)

egocentric or personal and the sociometric network. Based on the first type, it is possible to study the dynamic relationship between the groups and its neighborhood, generally, centered on those groups. With the second type of analysis, it is possible to study the influence of individuals in a population and all the links between them. For composing sociometric networks, the data could be collected as part of research specifically designed to this end, as it possesses still other complexities, such as the definition of population to be studied, ethical problems in the search for partners, and problems with data analysis [16].

Alternatively, analysts use graph theory and its applications to sociometric networks where the people are nodes and constitute the vertices of graphs, so the vertices are connected by lines with diverse characteristics. Diverse measures based on graph theory have been developed for this type of social network (e.g., centrality, proximity, the shortest path between two people) [14].

Social network analysis (SNA) combines the study of relations and patterns of communication within social groups. In SNA, a social group is modeled as a graph composed of nodes and edges. The nodes in the graph represent social actors and link the relationship between them. A graph consisting of n nodes and m edges is defined as $G=[V,E]$ where $V_{i,}$ $i=1,\ldots,n$ is the set of nodes and E_j, $j=1,\ldots,m$ is a set of links or edges. Graphs where the edges do have an associated direction are directed graphs (Fig. 13.1). The nodes represent variables, and probabilities are provided for each node given its parents. If we have a directed edge from node A to node B, then A is called the parent of C, and C is called the child of A.

Considering Fig. 13.1, we have the set of vertices $V=\{A,B,C,D,E\}$ and the set of edges $E=\{(A,C), (B,C), (C,E), (D,E)\}$. Nodes A and D do not have any parents. Node C is the child of nodes A and B, and the parent of node E. The graphical structure has to take the form of a directed acyclic graph or DAG. Nodes represent random variables; edges indicate conditional dependence relations. The joint probability $P(A,B,C,D,E)$ factorizes into the product $P(A)P(B)P(C|A,B)P(E|C,D)P(D)$.

A BN is characterized by a simple and unique rule for expanding the joint probability in terms of simpler conditional probabilities. Let $X_1,X_2,\ldots, X_n$ be a set of random variables represented by the nodes $i \in \{1,\ldots, n\}$ in the graph, define $pa[i]$ to be the parents of node i, and let $X_{pa[i]}$ represent the set of random variables associated with $pa[i]$. Then

$$P(X_1, X_2, \ldots, X_n) = \prod_{i=1}^{n} P(X_i \mid X_{pa[i]})$$

where $pa(X_i)$ represents the set of parents of variable X_i with $P(Y = y_j) = \sum_i P(X = x_i) \cdot P(Y = y_j \mid X = x_i)$.

The distance between two nodes i and j, denoted $d(i, j)$, is the minimum path length between i and j (and set to be infinite if no such path exists). The diameter of a network g is defined as $d(g) = \max_{i,j} d(i,j)$, the maximum distance between any two nodes. If a network is not connected (there are at least two nodes that have no path between them), then the diameter is infinite [4, 5]. As many social networks are not connected, the diameter is often reported for the largest component.

The main goal in social networks is to investigate diagrammatical spatial interaction between nodes applying probabilistic modeling techniques. Statistical modeling of social networks is implemented based on MRF [8] and exponential random graphical models (ERGMs) [1, 25]. Spatial interaction between neighboring nodes (indicating cliques) defines homogeneous regions without spatial variability.

Graphs and directed graphs can be represented by a binary *adjacency matrix*. For example, in the case of a graph, we can define **x** to be an $n \times n$ matrix with entries: $x_{ij} = 1$ if there is an edge between i and j and $x_{ij} = 0$, otherwise. Since $x_{ij} = 1$ if and only if $x_{ji} = 1$, **x** is necessarily a *symmetric* matrix. In the case of a directed graph, unit entries in **x** correspond to arcs in E (i.e., $x_{ij} = 1$ if and only if there is an arc from i and j and $x_{ij} = 0$, otherwise). In this case, symmetry is not necessarily implied.

In environmental epidemiology, the main aspect is the fraction of a community that must be vaccinated in order to prevent major epidemics of a disease that it is crucial health problem. Initially all members of the population are susceptible to infection. The epidemic starts when one or more infectious individuals enter the population and come into contact with its members. A susceptible person is infected if it has adequate contact with the infectious individual. Graphically the above process is represented in Fig. 13.2, where a Markov social network could be introduced.

The process could be considered as a finite connected graph, with certain properties. A finite directed graph has nodes representing entries and arcs (ordered sets of nodes) representing relationships between entries. An arc(g_1, g_2) has a direction $g_1 \rightarrow g_2$. A sequence of arcs $(g_1, g_2), \ldots, (g_{n-1}, g_n)$ is a path. If $g_1 = g_2$, the path is a circuit. A sequence is a chain if each edge has one node in common with the preceding and one common with the succeeding edge. A graph is connected if a chain exists between each pair of nodes, and a tree is a connected graph without cycles or circuits.

Bayesian statistical methods quantify uncertainty by calculating probabilistic predictions. The procedure has three stages: (1) determination of the prior probability distribution for model parameters, (2) construction of a likelihood function for the statistical model, and (3) derivation of the posterior probability distribution for

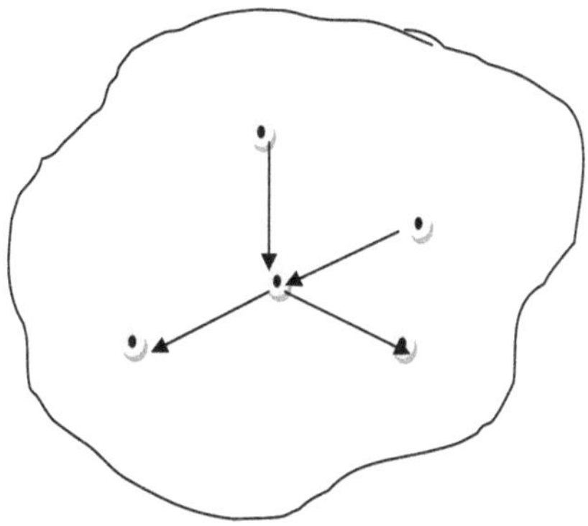

Fig. 13.2 Social network in epidemics: connections between regional disease nodes

the parameters by using the Bayes rule to adjust the prior distribution based on the observed data. Let $X=(X_1, X_2,\ldots, X_n)$ be the spread virus (environmental pollution) for individuals (denoted as nodes). We cannot observe directly the parameters of the spread virus (hidden variables) but some of the inflections $Y=(Y_1, Y_2,\ldots, Y_n)$. The stochastic model has the data, the spread virus for the subset D and the whole population G. Thus, the spreading probabilities are

$$P(Y_i = y \mid X_i = x) = S(y \mid x)$$

The transition probabilities are

$$P(X_i = x \mid X_{\mathrm{F}_i} = x_{\mathrm{F}}) = T(x \mid x_{\mathrm{F}})$$

where F_i denotes the father of i. Finally, the infection probability distribution is

$$P(\text{random founder } i \text{ has infected by } x) = P(X_i = x) = I_i(x)$$

Thinking $I_i(x)$ as a prior distribution on the virus of founder i and assuming that the spreading virus is conditionally independent given the parents spreading virus, the observed Y_D has probability function:

$$P(Y_D = y_D) = \sum_x \left\{ \prod_{i\in \mathrm{F}} I_i(x_i) \prod_{j\notin \mathrm{F}} T(x_j \mid x_{\mathrm{F}_j}) \prod_{k\in D} S(y_k \mid x_k) \right\}$$

where F is the founder. The conditional probabilities that a particular individual i infected by a virus x_i given the remaining individuals $x_{G\setminus i}$ is given by

$$P(X_i = x_i \mid x_{G\setminus i}) = \frac{P(X=x)}{\sum_{x=1}^{k} P(X_i = x, x_{G\setminus i})} = \frac{\prod_{j\in \mathrm{F}} I_j(x_j) \prod_{l\notin \mathrm{F}} T(x_l \mid x_{Fl})}{\sum_{x=1}^{k} \prod_{j\in \mathrm{F}} I_j(x_j) \prod_{l\notin \mathrm{F}} T(x_l \mid x_{Fl}) \big|_{x_i = x}}$$

The denominator involves the sum over all possible viruses for i, so terms that do not involve i cancel. The remaining terms have entries corresponding to i parents F_i and to the children C_i. Hence,

$$P(X_i = x_i \mid x_{G\setminus i}) = \begin{cases} \dfrac{I_i(x_i)\prod_{c\in C_i} T(x_c \mid x_i)}{\sum_{x=1}^{k} I_i(x_i)\prod_{c\in C_i} T(x_c \mid x_i)}, \text{if } i \in F \\ \dfrac{T(x_i \mid x_{F_i})\prod_{c\in C_i} T(x_c \mid x_i)}{\sum_{x=1}^{k} T(x_i \mid x_{F_i})\prod_{c\in C_i} T(x_c \mid x_i)}, \text{if } i \notin F \end{cases}$$

So $P(X_i = x_i \mid x_{G\setminus i}) = P(X_i = x_i \mid x_{\delta_i})$, where δ_i consists the neighborhood of the parents and children of i.

Hierarchical models, whereby a problem is decomposed into a series of levels linked by simple rules of probability, assume a very flexible framework capable of accommodating uncertainty and potential a priori scientific knowledge while retaining many advantages of a strict likelihood approach. Estimation of the parameters of the models could be achieved applying MCMC techniques.

Hierarchical modeling is based on a simple fact from probability that the joint distribution of a collection of random variables can be decomposed into a series of conditional models. For example, if a, b, and c are random variables, then basic probability allows the factorization

$$[a,b,c] = [a \mid b,c][b \mid c][c],$$

where the notation [.] is used to specify a probability distribution and $[x|y]$ refers to the distribution of x conditioned on y. In the case of spatial and spatiotemporal models, the joint distribution describes the behavior of the process at all spatial locations of potential interest (and, possibly, all times). The goal is to estimate the distribution of the process and parameters given the data. Bayesian statistics involves drawing statistical conclusions from the posterior distribution which is proportional to the data model (i.e., the likelihood) times the a priori knowledge (i.e., the prior).

Some methodological tools also stem from the field of geostatistics based upon the recognition that in the earth sciences there is usually a lack of sufficient knowledge concerning how properties vary in space. Therefore, a deterministic model may not be appropriate. If we wish to make predictions at locations for which we have no observations, we must allow for uncertainty in our description as a result of our lack in knowledge. So, the uncertainty inherent in predictions of any property we cannot describe deterministically is accounted for through the use of probabilistic models.

It thus provides the practitioner with a methodology to quantify spatial uncertainty. Statistics come into play because probability distributions are the meaningful way to represent the range of possible values of a parameter of interest. In addition, a statistical model is well suited to the apparent randomness of spatial variations. It must be noted that there is considerable variety of statistical methods that have been applied in the analysis of spatial variation in ecological data, summarized by Dale [7]. These include dispersal analysis, spectral analysis, wavelet analysis, kriging and spatial Monte Carlo simulations, and many geostatistics methods. Kriging was developed for estimating thresholds of continuous variables. It has been used for interpolation and simulation of categorical variables and for spatial uncertainty analysis. Autocorrelation of the spatial variables was represented by indicator autovariogram models. The kriging estimator for the occurrence probability of a class C_i at the location x_o is defined as a linear combination of the surrounding indicator data I_a with

$$P\left(x_o \mid x_{i_a}\right) = \sum_{i=1}^{a} \lambda_{i_a} I_{i_a}$$

where the set of weights λ_{ia} are obtained by solving a system of linear equations

$$\begin{cases} \sum_{a=1}^{n} \lambda_{i_a} \gamma_{ii}\left(h_{\alpha\beta}\right) + \mu_i = \gamma_{ii}\left(h_{\beta 0}\right) \\ \sum_{i=1}^{a} \lambda_{i_a} = 1 \end{cases}$$

where γ_{ii} $(h_{\alpha\beta})$ denotes the indicator autovariogram between data locations x_a and x_β and γ_{ii} $(h_{\beta 0})$ denotes the indicator autovariogram between data locations x_β and x_0; μ is the Lagrange parameter.

Markov chain geostatistics is a new nonkriging geostatistics. The basic idea of this geostatistics is to use Markov chains to perform multidimensional interpolation and simulation. Compared with the covariance-based (or variogram-based) geostatistics, MCG is transition probability-based. Compared with the kriging-based geostatistics, MCG is Markov chain-based. MCG directly uses Markov chains to accomplish conditional simulation. The basic idea of MCG is that an unknown location is related on its nearest known neighbors in different directions. With a Markov chain moving around in a space, its conditional probability distribution at any unknown point is entirely dependent on its nearest known neighbors in different directions. The interaction between each nearest known neighbor and the unknown location is expressed by a transition probability at the corresponding distance. Therefore, transiograms are the explicit components of the conditional probability function.

The MCG estimator for the occurrence probability of a class C at the location x is defined as a nonlinear combination of the surrounding data with

$$P\left(x=k \mid X_1=l_1,\ldots,X_m=l_m\right)=\frac{\prod_{i=1}^{m} p_{kl}^{i}\left(h_i\right)p_{lk}^{l}\left(h_l\right)}{\sum_{j=1}^{n}\left[\prod_{i=1}^{m} p_{jl}^{i}\left(h_i\right)p_{lj}^{l}\left(h_l\right)\right]}$$

where $p_{lk}^{i}(h)$ denotes a transiogram from state l to state k over the lag h in the ith direction and m is the number of data considered in different directions.

13.4 Conclusions

Social networks examine the relationships between social factors into various individuals. Social factors could be explained by social networks affecting the spatial variability of the regional neighborhood systems. These connections could be analyzed by directional diagrams introducing paths inside regions.

In this chapter, a general introduction of the social epidemics via environmental epidemiology was represented. Combination between environmental epidemics (virus spreading) and social networks would be explained involving Markovian and Bayesian statistical methodology. Finally, spatial connectivity and variability between neighborhood structures inside the social networks could be applied considering geostatistical tools (like kriging or variograms).

References

1. Anderson, C., Wasserman, S., & Crouch, B. (1999). A p^* primer: Logit models for social networks. *Social Networks, 21*, 37–66.
2. Berk, R. A., Bickel, P., Campbell, K., Keller-McNutly, S., Kelly, E., & Sacks, J. (2002). Workshop on statistical approaches for the evaluation of complex computer models. *Statistical Science, 17*, 173–192.
3. Berkman, L. F., & Kawachi, I. (2000). A historical framework for social epidemiology. In L. F. Berkman & I. Kawachi (Eds.), *Social epidemiology* (pp. 3–12). New York: Oxford University Press.
4. Bollobás, B. (2000). *Modern graph theory*. New York: Springer.
5. Bollobás, B. (2001). *Random graphs* (2nd ed.). Cambridge, UK: Cambridge University Press.
6. Bradford-Hill, A. (1965). The environment and disease: Association or causation? *Proceedings of the Royal Society of Medicine, 58*, 295–300.
7. Dale, M. R. T. (1999). *Spatial pattern analysis in plant ecology*. Cambridge, UK: Cambridge University Press.
8. Frank, O., & Strauss, D. (1986). Markov graphs. *Journal of the American Statistical Association, 81*, 832–842.

9. Greenland, S., & Brumback, B. (2002). An overview of relations among causal modelling methods. *International Journal of Epidemiology, 31*, 1030–1037.
10. Höfler, M. (2005). The Bradford Hill considerations on causality: A counterfactual perspective? *Emerging Themes in Epidemiology, 2*, 11.
11. Howick, J., Glasziou, P., & Aronson, J. K. (2009). The evolution of evidence hierarchies: What can Bradford Hill's 'guidelines for causation' contribute? *Journal of the Royal Society of Medicine, 102*(5), 186–194.
12. Jain, A. K., Kheshgi, H. S., & Wobbles, D. J. (1997). Is there an imbalance in the global budget of bomb-produced radiocarbon? *Journal of Geophysical Research, 102*, 1327–1333.
13. Jansen, M. J. W. (1998). Prediction error through modeling concepts and uncertainty from basic data. *Nutrient Cycling in Agroecosystems, 50*, 247–253.
14. Jolly, A. M., Muth, S. Q., Wylie, J. L., & Potterat, J. J. (2001). Sexual networks and sexually transmitted infections: A tale of two cities. *Journal of Urban Health, 78*, 433–445.
15. Klepper, O. (1997). Multivariate aspects of model uncertainty analysis: Tools for sensitivity analysis and calibration. *Ecological Modelling, 101*, 1–13.
16. Morris, M. (2004). Overview of network survey designs. In M. Morris (Ed.), *Network epidemiology: A handbook for survey design and data collection* (pp. 8–21). Oxford, UK: Oxford University Press.
17. O'Neill, R. V. (1979). Natural variability as a source of error in model predictions. In G. S. Innis & R. V. O'Neill (Eds.), *Systems analysis of ecosystems* (pp. 23–32). Fairland, MD: International Co-operative.
18. Phillips, C. V., & Goodman, K. J. (2006). Causal criteria and counterfactuals; nothing more (or less) than scientific common sense? *Emerging Themes in Epidemiology, 3*, 5.
19. Reynolds, J. F., Hilbert, D. W., & Kemp, P. R. (1993). Scaling ecophysiology from the plant to the ecosystem: A conceptual framework. In J. R. Ehleringer & C. B. Field (Eds.), *Scaling physiological processes: Leaf to globe* (pp. 127–140). San Diego, CA: Academic Press.
20. Scherm, H., & van Bruggen, A. H. C. (1994). Global warming and nonlinear growth: How important are changes in average temperature? *American Phytopathological Society, 84*, 1380–1384.
21. Singh-Manoux, A., Clarke, P., & Marmort, M. (2002). Multiple measures of socioeconomic position and psychosocial health: Proximal and distal effects. *International Journal of Epidemiology, 31*(6), 1192–1199.
22. Thacker, S. B., Stroup, D. F., Parrish, R. G., Anderson, H. A. (1996). Surveillance in environmental public health: issues, systems and sources. *Am J Public Health 86*, 633–638.
23. Ward, A. C. (2009a). The role of causal criteria in causal inferences: Bradford Hill's "aspects of association". *Epidemiological Perspectives and Innovations, 6*, 2.
24. Ward, A. C. (2009b). The environment and disease: Association or causation? *Medicine, Health Care and Philosophy, 12*, 333–343.
25. Wasserman, S., & Pattison, P. (1996). Logit models and logistic regression for social networks: I. An introduction to Markov graphs and *p**. *Psychometrika, 61*, 401–425.